T0076267

Get the eBook FREE!

(PDF, ePub, Kindle, and liveBook all included)

We believe that once you buy a book from us, you should be able to read it in any format we have available. To get electronic versions of this book at no additional cost to you, purchase and then register this book at the Manning website.

Go to https://www.manning.com/freebook and follow the instructions to complete your pBook registration.

That's it!
Thanks from Manning!

Software Mistakes and Tradeoffs

Software Mistakes
and Tradeoffs

How to make good programming decisions

TOMASZ LELEK
JON SKEET

MANNING
SHELTER ISLAND

For online information and ordering of this and other Manning books, please visit www.manning.com. The publisher offers discounts on this book when ordered in quantity. For more information, please contact

Special Sales Department
Manning Publications Co.
20 Baldwin Road
PO Box 761
Shelter Island, NY 11964
Email: orders@manning.com

 Manning Publications Co.
20 Baldwin Road
PO Box 761
Shelter Island, NY 11964

Development editors:	Doug Rudder
Technical development editor:	Jeanne Boyarsky
Review editor:	Mihaela Batinic
Production editor:	Deirdre S. Hiam
Copy editor:	Christian Berk
Proofreader:	Jason Everett
Technical proofreader:	Jean-François Morin
Typesetter:	Dennis Dalinnik
Cover designer:	Marija Tudor

ISBN: 9781617299209
Printed and bound by CPI Group (UK) Ltd, Croydon, CR0 4YY

Tomasz dedicates this book to all of the open source community. Most of the tools and architectures emerge from your devotion and contributions. You are the reason why software is progressing and meeting today's world demands.

Jon dedicates the chapters he authored to every software engineer who has ever been utterly perplexed by a problem caused by either time zones or diamond dependencies. (That covers a pretty large proportion of the developer population. . . .)

brief contents

contents

preface

The work of everyone involved in delivering software is full of tradeoffs. We tend to operate with limited time, limited budgets, and limited knowledge. Therefore, today's decisions about the software we are creating will have consequences in the future, such as maintenance cost, inflexibility of our software when it needs to change, limited performance when we need to scale, and many others. It is important to note that every decision is made in a specific context. It's easy to judge past decisions without complete knowledge about the context in which they were made. However, the more knowledge and the more deep analysis we do at decision time, the more aware we can be about the tradeoffs our decisions carry.

Throughout our professional careers, we were involved in and observed many software decisions and learned what tradeoffs they impose. Along the way, Tomasz started writing a personal decision log of the circumstances in which a specific decision was made. What was its context? What were the alternatives? How did we evaluate a particular solution? And finally, how did it end up? Did we anticipate all possible tradeoffs of a specific solution? Or were we surprised by something? It turns out that this personal list of lessons learned actually reflected problems and decisions that need to be tackled by many engineers out there. At this point, Tomasz decided that this was an excellent time to share that knowledge with the world. This is how the idea for this book was born.

We want to share our lessons learned from the experience with various software systems: monoliths, microservices, big data processing, libraries, and many more. This book deeply analyzes decisions, tradeoffs, and mistakes from real-life production systems.

By presenting those patterns, mistakes, and lessons, we hope to widen your context and equip you with better tools which will help you make better decisions in your day-to-day job. Seeing potential problems and limitations of a design upfront can save you a lot of time and money in the future. We won't try to give you definite answers. When the problem is complex, it can often be solved with more than one approach. We will present some of those challenging problems and ask questions without definite answers. Each solution will have its pros and cons, and we will analyze those. Every solution will result in its tradeoffs, and it will be up to you to decide which one suits your context the best.

acknowledgments

Writing a book involves a lot of effort. However, thanks to Manning, it was a pleasure to work on it.

First and foremost, I want to thank my wife, Małgorzata. You've always supported me and listened to my ideas and problems. Because I have you, I could focus on the book.

Next, I'd like to acknowledge my editor at Manning, Doug Rudder. Thank you for working with me. Your comments and feedback were invaluable. I was able to progress my writing skills to the next level because of your involvement. Thanks as well to all the other folks at Manning who worked with me on the production and promotion of the book. It was truly a team effort. Another big thank you to the rest of the staff at Manning: my production editor, Deirdre Hiam; my copyeditor, Christian Berk; my reviewing editor, Mihaela Batinic; and my proofreader, Jason Everett.

I'd also like to thank the reviewers who took the time to read my manuscript at various stages during its development and who provided invaluable feedback—your suggestions helped make this a better book: Alex Saez, Alexander Weiher, Andres Sacco, Andrew Eleneski, Andy Kirsch, Conor Redmond, Cosimo Atanasi, Dave Corun, George Thomas, Gilles Iachelini, Gregory Varghese, Hugo Cruz, Johannes Verwijnen, John Guthrie, John Henry Galino, Johnny Slos, Maksym Prokhorenko, Marc-Oliver Scheele, Nelson González, Oliver Korten, Paolo Brunasti, Rafael Avila Martinez, Rajesh Mohanan, Robert Trausmuth, Roberto Casadei, Sau Fai Fong, Shawn Lam, Spencer Marks, Vasile Boris, Vincent Delcoigne, Vitosh Doynov, Walter Stoneburner, and Will Price.

Special thanks to Jeanne Boyarsky, development editor, for her careful review of the content from a technical perspective.

This book is a consequence of all the professional decisions I made and the people I met throughout my career. There are many people who shaped me as a software engineer and positively influenced my career. I have had the luck to meet and work with such people from the beginning of my career. I would like to thank all my colleagues from Schibsted, Allegro, DataStax, and Dremio. Some of them who deserve special thanks are

- *Paweł Wołoszyn*—For being a great university lecturer and teaching me that programming can significantly impact our world
- *Andrzej Grzesik*—For encouraging me toward very ambitious goals
- *Mateusz Kwaśniewski*—For igniting an infinite spark of hunger for learning
- *Łukasz Bancerowski*—For giving me the initial directions and shaping my future JVM career
- *Jarosław Pałka*—For providing trust and space for experiments and learning
- *Alexandre Dutra*—For leading by example and showing the highest possible work ethic

—Tomasz Lelek

I thank everyone I've bored with time zone trivia over the years, particularly my long-suffering family. My colleagues at Google have been essential to my thinking on the aspects I've written about in this book, along with open source collaborators on Noda Time and other projects.

—Jon Skeet

about this book

Software Mistakes and Tradeoffs: How to make good programming decisions was written as a list of real-world problems you may encounter in your production systems. It tries to analyze every situation in a variety of contexts and consider all its tradeoffs. It also presents some non-obvious mistakes that may significantly impact your systems from various perspectives (not only correctness).

Who should read this book

Software Mistakes and Tradeoffs: How to make good programming decisions is for every software engineer who wants to understand tradeoffs and patterns used in production systems. It also teaches how to avoid nonobvious mistakes. The book begins with lower-level topics that can also be very valuable for software engineers starting their careers. Then, the content progresses toward more advanced topics that even the most advanced readers will benefit from. The primary language in which examples, patterns, and code samples are created is Java, but the decisions themselves are not specific to Java.

How this book is organized

The book contains 13 chapters. The first one provides an overview of the tradeoff analysis used in this book. The rest of the chapters are relatively independent of each other and focus on different aspects of software engineering. To get the most benefit from this book, we recommend reading it in the original order. However, if you are interested in a specific aspect of software engineering, you can jump ahead to a particular chapter:

- Chapter 1 presents the approach this book will take in analyzing tradeoffs in a specific context. It shows example tradeoffs at the software architecture, code, and quality assurance levels.

- Chapter 2 demonstrates that code duplication is not always anti-pattern. It considers different architectures and analyzes how they influence the loose coupling of our systems. Finally, it uses Amdhal's law to calculate the cost of coordination within and between teams.

- Chapter 3 describes strategies for handling abnormal situations in your code. It shows a use case for both checked and unchecked exceptions. It also demonstrates how to develop exception strategies for public APIs (libraries). Finally, it considers tradeoffs between object and functional programming approaches for handling errors.

- Chapter 4 teaches how to balance the flexibility versus complexity of our code and API. It shows that, often, the evolution of our code in one of the directions impacts the other direction.

- Chapter 5 teaches that premature optimization is not always evil. With proper tools and defined SLA, we can detect the hot path and optimize it. Furthermore, it demonstrates how leveraging the Pareto Principle can help in focusing optimization efforts on a system's appropriate place.

- Chapter 6 teaches how to design UX-friendly APIs. It shows that UX friendliness is a characteristic of not only UI interfaces but also programming interfaces, such as REST APIs, command-line tools, and others. However, it also shows that, sometimes, for UX friendliness, we need to pay with increased maintenance cost.

- Chapter 7 addresses the thorny issues associated with handling date and time information. Considering how much of our data includes at least some date and time elements, such as a date of birth or a log timestamp, there's a lot of opportunity for things to go wrong. It's a tractable domain, but it does need special attention.

- Chapter 8 teaches why data locality is crucial in big data processing. It also demonstrates the need for partitioning algorithms that help with distributing the data and traffic.

- Chapter 9 shows that the libraries we use become our code. It demonstrates different problems and tradeoffs we need to consider when importing a third-party library to our codebase. Finally, it tries to answer whether we should import a library or try to reimplement small parts of it.

- Chapter 10 focuses on a tradeoff between consistency and atomicity in distributed systems. It analyzes possible race conditions in a distributed system and shows how idempotency influences the way we design our systems.

- Chapter 11 explains how to deal with delivery semantics in distributed systems. It helps you understand the at-least-once, at-most-once, and effectively exactly-once semantics.

- Chapter 12 considers how software, APIs, and stored data all evolve over time as well as how they can do so while maintaining compatibility with other systems.

- Chapter 13 demonstrates that it is not always wise to keep up with the newest possible trends in the IT industry. It analyzes some of the widely used patterns and frameworks, such as reactive programming, but it also discusses whether we should use it in some specific contexts.

About the code

This book contains many examples of source code both in numbered listings and in line with normal text. In both cases, source code is formatted in a `fixed-width font like this` to separate it from ordinary text. Sometimes code is also **in bold** to highlight code that has changed from previous steps in the chapter, such as when a new feature adds to an existing line of code.

In many cases, the original source code has been reformatted; we've added line breaks and reworked indentation to accommodate the available page space in the book. In rare cases, even this was not enough, and listings include line-continuation markers (➥). Additionally, comments in the source code have often been removed from the listings when the code is described in the text.

This book contains many examples of source code, both in numbered listings and in snippets. The source code is formatted using the automated plugin according to the Google code guidelines. Code annotations accompany many of the listings, highlighting important concepts. Each chapter has a dedicated folder in the code repository. There is a substantial amount of unit and integration tests for all the code used in this book to assure the best code's quality. Not all the tests are shown in the book's listings. You may run and read tests to understand the specific part of logic more deeply. All the instructions for importing and running the examples are provided in the README.md file in the code's repository.

You can get executable snippets of code from the liveBook (online) version of this book at https://livebook.manning.com/book/software-mistakes-and-tradeoffs. The complete code for the examples in the book is available for download from the Manning website at https://www.manning.com/books/software-mistakes-and-tradeoffs, and from https://github.com/tomekl007/manning_software_mistakes_and_tradeoffs.

liveBook discussion forum

Purchase of *Software Mistakes and Tradeoffs* includes free access to liveBook, Manning's online reading platform. Using liveBook's exclusive discussion features, you can attach comments to the book globally or to specific sections or paragraphs. It's a snap to make notes for yourself, ask and answer technical questions, and receive help from the authors

and other users. To access the forum, go to https://livebook.manning.com/book/
software-mistakes-and-tradeoffs/discussion. You can also learn more about Manning's
forums and the rules of conduct at https://livebook.manning.com/discussion.

Manning's commitment to our readers is to provide a venue where a meaningful
dialogue between individual readers and between readers and the authors can take
place. It is not a commitment to any specific amount of participation on the part of
the authors, whose contribution to the forum remains voluntary (and unpaid). We
suggest you try asking the authors some challenging questions lest their interest stray!
The forum and the archives of previous discussions will be accessible from the publisher's website as long as the book is in print.

about the authors

Tomasz Lelek

In his professional Software Engineering career, Tomasz has worked on various production services, architectures, and programming languages (mostly JVM). He has production experience with monolith and microservices architectures. He has designed systems that handle tens of millions of unique users and hundreds of thousands of operations per second. He has worked in

- Microservices architecture with CQRS (using Apache Kafka)
- Marketing automation and event stream processing
- Big data processing with Apache Spark and Scala

Tomasz now works at Dremio, where he helps create a modern data lakehouse solution. Before that, he was working at DataStax, building a variety of products around the Cassandra Database. He designed tools for thousands of developers for whom API design, performance, and UX friendliness play a crucial part. He contributed to Java-Driver, Cassandra Quarkus, Cassandra-Kafka connector, and Stargate.

Jon Skeet

Jon is a staff developer relations engineer at Google, currently working on the Google Cloud Client Libraries for .NET. His contributions to Open Source include the Noda Time date and time library for .NET (https://nodatime.org), and he's possibly best known for his contributions to Stack Overflow. Jon is the author of the Manning book *C# in Depth* and also contributed to *Groovy in Action* and *Real-World Functional Programming*. Jon has interests in date and time APIs and versioning that are often regarded as unusual at best.

about the cover illustration

The figure on the cover of *Software Mistakes and Tradeoffs* is "Groenlandaisse," or "A Woman from Greenland," taken from a collection by Jacques Grasset de Saint-Sauveur, published in 1797. Each illustration is finely drawn and colored by hand. In those days, it was easy to identify where people lived and what their trade or station in life was just by their dress. Manning celebrates the inventiveness and initiative of the computer business with book covers based on the rich diversity of regional culture centuries ago, brought back to life by pictures from collections such as this one.

Introduction

When designing our code, APIs, and system architectures, we need to make decisions that impact maintenance, performance, extensibility, and many other factors. Almost always, the decision to go in one direction limits the possibility to evolve in a different one. The longer systems live, the harder it is to change their design and withdraw from previous decisions. The design and programming tradeoffs presented in this book focus on choosing between two or more directions in which your system can evolve. It's important to understand that, whatever you decide, you will need to live with one direction's pros and cons.

Depending on the context, time to market, service-level agreements (SLAs), and other factors, the team needs to make those hard decisions. We will show you the tradeoffs that we need to make in production systems and compare them with alternative ways of doing things. We hope that after reading this book, you will start to notice the design decisions that you make every day. Noticing these allows you to make conscious choices when considering their pros and cons.

The first part of this book focuses on the low-level design decisions that every software engineer needs to make in their code and APIs. The second part focuses on the bigger picture of your systems—the architecture and data flow between components. We will consider the tradeoffs that you need to make when working in distributed systems.

The next sections in this chapter demonstrate the approach that this book will take regarding analyzing tradeoffs. First, we will focus on the tradeoffs that every software engineer needs to make: the balance between unit, integration, end-to-end, and other types of tests. In the real world, we have a limited amount of time to deliver value through our software. Due to this, we need to decide whether we should invest more time into unit, integration, end-to-end, or other types of tests. We will analyze the pros and cons of having more tests of a specific type.

Next, we will show the well-proven singleton pattern and explain how the usability of this pattern is changing, depending on the context, which we will analyze in a single-threaded and multithreaded context. Finally, we will take a look at higher-level architecture tradeoffs: microservices versus monolith.

Note that, often, the architectures cannot be described as only monolithic or only microservices. It is common to see a hybrid approach: some functionalities are implemented as services, whereas other parts of a system may live as a monolith. For example, a legacy system may be built as a monolith, and only a tiny piece of it is moved to a microservices architecture. Also, it may be more reasonable for a greenfield project to start from one application approach and not split into microservices if that comes with a nonnegligible cost. We will concisely analyze tradeoffs between microservices and monoliths. You should apply some of that argumentation to your context, even if it is a hybrid architecture.

Those sections will show you the approach that every chapter will take: solving a problem in a particular context, then analyzing the alternative solution, and, finally, adding context that involves tradeoffs and decisions. We will explore pros and cons of every solution in a specific context. The subsequent chapters will dive a lot deeper into the tradeoffs.

1.1 *Consequences of every decision and pattern*

The goal of this book is to show design and programming tradeoffs and mistakes. When presenting tradeoffs and design choices in this book, I will assume that the overall quality of the code that you write is good enough. Once your code's quality is sufficient, you need to decide the direction in which it should evolve.

To understand the flow of each chapter in this book, let's first examine the tradeoffs between the two most useful and obvious techniques that you should use in your code: integration and unit tests. The ultimate goal of the test coverage is to have almost every path covered with unit and integration tests. In reality, it often is not feasible because you have a finite time with which to write and test your code. Thus, deciding about the proportions of unit and integration testing is an everyday tradeoff that you need to make.

1.1.1   *Unit testing decisions*

When writing tests, you need to decide which part of the code to test. Let's consider a simple component that you need to unit test. Suppose that we have a `SystemComponent` that exposes one public API method: `publicApiMethod()`. Other methods are hidden from clients by using a private access modifier. The following listing shows the code for this scenario.

Listing 1.1   Component to unit test

```
public class SystemComponent {

  public int publicApiMethod() {
    return privateApiMethod();
  }

  private int privateApiMethod() {
    return complexCalculations();
  }

  private int complexCalculations() {
    // some complex logic
    return 0;
  }
}
```

The decision that you need to make here is whether to unit test `complexCalculations()` or to keep this private method hidden. Such a unit test is a black-box test that covers only the public API. This is often a good enough level of unit testing. But sometimes, the private methods have complex logic that's worth unit testing as well. In such a situation, you might consider lowering the access modifier of `complexCalculations()`. The following listing shows this approach.

Listing 1.2   Component to unit test public visibility

```
@VisibleForTesting
public int complexCalculations() {
  // some complex logic
  return 0;
}
```

By changing the visibility to the public, you are allowing yourself to write a unit test that covers that part of the API that is not supposed to be public. Such a public method will be visible to clients of your API, so you are risking that the clients will use this API directly. In the listing, the `@VisibleForTesting` annotation (see http://mng .bz/y4wq) serves only an informational purpose. Nothing prevents the callers from calling the public method of your API. If they do not notice the annotation, they may ignore it.

Both unit testing approaches mentioned in this section are correct; the latter gives you more flexibility; however, the cost of maintenance may increase. You could end up with a middle ground solution between the two. This can be achieved by making your code package-private. Thus, when your tests are in the same package as your production code, you don't need to make your code public, but you will be able to use those methods in the test code.

1.1.2   *Proportions of unit and integration tests*

When testing your logic, you need to decide on the proportions of integration and unit tests for your system. Often, the decision to go in one direction limits the possibility to evolve in a different one. Moreover, this limitation may be imposed by the time we start to develop the system.

Because we usually have a limited timeframe for developing our features, we need to decide whether we should invest more time in unit or integration tests. Real-world systems should be tested using a combination of both unit and integration tests, so we need to decide how to proportion those.

Both approaches have pros and cons, which makes this is a typical tradeoff that you will encounter when writing your code. Unit tests are quicker and have faster feedback time, so the debugging process is often faster. Figure 1.1 demonstrates the pros and cons for both tests.

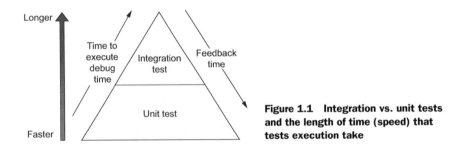

Figure 1.1   Integration vs. unit tests and the length of time (speed) that tests execution take

The diagram in figure 1.1 is a pyramid because, most often, the software systems have more unit tests than integration tests. The unit tests give almost instantaneous feedback to the developer, thereby increasing productivity. They are also faster to execute and decrease the debug time of your code. If you have 100% of your codebase covered in unit tests, when a new bug is introduced, chances are good that one of the unit tests will catch this problem. You will be able to detect it at the method level that the particular unit test is covering.

On the other hand, when your system has no integration tests, you won't be able to reason about the connections between components and how these integrate. You will have well-tested algorithms but without testing the bigger picture. You may end up with a system that does everything correctly at a lower code level, but the components in your system are not tested, so you cannot reason about the correctness of it at a higher level. In real life, your code should have a mix of unit and integration tests.

It is important to note that figure 1.1 focuses only on one aspect of testing: its execution time and, therefore, feedback time. In a real-production system, we have other layers of testing. We might have end-to-end tests that holistically validate business scenarios. In more complex architectures, we might need to start N services that are connected to provide this business functionality. Such tests will probably give us slower feedback time due to test infrastructure setup overhead. On the other hand, they will give us higher assurance regarding the end-to-end flow and correctness of our system. When comparing those tests to unit or integration tests, we might analyze them using different dimensions. For example, how well do they validate our system holistically, as figure 1.2 illustrates?

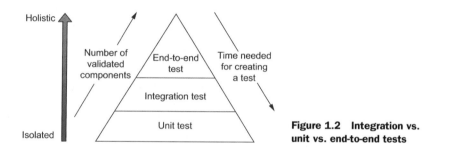

Figure 1.2 Integration vs. unit vs. end-to-end tests

Because unit tests run in isolation, these don't give us much information regarding other components in our system and how they interact with each other. Integration tests attempt to validate more components and the interactions between them. However, these often do not span multiple (micro)services that deliver given business functionality. Lastly, although the end-to-end tests validate our system holistically, the number of tested components may be substantial because we need to spin up all infrastructure, which can be N microservices, databases, queues, and so forth.

The other dimension (resource) that we need to consider is the time required for creating our tests. Unit tests are relatively easy to develop, and we can make many of them in a small amount of time. Integration tests are often more time-consuming to create. Finally, the end-to-end tests require a substantial investment upfront to create the infrastructure needed for them.

In reality, we have finite resources (e.g., budget and time), so we need to maximize the quality of our software considering those constraints. But covering our code with tests allows us to deliver better quality software and to reduce the number of released bugs. It also improves the maintainability of our software in the future. For this, we need to pick which type of tests to use and how many we want to implement; we need to find a balance between the number of unit, integration, and end-to-end tests because of those finite resources. By analyzing different dimensions, pros, and cons of the particular test type, we can make more rational decisions.

It is important to note that implementing tests increases development time. The more tests we want, the more time needs to be dedicated to that. Sometimes, it is hard to implement good end-to-end tests when not planning for those with a given deadline. Therefore, some types of tests should be planned accordingly—in the same way that we add new features rather than as an afterthought.

1.2   *Code design patterns and why they do not always work*

The code design patterns, such as Builder, Decorator, Prototype, and many more, were introduced years ago. They provide production-proven solutions for most well-known problems. I strongly recommend knowing those patterns (see *Design Patterns: Elements of Reusable Object-Oriented Software* by Erich et al. for more information) and using them in your code to make it more maintainable, extensible, and just better. On the other hand, you should use them with caution because implementing those patterns depends strongly on the context. As you already know, I am trying to show that every decision in your software involves tradeoffs and has consequences.

To understand tradeoffs at the code level, I will demonstrate the singleton pattern (https://refactoring.guru/design-patterns/singleton). This pattern was introduced as a way to share the common state between all components. The singleton is one instance that lives throughout the lifetime of your application. This one instance is referenced by the other classes. Say you need to create a private constructor to prevent creating a new instance of it. Creating a singleton for this is easy, as the following listing shows.

Listing 1.3   Implementing the singleton

```
public class Singleton {
  private static Singleton instance;
  private Singleton() {}

  public static Singleton getInstance() {
    if (instance == null) {
      instance = new Singleton();
    }
    return instance;
  }
}
```

The only way to get the singleton is through the getInstance() method, which returns the only one instance that you can safely share between components. The assumption here is that every time the caller's code wants to access the singleton, it does that via getInstance(). Later, we will consider a different use case that does not require accessing it every time via this method. This pattern seems like a quick win; you will be able to share code through the global singleton instances. You may ask yourself, "Where is the tradeoff here?"

Let's consider using this pattern in a different context. What happens if we use this pattern in a multithreaded environment? When you have more than one thread that is calling getInstance() simultaneously, you can have a race condition. In such a situation, your code creates two instances of a singleton. Having two instances of a singleton breaks the invariants of this pattern, and you may end up with system failures. To prevent this behavior, you need to add synchronization before performing the initialization logic, as the following listing shows.

Listing 1.4 Synchronizing for a thread-safe singleton

```
public class SystemComponentSingletonSynchronized {
  private static SystemComponent instance;

  private SystemComponentSingletonSynchronized() {}

  public static synchronized SystemComponent getInstance() {
    if (instance == null) {
      instance = new SystemComponent();
    }

    return instance;
  }
}
```

Starts the synchronization block

The synchronized block prevents accessing this logic by two threads. All but one thread will block and wait for the initialization logic. At first glance, everything works as expected. But if the performance of your code is a priority for you, using a singleton with multiple threads may decrease the performance of your code significantly.

Initialization is the first place at which multiple threads need to lock and wait. And once you create a singleton, every access to the object will need to be synchronized. A singleton can introduce thread contention (http://mng.bz/M2nn), which is a severe performance hazard. This happens when we have a shared instance of an object, and multiple threads are accessing it concurrently.

The synchronized getInstance() method allows only one thread to enter the critical section, whereas other threads will need to wait on that lock. Once the thread leaves the critical section, the second thread in the queue can enter it. The problem with this approach is that it introduces a need for synchronization and may slow the program substantially. In short, every time the code executes a call that is synchronized, there may be some additional overhead.

From this example, we can conclude that there is a tradeoff regarding your code's performance when using a singleton in a one-thread versus multithreading context. But what is essential is the context in which your code is executing. If your code works in a non-concurrent way or your singleton is not shared between multiple threads, the tradeoff does not appear. But if your singleton is shared between threads, you need to make it thread-safe, which potentially impacts performance. Knowing this tradeoff allows you to make a rational decision about your design and code.

If you decide that there are more cons for the specific design choice, you may end up changing your decision. In this singleton example, for instance, we can improve our solution with one of two patterns.

The first one employs the double-checked locking technique. The difference with this approach is that before entering the critical (synchronized) section, we must check whether the instance is null. If it is, we can continue to the critical section. If it's not, we don't need to enter the critical section, and we just return the existing singleton object. The following listing demonstrates this locking technique.

Listing 1.5   Singleton double-checked locking

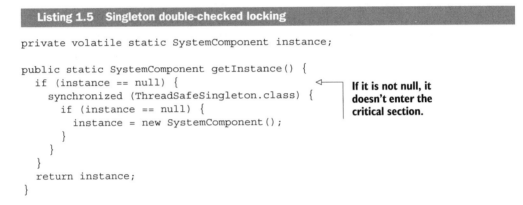

```
private volatile static SystemComponent instance;

public static SystemComponent getInstance() {
    if (instance == null) {                            ◁─────  If it is not null, it
        synchronized (ThreadSafeSingleton.class) {            doesn't enter the
            if (instance == null) {                           critical section.
                instance = new SystemComponent();
            }
        }
    }
    return instance;
}
```

Using this pattern, we can significantly reduce the need for synchronization and thread contention. This synchronization effect will be observed only on startup when every thread tries to initialize the singleton.

The second pattern that we might choose is thread confinement. It allows us to pin the state to the specific thread. However, you need to be aware that it won't be a singleton pattern at the global application level anymore. You will have a single instance of your object per thread. Assuming that you have *N* threads, you will have *N* instances as well.

When using this pattern, every thread in our code owns the instance of an object that is visible and tied to that specific thread. Due to this, there is no contention on access to an object shared between multiple threads. The object is owned by one thread and not shared. In Java, you can achieve this by using the ThreadLocal class (http://mng.bz/aD8B). It allows us to wrap a system component that should be tied to a specific thread. From the code's perspective, an object is inside of the ThreadLocal instance, as the following listing shows.

Listing 1.6   Thread confinement with ThreadLocal

```
private static ThreadLocal<SystemComponent> threadLocalValue = new
    ThreadLocal<>();
```

```
public static void set() {
  threadLocalValue.set(new SystemComponent());
}

public static void executeAction() {
  SystemComponent systemComponent = threadLocalValue.get();
}

public static SystemComponent get() {
  return threadLocalValue.get();
}
```

The logic for pinning `SystemComponent` to a specific thread is encapsulated in the `ThreadLocal` instance. When thread A calls the `set()` method, a new instance of `SystemComponent` is created inside `ThreadLocal`. What is important is that this instance is accessible only to this thread. If another thread (B, for instance) calls `execute-Action()` without previously calling `set()`, it gets a null `SystemComponent` instance because there is no component `set()` for this thread yet. The new instance dedicated for this thread will be created and accessible only after thread B calls the `set()` method.

We can simplify this by passing a supplier to the `withInitial()` method. This will be invoked if the thread-local has no value, so we are not risking getting a null. The following listing shows this implementation.

Listing 1.7   Thread confinement with an initial value

```
static ThreadLocal<SystemComponent> threadLocalValue =
    ThreadLocal.withInitial(SystemComponent::new);
```

By using this pattern, you are removing contention, which increases performance. But the drawback is in the complexity of such a solution.

> **NOTE** Every time the caller's code wants to access the singleton, it does not need to access it via the `getInstance()` method. It can access a singleton instance once and assign it to a variable (reference). Once it is assigned to a variable, subsequent calls can get the singleton object via this reference without the need to call `getInstance()`. This reduces the contention.

The singleton instance can also be injected into other components that need to use it. Ideally, your application creates all the components in one place and injects them into services (using, for example, the dependency injection technique). In this case, you may not need a singleton pattern at all. You can create just one instance of the object that should be shared and inject it into all dependent services (see http://mng.bz/g4dE). The other alternative would be to use an enum type that leverages the singleton pattern underneath. Let's now validate our assumptions by measuring the code.

1.2.1 *Measuring our code*

So far, we've created three thread-safe implementations of the singleton pattern by

- Using synchronization for all operations
- Employing double-checked locking
- Using thread confinement (via `ThreadLocal`)

We assumed that the first version would be the slowest, but we don't have any data yet. Let's create a performance benchmark that will validate all three implementations. We will use the JMH performance test tool (https://openjdk.java.net/projects/code-tools/jmh/), which we will use a couple of times in this book for validating our code's performance.

Let's create a benchmark that executes 50,000 operations of getting the System-Component (singleton) object (listing 1.8). We'll implement three benchmarks, each of those using a different singleton approach. To validate how the contention is impacting our performance, we'll run the code for 100 concurrent threads. Finally, we'll report the results (the average time) in milliseconds.

Listing 1.8 Creating a singleton implementation benchmark

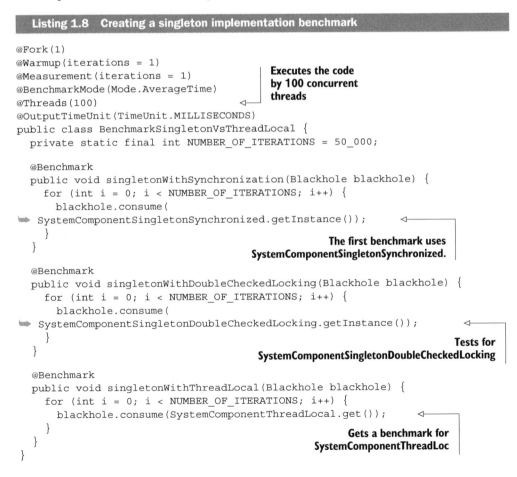

```
@Fork(1)
@Warmup(iterations = 1)
@Measurement(iterations = 1)          Executes the code
@BenchmarkMode(Mode.AverageTime)      by 100 concurrent
@Threads(100)                 <───    threads
@OutputTimeUnit(TimeUnit.MILLISECONDS)
public class BenchmarkSingletonVsThreadLocal {
  private static final int NUMBER_OF_ITERATIONS = 50_000;

  @Benchmark
  public void singletonWithSynchronization(Blackhole blackhole) {
    for (int i = 0; i < NUMBER_OF_ITERATIONS; i++) {
      blackhole.consume(
      SystemComponentSingletonSynchronized.getInstance());   <───
    }                                 The first benchmark uses
  }                      SystemComponentSingletonSynchronized.

  @Benchmark
  public void singletonWithDoubleCheckedLocking(Blackhole blackhole) {
    for (int i = 0; i < NUMBER_OF_ITERATIONS; i++) {
      blackhole.consume(
      SystemComponentSingletonDoubleCheckedLocking.getInstance());  <───
    }                                               Tests for
  }            SystemComponentSingletonDoubleCheckedLocking

  @Benchmark
  public void singletonWithThreadLocal(Blackhole blackhole) {
    for (int i = 0; i < NUMBER_OF_ITERATIONS; i++) {
      blackhole.consume(SystemComponentThreadLocal.get());   <───
    }                           Gets a benchmark for
  }                         SystemComponentThreadLoc
}
```

When we run this test, we will see an average time per 50,000 invocations for 100 concurrent threads. Note that the actual numbers may differ in your environment, but the overall trend will stay the same, as the following listing shows.

Listing 1.9 Viewing the singleton implementation benchmark results

Benchmark	Mode	Cnt	Score	Error	Units
CH01.BenchmarkSingletonVsThreadLocal.singletonWithDoubleCheckedLocking	avgt		2.629		ms/op
CH01.BenchmarkSingletonVsThreadLocal.singletonWithSynchronization	avgt		316.619		ms/op
CH01.BenchmarkSingletonVsThreadLocal.singletonWithThreadLocal	avgt		5.622		ms/op

Looking at the result, the `singletonWithSynchronization` implementation was indeed the slowest. An average time for completing our benchmarking logic was above 300 ms (milliseconds). Next, we have two solutions that improve this behavior. The `singletonWithDoubleCheckedLocking` performed the best (around ~2.6 ms), and the `singletonWithThreadLocal` solution completed in ~5.6 ms. We can conclude that improving the initial version of singleton pattern gives us around a 50-times performance increase for the thread local solution and 115 times for the double-checked locking solution.

By measuring our assumptions, we can make good decisions for our multithreading context. If we need to pick one solution over another when the performance is comparable, we may decide to choose a more straightforward solution. However, without the actual data, it is hard to make an entirely rational decision.

Let's now take a look at the design tradeoffs that involve an architectural decision. In the next section, we will learn about microservices versus monolithic architectures and their design tradeoffs.

1.3 *Architecture design patterns and why they do not always work*

Up to now, we've considered low-level programming patterns and tradeoffs that lead to different code designs. Although vital, you're probably more comfortable modifying these low-level parts if the application's context changes. The second part of this book will focus on architecture design patterns: those patterns that are harder to change because they span the whole architecture of multiple services that create your system. For now, we will focus on microservices (see http://mng.bz/enlv) architecture, which is one of the most common patterns when creating today's software systems.

The microservices architecture provides many advantages over the approach of creating one monolithic system where all business logic is implemented. However, it also has nonnegligible maintenance costs and increased complexity. Let's look at a few of the most essential advantages of microservices architecture over monolithic architecture.

1.3.1   *Scalability and elasticity*

The systems that we create need to handle high traffic, but they also need to adapt and scale, depending on demand. If one node of your application can process N requests per second and has a surge in traffic, the microservices architecture allows you to scale out horizontally quickly (see figure 1.3). Of course, the application needs to be written in a way that enables easy scaling. It should also use the underlying components.

For example, you can add a new instance of the same microservice to enable your system to process ~$2 \times N$ requests per second (where 2 is the number of services, and N is the number of requests that one service can serve). But this can only be achieved if the underlying data access layer can scale up as well.

Of course, there may be some upper threshold of scalability, after which adding new nodes does not give much improvement in the throughput. It may be caused by the scalability limit of the underlying components, such as database, queue, network bandwidth, etc.

However, the overall scalability of the microservices architecture tends to be easier compared to the monolithic approach. Monolithic architectures do not allow you to scale up as quickly after some upper resource limit is hit.

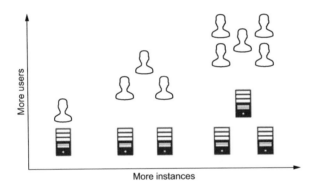

Figure 1.3   **Scaling out horizontally means adding more machines to your pool of resources as the demand increases.**

You can scale your app vertically (scaling up) by adding more CPUs, memory, or disk capacity to the computing instance, and here, too, there is a hard limit over which scaling up is not possible. For example, when you have a monolithic app deployed to the cloud, you can scale it up by deploying it using a more powerful cloud type instance (more CPUs or memory). As long as you can add more resources, this approach is fine. However, the cloud provider may not offer a more powerful machine to deploy to at some point. In such a case, scaling out (horizontally) is more flexible. If your app is written in a way that can be deployed to N instances, you can add more instances to your deployment to increase the total throughput of your service.

1.3.2   *Development speed*

In the microservices architecture, the work can be easily divided between multiple teams. Team A can work on the business functionality that will be implemented in a separate microservice. At the same time, team B can focus on a different part of the business domain. The work of both teams is independent, and they can move faster.

With microservices, there is no coordination at the codebase level. Teams can make their own decisions about technologies and evolve more quickly. When a new team member joins the team that works on part of the business domain, it is easier to understand the system and to start working on it.

The deployment process is more robust because each team can deploy its codebase independently. This results in more frequent deployments that carry less risk. Even if the team accidentally introduces a bug, the change that is deployed is smaller. Because of that, debugging the potential issue is faster. The problems with debugging may arise when the error comes from the integration between too fine-grained microservices. In that case, we need to request tracing to track the requests that are flowing through multiple microservices (see http://mng.bz/p2w8).

Contrary to that, in monolithic architectures, the codebase is often shared between many team members. If your application code lives in one repository and the application is complex, multiple teams may work on it simultaneously. In such a situation, there is a high potential for conflicts in code. Therefore, a significant part of development time may be sacrificed on resolving those conflicts. Of course, if your product's code can be structured in a modularized fashion, you can reduce that effect. However, there will always be a need for more frequent rebasing, as your product's main codebase changes faster if more people are working on it. When we compare monolithic to microservices, it is easy to see that the code for a dedicated business domain is most often smaller. Therefore, there is a high probability that there will be fewer conflicts.

In monolithic applications, the deployment is done less frequently. The reason for this is that more features are merged to the main code branch (because more people work on it). The more features it has, the longer it takes to test them. As more features are deployed in the same release, the chances for introducing a bug into the system grows.

It is worth noting that all of those pains could be reduced by creating a robust continuous integration (or continuous deployment) pipeline. We can run such a pipeline more frequently and build a new application version more often, and every version will contain fewer features. The new release code will be easier to reason about and debug if it introduces a problem. It is faster to find an underlying problem when the list of new features in a release is smaller. If we compare this approach to a release cycle that builds a new app less frequently, it is obvious that such a release will contain more features that will be deployed to production at the same time. The more features one release has, the more potential problems it will have, which will be harder to debug.

1.3.3   *Complexity of microservices*

Once you are aware of the pros of the microservices architecture over monolithic, you need to be aware of the cons. A microservices architecture is a complex design that involves a lot of moving parts. You can achieve scalability if you have a proper load balancer that keeps the list of running services and routes the traffic. The underlying services can be scaled up and down, meaning that they can appear and disappear. Tracking such changes is not an easy task. To make it work, a new service registry component is needed (figure 1.4).

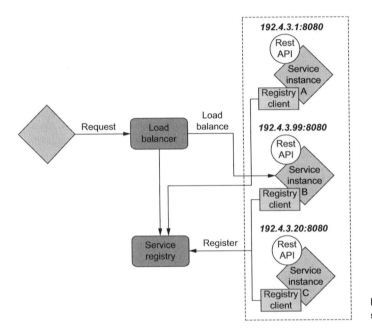

Figure 1.4   Microservices service registry

Every microservice needs to have a running registry client that is responsible for registering it with the service registry. Once it is registered, the load balancer can route the traffic to the new instance. The service registry handles the deregistration process by checking the health of the service instances. This is one of the complexities of this architecture that makes deployment significantly more difficult and complex.

Once you know the pros and cons of your problem, you need to add context to make a good decision about the design. If your context shows that you don't have high flexibility regarding scalability and your team of developers is small, you may decide that the monolithic architecture is right for you. Every chapter in this book follows a similar process to that presented in this chapter for assessing your design choices: finding the pros and cons of each of the designs, adding context, and answering the question of which design may be better in this specific context.

In this chapter, you were introduced to an example of the types of design tradeoffs that we will cover in this book. You learned about the low-level tradeoffs that involve choosing the proportion of unit versus integration tests for your apps. We also discussed that well-proven patterns like singletons may not be the best choice, depending on the context in which they are used. These may impact the performance of your system in multithreaded environments by, for example, introducing thread contention. Finally, we looked at the microservices versus monolithic architecture design patterns, which serves as an example of a higher-level design choice.

In the next chapter, we'll walk through the tradeoff of code duplication versus reusability. We will consider that code duplication is not always bad, again, depending on the context.

Summary

- When you have a finite time in which to develop your software, there are also design consequences, such as covering your code in unit or integration testing, that you need to consider.
- Well-proven, low-level code design patterns (like singleton) may not turn out to be good (in terms of thread safety, for example) design choices, depending on the context of your application.
- High-level microservices architectures do not fit every problem; we need a framework for accessing architecture design choices.

Code duplication is not always bad: Code duplication vs. flexibility

This chapter covers

- Sharing common code between independent codebases
- Tradeoffs between code duplication, flexibility, and delivery
- When code duplication is a sensible choice giving us loose coupling

The DRY (don't repeat yourself) principle is one of the most well-known software engineering rules. The main idea behind this is to remove duplicated code, which leads to fewer bugs and better reusability of our software. But over focusing on the DRY principle when building every possible system may be dangerous and hides a lot of complexities. It is easier to follow the DRY principle if the system we are building is monolithic, meaning that almost the whole codebase is in one repository.

In today's evolved systems, we tend to build distributed systems with many moving parts. In such architectures, the choice of reducing code duplication has more tradeoffs like, for example, introducing tight coupling between components or reducing the development speed of the team. If you have one piece of code used in multiple places, changing it may require a lot of coordination. Where coordination is needed, the process of delivering business value slows down. This chapter will delve into patterns and tradeoffs involving duplication of code. We will try to answer the question: when is code duplication a reasonable tradeoff, and when should we avoid it?

We will start with some duplicated code in two codebases. Next, we will reduce the duplication by using a shared library. Finally, we will use a different approach for extracting a common functionality, using a microservice that encapsulates this behavior. After this example, we will consider inheritance as a pattern to remove duplication in code. However, we will see that this has a nonnegligible cost as well.

2.1 *Common code between codebases and duplication*

We can analyze the first design problem with sharing code in the context of a microservices architecture. Let's imagine a scenario in which we have two teams. Team A works on the payment service, and team B works on the person service. Figure 2.1 illustrates this scenario.

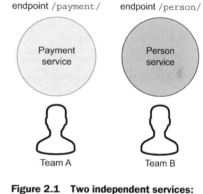

Figure 2.1 Two independent services: payment and person

The payment service exposes an HTTP API with the /payment URL endpoint. The person service exposes its business logic under the /person endpoint. Let's assume that both codebases are written in the same programming language. At this point, both teams are progressing with their work and can deliver the software quickly.

One of the most important reasons why there is a high development turnover (speed) is that there is no need for synchronization between teams. We can even calculate how synchronization impacts the overall time of the software delivery process using Amdahl's law. This formula states that the less synchronization is needed (and, thus, there is a more parallel portion of work), the more gain we get from adding more resources for solving a problem. Figure 2.2 illustrates this principle.

For example, when your task is parallelized 50% of the time (and 50% time requires synchronization), you will not gain any substantial processing speed improvement by adding resources (number of processors in the diagram). However, the more parallelized your task and the less synchronization overhead, the more processing speed you will gain from adding more resources.

We can use Amdahl's formula to calculate the parallelization of concurrent processing and the gains from adding new cores, but we can also adapt it to team members working on a specific task (http://mng.bz/OG4R). The synchronization that reduces parallelism can be the time spent on meetings, merge problems, and other actions that require the whole team's presence.

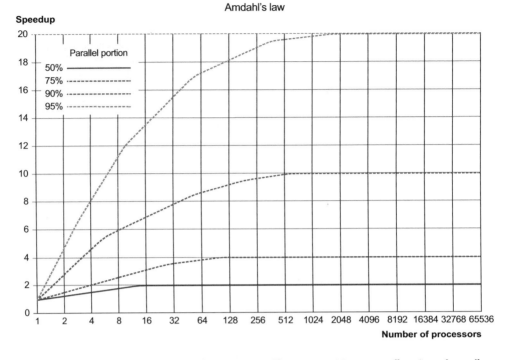

Figure 2.2   Amdahl's law finds the maximum expected improvement to an overall system, depending on the proportion of parallelizable work.

When the code is duplicated, it is developed independently by both teams, and there is no synchronization needed between those teams. Adding a new team member to a team would therefore increase performance. This situation differs when reducing code duplication and the two teams need to work and block each other on the same piece of code.

2.1.1   Adding a new business requirement that requires code duplication

After some time developing both services, a new business requirement to add authorization to both HTTP APIs is made. The first choice of both teams is to implement the authorization component in both codebases. Figure 2.3 shows the modified architecture.

Both teams develop and maintain a similar authorization component. The work of both groups is still independent, however.

In this scenario, be aware that we are using a simplified version of token-based authentication, but this solution is vulnerable to replay attacks (http://mng.bz/YgYB), so it is not suitable for production use. We are using a simplified version to avoid obscuring the main aspects discussed in this chapter. It is worth emphasizing that security is

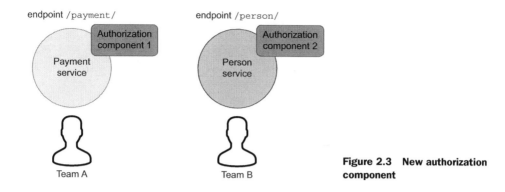

endpoint /payment/

Authorization component 1

Payment service

Team A

endpoint /person/

Authorization component 2

Person service

Team B

Figure 2.3 New authorization component

hard to get right. If each team works independently, the chances of them both getting security right are pretty low. Even if it takes longer to develop a shared library, the upside could be significant in avoiding a security incident.

2.1.2 Implementing the new business requirement

Let's take a look at the Payment service. It exposes the payment HTTP endpoint, /payment. It has only one @GET resource to retrieve all payments for a given token as the following listing shows.

Listing 2.1 Implementing the /payment endpoint

```
@Path("/payment")                                          ⊲─── Exposes the interface
@Produces(MediaType.APPLICATION_JSON)                           for the payment
@Consumes(MediaType.APPLICATION_JSON)                           microservice
public class PaymentResource {

  private final PaymentService paymentService = new PaymentService();
  private final AuthService authService = new AuthService();   ⊲───
                                                               Creates the
                                                               AuthService instance
  @GET
  @Path("/{token}")
  public Response getAllPayments(@PathParam("token") String token) {
    if (authService.isTokenValid(token)) {                   ⊲───
      return Response.ok(paymentService.getAllPayments()).build();
    } else {
      return Response.status(Status.UNAUTHORIZED).build();   Validates the token
    }                                                        using AuthService
  }
}
```

As you can see in listing 2.1, AuthService validates the token, so the caller proceeds to the payment service, which returns all payments. In real life, AuthService would have more complex logic. Let's take a look at a simplified version in the following listing.

Listing 2.2   Creating the authorization service

```
public class AuthService {

  public boolean isTokenValid(String token) {
    return token.equals("secret");
  }
}
```

> **NOTE** In reality, the two teams are unlikely to come up with exactly the same interfaces, method names, signatures, and so forth. That's one advantage of deciding to share code early: there is less time for both implementations to diverge.

The second team works on developing the person service, which exposes an HTTP /person endpoint. It also performs the token-based authorization, as the following listing shows.

Listing 2.3   Implementing the /person endpoint

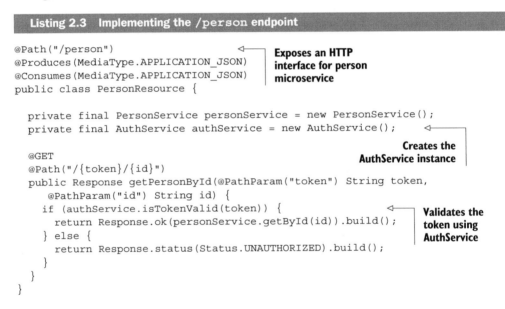

```
@Path("/person")                                      Exposes an HTTP
@Produces(MediaType.APPLICATION_JSON)                 interface for person
@Consumes(MediaType.APPLICATION_JSON)                 microservice
public class PersonResource {

  private final PersonService personService = new PersonService();
  private final AuthService authService = new AuthService();

                                                      Creates the
  @GET                                                AuthService instance
  @Path("/{token}/{id}")
  public Response getPersonById(@PathParam("token") String token,
      @PathParam("id") String id) {
    if (authService.isTokenValid(token)) {            Validates the
      return Response.ok(personService.getById(id)).build();   token using
    } else {                                          AuthService
      return Response.status(Status.UNAUTHORIZED).build();
    }
  }
}
```

The service integrates an AuthService as well. It validates the token provided by the user and then retrieves the Person using PersonService.

2.1.3   Evaluating the result

At this point, because both teams are developing independently, there is code and work duplication.

- *The duplication may lead to more bugs and mistakes.* When team Person, for example, fixes a bug in its authorization component, this does not mean that team Payment cannot make the same mistake.

- *When the same or similar code is duplicated between independent codebases, there is no knowledge sharing between engineers.* For example, team Person finds a bug in the token calculations and fixes it in their codebase. Unfortunately, such a fix is not automatically propagated to team Payment's codebase. Team Payment will need to fix this bug at a later time, independently from team Person.
- *Work without coordination may progress faster.* Even so, there can be a lot of similar work done by both teams.

In reality, you would probably use the production-proven authentication strategies, such as OAuth (https://oauth.net/2/) or JWT (https://jwt.io/) instead of implementing the logic from scratch. These strategies are proven to be even more useful in the context of microservices architecture. Both methods offer many advantages where multiple services need to authenticate to access resources from other services. We won't focus on the specific authentication or authorization strategies here. Instead, we will focus on the code aspects, such as flexibility, maintainability, and complexity. In the next section, we will see how to solve duplication by extracting common code to a shared library.

2.2 Libraries and sharing code between codebases

Let's assume that, because a substantial portion of code is duplicated between two independent codebases, both teams decide to extract common code to a separate library. We will extract the authorization service code to a separate repository. One team needs to create a deployment process for a new library. The most common scenario is to publish a library to an external repository manager, such as JFrog's Artifactory (https://jfrog.com/open-source/). Figure 2.4 illustrates this scenario.

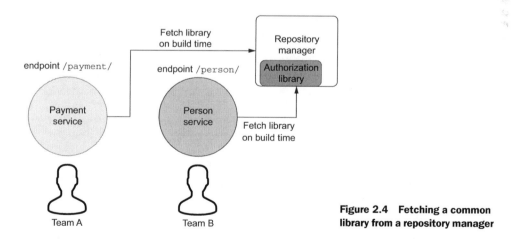

Figure 2.4 Fetching a common library from a repository manager

Once the common code is in the repository manager, both services can fetch the library at a build time and use the classes shipped with it. Using this approach, we can remove any duplication of code by storing it in one place.

One of the apparent benefits of eliminating duplication is the overall quality of the code. Storing a common library allows cooperation between both teams and improves the same codebase. Because of that, when one bug is fixed, the fix is immediately available to all library clients, so there is no duplication of work. Let's now take a look at the disadvantages and tradeoffs that you need to make if you decide to choose this approach.

2.2.1   *Evaluating the tradeoffs and disadvantages of shared libraries*

Once we extract a new library, it becomes a new entity with its own coding style, deployment process, and coding practices. In this context, a library means code that is packaged (into JAR, DLL, or *.so files on Linux platforms and so on) and can be used by multiple projects. A team or person needs to take responsibility for the new codebase. Someone will need to set up the deployment process, validate the project's code quality, develop new features, and so forth. However, it is a bit of a fixed cost.

If you decide to embrace shared libraries, you'll need to develop the processes for that, including coding practices, deployment, and so on. If you create the process once, however, you will be able to apply that multiple times. The cost of adding the first shared library may be high; the cost of adding the second should be much, much less.

One of the most apparent tradeoffs of this approach is that the language in which the new library is created needs to be the same as for the clients that will use it. If, for example, the payment and person services are developed using different languages, such as Python or Java, creating a new library is not feasible. In real life, however, this is rarely an issue because services are created using the same language or family of languages (e.g., JVM languages).

It is possible to create an ecosystem of services where services are written using different technology. However, this substantially increases the complexity of the whole system. It also means that we need to have people with expertise in a variety of technologies. We would also need to use a lot of tools, such as build systems and package managers from different technology stacks. Depending on your language of choice, you have a different ecosystem that surrounds this language.

> ### Open source contributions
> In the JVM ecosystem, there is a vibrant open source community that develops and maintains various libraries. Before you decide on extracting a separate library, you should do some research to find out if an open source library that solves your problem already exists. However, you may need to adapt or extend it a little bit to meet your needs.
>
> You can also donate your code to open source if there is no similar library available. By contributing to an existing open source project, you give your code to other potential users. In addition, you will get a deployment process and advertising for free. Then, chances are that other people will also find your library and reuse the code.

Often, it is possible to write a library in a different language (e.g., C) and wrap it into a native interface (i.e., Java Native Interface) language of your choice. However, using such an approach can be problematic because our code will need yet another layer of indirection. The code that is wrapped in the native interface may not be portable between operating systems, and its method calls may also be slower (compared to Java method calls). For these reasons, let's assume that our further discussion focuses on an ecosystem with the same technology stack.

The new library needs to be advertised within the company to allow other teams to know about it and use it if needed. Otherwise, you end up with a hybrid approach in which some teams use this new library, and others are still duplicating the code.

A repository manager is a good place for a shared library, but you also need to maintain good documentation for the library. Often, good coverage of tests allows other developers to contribute to a library more easily. If you have a test suite that other developers can use and experiment with, this will boost your library usage and contributions. Another thing to note is that the documentation may sometimes become outdated. It's therefore important to update the documentation regularly.

Tests, as well, need to be maintained and updated with your code, which serves as a good marketing tool for your library within the company and also assures potential users about the overall quality of your library. Of course, if you choose a duplication approach, you should test the duplicated code in all places. This means that you should also have a duplicated testing code.

Good test coverage should not be an excuse for not maintaining the documentation for your library. Trying to learn how to use a new library by looking at the tests may be difficult, unless they are written specifically for that purpose. Tests need to cover all kinds of ways to use the library—not just the encouraged ones. They might help answer a specific question, but they're not as useful as a dedicated page with teaching examples and a getting started guide.

2.2.2 *Creating a shared library*

When creating a library, we should strive for simplicity. This is most important when you need to depend on a third-party library. Let's assume that our authorization component needs to have a dependency on a popular Java library, Google Guava (https://github.com/google/guava), so you declare this dependency explicitly. When the payment service imports the new authorization library, it will also have a transitive dependency on Google Guava. Everything works well until the payment service needs to import another third-party library that has a direct dependency on Google Guava but in a different version. Figure 2.5 shows this scenario.

In such a situation, the payment service will have two versions of the same library. It starts getting more problematic if the major version of the underlying library is different. It means they may or may not be binary compatible. Moreover, if two libraries are present on your classpath, the newer one most often is automatically picked by your build system (e.g., Maven or Gradle) if not configured otherwise. For example,

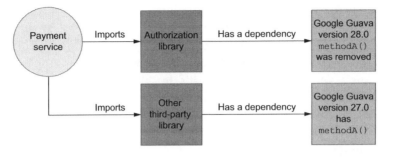

Figure 2.5   Transitive dependencies required to implement the payment service

there could be a situation in which the third-party library code relies on the older version of Guava and calls a `methodA()` that is not in the newer version. If your configuration does not specify which version to use, the build tool may pick the newer version of the library. In such a case, you may get a `MethodNotFound` exception or something similar. This is because the third-party library expects Guava version 27.0 with the called `methodA()`, but the build tool picked the Guava version 28, so the third-party library must use it. This creates the mentioned problems.

Such conflicts are hard to resolve and may discourage other teams in the organization from using your extracted library. So your library should try to have as few direct dependencies as possible. We will discuss this more in chapter 9 and chapter 12 that focus on the decisions that we need to make when choosing libraries for our systems.

In this scenario, we are assuming that the newly extracted library will be used in both the payment and person services. At this point, there is no dedicated team that works on the authorization service itself, so both teams will be involved in the development of the new authorization library. The development of such a library will require some planning and coordination between members from both teams.

2.3   *Code extraction to a separate microservice*

Sharing the code by using libraries may be a good start, but as we saw in section 2.2.1 about tradeoffs and drawbacks, this has a couple of problems. First, the developers working on the library need to take care of compatibility and many other factors. They cannot use third-party libraries freely. Also, importing the library's code means that you have tight coupling between your code and the library at the dependencies level. That does not mean that the microservices architecture does not involve any tight coupling; the services can be coupled at the API level, in requests formats, and so forth. The coupling in a library is in a different place than in the microservices architecture.

If the functionally that is duplicated can be captured as a separate business domain, we can consider creating yet another microservice that exposes the functionality as an HTTP API. For example, we can define a separate business domain that extracts and offers functionalities that were initially implemented elsewhere. Our authorization component is a good candidate for that because it provides the orthogonal functionality that validates the tokens, and the authorization service has its own business domain. We can find a business entity that this new service will handle, such as a user entity with a username and password.

> **NOTE** Our example is a bit simplified, but often, the authorization logic needs to access other information (e.g., in a database). In that case, when the permissions are stored in, say, a database, extracting the logic to separate microservices is even more reasonable. For the simplicity of our example, our authorization does not require access to an external service.

Adding new services requires nonnegligible efforts. These are related not only to its development but also to maintenance. The authorization service clearly has its own business domain with its separate business model. The authentication functionality is orthogonal to the existing platform. Both person and payment services are not related to the authentication functionality. With that justification, let's look at ways to implement the authorization service. Figure 2.6 shows the relationship among our three services.

As you can see in figure 2.6, our new architecture has three separate microservices that are connected with each other using an HTTP API. This means that the person and payment services will need to execute one additional request to validate their tokens. If your application does not have high performance requirements, making one additional HTTP call should not be problem-

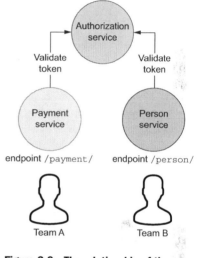

Figure 2.6 The relationship of the authorization service to the person and payment services

atic (assuming that this request is within a cluster or a *closed* network and not to some random server on the internet that might be on the other side of the globe).

With this new solution, the authorization service logic that was previously duplicated or extracted to the library will be abstracted away, using our HTTP API that is accessible under the /auth endpoint. Our clients will send requests to validate the token, and if the validation fails, then an unauthorized (401) HTTP response code is returned. If the token is valid, an HTTP API returns a 200 OK status code instead. The following listing shows our new authorization service.

Listing 2.4 Authorization service HTTP endpoint

```
@Path("/auth")
@Produces(MediaType.APPLICATION_JSON)
```

```
@Consumes(MediaType.APPLICATION_JSON)
public class AuthResource {

  private final AuthService authService = new AuthService();

  @GET
  @Path("/validate/{token}")
  public Response getAllPayments(@PathParam("token") String token) {
    if (authService.isTokenValid(token)) {
      return Response.ok().build();
    } else {
      return Response.status(Status.UNAUTHORIZED).build();
    }
  }
}
```

Because `AuthService` still encapsulates the token validation logic, it now executes
HTTP requests instead of calling a library. The code will live in the dedicated authorization microservice repository. The payment and person services will no longer need
to import authorization directly nor will they need to implement this logic in their
codebases. Both services only need an HTTP client that sends an HTTP request to the
`/auth` endpoint to validate the token. The following listing shows the code for sending this request.

Listing 2.5   Sending an HTTP call to an `AuthorizationService`

```
// send request to a separate service
public boolean isTokenValid(String token) throws IOException {
  CloseableHttpClient client = HttpClients.createDefault();
  HttpGet httpGet = new HttpGet("http://auth-service/auth/validate/" +
   token);
  CloseableHttpResponse response = client.execute(httpGet);      ◁
  return response.getStatusLine().getStatusCode() == HttpStatus.SC_OK;
}
```
**Sends an HTTP request to an
external authorization service**

In listing 2.5, we create the HTTP client that executes HTTP requests. In real-life systems, a client will be shared between calls and components to reduce open connections and resource consumption.

An HttpClient (https://hc.apache.org/) executes an HTTP GET request to validate the token. If the response status line is equal to the OK status code, it means that
the token is valid. Otherwise, the token is invalid.

> **NOTE**   The authorization service can be exposed using the `auth-service`
> domain name system (DNS). You can use a different service discovery mecha-
> nism as well, such as Eureka (https://github.com/Netflix/eureka), Consul
> (https://www.consul.io/), and so forth. The `auth-service` can be exposed by
> using a static IP address as well.

2.3.1 *Looking at the tradeoffs and disadvantages of a separate service*

The separate microservice fixes some of the problems that we encountered when extracting common code to a separate library. The approach of having a separate library involves a different mindset from the team that uses the code. When you import a library into your codebase, this code becomes your code, and you should be responsible for it. Using such a library also involves more tight coupling than using a separate microservice.

When we integrate with other microservices, we can treat them as a black box. The only integration point is an API, which can be HTTP or a different protocol. Theoretically, the library could be treated similarly. Unfortunately, as we saw in section 2.2, in practice, we cannot treat a library as a black box because of the dependencies that it brings to your code.

Calling a microservice means that you also need to add a new dependency to the client library used to execute the actual code. Theoretically, you may end up with the same transitive dependencies problem described in the previous section. Again, in practice, most microservices must use a client library for calls to other services. This can be an HTTP client or something else, depending on the protocol that you use. Therefore, when you need to call microservices from your service, you will probably use the same HTTP client. Because of that, the problem of additional dependencies for every called service does not exist.

Let's consider our authorization service as a separate microservice with its own API. We already saw that this solves some of the library's approach problems. But, on the other hand, maintaining a separate microservice takes significant effort. With this approach, we need to do a lot more than simply code the service and authorization logic.

A separate microservice means that you need to create a deployment process that will publish your code into a cloud or on-premise infrastructure. A library also needs to have a deployment process, but it is substantially more straightforward. You only need to package a JAR file and deploy it to a repository manager. Someone will need to monitor the health of the service and react if there are some problems. Note that the cost of creating the process for deploying, maintaining, monitoring, and so forth is a significant upfront expense. Once the process is in place, however, developing subsequent microservices may be easier and faster (a similar upfront cost needs to be done for libraries). Let's look at a couple of the most important things to consider when choosing an approach with a separate service.

THE DEPLOYMENT PROCESS

The microservice needs to be deployed and run as a process. This means that such a process needs to be monitored, and the team needs to react if there is a problem or failure. Therefore, creating, monitoring, and alerting are other factors you need to consider when extracting a separate microservice. If your company has an ecosystem for microservices, the alerting and monitoring solutions are probably already set up. If you are one of the first people in a company who wants to use such an architecture, it would mean that you need to set up those solutions yourself. This means a lot of integration points that will add a substantial amount of work.

VERSIONING

Versioning of the microservice may be a bit easier than versioning a library in some respects. Your library should follow semantic versioning, and you should not break the compatibility of your APIs in major versions. Microservice API versioning should also follow the same guidelines of not breaking backward compatibility. Still, in practice, it is easier to monitor the use of endpoints and deprecate them quickly if they are not used anymore. If you are developing a library and switching to a new major version is not possible, you need to be careful to not break its compatibility. Breaking it would mean that clients, after updating the version of your library, will not compile. Such a change is not acceptable.

When you have an HTTP API, you can measure every endpoint usage by a simple counter, using a metrics library, such as Dropwizard metrics (https://metrics.dropwizard .io/4.1.2/). If the counter for a specific endpoint does not increase for a long time and your service is used only internally within your company, you may decide to drop support for such an endpoint. If the endpoint is public and documented, you may need to support it longer. Even if the specific endpoint metric does not increase, that does not mean that you can delete it. If it is public and documented, someone may start using it.

For now, you can see that the microservices approach gives you more flexibility regarding API evolution. We will describe compatibility in detail in chapter 12.

RESOURCE CONSUMPTION

A library used by the client means that the computation and resource consumption of the client code can increase. For every request your payment service processes, the validation token needs to be handled in your code. If this code has substantial resource consumption, you will need to increase CPU or RAM, depending on the usage.

If the validation logic is hidden against the API exposed by a separate service, scaling and resource consumption is no longer a direct problem for the client. The processing will be executed at a particular microservice instance. If there are too many requests to process, the team responsible for the service will need to react accordingly and scale the service up as appropriate.

You need to be aware that your client code will require an extra HTTP call in such a case because every validation will need a round trip to the microservice. If the logic hidden via the microservice API is straightforward, it may turn out that the extra cost of an HTTP call is higher than the cost of executing the logic clientside. If the logic is more complex, the HTTP cost may be negligible compared to the microservice work. You should consider this tradeoff when deciding whether to extract the functionality externally.

PERFORMANCE

Finally, you need to calculate the impact on performance that executing additional HTTP requests will have. The tokens used to authorize usually have some expiration time associated with them. Therefore, you can cache them to reduce the number of requests that your service needs to make. For caching functionality, you will need to use a caching library in the client code.

It is often the case that both approaches (libraries and external services) are used to deliver business functionalities. Extracting the logic to a separate microservice imposes the need to execute an additional HTTP call for every user's request to your service, which may be a substantial drawback. You need to calculate how this will impact your response latencies and the service-level agreement (SLA) of your service. Figure 2.7 shows one such scenario.

If, for example, your 99th percentile latency according to your SLA needs to be less than n milliseconds, adding calls to other microservices may break your SLA. If the

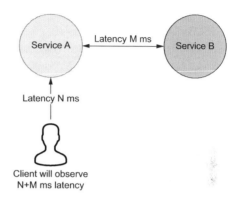

Figure 2.7 Adding additional latency can impact your services.

microservice 99th percentile latency is less than n, however, you can hide the additional HTTP call by executing some requests in parallel, by retrying, or by using speculative execution. This will worsen if a second microservice 99th percentile latency is greater than n. In that case, you won't fulfill your SLA. You will need to increase the latency in SLA requirements if possible. If this is not possible, you will need to invest more time to reduce the 99th percentile of the second service or use the approach of extracting a library.

If you are not concerned strictly about the latency, you still need to be careful about cascading failures (http://mng.bz/GGrv) and guard against the dependent microservice's temporary unavailability. The problem of cascading failures is not specific to microservices and can occur with any external system that you need to call (e.g., a database, an authentication API, and so on).

If your business flow requires an additional external request, you need to decide how to handle situations when this service is down. You may implement retry with exponential backoff to allow the downstream service to get back online without overwhelming the service with the request. Using this technique, you can probe the downstream service every x milliseconds, and when it gets back online, you can gradually increase the traffic. By adding an exponential backoff behavior, your retry strategy should be executed with a decreasing frequency. For example, the first retry after 1 second, the second retry after 10 seconds, the third retry after 30 seconds, and so on. If it does not help, and the service is down nontemporarily, you need to guard against that by using a circuit breaker pattern (https://martinfowler.com/bliki/CircuitBreaker.html).

You should provide fallback behavior that will be executed when the downstream system is down. For example, if you have a payment system and the payment provider is down, you may decide to validate the payment and debit the account after some period of time only after the downstream system is back online again. Such a solution needs to be implemented carefully, and it must be a conscious business decision.

MAINTENANCE

As you can see, there are many tradeoffs for separate microservices. In real life, this approach will need more planning and more maintenance. It would be best to compare it with a more straightforward method of sharing libraries and list all the pros and cons. If the logic that you need to share is simple and does not have many dependencies, you may end up extracting the library. On the other hand, if the logic is complex and can be extracted as a separate business component, you may consider creating a new microservice. With the latter approach, you need to keep in mind that it requires more work and probably a dedicated team that can support this running process.

2.3.2 *Conclusions about separate service*

Looking at all the tradeoffs for microservices, you can see that it has a lot of drawbacks. You need to implement a lot of new parts. Even if you do that correctly, the failure of a request that executes an external call via a network that can be unreliable is still unavoidable. You should take all those pros and cons into consideration when choosing the approach of a library versus a microservices approach.

> **NOTE** It is easier to outsource when a given functionality is abstracted away into a separate service or a library. For example, we could outsource the implementation of the authentication logic to an external vendor. However, this approach also has many drawbacks, including possibly a higher price, coordination problems, inflexibility of changes, and many more.

In the next section, we will analyze duplication at a lower level. We will see how it favors loose coupling.

2.4   *Improving loose coupling by code duplication*

In this section, we will look at the problem of duplication at the code level. Specifically, we will look at the design of two request handlers that process two types of trace requests.

Let's assume that our system needs to handle two types of requests. The first one is a standard trace request, and the second is a graph trace request. Both requests may arrive from a different API, using different protocols and so forth. For that reason, we have two code paths that handle both request types independently.

Let's start the discussion from the most straightforward approach of having two separate handler processor components. The GraphTraceHandler processes graph trace requests, whereas the TraceHandler processes normal trace requests. Figure 2.8 shows this arrangement.

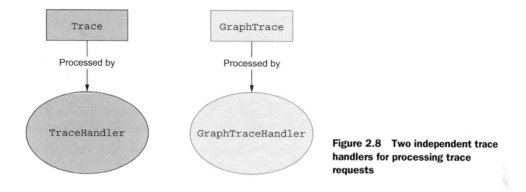

Figure 2.8 Two independent trace handlers for processing trace requests

The logic is isolated, and there is no coupling between these two handlers. The Trace and GraphTrace objects are similar; they carry information if the trace is enabled, and they both take actual data. For the GraphTrace class, this information is of an int type, whereas for the Trace class, it is a String, as the following listing shows.

Listing 2.6 Decoupled Trace and GraphTrace classes

```
public class Trace {
  private final boolean isTraceEnabled;       Specifies the data
  private final String data;              ⊲—  type for Trace

  public Trace(boolean isTraceEnabled, String data) {
    this.isTraceEnabled = isTraceEnabled;
    this.data = data;
  }
  public boolean isTraceEnabled() {
    return isTraceEnabled;
  }

  public String getData() {
    return data;
  }
}

public class GraphTrace {                    Notice that the data
  private final boolean isTraceEnabled;      types for GraphTrace
  private final int data;               ⊲—  and Trace differ.

  public GraphTrace(boolean isTraceEnabled, int data) {
    this.isTraceEnabled = isTraceEnabled;
    this.data = data;
  }
```

```
  public boolean isTraceEnabled() {
    return isTraceEnabled;
  }

  public int getData() {
    return data;
  }
}
```

At first glance, the classes look similar, but there is no common structure shared between them. They are totally decoupled.

Let's now take a look at the handlers that process the trace requests. The first handler that we will analyze is `TraceRequestHandler`. The responsibility of this handler is to buffer incoming requests. Figure 2.9 illustrates the process for the `TraceRequestHandler`.

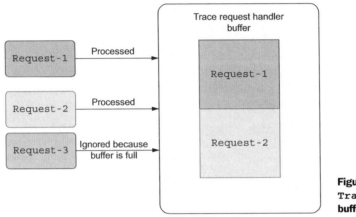

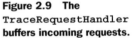

Figure 2.9   The `TraceRequestHandler` buffers incoming requests.

As you can see, `TraceRequestHandler` buffers the request as long as there is available space in the buffer. When the buffer is full, the request (Request-3 in figure 2.9) is ignored.

A `bufferSize` parameter limits the size of the buffer passed to the constructor of this handler by specifying how many items the `TraceRequestHandler` can process. Requests are buffered in the list data structure. When the buffer is full, the processed flag is set to true. The following listing shows the code for decoupling this handler.

Listing 2.7   Decoupled `TraceRequestHandler`

```
public class TraceRequestHandler {
  private final int bufferSize;
  private boolean processed = false;
  List<String> buffer = new ArrayList<>();

  public TraceRequestHandler(int bufferSize) {
    this.bufferSize = bufferSize;
  }
```

```
public void processRequest(Trace trace) {
  if (!processed && !trace.isTraceEnabled()) {
    return;
  }
  if (buffer.size() < bufferSize) {
    buffer.add(createPayload(trace));
  }

  if (buffer.size() == bufferSize) {
    processed = true;
  }
}

private String createPayload(Trace trace) {
  return trace.getData() + "-content";
}

public boolean isProcessed() {
  return processed;
}
}
```

If the size of the underlying buffer is less than bufferSize, then append to it.

If the size is full, then set the processed flag to true.

In the listing, note the `createPayload()` method. It has the only logic that is specific to the `Trace` class. It takes the trace request, extracts its data, and creates a string that is appended to the buffer.

To understand this component, let's take a look at a unit test. It will process five requests. However, the buffer limit will be set to four. In this case, after the buffer receives four requests, the fifth one will not be appended. In the following listing, we create the new `TraceRequestHandler` with buffer size four to implement this strategy. The last request (with the e value) should be ignored because it exceeds the buffer.

Listing 2.8 Creating the `TraceRequestHandler` unit test

```
@Test
public void shouldBufferTraceRequest() {
  // given
  TraceRequestHandler traceRequestHandler = new TraceRequestHandler(4);

  // when
  traceRequestHandler.processRequest(new Trace(true, "a"));
  traceRequestHandler.processRequest(new Trace(true, "b"));
  traceRequestHandler.processRequest(new Trace(true, "c"));
  traceRequestHandler.processRequest(new Trace(true, "d"));
  traceRequestHandler.processRequest(new Trace(true, "e"));

  // then
  assertThat(traceRequestHandler.buffer)
      .containsOnly("a-content", "b-content",
  "c-content", "d-content");
  assertThat(traceRequestHandler.isProcessed()).isTrue();
}
```

The actual buffer content has no e-content element.

After processing, isProcessed should return true.

As you can see, the buffer contains only four records. To understand why there is duplication between the handlers, we need to analyze the code of the GraphTrace-RequestHandler. In fact, the only difference between the graph and normal trace handlers is the createPayload() method that we implement in the following listing. The graphTrace extracts the data and appends the nodeId suffix to it.

Listing 2.9   Creating the payload for the `GraphTraceRequestHandler`

```
private String createPayload(GraphTrace graphTrace) {
    return graphTrace.getData() + "-nodeId";
}
```

The rest of the processing code is the same between the two components. At this point, we can see that both trace requests and also both handlers are similar. They are independent and loosely coupled, but the processRequest() method for the Trace-RequestHandler is quite complicated, and evolving this logic in two places in our code can be error prone and hard to maintain.

We know enough details about this code to decide that the common logic can be extracted to a separate parent class, and both handlers can inherit the most complex parts. In the next section, we will analyze this refactoring.

2.5   *An API design with inheritance to reduce duplication*

In this section, we will use an inheritance technique to reduce code duplication. The most complex method that we want to share for our request handlers is process-Request(). If you refer back to this method in listing 2.7, you will notice that it uses the isTraceEnabled() method to detect whether a trace request should be buffered. Because both Trace and GraphTrace are similar, we can extract the common parts to a new TraceRequest class, as the following listing shows.

Listing 2.10   Creating a `TraceRequest` parent class

```
public abstract class TraceRequest {
    private final boolean isTraceEnabled;        ◁──┐   isTraceEnabled
                                                     │   is shared by both
    public TraceRequest(boolean isTraceEnabled) {    │   GraphTrace and Trace.
        this.isTraceEnabled = isTraceEnabled;
    }

    public boolean isTraceEnabled() {
        return isTraceEnabled;
    }
}
```

With this new structure, both requests can extend the new abstract TraceRequest, providing only the data that is specific to each kind of request. The following listing shows how GraphTrace and Trace can extend TraceRequest.

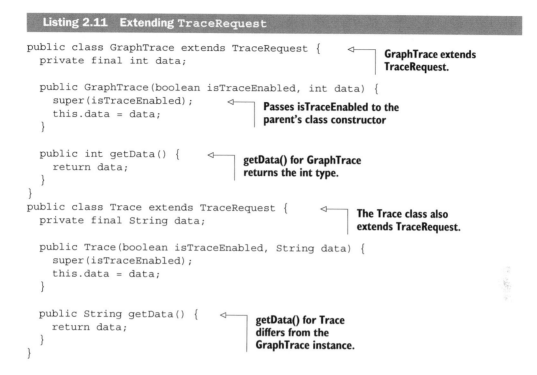

Listing 2.11 Extending `TraceRequest`

```
public class GraphTrace extends TraceRequest {          ◁─────  GraphTrace extends
  private final int data;                                        TraceRequest.

  public GraphTrace(boolean isTraceEnabled, int data) {
    super(isTraceEnabled);            ◁─────  Passes isTraceEnabled to the
    this.data = data;                         parent's class constructor
  }

  public int getData() {         ◁─────  getData() for GraphTrace
    return data;                          returns the int type.
  }
}
public class Trace extends TraceRequest {          ◁─────  The Trace class also
  private final String data;                               extends TraceRequest.

  public Trace(boolean isTraceEnabled, String data) {
    super(isTraceEnabled);
    this.data = data;
  }

  public String getData() {          ◁─────  getData() for Trace
    return data;                              differs from the
  }                                           GraphTrace instance.
}
```

Figure 2.10 shows how the `Trace` and `GraphTrace` hierarchy will look after extracting the common parts.

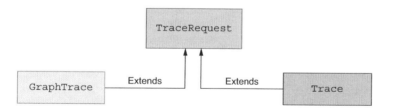

Figure 2.10   The new `TraceRequest` class that `GraphTrace` and `Trace` can extend to reduce code duplication

Thanks to our refactoring, we can use `TraceRequest` and the classes inheriting from this class in a new handler base class that we will extract in the next section.

2.5.1 Extracting a base request handler

The goal of our refactoring is to remove code duplication in the handlers. For this, we want to extract a new `BaseTraceRequestHandler` class that will operate on the `Trace-Request` class. The `createPayload()` method that is specific to a request type will end up in the child classes that provide this concrete behavior. Figure 2.11 illustrates this new arrangement.

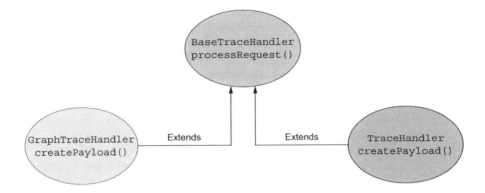

Figure 2.11 Extracting the BaseTraceHandler parent class

We need to parameterize the new BaseTraceRequestHandler class, so it can operate on any class that extends TraceRequest. Let's take a look at a revised BaseTrace-RequestHandler class in the following listing. It will work for all classes that call TraceRequest or that extend it. The <T extends TraceRequest> is a Java technique to achieve this invariant.

Listing 2.12 Creating the BaseTraceRequestHandler parent class

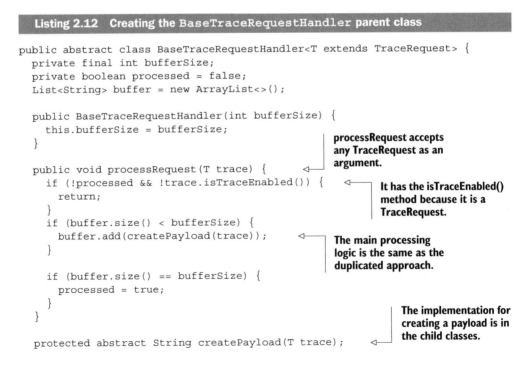

```
public abstract class BaseTraceRequestHandler<T extends TraceRequest> {
  private final int bufferSize;
  private boolean processed = false;
  List<String> buffer = new ArrayList<>();

  public BaseTraceRequestHandler(int bufferSize) {
    this.bufferSize = bufferSize;
  }

  public void processRequest(T trace) {
    if (!processed && !trace.isTraceEnabled()) {
      return;
    }
    if (buffer.size() < bufferSize) {
      buffer.add(createPayload(trace));
    }

    if (buffer.size() == bufferSize) {
      processed = true;
    }
  }

  protected abstract String createPayload(T trace);
```

processRequest accepts any **TraceRequest** as an argument.

It has the **isTraceEnabled()** method because it is a **TraceRequest**.

The main processing logic is the same as the duplicated approach.

The implementation for creating a payload is in the child classes.

```
  public boolean isProcessed() {
    return processed;
  }
}
```

The processRequest() logic works now on any TraceRequest class. The isTrace-Enabled() method is accessible here because the TraceRequest class defines this method. Note that createPayload() is an abstract method. The concrete implementation will be provided by the child classes that can process Trace or GraphTrace requests.

After this refactoring, both handlers can extend the base class, providing only the necessary parts of code for their implementation. The TraceRequestHandler and GraphTraceRequestHandler classes only need to provide the implementation for the createPayload() method. The parent class takes a bufferSize, which is used in the main processing logic to limit the buffer size as a parameter. The constructor of the child class then needs to call the super constructor with this argument. The new TraceRequestHandler extends the base class that we extracted. It is parameterized using the Trace class, as the following listing shows.

> **Listing 2.13 Adding inheritance to `GraphTraceRequestHandler` and `TraceRequestHandler`**

```
public class TraceRequestHandler extends BaseTraceRequestHandler<Trace> {

  public TraceRequestHandler(int bufferSize) {
    super(bufferSize);
  }

  @Override
  public String createPayload(Trace trace) {
    return trace.getData() + "-content";
  }
}

public class GraphTraceRequestHandler extends
    BaseTraceRequestHandler<GraphTrace> {

  public GraphTraceRequestHandler(int bufferSize) {
    super(bufferSize);
  }

  @Override
  public String createPayload(GraphTrace graphTrace) {      ◁─── Provides an algorithm
    return graphTrace.getData() + "-nodeId";                       for processing
  }                                                                 GraphTrace
}
```

By using inheritance, we were able to simplify the handlers substantially. We removed the duplicated code using the DRY principle. Our code is now more maintainable, but it is also more tightly coupled. After our hard work, we might think that this design decision does not involve a tradeoff. Our perspective will change a little bit when the new business requirement arrives. We will look at this in the next section.

2.5.2   *Looking at inheritance and tight coupling*

Our code uses inheritance now, and the handlers only provide the `createPayload()` method. Let's assume that a new business requirement arrives: we need to change the `GraphTraceRequestHandler` to work using an unbounded `bufferSize`. (Although it is not advisable to have unbounded buffers in production systems, we will consider this scenario for simplicity reasons.) This also means that this handler no longer needs the `bufferSize` parameter.

As you know, the `processRequest()` logic is in the parent class and is shared between all client classes. The new business requirement means that the method responsible for processing requests can be simplified, as the following listing shows.

Listing 2.14   Simplifying `processRequest`

```
public void processRequest(T trace) {
    if (!processed && !trace.isTraceEnabled()) {
      return;
    }

    buffer.add(createPayload(trace));          ◁───  The logic for limiting the
}                                                     number of trace requests in
                                                      the buffer is no longer in place.
```

One problem that we can see here is that the `processRequest()` method can be simplified only for graph trace handlers. The logic for the standard handler needs to track the buffer. So reducing duplication introduced a tight coupling to the design. Due to that fact, it is not feasible to change the `processRequest()` method for one child class without impacting other child classes. This lack of flexibility is the tradeoff that we need to make, and it limits our design substantially.

One solution to this problem is to create a special case for process requests using `instanceof` and then not buffering if the trace class is a `GraphTrace`. The following listing provides this solution.

Listing 2.15   Using `instanceof` as a workaround

```
if(trace instanceof GraphTrace){
  buffer.add(createPayload(trace));
}
```

Such a solution would be fragile and would defy the purpose of introducing inheritance in the first place. It introduces tight coupling between the parent and child classes. Suddenly, the parent class needs to know about all the request types that it needs to handle. It no longer operates on the generic `TraceRequest` class only. Now, it needs to know about one of the actual implementations: `GraphTrace`. The logic from the specific graph handler is leaking to the generic handler. Therefore, handling the

`GraphTrace` requests is no longer encapsulated in the code responsible for processing this request.

To alleviate this problem, we can return to the solution with duplicated code. However, in a real-life situation, such decisions are problematic because the components that we refactor are substantially more complex and involve a lot more work.

The thoughtful reader can see that, for our simple example, passing the `Integer` `.MAX_INT` in the constructor of the `GraphTraceRequestHandler` as the `bufferSize` would solve the problem. This would theoretically mean that we can achieve the business goal of having the unbounded buffer without changing more code. In real-world systems, however, a change of business requirements that you may encounter will be more complicated. You might not be able to solve them without reducing the tight coupling and removing the inheritance again.

I've chosen inheritance as a solution here due to the context in which the original code worked. Suppose you want to provide the caller with a possibility to provide an implementation of the handler but let the caller provide some implementation parts (as in `BaseTraceRequestHandler`). This is known as the *strategy pattern*. In that case, it may be easier to choose an inheritance in which the main logic and the skeleton are provided in the parent class and the client implements the missing parts.

You can try a different approach to reduce duplication, such as composition or design patterns that fit your needs. However, any solution will have its pros and cons, and you need to consider its tradeoffs. You need to decide whether the flexibility you want to achieve is worth maintaining code duplication that can evolve in different directions. One alternative approach you might want to consider is using composition of independent building blocks instead of tying multiple aspects of behavior together with inheritance.

2.5.3 *Looking at the tradeoffs between inheritance and composition*

The strategy pattern is a good fit for our example if each subclass always has a well-specific set of requirements that are somewhat separate to each other. If the set of requirements grows, however, you may want to consider using composition instead of inheritance. This would require separating the requirements into different responsibilities. In our existing system, we already have a transformation of the data into its eventual payload format and buffering.

Currently, the buffering is relatively straightforward and is always based on the number of elements added to it. Let's suppose we want to apply different buffering strategies, which might include infinite buffering, no buffering at all, the existing buffering based on the number of elements in the buffer, or, perhaps, a space-based buffer that takes into account the size of each element. With the inheritance approach, we might implement this with a `tryAddEntry()` method that can either be abstract or have a default implementation in `BaseTraceHandler`. Is this still the best design?

Separating the transformation and buffering responsibilities into different abstractions (potentially reusing existing functional interfaces) allows the handler code to just be plumbing that joins the abstractions together appropriately. This allows better flexibility and mixing and matching arbitrary buffering with arbitrary data transformations, for example. But this comes at the cost of increasing the number of abstractions the reader needs to understand when approaching the code. Figure 2.12 shows the two approaches side by side.

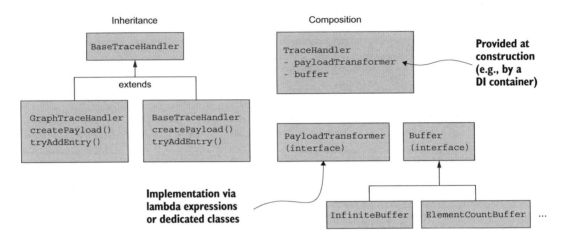

Figure 2.12   Composition and inheritance approaches to `TraceHandler`

If the handler abstraction itself is sufficiently isolated from the rest of the code, perhaps being configured in a dependency injection phase, and then simply used, you can switch from an inheritance-based approach to a composition-based approach (or vice versa) without disturbing the rest of the codebase. All of this discussion of how to avoid duplication presupposes that there is genuine duplication in the first place. That's not always the case, even when it looks like it at first glance.

2.5.4   *Looking at inherent and incidental duplication*

In the real world, software engineers tend to overfit for pattern matching. One example of this is creating a shared abstraction and then adapting the code in multiple places to share this abstraction. The fact that two things look identical doesn't mean they will solve the same business goal. They may also evolve differently. This is *incidental* duplication rather than something *inherent* in the code you're working with.

It's usually easier to merge two concepts into one if they turn out to be the same rather than to separate them if they turn out to be different. Once you have abstraction and multiple usages, the coupling of the components can be high. This means that splitting the shared code into separate classes can be challenging.

Sometimes, what looks like duplication is just two different things that happen to be treated the same way in current requirements but which may vary later and shouldn't be treated as equivalent. It may be difficult to distinguish between those two situations at the beginning of a system design.

Sometimes starting from an abstraction and adapting all possible usages to it may not be optimal. Instead, we can implement our system by creating independent components and letting them live independently for some time (even if it requires some code duplication). Later, we may begin to see some common patterns between those components, and abstraction may emerge. That might be the proper time to remove duplication by creating some abstraction instead of starting from it.

In this chapter, we analyzed solutions for reducing duplication in your code. We started from the code that was shared between two codebases and extracted it to a separate library. We analyzed the tradeoffs and problems that you need to tackle during the lifecycle of the library. Next, we saw a different approach of sharing common code via a specialized service that can extract its API and can be treated in a black-box way. The separate microservice was solving some of the problems of the library approach but also introduced a variety of issues and tradeoffs. The second part of this chapter was focusing on finding abstraction between two handler components that were decoupled from each other. We created a solution using inheritance that allows us to solve problems with less code. Inheritance solved some problems, but when there was a need for flexibility, we saw that it limits our design possibilities and has its tradeoffs.

In the next chapter, we'll learn how to handle exceptions and errors in our code. We will also learn how to handle exceptions from third-party code and about the best practices of handling exceptions in the multithread environment.

Summary

- Sharing common code between codebases can be achieved by extracting a separate library. Conversely, reusing code via the library comes with various problems, such as tight coupling and less flexibility.
- Extracting common business logic to a separate service may be the right choice for more complex problems, but it has a high maintenance cost.
- Inheritance helps us remove code duplication and share common code between child classes. Unfortunately, it has a lot of tradeoffs that limit the flexibility of our code.
- Sometimes it is worth keeping duplicated code because it provides flexibility and reduces coordination between teams.

Exceptions vs. other patterns of handling errors in your code

This chapter covers

- The best patterns for handling exceptions
- Exceptions from third-party libraries
- Exceptions in multithreaded and async code
- Exceptions in functional and object-oriented programs

Errors and exceptions are inevitable in our code. Almost every code path fails if something unexpected happens. Imagine that you are executing a simple addition of two numbers. At first glance, such a code path cannot fail. However, you need to be aware that your program executes in some context. For example, you may get an out of memory error if there is not enough memory to run any operation on your machine. You may get an interrupted exception in the multithreaded context if your code is executed in a separate thread, and this thread gets the interruption signal. Many potential problems can occur.

Most often, our code is not trivial, and it can fail in a variety of ways. Handling failures should be our first thought when creating our code. Our code should be *fault-tolerant*, meaning that it should recover from problems whenever possible. Before you can decide how to handle exceptions, you need to design an API that tackles problems and signals them in an explicit way. However, if we signal the possibility of every error explicitly, our code would become hard to read and maintain.

Not every error pattern requires recovery in code. According to the *let-it-crash* philosophy that was first defined in the Erlang ecosystem, it is better not to recover from critical failures. In such a scenario, a supervisor may monitor the process, and if the program crashes from some nonrecoverable error (out of memory, for instance), the supervisor simply restarts it. This philosophy does not require programmers to code defensively and to try to guard against every possible exception-causing behavior. It is a different approach than the one mainly used in the Java ecosystem. However, some Java-related technologies, such as Akka, follow this pattern.

In the standard Java-based application, the let-it-crash approach would be problematic because processing users' requests is not separated into independent processes. A typical Java application contains n processing threads, and each of those process requests for some users. Because we are working within one application, if we crash the whole application due to one user's request, it impacts other users.

In the actor approach with Erlang, Akka, and others, the processing model is more fine-grained. Usually, the application can contain hundreds of actors (or more), and each of those actors is responsible for processing a small amount of user traffic. If we crash one actor, it won't impact others. This approach has some valid use cases, but it depends heavily on the structure of your application and its threading model.

We will look at the tradeoffs of both approaches and when to use them. Once we know about the best patterns, we will add one more complexity level—handling problems in async code that works in a multithreaded environment.

When we can design an API upfront, we can make it robust and verbose where it should be explicit. But there are some errors we can't do much about when they happen. Such errors should remain implicit, and we do not need to include them in our API contract. And unfortunately, there are APIs and third-party libraries that hide problems from us. We will delve into techniques to handle such problems.

Finally, we will compare throwing exceptions in an object-oriented fashion with a functional approach that uses the `Try` monad to address problems. Let's start our journey into exceptions by understanding the hierarchy of problems that our code can signal and handle.

3.1 Hierarchy of exceptions

Before we delve into more advanced topics like designing our API's exception handling scheme, let's take a brief look into a hierarchy of exceptions and errors that we often use in our code. Figure 3.1 illustrates this hierarchy.

In Java, every exception is an object. A special `Throwable` type (extends `Object`) gives useful information for every error. It wraps the cause with a message that signals the problem. What is more important, it contains the stack trace. This is an array of elements where each element identifies a particular line in code in a specific class that leads to an exception. For diagnostic purposes, this information is essential. It helps

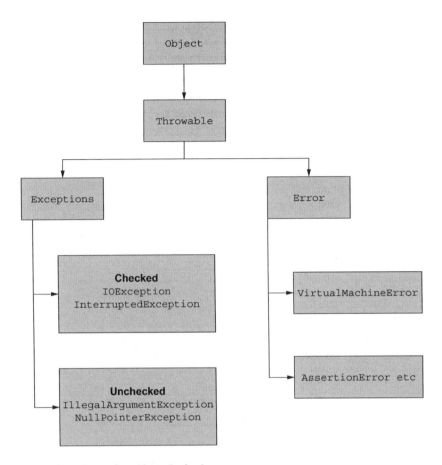

Figure 3.1 Exceptions hierarchy for Java

you trace back to the line where the problem occurred, so you can debug it. Next, we have two types of classes that extend a `Throwable` (`Error` and `Exception`). If your application throws an `Error`, it means that a critical problem has occurred, and most often, you should not try to catch or handle it. It can be, for example, a virtual machine error that signals a critical problem with the environment.

In this chapter, we won't focus on Java error handling because we don't have much control over it. We will, however, consider different strategies for exception handling. Also note that in the rest of the chapter, I will use the words *error* and *exception* interchangeably for the same concept.

On the left side of figure 3.1, you can see the exceptions. We should use those to signal problems within our code. Moreover, we should also handle them if there is a way to recover gracefully. In fact, if a method declares a checked exception, then the compiler requires a caller to handle such an exception (it can be caught or rethrown). This means that your code will not compile until you handle it. For example, if you load some files and get an IOException, it may be reasonable to recover and try to load it from a different place on your filesystem. Later, we will use those exceptions to design an error-handling API explicitly.

On the other hand, we are not required to handle unchecked exceptions. But if your code does not handle these, they are propagated to the main application thread and will stop your application. They often signal some usage error that cannot be recovered, and it is better to fail fast than to try to recover from such an error. For example, if you pass a negative number as an argument to a method that expects a positive number, you may decide to throw an unchecked exception because there is no point in trying to recover. The callers may also prefer to use unchecked exceptions to simplify using them from a functional interface (lambda) API, for example. This is the implicit part of the error handling code.

The concept of checked or unchecked exceptions is also present in other languages, but most of those pick one strategy or the other. For example, in the Scala and C# programming languages, every exception is treated as unchecked; therefore, you don't need to catch them. However, you need to be careful not to propagate exceptions up to the main thread. Otherwise, your program will stop.

3.1.1 *Catch-all vs. a more granular approach to handling errors*

Let's look at understanding exceptions and their hierarchy in an empirical way. We'll assume that we have a method that declares throwing two exceptions that are checked, as the following listing shows.

Listing 3.1 Method that throws checked exceptions

```
public void methodThatThrowsCheckedException()
    throws FileAlreadyExistsException, InterruptedException
```

Both FileAlreadyExistsException and InterruptedException are checked exceptions. This means the caller of this method needs to handle them at compile time. The first approach of handling those exceptions is to declare a catch clause for both types, as this listing demonstrates.

Listing 3.2 Handling checked exceptions

```
public void shouldCatchAtNormalGranularity() {
  try {
      methodThatThrowsCheckedException();
  } catch (FileAlreadyExistsException e) {          ◁    Catches
      logger.error("File already exists: ", e);          FileAlreadyExistsException
  } catch (InterruptedException e) {          ◁
      logger.error("Interrupted", e);             Catches other exception
  }                                               that is unrelated to the
}                                                 previous
```

By using two catch blocks, we can provide a different exception handling behavior, depending on the type. Often, this is a correct granularity level for handling exceptions.

Because of the exceptions hierarchy, we can alter the catch block to catch a wider type. For example, FileAlreadyExistsException (see http://mng.bz/zQwB) extends IOException, so the first catch block can directly catch IOException, as the following listing illustrates.

Listing 3.3   Handling checked exceptions with a wider type

```
public void shouldCatchAtHigherGranularity() {
  try {
     methodThatThrowsCheckedException();
    } catch (IOException e) {                      ◁──┐  FileAlreadyExistsException
     logger.error("Some IO problem: ", e);              │  extends IOException—
    } catch (InterruptedException e) {                 │  handle it instead.
     logger.error("Interrupted", e);
    }
}
```

There's one problem with this listing: we are losing the information that the File-AlreadyExistsException was thrown. Whereas this information will be present at run time, at compile time, we'll get only the information that it throws IOException.

We could broaden our exception type to Exception or any Throwable. However, we could also potentially catch exceptions that we didn't mean to catch initially. We may catch other potentially critical exceptions unrelated to our processing, which should be propagated to higher components.

If the method that is called throws more than one exception that extends IOException, we may consider creating one catch block instead of a couple lower granularity catch blocks. This is a rational solution if we don't need to create error handling logic per a specific type and we are OK with a more generic approach.

If we do not care about the type of exception, but we want to catch all the problems, it is possible to declare the catch for all exceptions. As you remember from the previous section, every exception, checked and unchecked, extends the Exception class, so this approach will catch all the problems of the called method. The following listing shows this approach.

Listing 3.4   Catching all exceptions

```
public void shouldCatchAtCatchAll() {
  try {
     methodThatThrowsCheckedException();
    } catch (Exception e) {            ◁──┐  Catches all exceptions,
     logger.error("Problem ", e);          │  checked and unchecked
    }
}
```

Such an approach may be convenient because it requires less code to write, but we lose a lot of information here. Also, you need to remember that you will catch *all* exceptions, even those that are not declared as checked exceptions thrown by the called method. This may not be the behavior that we expect. We are risking catching a problem that should be propagated higher in the call stack.

To reduce duplication and keep the information about expected exceptions, we can use a multi-catch block. In the following listing, we declare both IOException and InterruptedException in the catch signature.

Listing 3.5 Handling checked exceptions with a multi-catch block

```
public void shouldCatchUsingMultiCatch() {
  try {
    methodThatThrowsCheckedException();
  } catch (IOException | InterruptedException e) {
    logger.error("Problem ", e);
  }
}
```

To conclude our explanation of exceptions, let's consider a similar method that declares two checked exceptions but throws the unchecked one. RuntimeException is the unchecked one, so it does not need to be declared in the method signature, as the following listing shows.

Listing 3.6 Throwing an unchecked exception

```
public void methodThatThrowsUncheckedException()
    throws FileAlreadyExistsException, InterruptedException {
  throw new RuntimeException("Unchecked exception!");
}
```

Listing 3.4 will catch this problem even if we may not expect it to happen. If we narrow the catch blocks to catch only checked exceptions, RuntimeException will not be caught and will be propagated. The following listing demonstrates how to remedy this.

Listing 3.7 Calling a method that throws unchecked exception

```
public void shouldCatchAtNormalGranularityRuntimeWillBeNotCatch()
  assertThatThrownBy(
          () -> {
            try {
              methodThatThrowsUncheckedException();    ⟵  Throws an
            } catch (FileAlreadyExistsException e) {        unchecked
              logger.error("File already exists: ", e);     exception
            } catch (InterruptedException e) {
              logger.error("Interrupted", e);
            }
          })
      .isInstanceOf(RuntimeException.class);    ⟵  The propagated exception
}                                                  that was not caught is
                                                   RuntimeException.
```

Please note the catch blocks catch only exceptions that are declared in the `method-ThatThrowsUncheckedException()` signature. These do not declare catch for an `Exception`; therefore, the unchecked exception will not be handled.

In the following section, we'll refresh our knowledge about exceptions and their Java language types. Then, we'll see how we should design exception handling strategies for our APIs.

3.2 Best patterns to handle exceptions in the code that you own

When you are writing your software APIs, there is a high probability that someone else will use this code. If you work within a team, you may be responsible for developing logic for one part of the system, while another team member is responsible for a different part of a system.

The integration point between your code should be an interface that states the intent of your code. In fact, it should not matter if only other team members use your component or you are developing an open-source library used by more people. If you are designing an API, you should consider explicitly communicating exceptions to allow callers to decide how to treat those failures. However, you may develop components and methods that contain an internal logic and are not exposed publicly. In that case, maybe you don't need to be explicit about every possible problem the code can have.

3.2.1 Handling checked exceptions in a public API

Let's assume we are developing a component that exposes a public API and that other team members will use this API. When it comes to checked exceptions, we should clearly propagate our intent and annotate the public API methods with checked exceptions it can throw. For example, if you expect that your public method can fail on an I/O problem, you should declare the exception in the public API signature.

Some languages (e.g., Scala) tend to treat all exceptions as unchecked, allowing methods to not declare them. If you are designing such an API, know that it is error prone because clients of your code will not get the information about possible failure at compile time. This problem is deferred to the run time, which means your software may fail unexpectedly while running in production. If your API declares the exceptions explicitly, such a situation is not possible because you are forcing the client to decide about the exception handling strategy at compile time (when they are writing the code).

There is often the argument that declaring a couple (two, three, or even more) exceptions that your API may throw is too verbose, making the client's code harder to write. Let's assume that we are exposing such a method. Take a look at the following listing.

Listing 3.8   An API method with a couple of exceptions

```
void check() throws IOException, InterruptedException;
```

When clients of this API calls this method, they will need to make an explicit decision about handling it—every time this method is called. If this is problematic to a caller, it can catch all the exceptions using the pattern that we learned in the previous section and propagate the exception as an unchecked one. The following listing provides an example of this.

Listing 3.9 Propagating an exception as unchecked

```
public void wrapIntoUnchecked() {
   try {
     check();
   } catch (RuntimeException e) {          Catches all exceptions
     throw e;                              from the public API
   } catch (Exception e) {        ◄──┘     method call
     throw new RuntimeException(e);  ◄──┐  Wraps those into an
   }                                       unchecked exception
}
```

In the listing, note that we catch `RuntimeException` before `Exception` to avoid unnecessary wrapping to another `RuntimeException`. Also, it is important to wrap the underlying exception to a new unchecked one. By doing so, the caller gets all the information about the cause of the underlying exception. Other methods in the code can then use the wrapper method.

I do not recommend using an API that hides actual exceptions and propagates unchecked exceptions in your code as a solution for all problems. That will hide the expected exceptions and make your API less fault tolerant. However, it shows that the argument against making our API verbose is not rational. It is easy to convert checked exceptions into unchecked ones.

If our clients do not want to handle errors explicitly, they need to make a conscious decision to ignore those errors and propagate them up in the caller stack. Most often, this is not the right solution. At this point, we can see that declaring checked exceptions in the signature of the method in our public APIs has a couple significant advantages:

- *Such an API declares its contract explicitly.* The callers can, therefore, reason about the call outcome without looking into the method implementation.
- *The caller won't be surprised by any unchecked exceptions.* It is easier to write error handling code when we know what possible exceptions the called API can throw.

3.2.2 Handling unchecked exceptions in a public API

In our APIs, we often need to validate the arguments and state of the objects that are used by the caller. If such a state is invalid, we may decide to throw an unchecked exception. As you know, unchecked exceptions do not need to be declared in the method signature. They also don't need to be handled in the caller's code.

According to the guidelines on handling errors (see http://mng.bz/0wXN for a Java tutorial on unchecked exceptions), declaring the unchecked exception for every method reduces our program's clarity. However, there are some situations in which declaring unchecked exceptions is a viable solution. Let's assume that we have a method in our API that sets up a service, as the following listing shows.

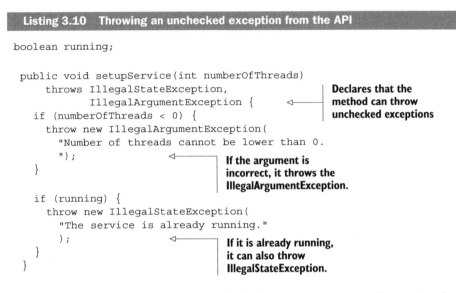

Listing 3.10 Throwing an unchecked exception from the API

```
boolean running;

public void setupService(int numberOfThreads)
        throws IllegalStateException,               Declares that the
                IllegalArgumentException {          method can throw
    if (numberOfThreads < 0) {                      unchecked exceptions
        throw new IllegalArgumentException(
          "Number of threads cannot be lower than 0.
          ");                                If the argument is
    }                                       incorrect, it throws the
                                            IllegalArgumentException.
    if (running) {
        throw new IllegalStateException(
          "The service is already running."
          );                               If it is already running,
    }                                      it can also throw
}                                          IllegalStateException.
```

The exceptions declared in this method signature serve an informational purpose. The caller of this method does not need to catch those exceptions, although it may be useful to know about those exceptions when interacting with other APIs.

If we create a method used by other components in our code, we should document the preconditions and expected behavior. Unfortunately, the documentation is not always read by developers, and it may become outdated over time. Declaring unchecked exceptions in a method signature can serve the purpose of documentation. Such documentation may be better because there are greater chances that the developer using our API will read it.

It is true that declaring too many exceptions can make our code too verbose and unclear. However, in real life, our software components declare only a subset of methods as a public API. The rest of the methods created to achieve the public API's functionality are hidden using private access modifiers. Such methods do not need to be so verbose. We can drop unchecked exceptions from their method signatures without losing much information.

If we modify the private methods of a specific component, we need to know their internals. We should examine these methods and know about the exceptions they can signal. When our component is used in a black-box way, only via a public API, we should not require the callers to know about this component's internals. Declaring the unchecked exceptions in these methods may be a good solution.

When making the decision of whether your API should throw checked or unchecked exceptions, you should consider many factors. Let's consider a situation in which the caller's code assumes that every code path of the API it calls can fail and may throw an exception. This probably means the application is structured in a way in which it catches all exceptions at some high level in the call stack. We can relate it to a situation in which you are writing the components and API used by your code. In this case, the decision to use unchecked exceptions is reasonable. You own both caller and implementation code. There is a low chance that the called code will surprise you in an unpredictable way.

However, when creating a public API that can be called by code unknown to you, you may choose to be more explicit and declare possible problems via checked exceptions. This approach gives potential callers explicit information about your API. They will know what they should expect from the called code, and they will guard against possible exceptions. When declaring exceptions explicitly in the API contract, we are not forcing callers to protect against all potential problems and guess the possible exceptions.

I am not trying to give a definite answer to which type of exceptions you should use. Both types have their use cases. What I am presenting is the tradeoffs of both types. You can take those tradeoffs and your context into consideration and then decide which type of exceptions are better suited for your code. In the next section, we will look at some anti-patterns that may prevent our code from being fault-tolerant.

3.3 Anti-patterns in exception handling

Let's assume that we've created a robust API that signals the problems and exceptions in an explicit way. Now, we need to use our API and react to problems properly. Unfortunately, in this scenario, it is easy to lose this information or not handle the exceptions properly. If the API that we want to use declares the exceptions, we need to handle them at compile time.

It is often tempting to analyze the underlying code and conclude that such an exception cannot be thrown under any circumstances. This may even be true for the time when the code is analyzed. However, if the method declares unchecked exceptions, we should treat it as the method contract. Even if it does not throw an exception when we are writing our caller code, the underlying behavior may change in the future. The following listing shows such an anti-pattern.

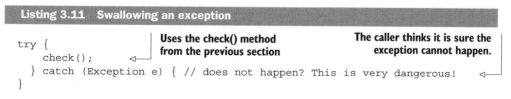

Listing 3.11 Swallowing an exception

```
try {                        Uses the check() method          The caller thinks it is sure the
    check();                 from the previous section         exception cannot happen.
} catch (Exception e) { // does not happen? This is very dangerous!
}
```

The exception that is swallowed never propagates up in the call stack. We will also lose that information, risking silent failure in our system. Those problems are tough to debug! We should never ignore an exception declared in the called method signature. It may also be tempting to just print the stack trace of the exception, as the next listing displays.

Listing 3.12   Print stack trace

```
try {
    check();
    } catch (Exception e) {
    e.printStackTrace();
}
```

This is also dangerous because printing the stack trace is printing the content of the exception to standard output by default. Instead, the destination can be something else—for example, a `FileOutputStream`. As well, if the standard output is not captured or propagated, we risk losing this information.

We need to decide whether the exception should be handled at this specific code level. If yes, then catching exceptions should extract as much information as possible. We can use a logger, as in the following listing, to extract the information about `Throwable`.

Listing 3.13   Using a log to catch an error

```
try {
    check();
} catch (Exception e) {
    logger.error("Problem when check ", e);
}
```

The logger.error method extracts the needed information.

The logger gets the stack trace of an exception and propagates it to the caller. It will be appended to the log file and will allow the caller to debug problems more efficiently.

If we decide to handle a particular error at a higher level, the method that calls `check()` should not try to catch it. Instead of catching it, it should only declare it in the method signature. By declaring the exception explicitly in the method contract, we are signaling to the clients what they should expect after calling a method. By using this pattern, we allow the clients to consider their own strategy for exception handling.

3.3.1 *Closing resources in case of an error*

Often, our code needs to interact with methods and classes that require some system resource consumption. For example, creating a new file requires opening a filesystem handle. Creating an HTTP client requires opening the socket that allocates the port from the pool of available ports. As long as the process progresses without problems and everything works as expected, then we need to close the client after the process completes.

Let's consider a simple example of creating an HTTP client, executing some requests, and closing the client. The following listing shows the code.

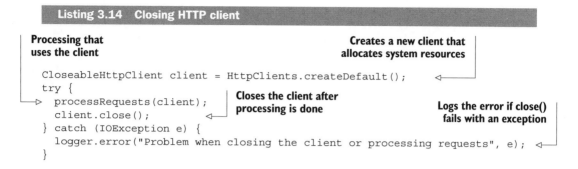

Listing 3.14   Closing HTTP client

Processing that uses the client

Creates a new client that allocates system resources

Closes the client after processing is done

Logs the error if close() fails with an exception

```
CloseableHttpClient client = HttpClients.createDefault();
try {
  processRequests(client);
  client.close();
} catch (IOException e) {
  logger.error("Problem when closing the client or processing requests", e);
}
```

At first glance, this code looks correct, and after processing, we close the client. (Here processing involves the logic that may fail if the network drops some packets.) Unfortunately, the processRequests() method may throw an IOException. If that exception is thrown at this place in code, the close() method will not be called. We are risking a resource leak that may lead to problems if we open too many socket connections or clients.

We need to convert this code to call close() even if processRequests() fails. We also need to handle problems from processRequests() separately. Only after those are handled can we close the client. The following listing shows how this would look.

Listing 3.15   Closing an HTTP client in case of process request problems

```
CloseableHttpClient client = HttpClients.createDefault();
try {
  processRequests(client);
} catch (IOException e) {
  logger.error("Problem when processing requests", e);
}
try {
  client.close();
} catch (IOException e) {
  logger.error("Problem when closing client", e);
}
```

Catches the process request problem

Calls close() only after processRequests() finishes.

Such a code is verbose and error prone. The verbosity comes from the fact that we need to handle the same IOException twice. Also, we need to guard against processing failures, and we need to fall back to the close() method call even if there is a processing problem. It is easy to forget about this if the API throws an unchecked exception. In such a case, we will not call the close method; thus, we risk resource leaks.

To improve our code a bit, we can use a try-with-resources statement to handle closing for us. This will work only if the class we use implements the AutoCloseable interface (see http://mng.bz/QWOv). Listing 3.16 shows how we can automatically close our HTTP client using this mechanism.

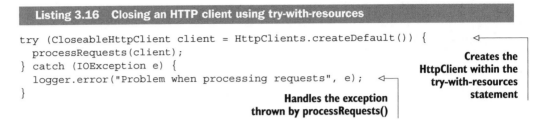

Listing 3.16 Closing an HTTP client using try-with-resources

```
try (CloseableHttpClient client = HttpClients.createDefault()) {
  processRequests(client);
} catch (IOException e) {
  logger.error("Problem when processing requests", e);
}
```

Creates the HttpClient within the try-with-resources statement

Handles the exception thrown by processRequests()

Using this technique allows our caller's code to focus only on the logic that needs to be executed. The lifecycle of the object that implements `Closeable` is handled for us. The `close()` method should provide the necessary logic for freeing resources. It also states our code's intent, clearly allowing our clients to reason about the types and their resource usage.

> **NOTE** If we design our API to return the object that involves some resource consumption that should be freed after the object is no longer used, we should implement the `Closeable` interface.

Although the try-with-resources abstraction is useful, your language may not support it. The main reason for using it is to close our resources, regardless of the processing outcome. If we execute code that throws an unchecked exception, that error may stop our code from progressing. In this case, we need to close the resources after the logic. Because of this, some languages allow programmers to execute code, regardless of whether an exception was thrown.

In Java, we can use the `finally` block to implement the logic responsible for closing resources. The code inside this block always executes, even if the code throws an exception. The following listing provides an example.

Listing 3.17 Closing resources using a `finally` block

```
CloseableHttpClient client = HttpClients.createDefault();
try {
    processRequests(client);
} finally {
    System.out.println("closing");
    client.close();
}
```

Now, even if `processRequests()` throws an exception, the `finally` block's closing logic will be executed. You can observe that because the closing message will appear in the standard output.

3.3.2 Anti-pattern of using exceptions to control application flow

The other common anti-pattern when implementing object-oriented exception handling is using exceptions to control our application flow (like the `goto` statement). In such an application, exceptions are over used and thrown to signal to the caller that the logic should follow a different code path.

It is also tempting to use exception(s) to overcome the one return type per method limitation. Let's assume that we have a method that returns a `String`. After some time, we want to change this method to return a special value if the string is too long. At first glance, throwing an exception in such a case seems like the correct solution, and as long as this exception is indeed an exceptional situation, using an exception is justified. Problems will start to appear if the caller builds conditional logic that executes different code paths, depending on the outcome of the method.

The more exception types the method throws, the more complex the caller logic becomes. Building complicated logic around exceptions is expensive (we'll look at performance in the last section of this chapter). Changing code paths depending on the exception makes our code complex, hard to reason about, and difficult to maintain.

Suppose we want to design our code so that it imposes on the caller a need for handling the edge cases in their logic. In that case, we may look at the functional programming constructs, such as `Try` (which we discuss later in this chapter) or `Either`. By using those constructs, we can design our code for handling edge cases without overusing exceptions.

Often, when we write our code, we use third-party libraries, and we do not have any (or we have very limited) influence over their codebase evolution. The next section focuses on error handling strategies when calling the code that we do not own.

3.4 *Exceptions from third-party libraries*

When we interact with the third-party libraries, our strategy of handling exceptions should be thoughtful. Let's consider an example of developing a software component responsible for saving information about a person to a catalog.

Our API will have two public methods. The first method gets the information about a person based on the person's name. The second method creates information about a person's name. The `getPersonInfo()` method loads the file from the filesystem, whereas the `createPersonInfo()` method creates a new file for the given person and saves the information to a file. The client code will interact with our API via two public methods, as figure 3.2 shows.

In our scenario, let's assume that we use a third-party library that provides the mechanism for saving and retrieving files in our filesystem. For that, we will use the Apache Commons IO library (http://mng.bz/9KW7). The library throws `IOException` or `File-ExistsException` (http://mng.bz/jynr) when there is a problem with any operation regarding file system access. As we know by now, every interaction with a filesystem involves a method call that can fail. Listing 3.18 shows how the API of our catalog component will look.

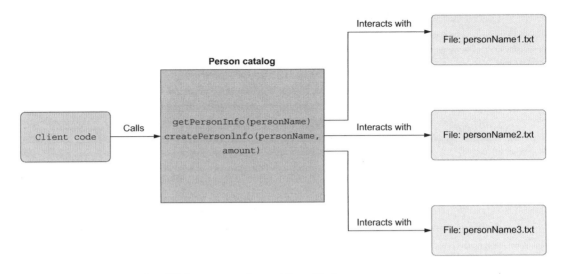

Figure 3.2   A person catalog API that exposes two public methods

Listing 3.18   An API with declared exceptions

```
import java.io.IOException;
import org.apache.commons.io.FileExistsException;        ◁──┤ Imports the third-party
                                                              class, which looks suspicious
public interface PersonCatalog {
  PersonInfo getPersonInfo(String personName) throws IOException;        ◁────────
  boolean createPersonInfo(String personName, int amount) throws
    FileExistsException;        ◁──────────┐                          Throws the
}                                           │                          IOException from the
              Throws an exception that leaks                          standard Java library
              the underlying implementation
```

The most important thing to note here is that both API method declarations may throw an exception. The getPersonInfo() method throws the IOException that is available in the Java standard JDK. The createPersonInfo() method throws the FileExistsException that is an exception specific to the underlying third-party library we imported. This is reasonable because both interact with the filesystem via the third-party library that also declares these exceptions.

On one hand, such a solution will work as expected: clients will need to handle the IOException and FileExistsException in their code when interacting with the PersonCatalog component. On the other hand, we will leak the internal exception used by the underlying third-party library. Once we propagate those exceptions and their types in the API, we will introduce tight coupling between the client's code and the third-party library, which we use internally in the PersonCatalog component. This defies the purpose of abstraction that we introduced because we cannot change the underlying library responsible for the filesystem operations. Changing that library would mean that other exceptions may be thrown, and our API method signature no longer reflects this.

It might also be possible that a different third-party library would not have a File-ExistsException class that we declared in the method signature. The IOException is less problematic because it is present in the JDK available in the client's code. You may wonder why we cannot just remove the throws FileExistsException and replace it with an exception from a different third-party library. Because this is a public interface, changing this type will mean that we'll break our library's compatibility. When clients use the new version of this method, the code will no longer compile!

We can conclude that propagating the third-party exception in our code's public API methods may not be an ideal solution. How can we solve that problem? We can introduce a library-specific exception and wrap the underlying exception within it. Let's introduce a PersonCatalogException that will wrap any underlying exception thrown by the third-party library responsible for interacting with the filesystem. The following listing shows this implementation.

Listing 3.19   Creating a domain-specific exception

The PersonCatalogException private constructor

```
public class PersonCatalogException extends Exception {
  private PersonCatalogException(String message, Throwable cause) {    ⟵
    super(message, cause);
  }
  public static PersonCatalogException getPersonException(String personName,
                                                         Throwable t) {
    return new PersonCatalogException("Problem when getting person file for: " +
      personName, t);
  }
  public static PersonCatalogException createPersonException(String personName,
                                                            Throwable  t) {
    return new PersonCatalogException("Problem when
➥ creating person file for: " + personName, t);
  }
}
```

PersonCatalogException takes a private constructor that encapsulates the actual Throwable and error message. For the getPersonInfo() method, we have a getPerson-Exception() factory that constructs the domain-specific exception. The createPerson-Info() API method presents a similar situation in which we wrap an underlying Throwable into our new PersonCatalogException.

Once we have a new domain-specific PersonCatalogException, we can propagate it easily in the public API without leaking the actual exception types of the underlying third-party library. The following listing shows the domain-specific exception.

Listing 3.20   `PersonCatalog` without leaking a third-party exception

```
public interface PersonCatalog {
  PersonInfo getPersonInfo(String personName) throws PersonCatalogException;
  boolean createPersonInfo(String personName, int amount) throws
    PersonCatalogException;
}
```

After those changes, both get and create methods declare that they throw the Person-CatalogException. Note that the third-party exception no longer leaks, and the client's code can use this API without tight coupling to the specific implementation that we are currently using. Such a solution gives us high flexibility when evolving the API and gives the clients code more information about the reason for the exception. By only looking at the exception type, the caller can infer the reason and place where the exception was thrown. If we use the low-level exceptions, such as IOException, the name of the exception itself carries a lot less information than it should.

We can see that wrapping exceptions can be useful in the public API and in our own code because this gives more context about the error. It basically carries more information with the same amount of exception output. This does not mean that we should wrap every exception propagated from the third-party libraries into our own codebase, but we should consider the cost of maintaining the new exception versus all the pros it gives us. Most often, introducing a domain-specific exception would give us more benefits than its cost of maintenance. If you are designing a private component that won't be exposed to clients directly, you should be OK with using the exceptions without wrapping them into custom ones.

Note also that, even if the exception type gives the caller a lot of information, the message that the exception carries should contain a detailed explanation of what happened. Besides that, the stack trace is recorded in the exception, and when an abnormal situation occurs, it also provides a lot of insight into what went wrong. When combining those three pieces of information together (i.e., exception type, message, and stack trace), it is easier to reason about what went wrong. The exception type is also useful for the compiler. When the error occurs at run time, we want to have all that information as well.

Up to this point, our design was concerned with code that worked synchronously. In the next section, we will see how to handle the code that works in a multithreaded and asynchronous way.

3.5   *Exceptions in multithread environments*

Handling exceptions in a multithreaded context is different than when our program is executed within a single-threaded context. When we submit a new action to an executor, we should get feedback about the success or failure of this action. Without a mechanism to get this information, we risk that the async action executed in a separate thread may fail without any signal. Such silent failures are dangerous and hard to diagnose.

When interacting with an executor, we have two ways to submit work. We can schedule a new action to be executed using the submit() method that returns the Future instance and then we can use this Future instance to get the result of the action. The second way of scheduling an async operation is to use the execute() method. This is basically the fire-and-forget approach, meaning that we will not get results from such action.

When we do get the result of our action, it means that such a result can succeed or fail if some exception is thrown from the code. Let's see how the exception handling code looks when we submit an action, as the following listing shows.

Listing 3.21 Submit and wait

**The action that is submitted will
throw an unchecked exception.**

**We will be using an executor with
one separate worker thread.**

```
ExecutorService executorService = Executors.newSingleThreadExecutor();
Runnable r =
    () -> {
        throw new RuntimeException("problem");
    };
Future<?> submit = executorService.submit(r);
assertThatThrownBy(submit::get)
    .hasRootCauseExactlyInstanceOf(RuntimeException.class)
    .hasMessageContaining("problem");
```

**The submit()
returns a Future.**

**The get() involves
blocking the main thread.**

It is important to note that the get() method blocks our flow, and the blocking operation must finish when get() is executed. If the underlying action finishes with an exception, it is propagated to the main thread. If you submit an action and don't use this result anywhere in code (fire-and-forget), the exception is not propagated, and you are risking silent failure. You need to remember, if the executor service returns a Future (promise), you must validate its correctness.

> **NOTE** You can find information about the Future interface at http://mng .bz/W70a. For .NET developers, a Future is similar to a Task.

The execute method is a bit different because it does not return any result. Let's look at the following listing to see its implementation.

Listing 3.22 Execute and forget

```
Runnable r =
    () -> {
        throw new RuntimeException("problem");
    };
executorService.execute(r)
```

The fact that our executor does not return a result means that the failure of an async action executed in a separate thread may fail silently. Such an exception can cause your thread to stop working. This may be problematic if you use a thread pool with a fixed number of threads. When the thread fails, it may not be recreated, and you are risking that, at some point, all threads will fail and the pool will be empty. If you have a thread pool that adapts to traffic, you are risking resource leaks. Every thread occupies a substantial amount of memory, and creating a lot of new threads may lead to out of memory problems.

The sane solution for such processing would be to register a global exception handler, which is executed for failures in any thread in our processing. We can register the exception handler for all threads using the UncaughtExceptionHandler (http://mng.bz/Ex5d), as figure 3.3 illustrates.

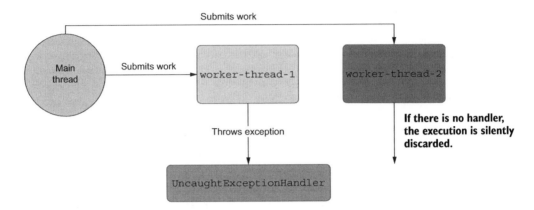

Figure 3.3   Global exception handling in a multithreading context.

As figure 3.3 shows, the main thread submits the work to worker-thread-1 using the execute() method (without getting the promise object back). Then, the worker thread executes this action asynchronously. If there is no promise returned, the main thread now has no way of letting us know if any problem occurs in the worker-thread processing. Fortunately, we can register a global exception handler that will be invoked if any exception in processing occurs. If there is no handler (as in worker-thread-2), we risk that the exception is silently discarded and the worker thread may stop working, leading to the resource leak described previously.

Let's take a look at a unit test that validates the global exception handler logic. We will call the execute() method with an action that will fail. Then, we will assert that the UncaughtExceptionHandler was called when the exception occurs. The following listing shows this use case.

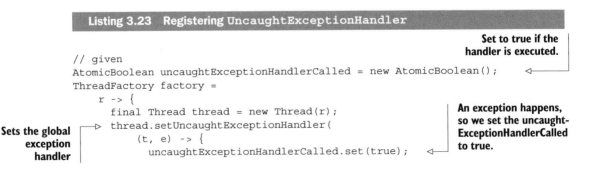

Listing 3.23   Registering UncaughtExceptionHandler

```
// given
AtomicBoolean uncaughtExceptionHandlerCalled = new AtomicBoolean();
ThreadFactory factory =
    r -> {
        final Thread thread = new Thread(r);
        thread.setUncaughtExceptionHandler(
            (t, e) -> {
                uncaughtExceptionHandlerCalled.set(true);
```

Set to true if the handler is executed.

Sets the global exception handler

An exception happens, so we set the uncaught-ExceptionHandlerCalled to true.

```
                    logger.error("Exception in thread: " + t, e);
                });
            return thread;
        };
```

```
Runnable task =
    () -> {
        throw new RuntimeException("problem");
    };
ExecutorService pool = Executors.newSingleThreadExecutor(factory);
// when
pool.execute(task);
await().atMost(5,
    TimeUnit.SECONDS).until(uncaughtExceptionHandlerCalled::get);
```

> **Sets the time to await until the handler is invoked (everything is async).**

> **execute() invokes the action in a separate worker thread.**

As you can see, exception handling in a multithreaded environment is tricky, especially if the API that we use allows or forces us to fire some action in an async way and forget about the results. But if we can get the Future object that wraps the async execution result, we should use this API because it forces us to think about the results and the possibility of an exception.

The promise API is a well-known construct that allows us to create async code and compose async operations fluently. This Java API has the CompletableFuture construct to create fluent async APIs that capture the failures explicitly (see http://mng .bz/NxMn). You will also find similar APIs in other programming languages. Let's take a look at how to handle exceptions using Java's promise API.

3.5.1 Exceptions in an async workflow with a promise API

Ideally, when creating an async workflow, we would interact with I/O, networks, and other external resources, using an API that works in an async way. Such an API should return a promise that we can use to chain async operations. Unfortunately, in the real world, sometimes we need to create a translation layer between sync and async APIs.

Let's assume that we need to call an external service. The method responsible for calling this external service works synchronously, so we need to wrap it into a Completable-Future API that allows us to change the subsequent async flow. The external call involves an I/O operation, so it declares that it can throw the IOException.

Because the IOException is a checked exception, we need to handle it somehow in an async fashion. We'll use the supplyAsync() method that wraps the blocking call and returns a nonblocking type, which is propagated to the callers that are expecting the async operation. The first approach would be to wrap this checked exception into unchecked one to propagate it to the caller, as the following listing shows.

Listing 3.24 Wrapping an exception in the async API

```
public int externalCall() throws IOException {
    throw new IOException("Problem when
```

> **The externalCall() methods can throw IOException.**

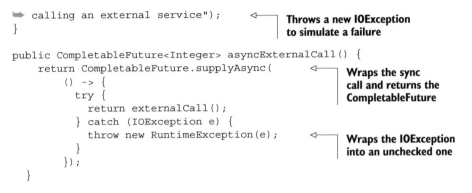

```
➡ calling an external service");                      Throws a new IOException
}                                                     to simulate a failure

public CompletableFuture<Integer> asyncExternalCall() {
    return CompletableFuture.supplyAsync(             Wraps the sync
        () -> {                                       call and returns the
            try {                                     CompletableFuture
                return externalCall();
            } catch (IOException e) {
                throw new RuntimeException(e);         Wraps the IOException
            }                                          into an unchecked one
        });
}
```

It is important to note that we are propagating IOException from the underlying
library directly without creating a domain exception that wraps it. We do this for
the simplicity of this example. For a detailed discussion about pros and cons, see
section 3.4.

This approach of wrapping the exception and propagating the unchecked one is
far from ideal. We are mixing two abstractions: one is a promise API, which should
encapsulate the result that can be fulfilled in the future or an exception if this action
fails. The other abstraction synchronously throws an exception that will propagate to
the caller. The Java API wraps this exception into CompletionException, captured in
the thread pool on which the async action is executed.

When calling the asyncExternalCall() method, you will see a stack trace denoting
that this exception was propagated to multiple layers of the concurrent API. Finally, you
will then find the underlying problem. The following listing shows the stack trace.

Listing 3.25 Stack trace of an exception that is not properly handled

```
ava.util.concurrent.CompletionException: java.lang.RuntimeException:
    java.io.IOException: Problem when calling an external service
    at java.util.concurrent.CompletableFuture.encodeThrowable(         A lot of
    CompletableFuture.java:273)                                        library calls
    at java.util.concurrent.CompletableFuture.completeThrowable(       that need
    CompletableFuture.java:280)                                        to handle
    at java.util.concurrent.CompletableFuture$AsyncSupply.run(         unexpected
    CompletableFuture.java:1592)                                       exceptions
    at java.util.concurrent.CompletableFuture$AsyncSupply.exec(
    CompletableFuture.java:1582)
    at java.util.concurrent.ForkJoinTask.doExec(ForkJoinTask.java:289)
    at java.util.concurrent.ForkJoinPool$WorkQueue.runTask(
    ForkJoinPool.java:1056)
    at java.util.concurrent.ForkJoinPool.runWorker(ForkJoinPool.java:1692)
    at java.util.concurrent.ForkJoinWorkerThread.run(
    ForkJoinWorkerThread.java:157)                                     After the library
Caused by: java.lang.RuntimeException: java.io.IOException:            code, you will find
➡ Problem when calling an external service                            the underlying cause.
```

Such a stack trace denotes that you didn't handle failure correctly because it involves
many intermediate steps to handle this in the concurrent library. Depending on your

language or library, you might not have much luck because such an exception may be not propagated, or it may kill the thread leading to a resource leak. How can we handle the errors and compose them with the promise API?

To solve this problem, we should create a new instance of `CompletableFuture` that returns the result or an exception. The latter case is crucial here. In the following listing, we fill the promise with the exception, but the exception is not thrown.

Listing 3.26 Fulfilling promise with the result or exception

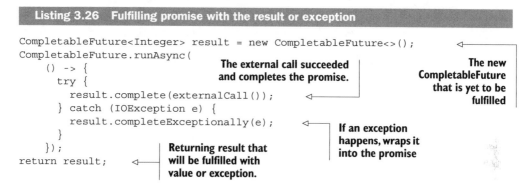

This above method's caller gets the value or the actual underlying cause by wrapping the exception into the promise API. You won't see any stack trace related to the concurrent library because we didn't rethrow the exception. Thanks to that, we are not risking that this exception will kill the thread or go unnoticed.

> **NOTE** The technique I presented in this section is common for most async APIs: you should find it useful in your chosen language.

We will compare our object-oriented way of handling errors using exceptions and throwing them with a functional programming approach in the next section. We will also look at a `Try` construct that encapsulates the success or failure, which will be similar to the promise API that we just learned.

3.6   *Functional approach to handling errors with Try*

Up to this point, we discussed the object-oriented way of handling exceptions. Let's now take a look at the functional approach to managing errors. We will focus on one of the main aspects of functional programming: code that is side effect free.

If a method throws an exception, it means that it has side effects. If we have a simple method that returns a value and throws an exception, we may consider that it throws the exception in the method's declaration. We're used to this pattern in the object-oriented world, but we need to remember that the exception is a side effect. The caller needs to handle the actual returned value, but it also needs to guard against exceptions. When the exception is explicitly mentioned in the method's contract, the functional code knows what to expect and can guard against this side effect, wrapping it within `Try` (more on that later).

On the other hand, when the exception thrown is unchecked and it is not declared in the method contract, the caller may not handle it, and the side effect will be propagated up in the call stack. This lack of handling may come from the caller not expecting the exception and, therefore, not guarding against it. Such behavior is problematic in a functional programming world.

The main philosophy in functional programming is to model every possible outcome of a function call with a type. If the function that we call can fail, this outcome should be modeled by the function's return type and a declared exception. Throwing an exception is explicit if we use the checked exception, but it may be implicit if the method throws an unchecked one. Such inconsistent behavior should be prohibited in a functional programming world. The type that a function returns must model every possible outcome of a function. This is a reason why the Try monad (also called an Error monad) is crucial when modeling error handling in functional programming (see http://mng.bz/la42 and http://mng.bz/BxV1).

Let's look at a simple construct. Try can carry one of two possible states: the first possible state is success, and the second is failure. The state of this type can be one or another but never both. Figure 3.4 shows the possible states.

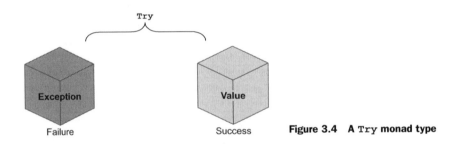

Figure 3.4   **A Try monad type**

In the previous section, we saw a promise type using the CompletableFuture API. This type is similar because it carries the result of the async computation or returns failure, showing what happened during the API's processing. It has one substantial limitation—it should only be used in the context of async processing.

The Try monad, however, can encapsulate the processing state in both synchronous and asynchronous contexts. The Try type is more general and flexible, and because of that, it serves as the primary abstraction to capture the failure or success in a functional programming approach. Let's see how the functional approach of handling errors will look in the Java programming language. We will use the Vavr library (https://www.vavr.io/), which provides the Try type for us to use.

NOTE   If your method returns a Try type, the caller of this method will always need to handle the fact that such a method may fail. Further processing can be chained using functional programming methods, such as a map, filter, or something similar.

Let's now look at how the caller of the method that returns Try can handle the processing. Our client's action is the task that may fail; therefore, it can throw an exception. We are mocking it for the purpose of this test to demonstrate the behavior of Try when the wrapped call does not fail, as the following listing demonstrates. In a real-life system, we would wrap calls to components or external systems that can fail.

Listing 3.27 A Try monad with success

```
// given
String defaultResult = "default";
Supplier<Integer> clientAction = () -> 100;

// when
Try<Integer> response = Try.ofSupplier(clientAction);
String result = response.map(Object::toString).getOrElse(defaultResult);

// then
assertTrue(response.isSuccess());
response.onSuccess(r -> assertThat(r).isEqualTo(100));
assertThat(result).isEqualTo("100");
```

It is important to note that the integration point with the action that may fail (client action) is wrapped into a Try type. A Try abstraction should be returned from the methods that can fail. The caller can chain subsequent processing on the Try type instead of worrying about exceptions. The Try monad already encapsulates the exceptions if that happens.

If we want to extract the actual String value from Try, we can get the value from the monad using the getOrElse() method. However, if the Try monad carries the exception, it won't have a return value. For that situation, we need to provide a default result that can be returned if the action wrapped into a Try fails. This is achieved via the getOrElse() method call.

If we want to create a process based on whether the action succeeds or fails, we can use the isSuccess() method to check that (because the Try abstraction is a functional programming construct). We can chain functional processing, using methods such as a map. If the Try is successful, then the map is called. Otherwise, the map is not invoked. On success, the callback is executed only if it contains a value—not an error.

One of the biggest benefits of the Try monad usage is that we don't need to handle the exception in standard try-catch blocks. The exceptions are still caught, instead by using the Try functional programming API. Therefore, the exception handling code does not pollute our business logic. Let's now look at how functional error processing behaves if the wrapped action throws an exception.

When the client action fails, the same Try abstraction interacts with the type system. Note that this time, the clientAction throws an exception. By doing that, we simulate a call to the component that fails. We can use that to test how the Try abstraction looks now.

Listing 3.28 shows the same `Try` type that wraps the action. There is no difference in our processing at this stage. Our API caller should interact with the component that may fail only through this `Try` type if we want to create some logic that is not polluted with the `try-catch` blocks.

Listing 3.28   A `Try` monad with failure

```
Supplier<Integer> clientAction =
    () -> {
      throw new RuntimeException("problem");
    };

// when
Try<Integer> response = Try.ofSupplier(clientAction);
String result = response.map(Object::toString).getOrElse(defaultResult);
Option<Integer> optionalResponse = response.toOption();

// then
assertTrue(optionalResponse.isEmpty());
assertTrue(response.isFailure());
assertThat(result).isEqualTo(defaultResult);

response.onSuccess(r -> System.out.println(r));
response.onFailure(ex -> assertTrue(ex instanceof RuntimeException));
```

Note that the functional processing that we want to perform is chained in the same way as before. Our logic uses the `map()` method to execute some action if the underlying client's action succeeds. However, this time `map()` is not invoked because the underlying client action throws an exception. In our case, the `Try` carries the failure. Therefore, when `getOrElse()` is called, it returns a default value. It cannot return the processed value because there isn't one.

We can transform the `Try` to an `Option` (a construct from the Vavr library that's similar to the Java `Optional`), which is yet another functional programming type. It signals the presence or absence of a value. It is similar to `Try` but does not contain the reason why the value may be empty. Some functional APIs operate on the `Option` type. By using this conversion, we can integrate between those APIs easily. The `Try` caller can check whether the result failed with the `isFailure()` method in a similar way to the previous example when we executed the check `isSuccess()`. We can use both checks here. Finally, we chain two functional processes.

When using the `Try` in production, the caller of the code should handle both success and failure. It can be handled, for example, by creating both `onSuccess()` and `onFailure()` methods. For our case, when we simulate the failure, only the latter callback will be executed. The callback extracts the underlying cause of the problem.

3.6.1   *Using Try in production code*

Let's now take a look at a more real-life example of using `Try`. Suppose we want to execute an HTTP request to an external service. This service returns the JSON content. We need to extract only an ID from the JSON. To achieve that, we need to execute a couple of operations that may fail and throw exceptions.

The first action is an external HTTP call. Next, we need to extract the string content from the HTTP entity body. This operation may fail because it involves I/O operations. Finally, we need to map the string content to a Java entity class. This operation may also fail because we are deserializing the string content to a JSON. Once we have our entity, we can extract its ID.

Such processing can be easily chained using the `Try` API. Firstly, we need to wrap the client call into the `Try` monad. It will encapsulate the outcome of processing. Next, each stage of processing can be expressed using the `Try` API. If the action that we want to execute throws an unchecked exception, we need to execute our action within the `mapTry()` method. If the exception is thrown, the `Try` type is fulfilled, and the whole processing flow will be marked as failed. The following listing shows this call.

Listing 3.29   An HTTP service call with `Try`

```
private static final Logger logger =
    LoggerFactory.getLogger(HttpCallTry.class);

public String getId() {
  CloseableHttpClient client = HttpClients.createDefault();
  HttpGet httpGet = new HttpGet("http:/ /external-service/resource");
  Try<HttpResponse> response = Try.of(() -> client.execute(httpGet));   ← Wraps the external call into the Try monad
  return response
      .mapTry(this::extractStringBody)   ← Uses mapTry() because the extractStringBody() throws
      .mapTry(this::toEntity)
      .map(this::extractUserId)   ← In the last stage of our processing, extracts the ID
      .onFailure(ex -> logger.error("The getId() failed.", ex))   ← Logs the exception in case of a problem
      .getOrElse("DEFAULT_ID");
}
private String extractUserId(EntityObject entityObject) {
  return entityObject.id;
}

private String extractStringBody(HttpResponse r) throws IOException {
  return new BufferedReader(
          new InputStreamReader(r.getEntity().getContent(),
      StandardCharsets.UTF_8))
      .lines()
      .collect(Collectors.joining("\n"));   ← Returns the default if there was a failure at any stage of processing
}

private EntityObject toEntity(String content) throws JsonProcessingException {
  return OBJECT_MAPPER.readValue(content, EntityObject.class);
}
```

```
static class EntityObject {
  String id;

  public EntityObject(String id) {
    this.id = id;
  }
}
```

Only by looking at the processing definition can we reason about the stages that might fail and the stages that may not. The extractStringBody() and toEntity() calls can fail. If you look at the extractStringBody() method declaration, you will notice that it declares the IOException that the caller must handle. Similarly, toEntity() can throw a JsonProcessingException. Once all actions that may fail complete, we extract the user ID. Finally, we want to return the String type from our getId() method. In that situation, the caller of this method does not know about the Try monad that is used internally.

When we want to extract the underlying String from the Try monad, we have a couple of options. Here we use the getOrElse() method. If the processing succeeds, it will simply return the proper user ID. However, if any stage of our processing fails and we are able to provide a sane default to the caller, we can do that by returning the default value. Note that we also log the exception (if it occurs) by using the onFailure() method. If there is no way to provide a reasonable default, we may consider returning the Try type from our getId() and let the caller deal with it, which would be preferable.

Finally, we can transform our functional processing based on the Try to a standard throwing exception pattern via getOrElseThrow(). If the Try monad carries the exception, it will be thrown to the caller. The last approach has a couple of disadvantages, and we will discuss those in the next section. However, before we do that, let's compare the Try approach with the standard exception-based Java implementation, as the following listing shows.

Listing 3.30 An HTTP service call with the Exception API

```
public String getIdExceptions() {
    CloseableHttpClient client = HttpClients.createDefault();
    HttpGet httpGet = new HttpGet("http://external-service/resource");
    try {
      CloseableHttpResponse response = client.execute(httpGet);
      String body = extractStringBody(response);
      EntityObject entityObject = toEntity(body);
      return extractUserId(entityObject);
    } catch (IOException ex) {
      logger.error("The getId() failed", ex);
      return "DEFAULT_ID";
    }
  }
```

The actual logic looks similar to the `Try` approach. The one difference is that we need to create many of the intermediate variables used in the next processing step. The `Try` approach follows a more functional approach, and we can pass the function references (lambdas).

The main difference between the standard `try-catch` approach and the functional programming approach is the return type of the method. With the functional approach, we can return the `Try<String>` and let the caller decide what to do with the failure. The possible failure is communicated by the compile type (`Try`) and needs to be handled; otherwise, the code does not compile. The exception-based logic is more implicit, and there is no way to return one type that encapsulates success or failure. The caller needs to handle the `String` result and to guard against a possible exception. Those are different philosophies for handling abnormal situations. Let's discuss common pitfalls when using the `Try` abstraction with an API that uses `Exceptions`.

3.6.2 *Mixing Try with code that throws an exception*

The most important thing to note is that the caller code should interact with the component that may fail through `Try`. But by using the `Try` abstraction, we can model every possible outcome (success or failure) with the type system. Unfortunately, there are a couple of problems when introducing functional programming to handle errors in languages that use exceptions as the primary mechanism for signaling failures. When choosing the mechanism for handling exceptions—functional programming using `Try` or object-oriented programming using exceptions—we should stick to one of them and use it consistently in our codebase. Mixing both solutions would make our code hard to reason about. We would need to handle both states of `Try` (success and failure), but we would also need to use `try` and `catch` patterns to catch exceptions.

As you remember, unchecked exceptions can be thrown by any method. We don't need to declare them in method signatures. Because of that, it becomes problematic to wrap every possible method that can fail into `Try`. Imagine that we have a logic that interacts with more components, where every component may throw an unchecked exception. In such a scenario, every call to every component would need to be wrapped into a `Try` type. This would make our code hard to read and too lengthy.

When we call functional code from nonfunctional code, we need to transform it into a `try-catch` pattern. When we call nonfunctional code from functional code, we need to catch all possible exceptions and encapsulate them into `Try` monads to remove side effects.

If you remember the section about designing public APIs, I've mentioned that it is often useful to declare all exceptions (checked and unchecked) in method signatures. If you interact with such a component, it is easier to wrap such an API into a functional `Try` construct. Everything is explicit, and if you choose to use the functional approach of handling errors, it will be easier for you to wrap only methods that throw exceptions. On the other hand, let's assume that you integrate the functional programming approach with an API that throws unchecked exceptions that are not declared in the method's signature. You will end up wrapping almost every call into a `Try` monad, making your code hard to read and too verbose.

We can conclude that the functional approach of handling errors works best when using an explicitly typed system. If such an approach suits your style, using `Try` will prove beneficial. Unfortunately, it may be hard to create a unified exception handling system if the APIs you call are overusing unchecked exceptions. In the next section, we will compare the performance of different exception handling strategies.

3.7   *Performance comparison of exception-handling code*

Finally, let's compare the strategies of exception handling from the performance perspective. We will use the Java Microbenchmark Harness (JMH) tool for microbenchmarks. It will allow us to benchmark exception handling code at a fine-grained level. We will want to test a couple of strategies.

The first strategy to test is the standard `try-catch` approach. Next, we will compare that with the `Try` monad approach, wrapping the underlying cause into it. Finally, we will see how consuming the stack trace impacts performance. We will consume the exception using standard output and a logger that logs the `Throwable`.

To begin, we need a baseline method that does not involve exception handling. This will be used to compare how exceptions impact performance. We'll run every benchmarking operation 50,000 times to have more repeatable runs (running the test only once will not give us much insight). We will use a `for` loop to emulate this behavior. You can also use the JMH iterations parameter for this purpose instead of the manual `for` loop. Both solutions are good enough for our use case. The following listing shows the benchmark baseline.

Listing 3.31   Exceptions benchmark baseline

```
private static final int NUMBER_OF_ITERATIONS = 50_000;
@Benchmark
public void baseline(Blackhole blackhole) {
        for (int i = 0; i < NUMBER_OF_ITERATIONS; i++) {
            blackhole.consume(new Object());
        }
}
```

The `Blackhole` (see http://mng.bz/doVo) JMH construct simulates the actual usage of the benchmarked code. If we do not use it, we risk having the JIT compiler optimize it or remove it altogether. The actual benchmarking code does not do much. It only creates an object and lets the `Blackhole` consume it. Let's now create the first benchmark code, as the following listing shows. We will throw an exception and catch it in the `catch` block.

Listing 3.32 Throwing a catch benchmark

```
@Benchmark
public void throwCatch(Blackhole blackhole) {
    for (int i = 0; i < NUMBER_OF_ITERATIONS; i++) {
        try {
            throw new Exception();
        } catch (Exception e) {
            blackhole.consume(e);
        }
    }
}
```

This allows us to validate the performance of standard exception handling code. Note that the exception is consumed. It simulates usage from the real-life code, but it does not examine the exception's stack trace or log the exception. The following listing shows how we can enrich our benchmarks suite with those operations.

Listing 3.33 Consuming the stack trace benchmark

```
@Benchmark
public void getStackTrace(Blackhole blackhole) {
    for (int i = 0; i < NUMBER_OF_ITERATIONS; i++) {
        try {
            throw new Exception();
        } catch (Exception e) {
            blackhole.consume(e.getStackTrace());    ◁── Gets all stack
        }                                                traces associated
    }                                                    with the exception
}

@Benchmark
public void logError() {
    for (int i = 0; i < NUMBER_OF_ITERATIONS; i++) {
        try {
            throw new Exception();
        } catch (Exception e) {
            logger.error("Error", e);    ◁── Passes the
        }                                    exception to
    }                                        a logger
}
```

When using a logger, it is important to note that the error method will get the stack trace, but it will also append to the log using an appender. To conclude our benchmark suite, let's add a benchmark that uses the functional programming approach of handling failures, as the following listing shows. We will wrap the exception into a Try monad, and the Try should be consumed.

Listing 3.34 Try monad benchmark

```
@Benchmark
public void tryMonad(Blackhole blackhole) {
```

```
for (int i = 0; i < NUMBER_OF_ITERATIONS; i++) {
    blackhole.consume(Try.of(() -> { throw new Exception();}));
}
}
```

Wraps the Exception into a Try. The stack trace is not accessed.

Let's now take a look at the performance result of our benchmarks. Note that the exact numbers may differ if you run this on your machine, but the overall trend will be the same. Figure 3.5 shows the results of these benchmarks on my machine.

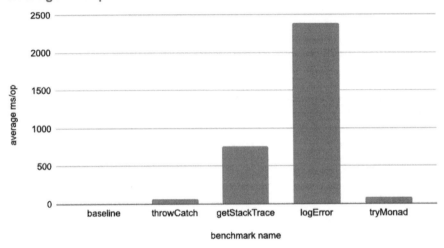

average ms/op vs benchmark name

Figure 3.5   **Our exception benchmark results (the results may differ on your machine).**

The baseline average takes less than one millisecond (ms). It shows the code that does not involve exception handling. Next, the throwCatch average operation takes less than 100 ms, and wrapping the exception to the Try monad is nearly identical. This means that when choosing an approach (functional or object-oriented) to handle errors, performance does not need to be taken into consideration. More interesting things happen if we need to examine the stack trace.

If we only get the stack trace, meaning that an array with all stack traces is created and consumed, the exception handling code takes around 750 ms per operation. Getting the stack trace is almost ten times slower than throwing and catching the exception without examining the stack trace. The most costly procedure is logging the exception. It involves getting the stack trace and constructing the string message out of it. Additionally, it might involve appender logic that may include an I/O operation to save the content to a disk file. The performance of logging the exception is around 30 times worse than the throw-catch approach or by using the functional Try. It is also three times slower than getting the stack trace. It is a reasonable conclusion because it needs to do a lot of additional work.

To finish this section about performance, you can see that you will be OK with both functional and object-oriented ways of handling errors, as long as you don't need to examine the stack trace. Even if you need to examine the stack trace, it should not be a problem in most cases. You may notice performance problems when your code is overusing exceptions and throwing them on almost every code path.

Of course, there will be times when you want to unwrap the exception stack trace and log it for debugging. The performance results give us one more bit of information in this regard. If you catch the exception and rethrow it, logging the exception in this intermediate step results in a substantial performance degradation. If you want to rethrow the exception to a higher level, then you should not log it; it will be handled at that level in the call stack and logged. If you are catching the exception without rethrowing, the one execution involving getting the stack trace is justified.

In most use cases (besides high-frequency, low latency processing), the performance impact discussed in this section will be negligible and can be safely ignored. Therefore, treat this section more as interesting information than as an excuse not to use exceptions where they should be used.

In this chapter, we learned about different strategies for handling exceptions. Exceptions and errors should not be used to control business logic. They serve the purpose of notifying you about the unexpected behavior of your code. As long as you are not over using exceptions, you should not observe performance problems related to them.

In the next chapter, we'll learn how to foresee the features needed by our users. We will see that the benefits of some features are lesser than the complexity and cost of their maintenance.

Summary

- A hierarchy of exceptions and errors exists for many object-oriented languages. For diagnostic purposes, understanding exceptions hierarchy is essential.
- To design error-handling APIs, we can choose either checked or unchecked exceptions. Checked exceptions are an explicit part of such APIs and must be handled; unchecked exceptions are an implicit part of error handling code and are not required to be handled.
- When designing exception handling logic for public APIs, we should analyze the pros and cons of checked versus unchecked exceptions, comparing them with the handling of exceptions in the code that we own.
- With our error-handling APIs, we need to react to problems properly. It is often tempting to analyze the underlying code and conclude that an exception cannot be thrown under any circumstances. Understanding common anti-patterns in exception-handling logic helps with this decision.
- When we interact with third-party libraries, we should develop a strategy of handling exceptions. When integrating with third-party libraries, leaking exception

types may lead to tight coupling, so it's important to understand the need for wrapping third-party exceptions.

- Handling failure in asynchronous processing that involves multithreading should be done with care; otherwise, we may risk silent failures.
- Throwing exceptions is not the only possible method of handling failures in our code. The `Try` monad construct encapsulates success or failure as well.
- We can use performance benchmarks for different exception handling strategies to determine which operations are most costly.

Balancing flexibility and complexity

This chapter covers

- Flexibility and extensibility versus cost of maintenance and complexity of APIs
- Providing maximum extensibility with the listener and hooks APIs
- Tackling complexity and guarding against unpredictable usage

When designing our systems and APIs, we want to find a balance between a set of features that it supports and the maintenance cost that arises from those features' complexity. In an ideal world, every API change, such as adding a new feature, would be backed by empirical studies. For example, we can analyze the traffic on our website and, according to a need, add a new feature. We can also conduct A/B (http://mng.bz/ragJ) testing to decide which feature should be retained and which is not needed. Based on the results of A/B testing, we can remove features that are not needed.

However, it is essential to note that removing functionality from a public API may be problematic or not feasible. If we need to keep backward compatibility, for example, removing a feature is a breaking change, and often we cannot do it. We can try to deprecate and migrate our clients to a new API without the removed elements, but this is a complex task. You will find more on compatibility in chapter 12.

When designing a public API, it is often better to start small. We can start with a limited set of features and extend a list of features based on the end users input rather than implementing many features upfront without the possibility of removing them.

On the other hand, when we build libraries used by other engineers and teams in our organization, we need to foresee a need for some features. If we create a library with a minimal set of features and design that is not extensible, we may end up in a situation where we need to refactor the code and change the API frequently. On the other hand, we can create a super extensive codebase and allow for its customization in all places. By doing so, we try to foresee all possible use cases for our code, but we also increase the complexity of our code, which often makes it over engineered. This chapter will help you find a balance between your codebase's flexibility and extensibility and the complexity and maintenance burdens that arise from it.

4.1   A robust but not extensible API

Let's assume that your team has a new task to create a software component shared with other teams and users. This means that once you write this component, it will be used by other people. We have a list of requirements that your code should meet.

4.1.1   Designing a new component

In our scenario, a new component's primary responsibility is to allow clients to execute a POST HTTP request for a given URL. Besides that, we need to add metrics to this code. If the request succeeds, the `requests.success` metrics should be incremented. If it fails, then we need to increment the `requests.failure` metric.

The third functionality that our code should provide is the possibility to retry an action. The caller of our code will specify the maximum number of retries. If the retries are exhausted, the processing fails. On the other hand, if it succeeds after one retry, the retry should be transparent for the client. We should increment the `requests.retry` metric denoting that there was a retry needed to fulfill the request. Note that failure is propagated to the client only after all retries are made. We can create a diagram that shows a set of features that our API should support, as figure 4.1 illustrates.

When designing such a component, we need to answer questions about third-party libraries we will use. But more importantly, we need to foresee use cases to allow proper extensibility points without over engineering this new component. Sometimes, engineers tend to start the implementation phase using patterns that would enable extending the code in the future. When we begin with this approach, we risk introducing many abstraction levels that add complexity to our system.

In this chapter, we will try a different approach. We will start with the most straightforward design without extensibility points. We will then progress to a more flexible code from the client's perspective. However, we will also observe that flexibility adds complexity to our code.

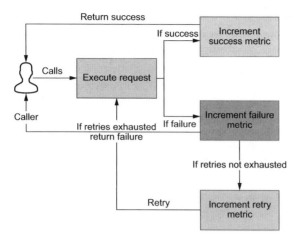

Figure 4.1 Set of supported features for our shared software component

4.1.2 Starting with the most straightforward code

We will start our refactoring journey from the most straightforward implementation. Let's first understand the implementation and then answer a question about its limitations. Next, we will try to foresee missing use cases and extensibility points we can provide.

We will call our new component `HttpClientExecution`. The constructor of this component takes `MetricRegistry` as an argument. This is a class from a third-party library that's used to expose metrics (https://metrics.dropwizard.io/4.2.0). The following listing presents a first look at this component.

Listing 4.1 `HttpClientExecution` parameters

```
import com.codahale.metrics.Meter;
import com.codahale.metrics.MetricRegistry;


private final int maxNumberOfRetries;
private final CloseableHttpClient client;
private final Meter successMeter;
private final Meter failureMeter;
private final Meter retryCounter;

public HttpClientExecution(
    MetricRegistry metricRegistry, int maxNumberOfRetries,
    CloseableHttpClient client) {
  this.successMeter = metricRegistry.meter("requests.success");
  this.failureMeter = metricRegistry.meter("requests.failure");
  this.retryCounter = metricRegistry.meter("requests.retry");
  this.maxNumberOfRetries = maxNumberOfRetries;
  this.client = client;
}
```

Sets an upper bound for retries that this component can execute

Creates metrics using MetricRegistry

The client is provided by the caller, who is responsible for configuring it.

Note that our code uses a third-party library that provides the `MetricRegistry` class (http://mng.bz/Vlzy). We will use this class to construct and publish metrics from our code. We can treat it as a black box, using its public API. However, by using this class in our component, we are coupling our `HttpClientExecution` to a specific metric library. There are a couple of metrics libraries available, and if the client wants to pick a different one, our code will not allow doing so. We will get back to this problem later.

Let's now focus on the algorithm implementation of execution with the retry method. To execute the POST request, this method should take only one parameter—a String path. The following listing is a reminder of how we increment metrics and provide retries.

Listing 4.2   Executing POST with retry logic

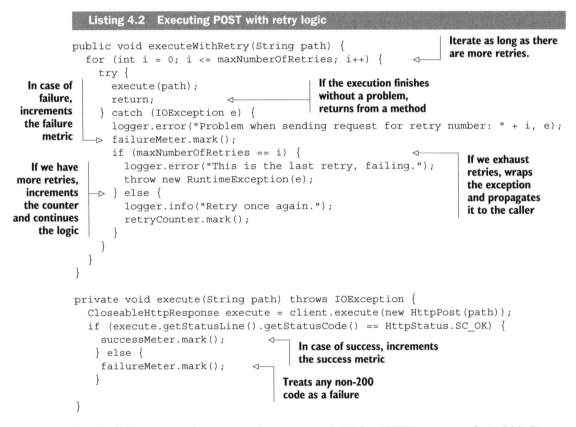

```
public void executeWithRetry(String path) {          Iterate as long as there
  for (int i = 0; i <= maxNumberOfRetries; i++) {    are more retries.
    try {
      execute(path);                 If the execution finishes
      return;                        without a problem,
    } catch (IOException e) {        returns from a method
      logger.error("Problem when sending request for retry number: " + i, e);
      failureMeter.mark();
      if (maxNumberOfRetries == i) {
        logger.error("This is the last retry, failing.");
        throw new RuntimeException(e);           If we exhaust
      } else {                                   retries, wraps
        logger.info("Retry once again.");        the exception
        retryCounter.mark();                      and propagates
      }                                           it to the caller
    }
  }
}

private void execute(String path) throws IOException {
  CloseableHttpResponse execute = client.execute(new HttpPost(path));
  if (execute.getStatusLine().getStatusCode() == HttpStatus.SC_OK) {
    successMeter.mark();              In case of success, increments
  } else {                           the success metric
    failureMeter.mark();
  }                                   Treats any non-200
}                                     code as a failure
```

In case of failure, increments the failure metric

If we have more retries, increments the counter and continues the logic

In the listing, note that we mark success only if the HTTP status code is 200. In any other case, regardless if it was an exception or non-200 status code, we increment `failureMeter`. We could also change this and treat all 2*xx* codes as success, but this is not essential for our example.

When you thoroughly analyze this algorithm, you will notice that it implements the logic from the figure 4.1 with supported features. Our code meets the requirements, but it does not provide any way to extend it. The only way the caller can alter its behavior is by passing the `maxNumberOfRetries` parameter. Later, we will modify this code, making it more flexible, so use it as a reference point before any refactoring.

Finally, to understand our end-to-end logic, let's take a look at unit tests that will validate the behavior of this component. The first unit test verifies that we should execute only one request if the first once succeeds. The following listing shows the code for this.

Listing 4.3 Validating success without retries

```
@Test
public void shouldNotRetryIfFirstRequestsSuccessful() throws IOException {
  // given
  MetricRegistry metricRegistry = new MetricRegistry();
  CloseableHttpClient client = mock(CloseableHttpClient.class);
  CloseableHttpResponse response = mock(CloseableHttpResponse.class);
  when(response.getStatusLine())
      .thenReturn(new BasicStatusLine(HTTP_1_1, HttpStatus.SC_OK, null));
  HttpClientExecution httpClientExecution = new
     HttpClientExecution(metricRegistry, 3, client);

  when(client.execute(any())).thenReturn(response);          ← Mocks the HTTP client
                                                               to return success
  // when
  httpClientExecution
➥ .executeWithRetry("http://localhost/user");     ← Executes
                                                     executeWithRetry(),
  // then                                             which is our public API
  assertThat(getMetric(metricRegistry, "requests.success"))
➥ .isEqualTo(1);                                                          ←
  assertThat(getMetric(metricRegistry, "requests.failure")).isEqualTo(0);
  assertThat(getMetric(metricRegistry, "requests.retry")).isEqualTo(0);
}
                                                          Increments the
                                                          request.success metric
```

If all subsequent retries fails, we should increment the failure and retry metrics. Finally, the underlying cause should be propagated to the client, as the following listing shows. In this test, we simulate failure for all retries.

Listing 4.4 Validating failure with retry

```
when(client.execute(any())).thenThrow(new IOException("problem"));
HttpClientExecution httpClientExecution = new
    HttpClientExecution(metricRegistry, 3, client);

// when
assertThatThrownBy(
        () -> {
          httpClientExecution.executeWithRetry("url");
        })
    .hasCauseInstanceOf(IOException.class);      ← After all retries, propagates
                                                   the underlying IOException
// then
assertThat(getMetric(metricRegistry, "requests.success")).isEqualTo(0);
```

```
assertThat(getMetric(metricRegistry,
➡  "requests.failure")).isEqualTo(4);
assertThat(getMetric(metricRegistry,
➡  "requests.retry")).isEqualTo(3);
```

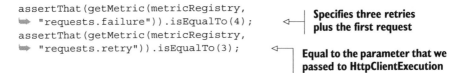

Specifies three retries plus the first request

Equal to the parameter that we passed to HttpClientExecution

NOTE   The requests.failure metric value will be higher than the client's retries by one. This happens because the first request is not counted toward the full retry count.

Finally, if the first request fails, but the second one succeeds, the retry logic should allow the call to pass. From the client's perspective, there will be no information about retries. Only metrics can tell the client if the retry happened or not. The following listing shows this last unit test, where the first request fails and the second succeeds.

Listing 4.5   Validating retry and success

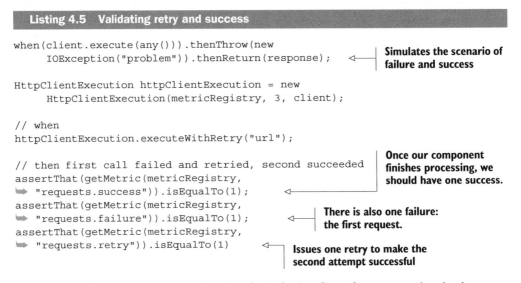

```
when(client.execute(any())).thenThrow(new
    IOException("problem")).thenReturn(response);

HttpClientExecution httpClientExecution = new
    HttpClientExecution(metricRegistry, 3, client);

// when
httpClientExecution.executeWithRetry("url");

// then first call failed and retried, second succeeded
assertThat(getMetric(metricRegistry,
➡  "requests.success")).isEqualTo(1);
assertThat(getMetric(metricRegistry,
➡  "requests.failure")).isEqualTo(1);
assertThat(getMetric(metricRegistry,
➡  "requests.retry")).isEqualTo(1)
```

Simulates the scenario of failure and success

Once our component finishes processing, we should have one success.

There is also one failure: the first request.

Issues one retry to make the second attempt successful

Although we have a component that is relatively simple and easy to maintain, it comes with a number of limitations. We don't have many extension points, and we impose on the client's code to use a specific metric library implementation. This means there is a tight coupling between our component and the third-party library.

Let's assume that we want to improve our component, allowing for more flexibility. End users should be able to pick their library and to provide the implementation. Our component should not care about the actual library used for collecting metrics. In the next section, we will see how trying to foresee this feature will impact our codebase.

4.2   *Allowing clients to provide their own metrics framework*

At this point, our component is not very flexible, and it has a hard dependency on a third-party library that is responsible for gathering metrics. This is not problematic at first sight, but other engineers and systems will use our code. By using any class from this third-party library in our codebase, we limit our component's future implementations. Moreover, we place the restriction that everywhere our piece of code is used, the same metrics library needs to be used.

When you look at the imports in our `HttpClientExecution` component, you will notice that we have dependencies to third-party libraries. The following listing shows these dependencies.

Listing 4.6   Metrics dependencies on third-party libraries

```
import com.codahale.metrics.Meter;
import com.codahale.metrics.MetricRegistry;
```

It turns out that our simple code has a tight coupling that makes it hard to test and to extend the code. For that reason, we abstract away the metrics-related code. The pattern of abstracting it out is quite simple. We need to define an interface that is generic and that can be an entry point to our system (see figure 4.2). But from this point on, our code will integrate with any metrics-specific implementation only via this new interface.

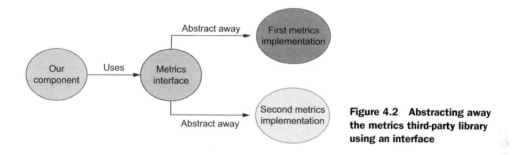

Figure 4.2   Abstracting away the metrics third-party library using an interface

The new metrics interface needs to define the contract between our component and any third-party library. It may look as simple as that shown in the following listing.

Listing 4.7   Defining our metrics interface

```
public interface MetricsProvider {
  void incrementSuccess();
  void incrementFailure();
  void incrementRetry();
}
```

This interface does not allow the caller to get the data back out of the component. It is, however, a sound limitation because the caller can inject their metric registry to track metrics. Due to that fact, the caller owns the metric registry code and can access the metrics directly. There is no need to add accessor methods in this `MetricsProvider` interface. And `MetricsProvider` does not need to import any class from a third-party metrics library, so we don't have a tight coupling between our new `MetricsProvider` and specific metrics implementation.

`HttpClientExecution` will interact with metrics via this abstraction. By doing so, we don't need to worry about the implementation details. They will need to be provided by the client. Let's assume the clients want to provide an implementation for the metrics Dropwizard library. Most importantly, the client needs to implement the `MetricsProvider` interface. The following listing shows this implementation.

Listing 4.8   Implementing a metrics provider

```
public class DefaultMetricsProvider implements MetricsProvider {
  private final Meter successMeter;
  private final Meter failureMeter;                    This implementation
  private final Meter retryCounter;                    provides internal details.

  public DefaultMetricsProvider(MetricRegistry metricRegistry) {
    this.successMeter =
    metricRegistry.meter("requests.success");        ◄──
    this.failureMeter = metricRegistry.meter("requests.failure");
    this.retryCounter = metricRegistry.meter("requests.retry");
  }

  @Override
  public void incrementSuccess() {        ◄──   Interface methods are
    successMeter.mark();                         the only integration
  }                                              points with our
                                                 component.
  @Override
  public void incrementFailure() {
    failureMeter.mark();
  }

  @Override
  public void incrementRetry() {
    retryCounter.mark();
  }
}
```

How did foreseeing this feature impact the flexibility and complexity of our component? First, we can see that the actual implementation details were abstracted away from our component, and the logic of `HttpClientExecution` is simplified. There's no longer a need to implement that in our system. The clear conclusion from this is that the complexity of our component decreased. And because clients can now provide any metrics implementation that they want, flexibility is also increased.

It would seem that increasing flexibility and decreasing complexity is a win–win situation. However, this approach has some drawbacks. The complexity that we removed from our system needs to live somewhere. If multiple clients use our component, they all need to implement a new metrics interface. Now, the complexity lives in various clients' repositories. In essence, we outsourced the complexity to external clients. It looks like we increased flexibility, but we also increased complexity. It just did not grow in our codebase.

From the client's perspective, using a component that requires many additional steps, such as providing its own metrics implementation, may be cumbersome, and clients may end up using a different system or component! A good middle ground here would be to extract the metrics interface but provide a default implementation that's used by most users. By doing so, we are allowing extensibility, but the complexity will be tacked on to our system. We do not outsource it to the client's code. If they want a different implementation, they can easily implement that and provide it to our component.

Our systems rely on many external components in real life, and abstracting them may not be feasible. Even for our simple example, we depended on the actual implementation of an HTTP client. The HTTP client provides more methods that may be hard to hide against abstraction. Developing an abstraction that hides an HTTP client when trying to foresee every use case of such a library will increase the complexity of our code.

In the next section, we will see one of the most flexible and extensive mechanisms for providing those extension points, knowing that the complexity of our design will increase substantially. We will look at a mechanism, a hooks API, that allows clients to provide their behavior in various places of our component life cycle. We will consider a different use case (that is not metrics related).

4.3 Providing extensibility of your APIs via hooks

Every framework and system has a life cycle with multiple steps. Instead of trying to foresee every possible use case for our clients, we may attempt to allow clients to provide their own behavior and inject it into our component. We no longer need to alter our API and code, based on the new feature requests. Clients can provide their logic, and our code does not need to know about it. In theory, this approach substantially increases extensibility, and we don't need to worry about that anymore. In practice, we need to be careful about code that is injected into our system. There are not many assumptions that we can make because we know nothing about the caller's provided behavior.

It's possible to make each phase of the life cycle extensible and flexible by using various patterns, such as abstracting away (shown in the previous section) or using inheritance. Often, if we want to give maximum flexibility to our code for our clients, we can employ a hook mechanism. This pattern allows clients to plug their code in between phases of the specific component's life cycle. In our example API, we want to enable clients to hook into code after preparing the HTTP request but before sending an actual HTTP request to a REST endpoint. Figure 4.3 shows this arrangement.

The client first executes the executeWithRetry() method. This starts the life cycle of our component, which creates an HTTP request method. Normally, once this phase of the life cycle completes, this method executes an external REST call, and the life cycle of our component finishes. By introducing the hooks API, we are allowing clients to *intercept* a specific call. The client only needs to implement a hook interface.

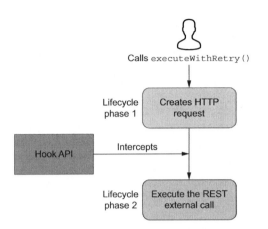

Intercepts

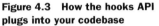

Figure 4.3   **How the hooks API plugs into your codebase**

Next, we call this hook in a proper life cycle of our component. This provides a flexible mechanism that removes the burden of foreseeing the exact features that our clients may need in the future.

The first step to support the hooks API is to create an interface that allows our code to call the hook in a specific phase of our code's life cycle. The new interface is simple. It has only one method, as the following listing shows. We will call this method passing `HttpRequestBase` as an argument, which is created in the first phase of our life cycle.

Listing 4.9   Implementing the hooks interface

```
public interface HttpRequestHook {
  void executeOnRequest(HttpRequestBase httpRequest);
}
```

The client of our component injects the hook implementation (clients can inject more than one hook). Therefore, we need to accept a list of hooks in our constructor, as the next listing shows.

Listing 4.10   Using a hook constructor

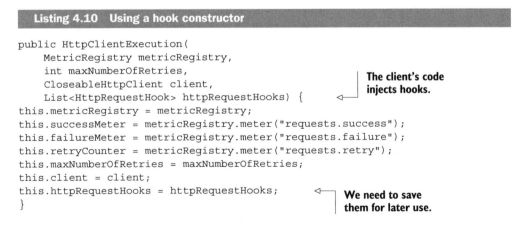

```
public HttpClientExecution(
    MetricRegistry metricRegistry,
    int maxNumberOfRetries,
    CloseableHttpClient client,
    List<HttpRequestHook> httpRequestHooks) {        ◁── The client's code injects hooks.
this.metricRegistry = metricRegistry;
this.successMeter = metricRegistry.meter("requests.success");
this.failureMeter = metricRegistry.meter("requests.failure");
this.retryCounter = metricRegistry.meter("requests.retry");
this.maxNumberOfRetries = maxNumberOfRetries;
this.client = client;
this.httpRequestHooks = httpRequestHooks;        ◁── We need to save them for later use.
}
```

Next, let's look at how the hooks API plugs into our component's existing life cycle. Because the client's code executes between life cycle phases, it iterates over every injected hook and passes the `HttpPost` object to the caller code. The following listing shows this procedure.

Listing 4.11 Executing without error handling

The first phase of the life cycle creates an HttpPost object.

Executes client's code between life cycle phases

```
private void execute(String path) throws IOException {
  HttpPost httpPost = new HttpPost(path);
  for (HttpRequestHook httpRequestHook : httpRequestHooks) {
    httpRequestHook.executeOnRequest(httpPost);
  }
  CloseableHttpResponse execute = client.execute(httpPost);
  if (execute.getStatusLine().getStatusCode() == HttpStatus.SC_OK) {
    successMeter.mark();
  }
}
```

The second phase of our life cycle executes an external REST call.

Using this mechanism allows clients to inject their code in the middle of our processing. Here we are passing the HTTP post request to the client code. The caller can execute any action on it. Thus, the flexibility of this solution is high.

4.3.1 Guarding against unpredictable usage of the hooks API

In this example, we iterate over all hooks provided by the client and then pass the `HttpPost()` method to the API. At this point, we can conclude that we were able to achieve high extensibility without increasing the complexity of our code substantially. Unfortunately, we need to realize that we don't have any influence over the client's code. Our hook interface does not declare any exceptions. However, as we learned in the chapter about exceptions, clients can still throw an unchecked exception from their code. It means that when the client's code does something unpredictable, it can lead to an unchecked exception.

Documenting contracts for hooks not throwing exceptions versus guarding against hooks that can throw exceptions

In an ideal world, when we expose an API for our users to our clients, we should document its contract. We may, for example, state that all hook implementations cannot throw exceptions. However, it is hard to impose that requirement on all our clients. Someone may forget to do so (or not read the documentation). Someone else may rely on some other code that throws unchecked exceptions, even if it shouldn't. For those reasons, if we state that no exception should be thrown, it's wise to guard against possible exceptions. Otherwise, the client's application that uses our code may fail with hard to detect problems (or silent failures).

We can validate that assumption by writing a unit test that provides a hook that throws an unchecked exception. The following listing shows such a test.

Listing 4.12   Testing for unpredictable problems in a hook

```
HttpClientExecution httpClientExecution =
    new HttpClientExecution(
        metricRegistry,
        3,
        client,
        Collections.singletonList(
        httpRequest -> {
          throw new RuntimeException("Unpredictable problem!");
        }));
```

An unexpected problem is thrown from the code we don't control.

In such a case, the life cycle of our component will be impacted; by providing flexibility to a client, we introduce complexity to our code. To guard against this problem, we need to wrap the code that we don't own into a try-catch block, as the following listing displays.

Listing 4.13   Guarding against failures

```
for (HttpRequestHook httpRequestHook : httpRequestHooks) {
  try {
    httpRequestHook.executeOnRequest(httpPost);
  } catch (Exception ex) {
    logger.error("HttpRequestHook throws an exception. Please validate your
    hook logic", ex);
  }
}
```

We must expect anything, so any Exception can be thrown.

We can't stop the lifecycle of our component if the client throws.

We can log the error to provide feedback to the client if the exception is not fatal from the perspective of our core business processing (the code that calls hooks). In other words, regardless of the type of logic injected by the caller, we don't want our processing to be impacted by those problems. If the code provided by the hook fails, we can log that for debugging, but we can still continue with our processing.

If we allow this exception to propagate, it will impact the logic of our library. We don't want to allow that behavior because our library code works as expected, but things may get even more complicated. If we pass a stateful object, such as the HTTP client object to a hooks API, we cannot influence how this object will be used. The code from the hooks API may execute code that alters the internals of the client. For example, it can be used to execute additional HTTP requests. This may be problematic if you have tweaked your HTTP client for your traffic (you've configured proper queue size, timeouts, and other settings).

The provided logic of your component may consume resources that are needed for a normal workflow. As a result, you may break the service level agreement (SLA), or the whole life cycle may fail. In the worst case, the client's code may execute some logic that makes the HTTP client fail. In such a case, your component will also fail.

NOTE You need to be careful when passing any internal state to the code you don't own. Documenting the hooks API code assumption is a good first step, but it will not prevent unexpected usages in real life.

In this section, we learned how to guard against unexpected usage from the correctness perspective. How does it look from the performance perspective? Let's take a look at this problem in the next section.

4.3.2 Performance impact of the hook API

From the correctness perspective, our code should handle unexpected failures of the client's provided code. But we need to be aware that the logic provided by the client may be blocking. This means that we don't have any influence over the time it takes to call the hooks API.

Let's assume that the caller provides the hook logic that executes some I/O call, such as a network or filesystem call that involves blocking. Every I/O call can be unpredictable, and it may result in high latency. Let's assume that the latency of the hooks API call is 1,000 ms. If our first life-cycle phase takes 100 ms and the second life-cycle phase takes 200 ms, we will have a total time of one call equal to 1,300 ms instead of 300 ms. This is four times slower! This impacts the performance of our component substantially. Figure 4.4 summarizes this scenario.

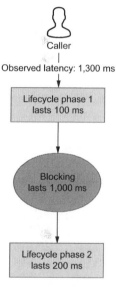

The caller will observe high latency, and looking at our component's current design, we can do nothing about it. The synchronous call inside of the hook uses the same thread that our component uses. Because of that, in some situations, we may even risk deadlock.

Imagine a scenario in which we have a minimal number of threads and the client's code provided in the hooks API blocks or waits for some external resource to be available. Even if this external resource is not available in one out of many situations, the thread shared between our component

Figure 4.4 The hooks API blocking call

and client's code will block. If this happens multiple times, we may risk a problem when there are not enough threads to process requests.

We can require clients to execute nonblocking calls in the callback code. This means that every client needs to manage a thread pool that will handle the hooks API actions. Again, even if we document it, we cannot enforce it easily. It is possible to detect a blocking call on our thread, but it will substantially complicate the design.

The described situation worsens if we have multiple independent hook actions, and each of them executes logic that involves blocking behavior. If we have two blocking hooks, and each of them takes 1,000 ms, our total processing time increases to 2,300 ms, which is eight times slower than the code without the hooks API, as figure 4.5 illustrates.

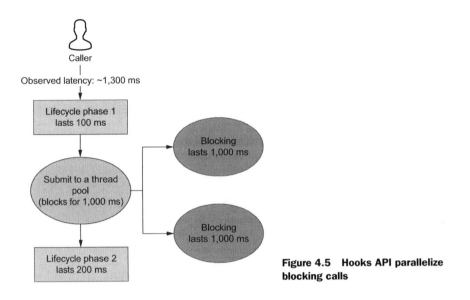

Figure 4.5   Hooks API parallelize blocking calls

One solution for this problem would be to assume that the hooks API code is not safe and always may be blocking. By introducing this assumption, we can wrap every hook API call into an action executed on a separate thread.

With the current design, every hook API is submitted to a separate thread pool, and the thread pool needs to be managed and maintained in our code. We need to decide about the number of threads needed, the queue size, and other factors such as allowing the addition of threads dynamically or not. We also need to monitor this thread pool usage and threads consumption.

Managing a separate thread pool increases the complexity of our codebase. The thread pool contains a queue of tasks that we can process, so we need to monitor this queue, so it does not risk exceeding memory with pending tasks. Also, we need to make sure that threads are not dying silently when some unexpected exception occurs.

We can submit n parallel hook executions, where n is a number of threads in our thread pool. Let's assume the caller provides two hooks. Each of these executes a blocking call that lasts 1,000 ms. Ideally, those hooks can be run separately without a need to wait between stages. In that case, they will not impact the latency of our component call. But if you remember, this new API allows clients to plug the code between phases of our life cycle. Because of that, there is a *happens-before* relationship between completing all the hooks API calls and proceeding to the next phase of our life cycle. Even if we can parallelize the calls, we need to wait for all of them to finish. So the latency that's added will be at least as high as the slowest operation provided via the hooks API. Our flexibility of this design decreases the performance by increasing latency.

Let's take a look at the design of our `HttpClientExecution` component that takes into account improvements regarding correctness and performance. We need to create a dedicated thread pool for the hooks API, which increases complexity and maintenance. In the following listing, note that every hook API is submitted to the dedicated thread pool.

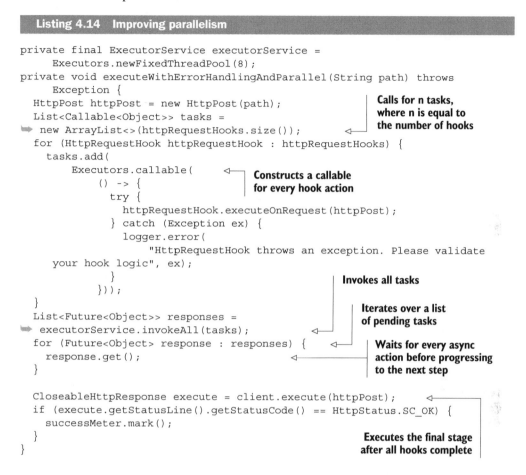

Listing 4.14 Improving parallelism

```
private final ExecutorService executorService =
    Executors.newFixedThreadPool(8);
private void executeWithErrorHandlingAndParallel(String path) throws
    Exception {
  HttpPost httpPost = new HttpPost(path);
  List<Callable<Object>> tasks =
  new ArrayList<>(httpRequestHooks.size());
  for (HttpRequestHook httpRequestHook : httpRequestHooks) {
    tasks.add(
        Executors.callable(
            () -> {
              try {
                httpRequestHook.executeOnRequest(httpPost);
              } catch (Exception ex) {
                logger.error(
                    "HttpRequestHook throws an exception. Please validate
    your hook logic", ex);
              }
            }));
  }
  List<Future<Object>> responses =
  executorService.invokeAll(tasks);
  for (Future<Object> response : responses) {
    response.get();
  }

  CloseableHttpResponse execute = client.execute(httpPost);
  if (execute.getStatusLine().getStatusCode() == HttpStatus.SC_OK) {
    successMeter.mark();
  }
}
```

Annotations:
- Calls for n tasks, where n is equal to the number of hooks
- Constructs a callable for every hook action
- Invokes all tasks
- Iterates over a list of pending tasks
- Waits for every async action before progressing to the next step
- Executes the final stage after all hooks complete

Compared to the first design of our component, our code gets complicated. We need to handle any failure to not risk killing the threads from the thread pool silently. Also, we need to parallelize the hooks execution, but this does not solve all performance issues that arise from using hooks. We still need to wait for them to finish. The flexibility that clients can achieve using the hooks API does not come for free. We will pay for that with more maintenance costs for dedicated thread pools and the complexity of our solution.

In the next section, we will look at another mechanism, the listener API, that allows us to make our API flexible without a need to foresee every possible feature that clients may request. We will also provide a way for propagating the information about the number of retries to a client. Finally, we will see how anticipating this feature later complicates the logic.

4.4   *Providing extensibility of your APIs via listeners*

At first glance, the listener API may appear to be similar to a hooks API, but there are differences that make it worth explaining separately. As you may remember, the hooks API design was synchronous because we needed to wait for all hooks completion before progressing to the next step. As depicted in figure 4.6, the observer design pattern, which provides a listener API, takes a different approach for providing extension points for the client. Our component (called a *subject* in the observer pattern) allows clients to register observers. Those observers will get a notification when some action in our component occurs.

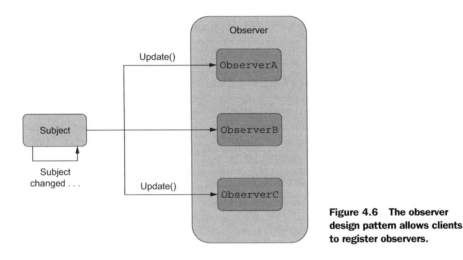

Figure 4.6   The observer design pattern allows clients to register observers.

We allow clients to provide multiple observers. Let's take a look at the most significant difference between a listener API and the hooks API.

4.4.1   *Using listeners vs. hooks*

When we send some event (e.g., denoting that our component finishes the life cycle phase), the notification is fully asynchronous. There will be no happens-before relationship between events and progressing to the next stage of our component. This means that there is no risk of performance degradation as long as we execute listeners in a separate thread pool. The only difference is that we don't need to wait on the listener's API actions to be completed.

It may be tempting to expose an internal state or signal that some event occurred using the listener API. It is a flexible abstraction because we can allow clients to provide their own behavior without modifying our code or API. Let's assume that we decide that we want to foresee a new use case and that we send a notification with a retry state when our component finishes executing, as figure 4.7 illustrates.

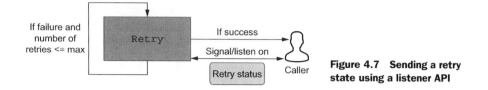

Figure 4.7 Sending a retry state using a listener API

We will expose the retry status when all retries finish. For that purpose, we need to create a new `RetryStatus` class that encapsulates the information that we want to propagate to a client. The following listing shows this new class.

Listing 4.15 Creating a `RetryStatus` class

```java
public class RetryStatus {
  private final Integer retryNumber;
  public RetryStatus(Integer retryNumber) {
    this.retryNumber = retryNumber;
  }
  public Integer getRetryNumber() {
    return retryNumber;
  }
}
```

For the sake of simplicity in this example, our retry status contains only the retry number. It returns the counter of a specific retry.

We will allow our clients to register the `OnRetryListener` that is invoked by our component when the expected action occurs. The `OnRetryListener` interface has only one `onRetry()` method to get the status of retries, and each retry will have a dedicated `RetryStatus`. The following listing shows this implementation.

Listing 4.16 `OnRetryListener`

```java
public interface OnRetryListener {
  void onRetry(List<RetryStatus> retryStatus);
}
public class HttpClientExecution {
  private final List<OnRetryListener> retryListeners = new ArrayList<>();
  public void registerOnRetryListener(OnRetryListener onRetryListener) {
    retryListeners.add(onRetryListener);
  }
// remaining methods
}
```

Keeps a list of listeners

Registers a new listener via a dedicated method

When the retry logic finishes, we can iterate over every listener and propagate all retry statuses for a given execution. We need to aggregate those into a list and then send the list to every retry listener. The following listing shows this implementation.

Listing 4.17 Invoking `OnRetryListener`

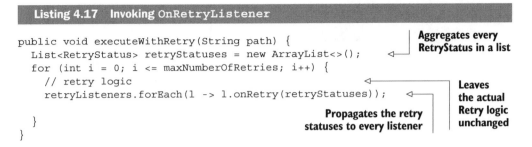

```
public void executeWithRetry(String path) {
  List<RetryStatus> retryStatuses = new ArrayList<>();
  for (int i = 0; i <= maxNumberOfRetries; i++) {
    // retry logic
    retryListeners.forEach(l -> l.onRetry(retryStatuses));

  }
}
```

Aggregates every
RetryStatus in a list

Propagates the retry
statuses to every listener

Leaves
the actual
Retry logic
unchanged

Note that the rules for handling failures and how to make our code run in parallel are the same rules discussed in section 4.3. At first sight, the logic looks correct, but we need to be aware of one caveat when propagating our internal state to the caller's code. We cannot prevent the caller from modifying the state that is passed. Modifying this state can make our logic corrupted. Let's look at this problem in the next section.

4.4.2   *Immutability of our design*

When propagating any state from our component, we cannot be sure that it will not be modified in the client's code. The following listing shows a unit test that we can create to simulate this behavior.

Listing 4.18   Modifying state via a listener

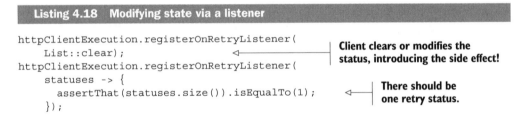

```
httpClientExecution.registerOnRetryListener(
    List::clear);
httpClientExecution.registerOnRetryListener(
    statuses -> {
      assertThat(statuses.size()).isEqualTo(1);
    });
```

Client clears or modifies the
status, introducing the side effect!

There should be
one retry status.

The list of retry statuses that is passed to `OnRetryListener` is a reference to an actual list. There is nothing preventing the client from calling `clear()` or from removing or adding an element to this list. If the first listener clears the statuses, the second listener will not see the modification. This means there is a side effect introduced by the caller's code. Such a situation makes our API error prone and nondeterministic. To prevent such a situation, we can create a copy of the actual list that is propagated to a client. The following listing shows this.

Listing 4.19   Copying the object propagated to listeners

```
retryListeners.forEach(l -> l.onRetry(new ArrayList<>(retryStatuses)));
```

For every listener, we create a copy of the retry status, which is sent to every listener. Because of that, even if the caller modifies the object, it will not impact any other listener or our API code. This has a couple of drawbacks.

First, we need to create a lot of copies of the data if this is a deep copy of the original object. A *deep copy* copies all values from the original object to the new one, and it may increase the memory usage of our application substantially. If we have *n* listeners, we need to copy the actual data *n* times, which increases memory consumption by this amount. The second drawback is the potential difficulty of silent problems in the listener's code. If the client modifies the list, it may be nonintentional, and sometimes, it is better to signal that such an operation is forbidden explicitly by throwing an exception.

We can solve both problems by wrapping the statue into an immutable wrapper. For a list, we can use the `ImmutableList` (http://mng.bz/xvzd) construct, as the following listing shows.

```
retryListeners.forEach(l -> l.onRetry(ImmutableList.copyOf(retryStatuses)));
```

Wrapping the actual state into an immutable abstraction does not create a copy. It will create a class that throws an exception on any modification of the underlying list. We don't need to copy the actual content of the list every time it is propagated to the listener. Only methods that make any modifications are forbidden. The second benefit of this approach is that it's explicit and fail-fast. If the code in the listener API modifies the content accidentally, the feedback is provided immediately, and there is no risk of failing silently.

If you are propagating any state to a code that you don't own, you should always assert that the state is immutable. You can make it immutable from the beginning by designing it that way. It can be achieved by using immutable classes and the final fields. If the API that you are using is immutable, you don't need to create a defensive copy. The memory footprint will be substantially lower.

In reality, we often need to use libraries that are not immutable. The majority of collections, such as lists or maps, are mutable. It would help if you were extremely careful when propagating these to a client. In such a case, you should wrap the state into an immutable class that hides or forbids the modification of the underlying data.

The other problem that you may have when propagating state to the listener API is the risk of overwhelming listeners with traffic. If you are invoking *n* listeners every time there is some action, it means that your application's memory consumption increases substantially. There is a risk that the caller's code will not keep up with the traffic and block, impacting the main processing of your application. You may consider adding back pressure or buffering more status events and sending them in batch in such a case. All solutions to this problem complicate your design substantially. You should exercise caution if you decide to send notifications from your component.

You can see that even a simple propagating state using a listener API makes your code complex: you need to assure that your data is immutable, and you need to assert that caller's code will be able to keep up with the traffic. Foreseeing use cases that look simple at first sight add a lot of complexity to your code.

4.5 *Flexibility analysis of an API vs. the cost of maintenance*

The most important conclusion you should take from the examples in this chapter is that every new feature increases the complexity at some level. For example, sometimes we want to abstract away a specific library that we depend on. We saw an example of this pattern when abstracting away the metric-specific library. Abstracting away the actual implementation decreases the complexity in our component but increases it in the client's code. Every client would need to provide the implementation for the concrete metrics library. For this, we found that a hybrid solution may be the best in the majority of use cases—abstracting away but providing the default, most used implementation.

If we try to guess and foresee the exact use case, we may be tempted to introduce fairly generic patterns, such as listeners or hooks APIs. At first sight, they are flexible and do not add a lot of complexity. This statement may be accurate, but we will pay for the extensibility with increased complexity.

When using a hooks API, you need to guard against any unpredictable usage. This means that your code should expect any exception. Also, you need to pay attention to the thread execution model of your API extension points. If your design allows synchronous client calls, we must assume that some clients will block these, impacting the SLA of your component and resource usage, such as threads. But introducing asynchronous logic that should work in parallel in your code adds additional complexity. You need to maintain a dedicated thread pool and monitor it.

Additionally, you need to pay attention to your component extensibility points and the happens-before relationship between phases of processing. If this is the case, even if you make your processing parallel, you cannot reduce the additional latency to zero. This is a complexity that you need to pay for by exposing the hooks API to the callers.

The listener API is similar to the hooks API, but it does not involve blocking between phases of your component's execution. The signals you emit are asynchronous, so it should not impact your component's overall latency. But you need to be careful about the emitted state. Once you pass some code to a caller component, you don't know if the client will modify it or not. Because of that, the immutability of state that is propagated in the listener API is crucial.

In general, the higher flexibility your API has, the more complexity you will introduce. It can be code complexity or the execution model complexity if you need to introduce async processing. Figure 4.8 illustrates these two approaches: flexibility versus complexity.

Comparing those approaches, abstracting away metrics library gives some flexibility, but we still have an explicit API contract that the clients should fulfill. On the

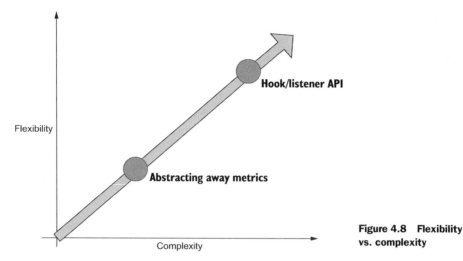

Figure 4.8 Flexibility vs. complexity

other hand, the hooks or listener APIs are a lot more flexible. However, they are exposing an internal event or state of our APIs. The client can do anything with it. This gives us a lot of flexibility, but we cannot reason about the client code; we'll need to guard against unpredictable failures. For this, we need to use an immutable state. Another disadvantage is that we are unable to reason about the client's concurrency model (if it will be a blocking or asynchronous execution). Because of that, sometimes making our system flexible will provide too much trouble. We need to find a place on the flexibility–complexity axis and design our systems accordingly.

I've demonstrated only a small subset of patterns and ways of making our APIs more flexible. There are several different patterns (such as decorator, factory, proxy, and many others) that we can use. This chapter's main purpose was to pick some of those patterns and demonstrate their pros and cons. When a given solution gives you a lot of flexibility, you may want to analyze its inherent complexity too. These general rules apply to all software engineering patterns.

In the next chapter, you'll learn that premature optimization is not always evil. You also learn about cases when optimizing the *hot path* is rational and how to detect the hot paths in your code to make a favorable decision about optimizing parts of your code.

Summary

- We can introduce flexibility to our API via abstracting away third-party logic.
- Introducing the hooks and listener APIs can provide the highest flexibility for our code. These APIs allow us to make our code extensible from the client's perspective.
- Making our system more generic and flexible may increase its complexity.
- Complexity can be added not only to the code and its maintenance but also to other parts of our system.

- When making our code highly extensible using the hooks API, we need to be careful about handling failures and the complexity of the execution model that arises from this API.
- Immutability helps us when reasoning about the system.
- There are various tradeoffs between complexity and flexibility when using different patterns.

Premature optimization vs. optimizing the hot path: Decisions that impact code performance

This chapter covers

- When premature optimization is *evil*
- Finding the hot path in your code using performance testing and measurements
- Optimizing the hot path

There is an old computer science saying that premature optimization is the root of all evil. This has a solid background because it's accurate for a lot of use cases. Without any input data about expected traffic and a service level agreement (SLA), it's hard to reason about your code and its required performance. Optimizing random paths in code in such a situation is like shooting in the dark. You will complicate your code without a sane reason.

> **NOTE** SLA specifies the amount of traffic the service should handle. It can also state the number of requests that it needs to execute and the given number of requests that must be executed with a latency lower than a specific threshold. A similar concept is nonfunctional requirements (NFR), which may specify the expected performance of a system.

At the design stage, we may know a lot about the expected traffic our system will need to handle. In such a scenario, we can design performance benchmarks that

97

will reflect the production traffic. Once we are able to simulate the traffic, we can measure paths in our code and find the hot path. The *hot path* is a part of your code that does most of the work and is executed for almost every user request. In this chapter, we will learn that the Pareto principle can be used to find and estimate where the hot path occurs. Once we have detected the hot path, we can optimize it.

Some can say that this is *premature optimization* because we optimize code before it's even deployed to production. The truth is that by having enough data, we can make rational decisions that allow us to make nonnegligible performance improvements before our system goes to production. The data should come from the performance benchmarks that are executed before the application is deployed to production. We can model the expected traffic when we have defined an SLA and expectations about the real production traffic for our system. When we have enough data that backs up our experiments and hypotheses, optimization is no longer premature.

This chapter will focus on finding a hot path in our code and how to benchmark it. We will see how to introduce improvements to our code with the assurance that our changes will improve our app's performance. Let's start by understanding when premature optimization is, indeed, evil or, at least, problematic.

5.1 When premature optimization is evil

Often, when we write our application code, we don't have much input data regarding its expected traffic. In the ideal world, we would always have information about the expected throughput and maximum latency requirements. In reality, we often need to follow a more ad hoc approach. We start by writing software that is maintainable and easy to change. However, as we write the code, we don't have strict performance requirements. In such a case, optimizing the code up front has too many unknowns.

When optimizing the performance of some code path, we often increase its complexity. Sometimes, however, we need to write parts of it in a specific way. In those parts of the system, we are trading performance over complexity. This may be code complexity, but it can also be maintenance or system complexity of the components we use. Without input data about the traffic, it may turn out that the given code is not impacting the overall performance of our main workflow. Because of that, we introduce additional complexity without the benefit of increasing performance.

Another pitfall we might encounter is optimizing code that's based on false assumptions. Let's see how easy it is to make this mistake.

5.1.1 Creating accounts processing pipeline

Let's consider a simple scenario where we have an account entity for which we want to build a processing pipeline that finds an account with a given ID. The following listing shows this entity.

Listing 5.1   Building an account entity

```
public class Account {
  private String name;
```

```
    private Integer id;
// constructors, getters and setters omitted
}
```

Our code operates on the list of accounts and takes the ID that it should find as an argument. The following listing presents the filtering logic for our account entity.

Listing 5.2 Initial filtering logic

```
public Optional<Account> account(Integer id) {
    return accounts.stream().filter(v -> v.getId().equals(id)).findAny();
}
```

This simple code uses the stream API and hides many performance optimizations already. The stream abstraction works lazily. This means that it executes the filter operation that checks if the account ID matches the argument as long as there is no account found yet.

findAny() vs. findFirst() methods

Let's clarify the use of findAny() and findFirst(), which are often used in the wrong context. Laziness is achieved by using findAny(). This method will stop processing when any element is found. If we use findFirst(), it mimics the same behavior as sequential processing. If this processing is split into parts, then find-Any() may perform better because we do not care about the ordering of processing. However, using findFirst() means that the processing must be done sequentially, which slows down the processing pipeline. This difference becomes more important when we use parallel streams.

We created this code as a first approach. It is important to note that we don't have any performance information. The list of accounts that we process could contain a couple of elements, but it can also hold millions of elements. Without this knowledge, it is hard to optimize the performance for the processing.

For a few accounts, however, our code will be good enough. But for millions of elements, we may consider splitting the work into different threads. One solution would be to create those threads manually, split the work into batches, and submit them to multiple threads. We can also use existing mechanisms, such as parallel streams that hide the creation of threads and split the work.

The problem that we have here is that the assumptions about this code may be false. We can safely assume that it will process maximum N elements, where N is equal to 10,000. As long as the system analysis backs this number, we can start optimizing this part of the code. Unfortunately, we often don't have this input data. It is problematic to optimize code in such a context because we will introduce additional complexity without clear benefit. Let's see how wrong assumptions can complicate our code.

5.1.2   *Optimizing processing based on false assumptions*

Let's assume that we decide to introduce performance optimization to our processing code. We notice that the processing works in one thread. This means that we do not split the work and execute it concurrently, leveraging all cores of our CPU. One of the possible optimizations we can make is to use the work-stealing algorithm, where we need to split the work into N independent stages: all input accounts will have N elements in them. Figure 5.1 illustrates this approach.

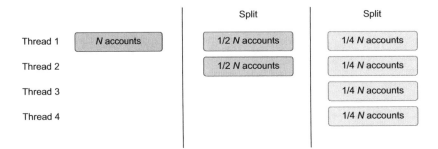

Figure 5.1   Work stealing as performance optimization

First, we will split the work in half into two threads. At this point, two threads will be responsible for processing half of the N accounts. Second, our code should undergo another split because not all threads are utilized, so the work will be split into four of N accounts. Now, every thread can start the actual processing. Our split phase should split the accounts into as many parts as there are available threads or cores. The following listing shows how the proposed logic can be written in a simple way, using the streams API.

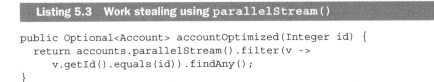

Listing 5.3   Work stealing using `parallelStream()`

```
public Optional<Account> accountOptimized(Integer id) {
  return accounts.parallelStream().filter(v ->
    v.getId().equals(id)).findAny();
}
```

The `parallelStream()` method splits the work into N parts. It uses the internal fork–join thread pool (http://mng.bz/Axro) with a number of threads equal to the number of cores −1. It looks simple, but this hides a lot of complexity. The most important change is that our code is multithreaded now, which means that the processing should be stateless (for example, we shouldn't modify state from any processing method used as a filter.) Because we use a thread pool, we should monitor its use and utilization.

Another hidden complexity that the work-stealing algorithm presents is the phase of splitting the work. This phase takes additional time, adding performance overhead to our code. This overhead can be higher than the gain we get from making it parallel.

And because we based our optimization work on false (or no) assumptions, we cannot reason how this code will perform in production. To verify that our performance optimization is efficient, we need to write a performance benchmark that validates both methods.

5.1.3 *Benchmarking performance optimization*

As you may remember, we assumed that the processing would work for *N* accounts, where *N* is equal to 10,000. Regardless, if this number is based on empirical data or on our assumption, we should at least write a performance benchmark to validate our optimization.

Our benchmarking code will generate *N* random accounts with IDs from 0 to 10,000. For this, we can create a random string using the UUID class. The fork parameter states that all tests should run in the same JVM. For this requirement, we will use the Java Microbenchmark Harness (JMH) tool for benchmarking (see https://github.com/openjdk/jmh). Other platforms have other tools available to help you benchmark your code properly, such as BenchmarkDotNet (https://benchmarkdotnet.org/) for .NET. There are many subtleties involved in benchmarking; it's worth investing time in learning the tried-and-tested tools for your platform rather than trying to roll your own.

Before the actual benchmarking logic, we need to run a warmup that allows JIT to optimize the code paths. This is configured using the @Warmup annotation. We will execute 10 iterations of measurements, which is good enough—the more iterations we execute, the more repeatable the results will be. We are interested in the average time the method takes, and the results will be reported using millisecond (ms) time units. Let's take a look at the benchmark initialization logic, as the following listing shows.

Listing 5.4 Initializing the account's benchmark

```
import org.openjdk.jmh.annotations.Benchmark;
import org.openjdk.jmh.annotations.BenchmarkMode;
import org.openjdk.jmh.annotations.Fork;
import org.openjdk.jmh.annotations.Measurement;
import org.openjdk.jmh.annotations.Mode;
import org.openjdk.jmh.annotations.OutputTimeUnit;
import org.openjdk.jmh.annotations.Warmup;
import org.openjdk.jmh.infra.Blackhole;

@Fork(1)
@Warmup(iterations = 1)
@Measurement(iterations = 10)
@BenchmarkMode(Mode.AverageTime)
@OutputTimeUnit(TimeUnit.MILLISECONDS)
public class AccountsFinderPerformanceBenchmark {
  private static final List<Account> ACCOUNTS =
      IntStream.range(0, 10_000)
          .boxed()
```

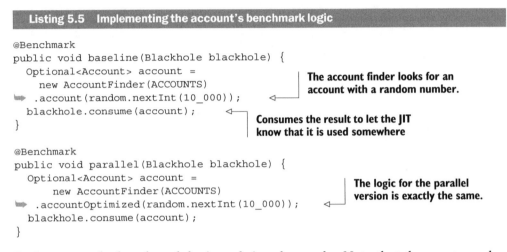

```
        .map(v -> new Account(UUID.randomUUID().toString(), v))
        .collect(Collectors.toList());
  private static final Random random = new Random();
// actual testing methods
```

Generates N accounts to use in this benchmark

Calls the random generator to get the ID we are searching for

The baseline method executes the first version of our accounts finder logic. The `parallel()` method then executes the improved version that uses `parallelStream`, as the following listing shows.

Listing 5.5 Implementing the account's benchmark logic

```
@Benchmark
public void baseline(Blackhole blackhole) {
  Optional<Account> account =
    new AccountFinder(ACCOUNTS)
  .account(random.nextInt(10_000));
  blackhole.consume(account);
}

@Benchmark
public void parallel(Blackhole blackhole) {
  Optional<Account> account =
      new AccountFinder(ACCOUNTS)
  .accountOptimized(random.nextInt(10_000));
  blackhole.consume(account);
}
```

The account finder looks for an account with a random number.

Consumes the result to let the JIT know that it is used somewhere

The logic for the parallel version is exactly the same.

Let's execute the benchmark logic and view the results. Note that the exact number may differ on your machine, but the overall trend will be the same. The following listing shows the result when I execute the benchmark logic on my machine. Notice that the performance of both solutions is almost the same.

Listing 5.6 Viewing the performance benchmark output

```
CH05.premature.AccountsFinderPerformanceBenchmark.baseline
  avgt   10   0.027 ± 0.002   ms/op
CH05.premature.AccountsFinderPerformanceBenchmark.parallel
  avgt   10   0.030 ± 0.002   ms/op
```

The parallel processing may be slightly slower because of the split overhead needed before the actual work. If you increase the number of accounts, however, you may notice that the parallel version is slightly faster. But overall, the difference between both solutions will be negligible.

From this simple test, we saw that the parallel solution's performance results do not justify adding the additional complexity that arises from using a multithreading solution. However, the code complexity doesn't increase, whether you choose a `parallel-Stream` or a standard stream. The complexity is hidden in the internals of the `parallelStream()` method. Further, our optimization can yield different results in production because we decided on performance improvements based on false assumptions.

In such a scenario, optimizing our code prematurely *before* we gain insight about the way it will be used in production may be problematic.

To summarize our efforts, we put some work into optimizing specific code parts in our system. It turns out our improvements didn't provide any value. In essence, we wasted time based on false assumptions. We assumed the code would be called for a specific number of elements. In such a context, the second version of our code did not perform better. The problem is that the numbers used to conduct the test were a guess. In a real-world system, it's probable that the number of elements to process will be substantially different (higher or lower). This means that we will have more empirical data that we can use to optimize the code, but this time it will be based on real-world assumptions. In that case, we can get back to optimizing the code—this time using the correct numbers.

If you know up front that your accounts will grow over time, you need to adapt your benchmarking code. Once you hit some threshold, you will notice that `parallel-Stream()` will perform better than the standard `stream()`. In such a case, it won't be premature optimization anymore.

We looked at one aspect of the input information needed for useful performance optimizations. In real-world systems, we have a lot of code paths. Even assuming that we know N for all input processing, it may not be feasible to optimize all of those paths. We should know how often the given code path will be executed to decide if it is worth optimizing. There are code paths that are executed rarely, such as code initialization. However, we have code paths that are executed for every user request. We call this code the *hot path*. Optimizing code on this path is often worth doing, resulting in a substantial performance improvement of the overall system. In the next section, we will learn how to reason about our hot paths.

5.2 *Hot paths in your code*

In the previous section, we saw an example of optimization based on false assumptions. We also saw that one of the essential data characteristics that's useful when optimizing your code is knowing the input number of elements (N). This may be the number of requests per second or the number of files you need to read. As we know, an algorithm's complexity can be calculated by knowing the input number of elements (N). We can pick the proper algorithm, but we can also estimate memory usage.

Knowing N is vital, but not all code in our applications has the same importance in real production systems. For example, let's consider a simple HTTP application that has different endpoints executed more or less often. Figure 5.2 shows this request frequency.

The first request endpoint exposes the main functionality of our application. It executes for almost every client call and does the main work in our code. Let's assume that this endpoint is executed by our clients 10,000 times per second. We can also assume that N for both endpoints is calculated based on the empirical data or the SLA that our service offers. In this example, the data we are using is based on assumptions backed up by actual data.

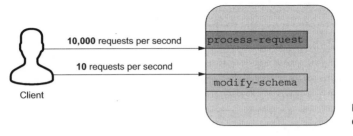

Figure 5.2   Endpoints with different request frequencies

On the other hand, we have a different method that does more of the heavy work. The *modify-user-details* manipulates the data structure in the underlying database that this HTTP application uses. It is called *rarely* because changing the user details is not a common task that clients will execute. Once the user details are changed, it will stay in the same structure for a long time.

Now, let's assume that we measure the 99th percentile of latency for both endpoints (i.e., 99% of the requests are faster than a specific number). After some time, we get the results, concluding that the p99 latency for our process-request is equal to 200 ms, and the p99 latency for the modify-user-details is 500 ms. If we look only at those measurements without the context of the number of requests per second, we could conclude that we should start optimizing the modify-user-details endpoint first. When you add context about the number of requests, however, it is easy to see that optimizing the process-request endpoint will give us more overall savings in resources and time.

For example, if we can reduce the p99 latency for process requests by only 20 ms (10%), we will get an overall reduction of latency equal to 200,000 ms:

$$(10{,}000 \times 200) - (10{,}000 \times 180) = 200{,}000$$

However, if we optimize the modify user details endpoint twice to 250 ms, we will get a substantially lower overall latency reduction that is equal to 2,500 ms: $(10 \times 500) - (10 \times 250) = 2{,}500$.

Based on that calculation, we can conclude that investing time in optimizing the endpoint that is called more often results in 80 times more savings than optimizing the endpoint that takes more time to execute: $200{,}000 \div 2{,}500 = 80$.

As previously mentioned, the path that is executed for the majority of requests is called a *hot path*. Finding and optimizing it is a crucial aspect if we want to optimize the performance of every application.

It turns out that in real-world systems, this pattern of unevenly distributed traffic between code paths in our application happens quite often. A lot of empirical studies conclude that the Pareto principle can simplify thinking about our systems. Let's take a look at this principle in the next section.

5.2.1 *Understanding the Pareto principle in the context of software systems*

Studies of multiple systems (organizations, work efficiency, and software systems) found interesting characteristics for most of them. We will analyze those characteristics in the context of software systems.

It turns out that a small fraction of code delivers a substantial proportion of the value produced by our software. The ratio that was detected most often was 80% to 20%. This means that 80% of the value and work that our system performs is delivered by only 20% of our code. Figure 5.3 depicts this ratio in a graph.

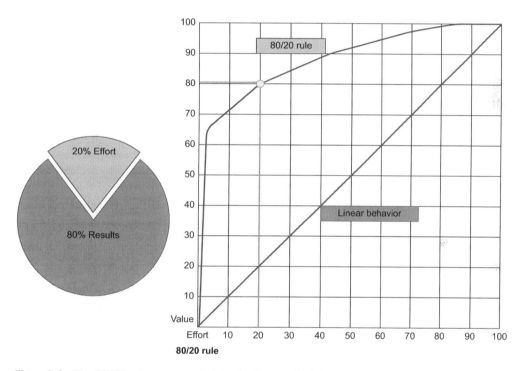

Figure 5.3 The 80/20 rule, as presented by the Pareto principle

If we have a linear behavior, every path in our code has the same importance. In such a scenario, adding a new component to our system means that the value delivered to our clients increases proportionally. In reality, every system has a core functionality that provides the most value for the core business. The rest of the functionalities, such as validation and handling edge cases and failures, are not crucial and do not produce much value (say, 20%). However, they require 80% of the time and effort to build.

Of course, the actual proportion differs, depending on the business domain and system. It may be 30% to 70% or even 10% to 90%. The actual number is not important.

What's the most important lesson from this characteristic? We can conclude that optimizing a smaller part of our codebase will impact most of our clients.

When creating a new system, we should have SLA requirements with an expected upper bound of traffic that our system can handle. Once we have those numbers, we can create performance tests that simulate real-world traffic.

5.2.2 Configuring the number of concurrent users (threads) for a given SLA

Let's assume that our service needs to provide an SLA for handling 10,000 requests per second. The average latency is 50 ms. If we want to examine such a system by a performance tool, it's essential to set the correct number of threads (concurrent users) to execute the requests to a system under stress.

If we pick one thread, we can run, at most, 20 requests per second (1000 ms ÷ 50 ms = 20). Such a performance setup won't allow us to examine the system SLA. However, once we know that one thread can handle 20 requests per second, we can calculate the total number of threads that we'll need. We can then divide the expected number of requests per second by the number of requests that one thread can handle: 10,000 ÷ 20 = 500.

This will tell us that we need 500 threads to saturate the system or the network traffic. Once we have that number, we can configure our benchmark tool accordingly. If the stress test tool is unable to create that many threads on one node, we can divide the traffic into N stress test nodes, where each test node handles a portion of the traffic. For example, we can execute requests from four stress test nodes. In that case, each of those nodes will need to execute requests for 125 concurrent users (500 threads ÷ 4 nodes = 125). Note that those calculations may be a bit different, depending on the performance tool that you use.

If your performance tool uses an event loop (nonblocking I/O), you may execute more requests from one thread. In such a case, you first need to measure the number of requests that one thread can handle and adapt the rest of the calculations to that number. Then, you should create a bit more threads than the number calculated because the calculations are based on average latency. There might still be some outliers that will slow down the concurrent threads. To see how many outliers we have, we can look at the latency of higher percentiles (e.g., p90, p95, p99). Due to that fact, we can multiply the total number of threads needed for an average SLA by some factor (e.g., 1.5) to allocate extra threads in the case of a temporary slowdown of a system under stress.

Finally, we can measure critical code paths for the number of invocations and the time that this takes. With those numbers, we can detect the hot path and calculate how significant performance gains we'll get from optimizing a small part of our code. Thanks to the characteristics of most of the systems that follow the Pareto principle, by optimizing our hot path, we can impact and deliver improvements to the majority of our clients. In the next section, we will apply this framework for optimizing a system that has a defined SLA, where we will build a new system and its domain. With our newly found understanding, we will optimize its hot path.

5.3 *A word service with a potential hot path*

Let's say that we want to build a word service that has two functionalities exposed under two API endpoints. Figure 5.4 shows the architecture of this service.

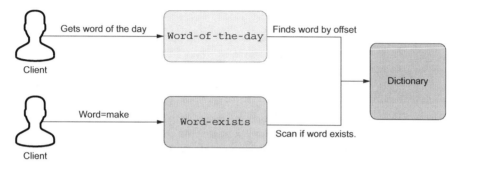

Figure 5.4 The architecture of a word service with two functionalities

The first functionality it offers is getting the word of the day. It calculates the offset specific for the current date and returns the word with the index equal to this offset.

The second functionality validates the word. The user passes the word as a query parameter, and the service scans the dictionary for its existence, returning the information about its existence in a response body. The word service, demonstrated in the following listing, is a core component of our system and is based on the Words-Service interface.

Listing 5.7 Implementing the `WordsService` interface

```
public interface WordsService {
  String getWordOfTheDay();
  boolean wordExists(String word);
}
```

The getWordOfTheDay() method does not take any arguments. It just returns the correct word. The wordExists() method takes the word that should be checked and returns whether it exists or not. The first implementation of WordsService does not do any premature optimizations, as we don't have any numbers regarding SLA or traffic yet.

5.3.1 *Getting the word of the day*

The core functionality for getting word of the day calculates the index for a given day. The following listing shows that this logic is simple, as it uses year and day of the year plus a multiplying factor to get a better distribution of the returned words.

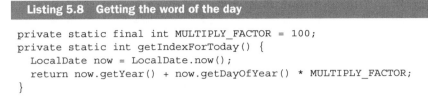

Listing 5.8   Getting the word of the day

```
private static final int MULTIPLY_FACTOR = 100;
private static int getIndexForToday() {
  LocalDate now = LocalDate.now();
  return now.getYear() + now.getDayOfYear() * MULTIPLY_FACTOR;
}
```

NOTE   We picked the multiplying factor to be equal to 100, but it can be any arbitrary number.

The implementation of the word service needs to take the path to the actual dictionary file as an argument to load the file and scan it. The function for providing an index for today can be mocked by passing a supplier function, as the following listing shows. This is useful for unit testing because we don't want to base our test on the state returned by the `LocalDate.now()` call.

Listing 5.9   Adding the `DefaultWordsService` constructor

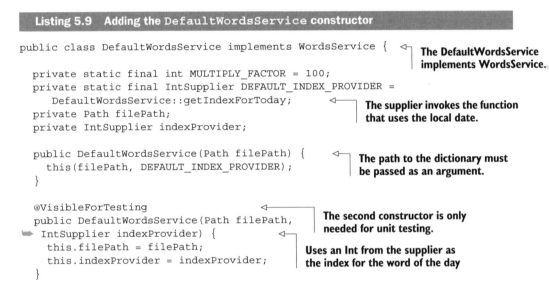

```
public class DefaultWordsService implements WordsService {          ⟵  The DefaultWordsService
                                                                        implements WordsService.
  private static final int MULTIPLY_FACTOR = 100;
  private static final IntSupplier DEFAULT_INDEX_PROVIDER =
      DefaultWordsService::getIndexForToday;            ⟵  The supplier invokes the function
  private Path filePath;                                    that uses the local date.
  private IntSupplier indexProvider;

  public DefaultWordsService(Path filePath) {          ⟵  The path to the dictionary must
    this(filePath, DEFAULT_INDEX_PROVIDER);                be passed as an argument.
  }

  @VisibleForTesting                          ⟵
  public DefaultWordsService(Path filePath,       The second constructor is only
    IntSupplier indexProvider) {          ⟵      needed for unit testing.
    this.filePath = filePath;                  Uses an Int from the supplier as
    this.indexProvider = indexProvider;        the index for the word of the day
  }
```

The logic for calculating the word of the day uses the `Scanner` class (http://mng .bz/ZzjR), which allows us to scan the file lazily. If we want the next line, we need to call the method that retrieves it. Once we are done processing, there is no need to load more lines.

The logic for this example is quite simple. It iterates over the file as long as the line number index denoting the day's expected word is not found. If there are more lines, we continue to execute our logic. Finally, if the current processing index equals the index for the expected word, we return the word and finish the processing. The following listing demonstrates the logic for getting the word of the day.

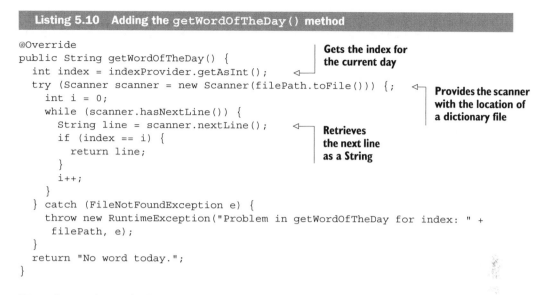

Listing 5.10 Adding the `getWordOfTheDay()` method

```
@Override
public String getWordOfTheDay() {
  int index = indexProvider.getAsInt();         ←   Gets the index for
  try (Scanner scanner = new Scanner(filePath.toFile())) {;   ←   the current day
    int i = 0;
    while (scanner.hasNextLine()) {
      String line = scanner.nextLine();          ←   Retrieves
      if (index == i) {                              the next line
        return line;                                 as a String
      }
      i++;
    }
  } catch (FileNotFoundException e) {
    throw new RuntimeException("Problem in getWordOfTheDay for index: " +
      filePath, e);
  }
  return "No word today.";
}
```

Gets the index for the current day

Provides the scanner with the location of a dictionary file

Retrieves the next line as a String

Note that at the end of processing, we are handling one edge case. If the index for the word of the day was too high, no word for today is returned. This can happen when the index for the given day is out of bounds of the underlying file.

5.3.2 Validating if the word exists

The second business functionality that our service delivers is validation of whether the specific word exists. The logic for getting this information is similar to word of the day, but to determine if the word exists, we need to iterate over the whole file. The `wordExists()` method searches for the word passed as an argument. If the line loaded from the file equals the word argument, we return true, which means that the word exists. Finally, if the word is not found after iterating the whole file, we return false. Let's look at the code in the following listing to see this functionality.

Listing 5.11 Adding the `wordExists()` method

```
@Override
public boolean wordExists(String word) {
  try (Scanner scanner = new Scanner(filePath.toFile())) {
    while (scanner.hasNextLine()) {
      String line = scanner.nextLine();
      if (word.equals(line)) {
        return true;
      }
    }
  } catch (FileNotFoundException e) {
    throw new RuntimeException("Problem in wordExists for word: " + word, e);
  }
  return false;
}
```

The logic for wordExists() is not optimized because we did not define the SLA. We don't have a performance test to find the performance of the current solution yet, but now we can expose our logic under an API endpoint.

5.3.3   *Exposing the WordsService using HTTP service*

The WordsController exposes two endpoints, as listing 5.12 shows. The first endpoint, /word-of-the-day, uses a GET HTTP request that does not take any query parameters. The request triggers loading the file with a dictionary and then loads a words.txt file from the resources folder. The first endpoint functionality is exposed as a /word-of-the-day API path. (The prefix for every path in our example is /words.) The second functionality is exposed under the /word-exists endpoint. It uses a word provided as a query parameter and checks if this word exists.

> **Listing 5.12   Adding the WordsController**

```
@Path("/words")
@Produces(MediaType.APPLICATION_JSON)
@Consumes(MediaType.APPLICATION_JSON)
public class WordsController {
  private final WordsService wordsService;

  public WordsController() {                              Constructs the default
    java.nio.file.Path defaultPath =                      implementation of
        Paths.get(                                        WordsService
          Objects.requireNonNull(
      getClass().getClassLoader().getResource("words.txt")).getPath());
    wordsService = new DefaultWordsService(defaultPath);   ◄
  }
  @GET                                          Wraps the word of the day
  @Path("/word-of-the-day")                     within the HTTP response body
  public Response getAllAccounts() {
    return Response.ok(wordsService.getWordOfTheDay()).build();   ◄┘
  }
  @GET
  @Path("/word-exists")
  public Response validateAccount(@QueryParam("word") String word) {
    boolean exists = wordsService.wordExists(word);            Wraps the information
    return Response.ok(String.valueOf(exists)).build();   ◄─┤ about the word's existence
  }                                                           into an HTTP response
}
```

Finally, we can start our HTTP application using the Dropwizard embedded HTTP server (see http://mng.bz/REpZ). Our application needs to extend the io.dropwizard .Application class that provides the functionality to start the HTTP server, as listing 5.13 demonstrates. Because of that, we need to extend the Application class with a default Configuration. This creates a WordsController that provides our business functionalities. Next, it registers this controller as an API endpoint. Finally, our app starts the HTTP web server, which is accessible under http://localhost:8080/words.

Listing 5.13 Starting an HTTP server

```java
public class HttpApplication extends Application<Configuration> {

  @Override
  public void run(Configuration configuration, Environment environment) {
    WordsController wordsController = new WordsController();
    environment.jersey().register(wordsController);
  }

  public static void main(String[] args) throws Exception {
    new HttpApplication().run("server");
  }
}
```

> **NOTE** If you run this main function, the `Words` application with both controllers will be up and running on your local machine.

In the next section, we will use information about expected traffic to detect our hot path. For this, we will use Gatling benchmarks (https://gatling.io/open-source/) to model the traffic and the Dropwizard's `MetricsRegistry` to measure the code paths. We will see if the structure of our application follows the Pareto principle described in the previous section.

5.4 Hot path detection in your code

Let's assume that our traffic estimations and SLA states that the `word-of-the-day` endpoint will serve one request per second. On the other hand, the `word-exists` endpoint will be called more frequently at 20 requests per second. Straightforward calculations will show us that this exceeds the values from the Pareto principle (the 80/20 rule):

$$1 \div (20 + 1) = {\sim}5\%$$

$$20 \div (20 + 1) = {\sim}95\%$$

This equation shows that the word-exists functionality serves 95% of the user's requests, while not serving 5% of them. Before we start optimizing this endpoint, however, we should create a performance test for both endpoints to give us latencies. By knowing both numbers of requests and latencies, we can calculate the overall benefits of optimizing one functionality or the other. For this, we will use the Gatling tool for performance testing.

5.4.1 Creating API performance tests using Gatling

We want to model two performance test scenarios. The first should target the `word-of-the-day` endpoints and execute one request per second. The duration of this benchmark will be 1 minute to get fast feedback. This will be enough for our use case to compare the initial and optimized versions. However, when you are performance testing real-life systems, this value should be substantially longer.

The simulations using Gatling are written with the Scala programming language, and every simulation needs to extend the Simulation class. The scenario for getting our word of the day is straightforward. We need to execute a GET request for a given endpoint, and every request will be executed in the context of the http://localhost:8080/words URL. If you want to deploy the Words application on a separate server, you will need to change this URL. Our API endpoint accepts and produces JSON format. The benchmarking scenario executes the GET HTTP request on the /word-of-the-day endpoint. We expect the result to be equal to the 200 HTTP response code. Any other code will be treated as an error. The following listing shows the implementation.

Listing 5.14   Getting the word-of-the-day's performance

```
class WordsSimulation extends Simulation {
  val httpProtocol = http
    .baseUrl("http://localhost:8080/words")
    .acceptHeader("application/json")

  val wordOfTheDayScenario = scenario("word-of-the-day")    ← Uses this scenario to generate traffic
    .exec(WordOfTheDay.get)

  object WordOfTheDay {
    val get = http("word-of-the-day").get("/word-of-the-day").check(status is
      200)

}
```

The second scenario is similar, but the HTTP get request needs to send the word to validate as an HTTP parameter. Because of that, we need to feed the scenario with words we want to validate. The following listing shows the words in our example words.csv file.

Listing 5.15   Words used for performance testing

```
word
1Abc
bigger
presence
234
zoo
```

Note that we have the word *bigger* from the beginning of the dictionary. We also have the word *presence* in the middle of it. Finally, we have the word *zoo*, which resides at the end of a dictionary. Besides that, we have two words that do not exist; they will trigger a full file scan.

The validate scenario uses the words.csv file and passes it as the query parameter to the API endpoint. The feeder fetches words from words.csv and executes them randomly. Finally, the scenario executes a GET request with the word query parameter. The following listing displays the code for this scenario.

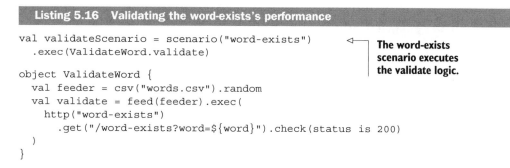

```
val validateScenario = scenario("word-exists")
  .exec(ValidateWord.validate)

object ValidateWord {
  val feeder = csv("words.csv").random
  val validate = feed(feeder).exec(
    http("word-exists")
      .get("/word-exists?word=${word}").check(status is 200)
  )
}
```

> **Listing 5.16 Validating the word-exists's performance**
>
> The word-exists scenario executes the validate logic.

Once we have defined our scenarios, we should inject them into the execution engine and specify the expected traffic. Listing 5.17 shows an example of how to do this. The first scenario executes one request per second. The second (validate) scenario, which is responsible for 95% of the client's requests, executes 20 requests per second.

Listing 5.17 Setting up the traffic profile

```
setUp(
  wordOfTheDayScenario.inject(
    constantUsersPerSec(1) during (1 minutes)
  ),
  validateScenario.inject(
    constantUsersPerSec(20) during (1 minutes)
  )).protocols(httpProtocol)
```

Now, we are able to start the actual performance benchmark. First, `HttpApplication` must be started. Once the application is running on our localhost, we can start using Gatling benchmarks by issuing the command: `mvn gatling:test`. This will start the performance test for our application. After some time, the results will be available as an HTML web page.

Let's analyze the performance results for both scenarios. As figure 5.5 shows, the performance for the word-of-the-day scenario seems good enough.

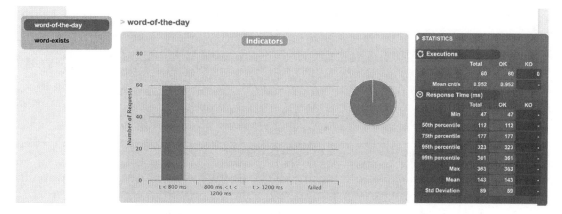

Figure 5.5 Viewing the word-of-the-day initial performance results

All requests for the `/word-of-the-day` endpoint succeed below 800 ms. The p99 latency is equal to 361 ms.

Let's now take a look at the results for our validate words scenario. As figure 5.6 shows, this endpoint executed the majority of requests.

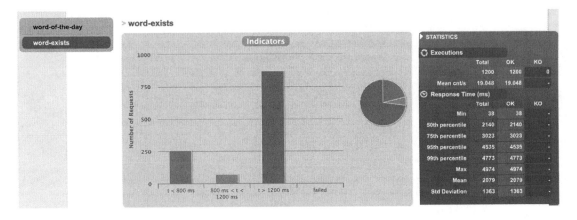

Figure 5.6   Viewing the word-exists initial performance results

The majority of requests for the `/words` endpoint have a latency higher than 1,200 ms. Here, the p99 is almost 5 s.

By looking at both results, we can see that the word-exists performance is problematic. Fixing it will impact 95% of our customers. There is no need to prematurely optimize the word of the day, as the performance is good enough, and it impacts only 5% of our customers.

Let's calculate the performance impacts of both endpoints using the formula from the second chapter. The word-of-the-day p99 is 360 ms, but we have only one request per second: $(1 \times 360) = 360$. On the other hand, the word-exists p99 is almost 5,000 ms: $(20 \times 5,000) = 100,000$. We can calculate that the word-of-the-day is responsible for less than 1% of our service requests handling work: $360 / (100,000 + 360) = 0.003 == 0.3\%$.

Once we have these calculations, it is obvious where we should focus our optimization efforts. The word-exists logic takes 99.7% of the total workload of our system.

Once we know that the word-exists logic is problematic, we need to get information from our code's lower level. We will need to understand what parts of the code path take most of the processing time. We can get this information by measuring the code that is on the hot path, which we will do in the next section.

5.4.2   *Measuring code paths using MetricRegistry*

Initially, in section 5.3, the code for validating if the word existed was simple and had no optimization. We didn't know at that point that optimization might be necessary. Now, we have input regarding the number of requests that our service will handle.

The performance tests showed that we have a problem with latencies on the /word-exists endpoint that serves 95% of our user's requests.

The Gatling tests were black box, meaning that we got the information on how the specific endpoints perform, but we don't have any internal information about the most time-consuming parts of the system. Let's look at that now.

The wordExists() method consists of two main functionalities. The first loads the file containing words to check. The second, the scan phase, finds whether the actual word exists. We can wrap both stages into separate timers to measure every invocation of those methods and give us more detailed information about their performance. In listing 5.18, we create two timers. The first timer measures the time it takes to load the file. The second timer measures the scan time (i.e., how long it takes to find whether or not the word is valid).

Listing 5.18 Measuring the word-exists logic

```
@Override
public boolean wordExists(String word) {
    Timer loadFile = metricRegistry.timer("loadFile");
    try (Scanner scanner = loadFile.time(() -> new
      Scanner(filePath.toFile())))) {          ◁──────  Measures the creation
                                                        of a new scanner to
                                                        access the file
        Timer scan = metricRegistry.timer("scan");
        return scan.time(          ◁──────
            () -> {                          Measures the main
                while (scanner.hasNextLine()) {   logic of our method
                    String line = scanner.nextLine();
                    if (word.equals(line)) {
                        return true;
                    }
                }
                return false;
            });

    } catch (Exception e) {
        throw new RuntimeException("Problem in wordExists for word: " + word, e);
    }
}
```

The timer will be executed for every operation, and it will give percentiles, average, and the number of invocations. You can measure your code at any granularity level that suits your needs. Measuring every code path may impact the processing logic's overall performance, so you should use it carefully. Once your logic is optimized, you may decide to remove some or all of the measurements.

The final step before rerunning the performance tests is to use the new Measured-DefaultWordsService in the WordsController. The following listing shows this code.

Listing 5.19 Using MeasuredDefaultWordsService

```
wordsService = new MeasuredDefaultWordsService(defaultPath);
```

When we restart the application, it will measure every request that hits the /word-exists API endpoint. After the Gatling performance test finishes, we can visit the `http://localhost:8081/metrics?pretty=true` endpoint to see all the metrics exposed by our application. You should see a section dedicated to `loadFile`, which will have data for percentiles. We are most interested with the 99th percentile, so let's take a look at it in the following listing.

Listing 5.20   Viewing the performance of `loadFile`

```
loadFile": {
"count": 1200,
"p99": 0.000730684,
"duration_units": "seconds"
}
```

The results are reported in seconds, and we can see that the 99th percentile of the load file action is equal to 7 ms. The load file operation is not causing the performance problems that we detected using the Gatling test.

You also have a `count` that shows the number of invocations of the specific code. Using that, you can compare different code paths and see where most of the time is spent. It may be handy if you don't have predefined information about expected traffic or SLA. If you have that information, you can use the metrics to validate your assumptions. In such a scenario, you can deploy the application to production with metrics and calculate which code paths were invoked most of the time. By having this information, you can detect the hot path and focus on improving its performance. The following listing shows the scan timer.

Listing 5.21   Measuring scan performance

```
"scan": {
"count": 1200,
"p99": 4.860273076,
"duration_units": "seconds"
}
```

We can see that the 99th percentile is almost 5 ss. It seems that we found the underlying cause of our performance problems. The scan operation takes a long time to execute, and it takes most of the request's processing time.

Once we detect the underlying cause, we can start optimizing the hot path. We will do that in the next section and validate if our improvement results in better performance.

NOTE   If we cannot add a measurement code to the application we are performance testing, we may consider using a profiling technique to get more insights into the time spent in specific parts of the code. In the JVM world, we can use, for example, the Java Flight Recorder (http://mng.bz/2jYg).

5.5 *Improvements for hot path performance*

We want to focus on optimizing the word-exists code path. When we experiment with `wordExists()` method and try a different approach, we should get feedback regarding its performance. We can use our existing Gatling performance tests, but they are high-level and more time consuming to run. For that, we need to start the actual web server, start the Gatling tests, and collect the results. Because we know the exact code path that should be optimized, we can write more low-level microbenchmarks that focus only on the specific code path. Using this approach, we will get faster feedback that will allow us to find a more performant solution.

It is worth noting that writing a microbenchmark for every change may not be necessary if we have those higher-level performance tests. The microbenchmarks require more work, but on the other hand, they provide faster feedback. If you want to test *N* solutions for solving the same low-level problem, you may find microbenchmarks more useful.

In this section, I will show how to implement microbenchmarks for learning purposes. You can, however, develop a different solution to solve our problem. You can also write another microbenchmark to compare it with the solution presented in this section.

5.5.1 *Creating JMH microbenchmark for the existing solution*

Before we optimize the code path, let's write a JMH benchmark for the existing code. We will call this benchmark the baseline. We will use this as a point of reference when improving our code. The benchmark will cover the logic from the hot path that takes the majority of request processing time.

Let's take a look at the setup logic for our benchmark (listing 5.22). It executes 10 iterations for our example run (the more iterations there are, the more accurate results will be). We want to measure the average time that the benchmarking method takes. One benchmark measures the invocation of `wordExists` `NUMBER_OF_CHECKS` * `WORDS_TO_CHECK.size()` times. Every iteration executes 100 checks to simulate a more realistic use case. The word service will be reused 100 times, then the next iteration will start.

Listing 5.22 Creating the word-exists benchmark

```
@Fork(1)
@Warmup(iterations = 1)
@Measurement(iterations = 10)
@BenchmarkMode(Mode.AverageTime)
@OutputTimeUnit(TimeUnit.MILLISECONDS)
public class WordExistsPerformanceBenchmark {
  private static final int NUMBER_OF_CHECKS = 100;
  private static final List<String> WORDS_TO_CHECK =
      Arrays.asList("made", "ask", "find", "zones", "1ask", "123");
```

Note that we pick words to check from the beginning, middle, and end of the dictionary file. We also have some words that do not exist.

The baseline creates the `DefaultWordsService` (the current logic without any optimization). Checking word existence will be done 100 times, and every word from the list of words to check will be examined once per iteration.

The `WordsService` is created once per JMH measurement iteration. It is reused `100 * WORDS_TO_CHECK.size()` times. The `wordExists()` method is invoked for every word. The following listing shows this approach.

Listing 5.23   Getting the baseline benchmark

```
@Benchmark
public void baseline(Blackhole blackhole) {
  WordsService defaultWordsService = new DefaultWordsService(getWordsPath());
  for (int i = 0; i < NUMBER_OF_CHECKS; i++) {
    for (String word : WORDS_TO_CHECK) {
      blackhole.consume(defaultWordsService.wordExists(word));
    }
  }
}
```

**Gets the path to
the dictionary file**

```
private Path getWordsPath() {         ◁─┘
    try {
      return Paths.get(
          Objects.requireNonNull(getClass().getClassLoader()
⇒ .getResource("words.txt")).toURI());
      } catch (URISyntaxException e) {
        throw new IllegalStateException("Invalid words.txt path", e);
      }
```

```
Benchmark                                         Mode  Cnt    Score    Error  Units
CH05.WordExistsPerformanceBenchmark.baseline      avgt       55440.923         ms/op
```

Once we measure the baseline, we can try to create another optimized variant of the `wordExists()` method and add a benchmark. By doing so, we will be able to validate whether or not our optimization influences the performance. The baseline results show us the number of milliseconds per operation. We will use those numbers to see how the improved version compares to this one.

5.5.2   *Optimizing word exists using a cache*

Let's assume the words file that we are using for checking a word's existence is static and does not change. This assumption is important in the context of our logic. It means that once we check whether the word exists, the value will not change in the future.

We could construct a static map where the key is a word and the value denotes if it exists. Constructing such a map would need to be done at the initialization time of our application. Figure 5.7 shows a theoretical map for our use case.

The dictionary file can contain millions of records, and constructing the map up front means our application's startup time increases substantially; in this case, we are

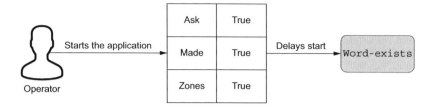

Figure 5.7 Eager initialization and computation

using eager optimization. This also means that we need to use substantial resources for precomputing data that may not be required in the future.

We will use some portion of RAM, regardless of the actual usage of our service. It may turn out that only a small percentage of words are checked, whereas others are not needed. Those unneeded words will occupy the memory space with no apparent reason, so the program will use more RAM than necessary.

The other solution we may choose is to construct a cache lazily. This means that we start with an empty cache and build it up as the request arrives. Our assumption is that the words file is static and does not change. If our file contains a small amount of data, we could cache it indefinitely without eviction. However, there can be a case in production systems that need to load a lot more data. For example, we can imagine an application that checks the word's existence for more languages (e.g., English, Spanish, Chinese, etc.) and needs to load all dictionaries. For such a case, we'll want to reduce unnecessary memory usage, so we may choose to utilize time eviction for data that is stale for some time.

The eviction time can be calculated based on the traffic information. For example, if we record the logs for requests, we can get statistics about the requested words. Based on the time of requests, we can get time intervals between requests. The next step is to construct the statistical distribution of those time intervals. Once we have that information, we can get, for example, the 90th percentile and set the eviction time for this value. This guarantees that the cache should serve 90% of our request. If the 99th percentile eviction time is not too high, we can also pick this value as eviction.

Our solution focuses on a situation in which the application is not yet deployed, and we don't have much information about traffic distribution besides the SLA and expected number of requests per second. In such a situation, we can pick some value based on prediction and record cache statistics. Once the application is in production, we can get the cache hit, cache miss, and other similar statistics to see if our cache performs well. If the miss ratio is high, we should consider increasing the eviction time.

Let's implement the solution based on the cache and measure its performance (listing 5.24). We need to construct a cache that calls the existing word-exists method if the given word is not present. For that, we will set the default eviction time to 5 minutes (min). This can be adapted once we have more data about production traffic distribution. We are constructing the cache, so a word is a key and the information about its existence is value. We will use Guava's `LoadingCache` (http://mng.bz/1jOX) for this.

> **NOTE** We are using a Google Guava library because it's one of the most commonly used caching libraries in Java. We could also choose other caching libraries (one such as Caffeinate), but still, the overall conclusion from this chapter will remain the same.

When the specific word is not accessed by the eviction time, it's removed from the cache. The following listing shows how to construct our cache.

Listing 5.24   Constructing a word-exists cache

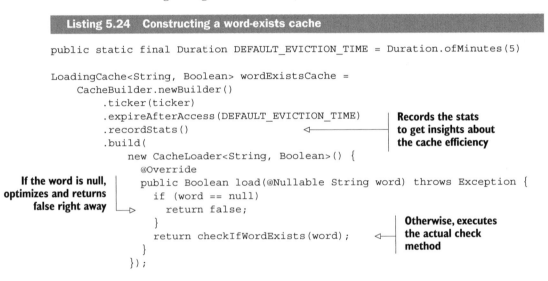

```
public static final Duration DEFAULT_EVICTION_TIME = Duration.ofMinutes(5)

LoadingCache<String, Boolean> wordExistsCache =
    CacheBuilder.newBuilder()
        .ticker(ticker)
        .expireAfterAccess(DEFAULT_EVICTION_TIME)
        .recordStats()                              ⟵———  Records the stats
        .build(                                            to get insights about
            new CacheLoader<String, Boolean>() {           the cache efficiency
                @Override
                public Boolean load(@Nullable String word) throws Exception {
                    if (word == null)
                        return false;
                }                                   Otherwise, executes
                return checkIfWordExists(word);  ⟵—  the actual check
            }                                          method
        });
```

If the word is null, optimizes and returns false right away

Before we test the performance of the improved solution, let's test its correctness. We will use `FakeTicker()` to simulate time movement without a need to use a sleep thread, as listing 5.25 demonstrates. The first check of word existence will trigger the actual check operation. After this check, the cache should have one entry.

Listing 5.25   Unit testing the word-exists cache

```
@Test
public void shouldEvictContentAfterAccess() {
    // given
    FakeTicker ticker = new FakeTicker();
    Path path = getWordsPath();
    CachedWordsService wordsService = new CachedWordsService(path, ticker);

    // when
    assertThat(wordsService.wordExists("make")).isTrue();

    // then
    assertThat(wordsService.wordExistsCache.size()).isEqualTo(1);
    assertThat(wordsService.wordExistsCache.stats()
        .missCount()).isEqualTo(1);
```

The first request triggers the actual load.

```
    assertThat(wordsService.wordExistsCache.stats()
    .evictionCount()).isEqualTo(0);
```
◁ **The entry was not evicted; it sits in the cache.**

```
    // when
    ticker.advance(
    CachedWordsService.DEFAULT_EVICTION_TIME);
```
◁ **Advances the time to simulate the eviction**

```
    assertThat(wordsService
    .wordExists("make")).isTrue();
```
◁ **Calls wordExists() to trigger the eviction**

```
    // then
    assertThat(wordsService.wordExistsCache.stats()
    .evictionCount()).isEqualTo(1);
}
```
◁ **After this operation, the entry is evicted: eviction count = 1.**

Finally, listing 5.26 shows how to write a microbenchmark, using JMH to validate whether our new design improves the wordExists() performance. The only difference with this benchmark is that we use a different implementation backed by our cache.

Listing 5.26 Writing the word-exists cache microbenchmark

```java
@Benchmark
public void cache(Blackhole blackhole) {
  WordsService defaultWordsService = new CachedWordsService(getWordsPath());
  for (int i = 0; i < NUMBER_OF_CHECKS; i++) {
    for (String word : WORDS_TO_CHECK) {
      blackhole.consume(defaultWordsService.wordExists(word));
    }
  }
}
```

Let's start the benchmarks again and compare the results between the first baseline version and the improved version based on cache. The following listing shows how to do this.

Listing 5.27 Benchmark results for baseline and cache version

Benchmark	Mode	Cnt	Score	Error	Units
CH05.WordExistsPerformanceBenchmark.baseline	avgt		55440.923		ms/op
CH05.WordExistsPerformanceBenchmark.cache	avgt		557.029		ms/op

We can conclude that the average performance of our solution increased by 100 times. That's an outstanding result, and we are ready to test the whole application in an end-to-end fashion. The only change we need to make so our Words application uses the new implementation based on cache is to initialize it in the WordsService. The following listing shows how this is done.

Listing 5.28 Using the `CacheWordsService` in the `WordsController`

```java
wordsService = new CachedWordsService(defaultPath);
```

We are ready to run the Gatling performance tests. To run the tests, follow the same procedure we followed in section 5.4. Let's open the results (see figure 5.8) from our performance test.

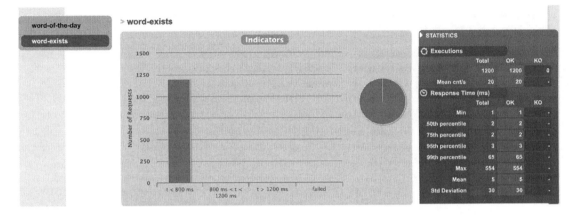

Figure 5.8   The performance results for improved word-exists

We can see that the performance of our solution increased substantially. The 99th percentile latency is equal to 65 ms. It is almost 80 times faster than the initial solution!

Once we perform our optimization, we should recalculate the impact that specific parts of the code will make. Our p99 latency is reduced to 65 ms now. We can use the second section's formula to calculate the performance impact of the word-of-the-day and word-exists logic:

- The word-exists traffic is 20 requests per second with p99 equal to 65:

$$(20 \times 65) = 1{,}300$$

- The word-of-the-day has one request per second with p99 equal to ~360 milliseconds:

$$(1 \times 360) = 360$$

Finally, we can calculate the percentage of traffic generated by both endpoints. We can do this by calculating the traffic for the word of the day:

$$360 \div (360 + 1{,}300) \sim= 0.21 == 21\%$$

Figure 5.9 shows that our calculations reveal that the word-of-the-day traffic generates 21% of the workload on our system, and the word-exists traffic is responsible for the other 79% of the workload. We reduced the word-exists workload from 99.7%, although it is still responsible for most of the workload. However, as we calculated

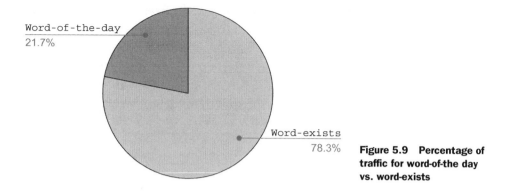

Figure 5.9 Percentage of traffic for word-of-the day vs. word-exists

before, that impacts 95% of our user's requests. After our optimization, the word of the day (which affects 5% of our user's request) takes 21% of the processing resources. If we seek further optimizations, we can calculate the possible time savings with section 5.2's formulas. Let's assume we can further improve the performance of both endpoints by 10%. For the word of the day, those formulas will give us 36 ms of time savings because we have only one request per second: $0.1 \times 360 \times 1 = 36$.

Improving the word-exists performance by a further 10% gives us 130 ms of time saved because we have 20 requests per second: $0.1 \times 65 \times 20 = 130$.

However, it may turn out that optimizing the word-exists performance by a further 10% is not practical or is hard to achieve. We can calculate that only by optimizing the word-of-the-day by 40%, which will give us more time savings than optimizing the word-exists by 10%: $0.4 \times 360 \times 1 = 144$.

If optimizing this endpoint by 40% is more feasible than optimizing the word-exists by 10%, we may decide that we should focus on the non-hot path optimization. However, as you noticed, optimizing the hot path gives more benefits with lower efforts. In real life, optimizing the specific code path by 10% is more realistic than 40%.

> **NOTE** When optimizing the performance of one endpoint, we often need to allocate more resources for handling the traffic. This may improve the latencies and/or throughput of a given endpoint, but it can also mean that those resources need to be taken from other endpoints. As a result, the performance of other endpoints may be impacted. For that reason, it is crucial to monitor the performance of all endpoints that are exposed to customers and to assure that the endpoints' performance don't drop. Also, the more resources we use, the higher utilization of the node on which the app is running will be. At some point, we would need to scale our application to more nodes (horizontal scaling) or have a more powerful node (vertical scaling). So increasing performance often (but not always) means that we need to allocate more resources, and the need for more resources impacts scalability.

5.5.3   *Modifying performance tests to have more input words*

There is one more important observation to make. Our final solution uses the cache to back our logic. It means that doing performance tests for only six input words does not validate our performance that well; we hit the cache with only a few existing values.

When performing performance tests of a solution using the cache underneath, we should test it using more input words. That way, it better validates whether the cache does not evict that data too soon. It also validates whether the cache does not put too much memory pressure on our system.

Let's take a random 100 words from the dictionary and put it into the words.csv file used by the Gatling simulation. The number of words should be picked according to expected traffic. Our test executes 20 requests per second for 60 s, which is a total of 1,200 requests. If we use more random words (e.g., 1,000), almost every request hits the cache with an unloaded value, and the performance improvement that we observed will not be seen.

We can choose a different approach, pick more random words, and, also, extend the performance test time. By doing so, we will fill the cache with data. Then, the next subsequent requests will hit the entries that exist in the cache already.

To get the random *N* words from words.txt, we can use a Linux sort command. The following listing shows the code for getting our random words.

> **Listing 5.29   Getting a random number of words**

```
sort -R words.txt | head -n 100 > to_check.txt
```

Finally, we need to copy words from the to_check.txt file to the words.csv used by the Gatling simulation and start the simulation once again. Figure 5.10 shows that the results are substantially different.

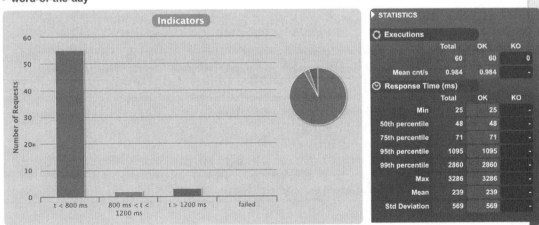

Figure 5.10   Words exists with more input words

The performance is still substantially better than the initial solution, but there are higher latencies. This is because almost 10% (100 ÷ 1,200) of requests hit a cold cache.

You can experiment with different traffic patterns and performance test times. The important lesson learned from this section is that when changing the details of a solution (say, to a cache), you may also consider adapting your performance tests to capture more realistic traffic distribution.

With analysis and gathering a lot of information before releasing your software, you are no longer doing premature optimization. Benchmarks will give you a lot of insights into your code. When you have benchmarks based on close to real-world traffic, you can produce realistic performance data. Once you have that data, you can optimize your code's proper parts and be certain that those optimizations will give you good results.

In this chapter, we were able to reduce the latency and increase our application's performance without it being deployed to production. Premature optimization when we have enough input data regarding SLA and expected traffic is possible and can yield great results. We need to remember to follow the strategy of finding the bottleneck before optimizing random code paths. If your application delivers functionality and follows the Pareto principle for traffic distribution in your code, you should find the hot path quite easily. Once you detect where the hot path is, you can narrow the scope using microbenchmarks. They will allow you to optimize your code more efficiently because of the faster feedback loop you will get. Remember that once you optimize your hot path, the bottleneck may shift into different parts of code.

In the next chapter, we'll learn how our user interfaces simplicity may increase maintenance costs. We will also learn about the benefits of abstracting away the underlying systems and their tradeoffs.

Summary

- Even if your code is not on the hot path, it may take a lot of time to execute. Such a situation often occurs if a non-hot path code is orders of magnitude slower than a hot path; thus, your code may require optimization.
- You can use the calculations from the second section of this chapter to find code paths to focus your optimizing efforts.
- Writing benchmarks using the Gatling performance tool allows us to detect the hot path based on the expected traffic.
- Parts of our code can be measured using metrics.
- Narrowing the scope of performance tests can be achieved using microbenchmarks and JMH.
- Often, we can optimize our hot path using cache.
- The Gatling output can be leveraged for validation and comparison of performance results.

Simplicity vs. cost of maintenance for your API

This chapter covers

- UX and maintenance tradeoffs when integrating with third-party libraries
- The evolution of settings exposed to clients
- Pros and cons of abstracting away things you don't own

When building our systems for end users, our API's simplicity and friendly user experience (UX) are essential. It is important to note that UX can apply to all interfaces. We can design a graphic user interface (GUI) that is clean and user friendly. We can also create our REST APIs in a UX-friendly way. Going one level deeper, the command-line tools can also be UX friendly or not UX friendly. Basically, every software that needs to interact with the user in any way requires a discussion and planning about its UX.

The configuration mechanism of our system is an entry point that we need to expose to clients. It is also a vital part of the UX friendliness of our component. Often, our systems depend on and use multiple components to provide the result of processing. Each of the dependent components exposes its configuration settings that need to be set in some way.

We can abstract away every downstream component (any element used by the system for which we are creating a UX) and not expose any of those component settings directly with the tool that interacts with the user. This will improve the UX of our system, but it will require substantial maintenance.

On the other side of the spectrum, we can directly expose all dependent settings. This option does not require much maintenance from us, but such an approach has a couple of tradeoffs. First, we are tightly coupling our clients with the downstream component used by our service or tool. This makes it hard to change the component. Additionally, handling changes to the downstream component in a UX-friendly (and backward compatible) way will be difficult if not impossible.

Both solutions have their tradeoffs and can be used as a base for a discussion regarding our API's simplicity versus its cost of the maintenance. I will elaborate on those tradeoffs in this chapter, as this chapter focuses on those aspects. Let's start our chapter by introducing and analyzing a cloud component that already has its configuration mechanism. Next, we'll use this component with two tools that take different approaches to costs of maintenance and UX simplicity.

6.1 A base library used by other tools

We need to integrate with and use various software systems when delivering business value from our system. For example, we may need to integrate with databases, queues, or cloud providers. We may also need to integrate with parts of an operating system, such as the filesystem, network interfaces, or disk. The majority of systems that we depend on provide their own software development kits (SDKs) or client libraries. These allow us to easily integrate with their systems without developing the whole integration from scratch. Figure 6.1 illustrates this aspect of integration.

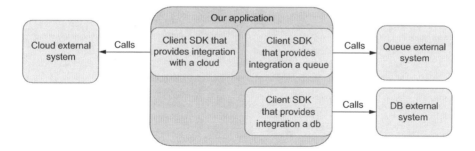

Figure 6.1 SDKs with a client that provides integration with external systems

As mentioned, in the real world, our application may need to integrate with databases, queues (such as Apache Kafka or Pulsar), and cloud services (e.g., EC2 and GCP). All these services provide client libraries. Using them, we can deliver a more robust software faster compared to a situation in which we would need to write every integration from scratch.

Almost every client needs to be configured before we can interact with the third-party system. It can be, for example, authentication credentials, timeouts, buffer size, or a variety of other settings. The configuration can be provided, for instance, via system properties, environment variables, or config files, and all users of the client component need to deliver their configuration to the client library.

For the examples in this chapter, and for clarity and simplicity, we will build a simple cloud client component that we will need to configure before using. Then, we will use this component from two tools that deliver value to our end users. Let's start by creating this component and understanding its usage.

6.1.1   Creating a cloud service client

Our cloud service client will provide a way for our component's callers to execute a request that loads data to a cloud service. Before the request is executed, it is authenticated. We have two ways of authenticating the requests. The first uses a token to validate it. The second uses a username and password. The authentication strategy is picked based on the configuration provided by the user. Figure 6.2 depicts these alternatives.

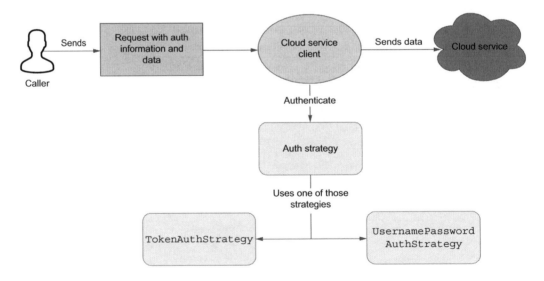

Figure 6.2   Cloud client component and two possible authentication strategies

Let's look at these components. The first entry point of the caller for our cloud component is the Request class. It carries the list of data elements and the information needed to perform authentication: username, password, or token. The following listing shows this implementation (see http://mng.bz/PWgw if you're unfamiliar with the @Nullable annotation in the listing).

Listing 6.1 Creating the cloud request

```
public class Request {
  @Nullable private final String token;          ◁┐  Tells the users
  @Nullable private final String username;         │  that token can be
  @Nullable private final String password;         │  a null value
  private final List<String> data;
  // constructors, hashCode, equals, getters, and setters omitted
}
```

The CloudServiceClient component handles the request (we can think of this component as a cloud client library for a cloud provider like AWS, Azure, GCP, etc.). The interface of our component is straightforward, as the following listing shows. It exposes only one public method that should be used by the clients of this component.

Listing 6.2 Creating the CloudServiceClient interface

```
public interface CloudServiceClient {
  void loadData(Request request);
}
```

The loadData() method takes the request and loads it into the cloud service. The implementation of this method also performs authentication. Now, let's take a look at some authentication strategies for this component that our clients can use.

6.1.2 Exploring authentication strategies

Our cloud component supports two strategies for authentication. The first is a simple username/password authentication strategy, as listing 6.3 shows. It requires both username and password to be nonnull in the incoming request. It's constructed based on this configuration and checks whether the Request's username/password matches the configuration.

Listing 6.3 Adding the username/password authentication strategy

```
public interface AuthStrategy {
  boolean authenticate(Request request);        ◁┐  AuthStrategy is
}                                                  │  implemented by both
                                                   │  authentication strategies.

public class UsernamePasswordAuthStrategy implements AuthStrategy {
  private final String username;
  private final String password;

  public UsernamePasswordAuthStrategy              Creates strategy
➥ (String username, String password) {    ◁┐    for username and
    this.username = username;                      │    password extracted
                                                    │    from the config file
```

```
    this.password = password;
  }

  @Override
  public boolean authenticate(Request request) {
    if (request.getUsername() == null
    || request.getPassword() == null) {
      return false;
    }

    return request.getUsername().equals(username) &&
      request.getPassword().equals(password);
  }
}
```

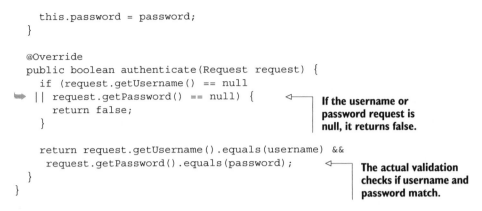

If the username or password request is null, it returns false.

The actual validation checks if username and password match.

Both strategies implement the `AuthStrategy` interface. If the request contains a username or password with a null value, the `authenticate()` method returns false. Note that storing a password as a `String` can be problematic because it can leak from our application. Thus, it can be stolen by an attacker. We will look at a better approach to handle this later.

The second authentication strategy is similar but uses a token to validate the request. If the token matches the one provided by the constructor, the `authenticate()` returns true.

Listing 6.4   `TokenAuthStrategy`

```
public class TokenAuthStrategy implements AuthStrategy {
  public TokenAuthStrategy(String token) {
    this.token = token;
  }

  private final String token;

  @Override
  public boolean authenticate(Request request) {
    if (request.getToken() == null) {
      return false;
    }
    return request.getToken().equals(token);
  }
}
```

Implements AuthStrategy

Checks if the token matches

The logic is the same as the previous authentication mechanism in listing 6.4, but it uses a token from the request.

6.1.3   *Understanding the configuration mechanism*

The client provides our cloud service configuration via a YAML file.

> **NOTE**   Many real-world frameworks and libraries use a very similar YAML-based configuration mechanism (i.e., Spring Boot), so you may relate the examples

from this chapter to some of them. However, to keep this chapter technology agnostic, we will use a custom code instead of an existing framework.

Based on the configuration in this file, we'll create a `CloudServiceConfiguration` class used by the cloud service implementation. At this stage of our client library, the configuration contains only the `AuthStrategy` that we'll use in our authentication mechanism. The following listing displays the code to create our cloud service configuration.

Listing 6.5   Implementing a `CloudServiceConfiguration`

```java
public class CloudServiceConfiguration {
  private final AuthStrategy authStrategy;

  public CloudServiceConfiguration(AuthStrategy authStrategy) {
    this.authStrategy = authStrategy;
  }

  public AuthStrategy getAuthStrategy() {
    return authStrategy;
  }
}
```

Loading the configuration from YAML should be abstracted away from the implementation of `CloudServiceClient`. This abstraction may be useful if we decide to support another configuration file, such as JSON, Hocon, and so forth. To do this, we will create a `DefaultCloudServiceClient` that injects the `CloudServiceConfiguration` via a constructor. The `loadData()` method first validates whether the request should be authenticated. It uses the `CloudServiceConfiguration#authStrategy` provided in the configuration object, as the following listing demonstrates.

Listing 6.6   Creating our default `CloudServiceClient`

```java
public class DefaultCloudServiceClient implements CloudServiceClient {
  private CloudServiceConfiguration cloudServiceConfiguration;
  public DefaultCloudServiceClient(CloudServiceConfiguration
    cloudServiceConfiguration) {
    this.cloudServiceConfiguration = cloudServiceConfiguration;
  }

  @Override
  public void loadData(Request request) {
    if (cloudServiceConfiguration.getAuthStrategy().authenticate(request)) {
      insertData(request.getData());        ◁──┐  After validation,
    }                                            inserts the data into
  }                                              a cloud service
}
```

The last step we need to implement is reading the YAML config file and constructing our cloud client. The YAML configuration file should contain a section dedicated to the authentication configuration. The following listing shows how the config file should look for the username/password strategy.

Listing 6.7   Cloud service config for username and password

```
auth:
  strategy: username-password
  username: user
  password: pass
```

We will use the `strategy` value, `username-password`, to construct a proper `Auth-Strategy` implementation. For the token strategy, the YAML configuration looks a bit different. For testing purposes, the actual token value can be any UUID. In a real production system, tokens won't be hardcoded. They are generated dynamically and refreshed based on some time interval. The following listing shows our token strategy.

Listing 6.8   Cloud service token

```
auth:
  strategy: token
  token: c8933754-30a0-11eb-adc1-0242ac120002
```

Let's finally construct the builder class responsible for loading the configuration and constructing the `DefaultCloudServiceClient`. We will use `ObjectMapper` (http://mng.bz/J14o) to read the YAML config file and parse it. Because we are using YAML, the configuration file has a structure that can be presented as a map of maps. The first outer map contains all the settings needed for the `auth` section. The second outer map contains other settings. Figure 6.3 provides a first look at our map of maps.

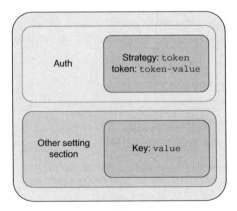

Figure 6.3   Configuration structure in our YAML file

In the figure, the inner map is keyed by the property name (e.g., `strategy`), and the value can be any object (e.g., `token`). Another outer map has a dedicated section in our configuration. Our `auth` section is a dedicated outer map. If we would like to add a config section in the future, it will have a new dedicated section (e.g., other setting section).

In listing 6.9, the CloudServiceClientBuilder constructor creates a map of map type to read the YAML file. We also have constants with strategy identifiers (e.g., USER-NAME_PASSWORD_STRATEGY) to construct the proper authentication strategy. For this example, we'll use the YAMLFactory class from the Jackson library (http://mng.bz/wnGO). The ObjectMapper reads the configuration from the YAML file.

Listing 6.9 `CloudServiceClientBuilder` **constructor**

```
public class CloudServiceClientBuilder {
  private static final String USERNAME_PASSWORD_STRATEGY = "username-password";
  private static final String TOKEN_STRATEGY = "token";
  private final ObjectMapper mapper;              ◁─── The mapper will be used
  private final MapType yamlConfigType;                to read the config file.

  public CloudServiceClientBuilder() {
    mapper = new ObjectMapper(new YAMLFactory());  ◁─── Because the file is a YAML,
    MapType mapType =                                   uses the YAMLFactory
        mapper.getTypeFactory().constructMapType(HashMap.class, String.class,
    Object.class);    ◁───────┐ The inner map type
    yamlConfigType =            has a string key and
        mapper                  object value.
            .getTypeFactory()
            .constructMapType(                         The outer map
                HashMap.class, mapper.getTypeFactory()  contains the inner
            ⇒  .constructType(String.class), mapType);  ◁─── map type.
  }
  // ...
```

Now, let's look at the final part of our cloud service client. As listing 6.10 shows, two methods are responsible for creating the object. We allow the callers of this code to pass the path to the YAML config file. Still, we also expose the way to provide Cloud-ServiceConfiguration programmatically without using the YAML configuration mechanism. The fact that those two config mechanisms are exposed allows the callers to configure the client in two ways. Both have their own tradeoffs, and we will analyze them later.

Listing 6.10 **Creating** `DefaultCloudServiceClient` **based on the config**

```
public DefaultCloudServiceClient
  ⇒ create(CloudServiceConfiguration cloudServiceConfiguration) {  ◁─── Passes the
    return new DefaultCloudServiceClient(cloudServiceConfiguration);     configuration
}                                                                        to the
                                                                         constructor
public DefaultCloudServiceClient create(Path configFilePath) {
    try {
```
Reads the YAML file using configFilePath
```
      Map<String, Map<String, Object>> config =
          mapper
          ⇒  .readValue(configFilePath.toFile(), yamlConfigType);
```

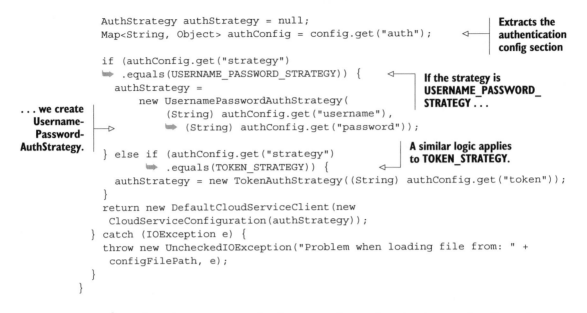

```
      AuthStrategy authStrategy = null;                              Extracts the
      Map<String, Object> authConfig = config.get("auth");    ◁──┤  authentication
                                                                    config section
      if (authConfig.get("strategy")
      ⟿ .equals(USERNAME_PASSWORD_STRATEGY)) {         ◁─┐   If the strategy is
        authStrategy =                                        USERNAME_PASSWORD_
            new UsernamePasswordAuthStrategy(                 STRATEGY . . .
                (String) authConfig.get("username"),
                ⟿ (String) authConfig.get("password"));
                                                          A similar logic applies
      } else if (authConfig.get("strategy")             to TOKEN_STRATEGY.
              ⟿ .equals(TOKEN_STRATEGY)) {        ◁─────┘
        authStrategy = new TokenAuthStrategy((String) authConfig.get("token"));
      }
      return new DefaultCloudServiceClient(new
      CloudServiceConfiguration(authStrategy));
    } catch (IOException e) {
    throw new UncheckedIOException("Problem when loading file from: " +
      configFilePath, e);
    }
  }
}
```

...we create Username-Password-AuthStrategy.

The YAML-based create() method extracts the authentication section from the configuration. Next, it checks if the strategy matches the CloudServiceConfiguration. If it does, then create() logic tries to construct the UsernamePasswordAuthStrategy class. Otherwise, if the strategy is TOKEN_STRATEGY, then it creates the TokenAuthStrategy.

Once we have our cloud client library ready, we can implement two tools that will use it. They both take a different approach to integration. The first exposes the settings of the cloud client directly; we will see how that impacts the maintenance cost. The second abstracts those settings away, exposing their configurations and mapping them to a cloud service. Let's start with the tool that exposes settings directly.

6.2   *Directly exposing settings of a dependent library*

The first tool we'll implement uses the cloud client as a batch service. Its primary responsibility is to batch the incoming requests until the buffer size exceeds the batch size parameter. Once the buffer is full, it calls the cloud client that performs authentication and sends the data to the cloud service, as figure 6.4 illustrates.

The client needs to configure the batch service before its use. Because the batch service uses a cloud client, we also need to pass the client's configuration to the cloud client. The configuration needs to be provided by the end user to construct the underlying CloudServiceClient used by the BatchService.

The batch service configuration is quite simple, as it contains only one setting—the batch size—which is specific to the batch service. Listing 6.11 shows this configuration.

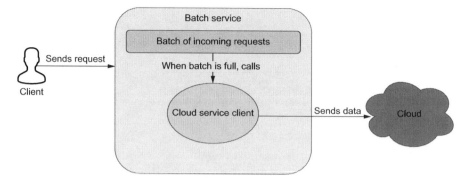

Figure 6.4   Batch service architecture for our cloud client

Listing 6.11   Implementing `BatchServiceConfiguration`

```
public class BatchServiceConfiguration {
  public final int batchSize;

  public BatchServiceConfiguration(int batchSize) {
    this.batchSize = batchSize;
  }

  public int getBatchSize() {
    return batchSize;
  }
}
```

The batch service uses its configuration to limit the number of aggregated events. When the data in a batch has enough elements (equals to or exceeds the `batchSize` parameter), it uses the cloud client to send the actual data. `BatchService` operates on the `Request` class we saw in the previous section. Let's look at the logic for `Batch-Service` in the following listing.

Listing 6.12   Viewing the `BatchService` logic

```
public class BatchService {
  private final BatchServiceConfiguration batchServiceConfiguration;
  private final CloudServiceClient cloudServiceClient;
  private final List<String> batch = new ArrayList<>();      ⟵─┐ Buffers the
                                                                │ data in the list
  public BatchService(
      BatchServiceConfiguration batchServiceConfiguration, CloudServiceClient
      cloudServiceClient) {                                   ⟵─────────────┐
    this.batchServiceConfiguration = batchServiceConfiguration;            │
    this.cloudServiceClient = cloudServiceClient;                          │
  }                                                        Uses an injected │
                                                           CloudServiceClient
  public void loadDataWithBatch(Request request) {
    batch.addAll(request.getData());
```

```
    if (batch.size() >=
  ⮑ batchServiceConfiguration.getBatchSize()) {
      cloudServiceClient.loadData(withBatchData(request));
    }
  }

  private Request withBatchData(Request request) {
    return new Request(request.getToken(), request.getUsername(),
      request.getPassword(), batch);
  }
}
```

When the batch size equals or exceeds the batch size . . .

. . . it uses the cloud service and loads the data.

It's important to note that the batch service uses the cloud client directly when executing these requests. Injecting `CloudServiceClient` in the constructor is our integration point between batch tool and cloud client.

Encapsulating the CloudServiceClient

In this example, we operate on the `CloudServiceClient` interface that is generic in the context of this particular cloud library. However, if we want to have higher flexibility, we may consider creating a separate class that encapsulates the concrete `CloudServiceClient`. By doing so, it will be easier to switch the underlying libraries without impacting the caller's code (because this code will use the cloud client via the abstraction layer).

6.2.1   Configuring the batch tool

The most important decision regarding the UX and the maintenance of the batch service is how we provide settings to the underlying cloud client. We've decided that the end user of the batch tool needs to provide a configuration as a YAML file. The `auth` section of this file is passed directly to the underlying cloud client configuration loader, as figure 6.5 shows.

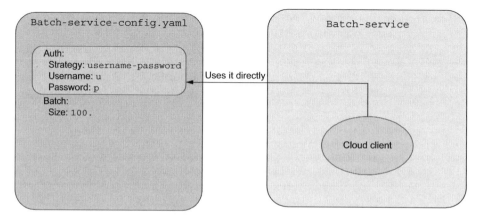

Figure 6.5   Passing the cloud client settings directly from the YAML config file

It is important to note that the auth section of the batch service configuration must have the same structure as the cloud-configured YAML. This also means we are exposing the internal details of the cloud client configuration to the batch service clients. Because of this approach, constructing the cloud configuration does not require any maintenance from our side when we implement this mechanism. The client of batch service provides the configuration, and the batch service passes it as is.

The batch service uses the batch section of the configuration. The batch service builder takes the YAML file as an argument and loads the file. Next, it extracts the batch section and uses it to construct the BatchServiceConfiguration. Finally, it passes the whole YAML file to the cloud client service builder. As you may remember from the previous section, the CloudServiceClientBuilder extracts the auth section from the file and constructs the client. The following listing shows this procedure.

Listing 6.13 Passing a YAML file to the cloud client

```
public class BatchServiceBuilder {
  public BatchService create(Path configFilePath) {
    try {

      Map<String, Map<String, Object>> config =
        mapper.readValue(configFilePath.toFile(), yamlConfigType);
      Map<String, Object> batchConfig = config.get("batch");     <-- Extracts the
      BatchServiceConfiguration batchServiceConfiguration =           batch section of
        new BatchServiceConfiguration                                 the configuration
          ((Integer) batchConfig.get("size"));     <--
                                                          Uses BatchConfig
      CloudServiceClient cloudServiceClient =                 to construct
        new CloudServiceClientBuilder()                       BatchServiceConfiguration
          .create(configFilePath);
      return new BatchService(batchServiceConfiguration, cloudServiceClient);
    } catch (IOException e) {
      throw new UncheckedIOException("Problem when loading file from: " +
      configFilePath, e);
    }
  }
}
```

Passes the YAML file path (raw configuration) to the builder

As long as the configuration structure passed to the cloud client builder is correct, the batch service doesn't need to do any specific processing. If there is a problem, an exception is thrown.

Let's analyze how creating the YAML configuration format and embedding the cloud client library structure in it impacts our software. The first issue is that we are introducing tight coupling between our service and the underlying cloud client library by passing the path to the config file directly to the cloud configuration loader. It expects the auth section in this file. In case the section is missing, an exception is thrown. If we want to migrate to a different cloud library in the future, it will be difficult. The auth section that is exposed by our tool becomes a contract (API). If this tool is used publicly, our software systems' clients will need to provide the YAML file with the authentication configuration in it. We cannot remove or change the auth section if it is no longer required or has a different format.

The second issue with this approach manifests if the cloud client changes or deprecates and removes some configuration setting. We will discuss this problem in greater detail later in this chapter.

There are also advantages to this approach. If you are integrating with a downstream system that exposes tens or hundreds of settings, passing configurations directly may be a good choice for you. It's also important to note that the caller must know the downstream system configuration format and use it in its code. Our use case satisfies that requirement because the cloud client allows callers to pass the settings directly. Also, the caller, in this case, knows the structure of the downstream settings: a YAML file with an auth section. You don't need to worry about mapping settings to the proper structure, so there is no maintenance cost here.

In the next section, we will create a streaming tool with a different approach to configuration and the UX of its API. Settings from the underlying cloud client will not be directly exposed.

6.3   *A tool that is abstracting settings of a dependent library*

Let's now focus on the second service that takes a different approach for configuring the dependent cloud client. The streaming service that we build in this section now exposes only the settings it owns. It uses those settings to construct a cloud client. However, it abstracts the creation and configuration of the cloud client from the user. The end users of the streaming tool will know nothing about the cloud client used underneath. The following listing provides the configuration specific to streaming service, which contains only one setting: maxTimeMs.

> **Listing 6.14   Building the `StreamingServiceConfiguration`**

```
public class StreamingServiceConfiguration {
  private final int maxTimeMs;

  public StreamingServiceConfiguration(int maxTimeMs) {
    this.maxTimeMs = maxTimeMs;
  }

  public int getMaxTimeMs() {
    return maxTimeMs;
  }
}
```

This value for maxTimeMs is used to track the time of the request in milliseconds. If the time of the request exceeds that value, a warning is logged. In this case, the streaming service does not batch requests because low latency of processing is critical. The loadData() method uses a Request object (the previous batch service used the same object). The total time of processing is calculated by subtracting the time after cloud service load from the start time. Let's look at this logic in the following listing, where the code validates if the total time is greater than the maximum time from the streaming tool configuration object.

Listing 6.15 Streaming tool logic

```
public void loadData(Request request) {
  long start = System.currentTimeMillis();
  cloudServiceClient.loadData(request);
  long totalTime = System.currentTimeMillis() - start;
  if (totalTime > streamingServiceConfiguration.getMaxTimeMs()) {
    logger.warn(
        "Time for a streaming request exceeded! It is equal to: {}, but
      should be less than: {}",
        totalTime,
        streamingServiceConfiguration.getMaxTimeMs());
  }
}
```

Let's now look at the mechanism for loading the streaming configuration. We'll also see how it abstracts away the cloud service configuration.

6.3.1 Configuring the streaming tool

The streaming service also uses a YAML file for its configuration. The most significant difference between its configuration format and the batch tool configuration from section 6.2 is that the streaming service exposes all the settings in the `streaming` section. It is also important to note that the streaming tool supports only username/password authentication. The following listing shows the pertinent section in the YAML file.

Listing 6.16 The streaming service configuration

```
streaming:
  username: u
  password: p
  maxTimeMs: 100
```

The dedicated `streaming` section defines all the settings for the streaming tool, which owns the configuration. Consequently, our clients know nothing about the underlying cloud service client. In other words, the configuration of the cloud service is abstracted away from the user. The `streaming` section defines a clear contract owned by the streaming tool. It looks simpler from the UX perspective, but it requires some maintenance to map the settings from the streaming format to the cloud client.

Let's now take a look at the streaming service creation logic in listing 6.17. All the settings related to the streaming tool are extracted from the `streaming` section: it pulls the `maxTimeMs` setting and constructs the `StreamingServiceConfiguration`. The most important part of the code happens when we are constructing a cloud client. The internal cloud library and its `UsernamePasswordAuthStrategy` are abstracted away from the user. The client of StreamingService does not know anything about its configuration mechanism. Additionally, the username and password settings construct the UsernamePasswordAuthStrategy. Next, this strategy creates a cloud service client using its programmatic configuration API.

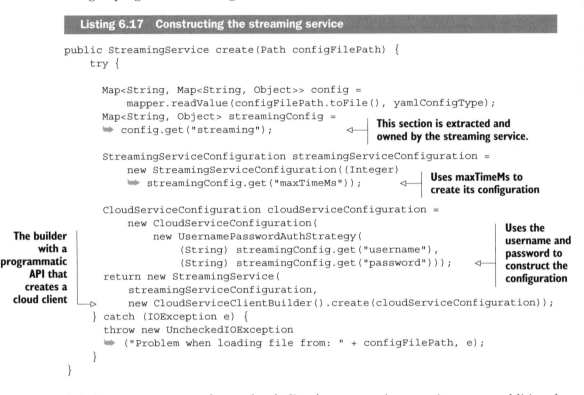

Listing 6.17 Constructing the streaming service

```
public StreamingService create(Path configFilePath) {
    try {

        Map<String, Map<String, Object>> config =
            mapper.readValue(configFilePath.toFile(), yamlConfigType);
        Map<String, Object> streamingConfig =
    ➥   config.get("streaming");                        ◁—┤ This section is extracted and
                                                            owned by the streaming service.

        StreamingServiceConfiguration streamingServiceConfiguration =
            new StreamingServiceConfiguration((Integer)
    ➥       streamingConfig.get("maxTimeMs"));          ◁—┤ Uses maxTimeMs to
                                                            create its configuration

        CloudServiceConfiguration cloudServiceConfiguration =
            new CloudServiceConfiguration(                        Uses the
                new UsernamePasswordAuthStrategy(                 username and
                    (String) streamingConfig.get("username"),     password to
                    (String) streamingConfig.get("password")));  ◁— construct the
        return new StreamingService(                              configuration
            streamingServiceConfiguration,
            new CloudServiceClientBuilder().create(cloudServiceConfiguration));
    } catch (IOException e) {
        throw new UncheckedIOException
    ➥   ("Problem when loading file from: " + configFilePath, e);
    }
}
```

The builder with a programmatic API that creates a cloud client

It is important to note that a cloud client's construction requires some additional work from our side. We need to map the settings exposed by the streaming service to a cloud configuration. Once the system is released, we need to maintain this mapping. Therefore, it involves an additional maintenance cost. On the other hand, the UX of our streaming tool configuration is better off because callers need to focus only on a dedicated configuration section. The cloud client used by this tool is abstracted away.

Let's assume that you are integrating with a downstream system that exposes tens or hundreds of settings. What is important is that we choose a configuration option that abstracts those settings away. Due to this, you need to map every downstream library setting to the setting in your tool. This may mean a substantial amount of code that only needs to rewrite those settings. This effect will be an order of magnitude higher if you have *N* services or tools that use a downstream system that exposes many of those settings. In such a scenario, the maintenance cost is nonnegligible.

In the next section, we will analyze both configurations when the new setting is added to the cloud client from the perspective of UX and cost of maintenance for both tools. You'll see that we pay the maintenance cost upfront. Fortunately, this cost will give us some benefit in the long run. Let's analyze these scenarios now.

6.4 Adding new setting for the cloud client library

Let's assume that the client service is modified and exposes a new setting responsible for timeouts. This new setting will have a dedicated `timeouts` section in the YAML configuration, as the following listing shows.

Listing 6.18 Adding a new timeout setting

```
auth:
  strategy: username-password
  username: user
  password: pass

timeouts:
  connection: 1000
```

We will also add this new setting to the `CloudServiceConfiguration`. The following listing shows this implementation.

Listing 6.19 A new timeout setting for `CloudServiceConfiguration`

```
public class CloudServiceConfiguration {
  private final AuthStrategy authStrategy;
  private final Integer connectionTimeout;
   // constructors, hashCode, equals, getters, and setters omitted
}
```

The builder of the cloud client extracts the `timeouts` section from the YAML configuration and uses it to construct the client. This next listing shows this part of our process for adding a new cloud client library setting.

Listing 6.20 Extracting timeout in the `CloudServiceClientBuilder`

```
Map<String, Object> timeouts = config.get("timeouts");
// ...
return new DefaultCloudServiceClient(
        new CloudServiceConfiguration(authStrategy, (Integer)
    timeouts.get("connection")));
```

From the perspective of both tools (streaming and batch), this is an important change because it is not backward compatible. Conversely, if the cloud client provides a default when the setting is *not* set, the change will be backward compatible. However, if the default and provided value are not explicitly set, the new version of the cloud client cannot be constructed. Both tools need to provide the new timeout value to be able to construct the cloud client. Let's first analyze how this change impacts the batch service that passes the settings directly to the cloud client builder.

6.4.1   *Adding a new setting to the batch tool*

The batch tool passes the settings directly from the caller to the cloud client builder. This means that the client needs to provide the new `timeouts` section to run the batch tool. The following listing shows how the new YAML batch configuration could look.

Listing 6.21   Adding a new `timeouts` section

```
auth:
  strategy: username-password
  username: u
  password: p
                          Adds the new
                          configuration
                          section
timeouts:      ◁┘
  connection: 1000
batch:
  size: 100
```

If we want our batch tool to construct the cloud client with new configuration settings, all clients need to add this section. If they do not add it, the cloud client and the construction of the batch service tool that uses it will fail.

There is one crucial remark regarding adding this new setting. As you may recall from section 6.2, the `BatchServiceBuilder` passes the YAML file directly to the cloud client. Because of that, there is no need to change any code for handling the new timeout parameter for our batch tool. The raw configuration is passed to the underlying cloud client library, as figure 6.6 illustrates.

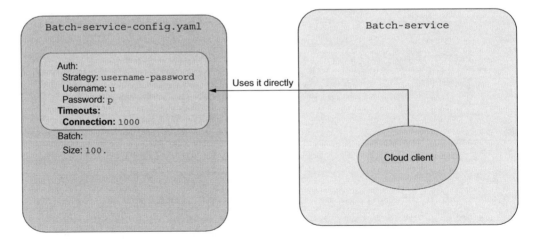

Figure 6.6   Passing cloud client settings directly with a new `timeouts` section

We can conclude that the UX of the solution did not change substantially. The clients still need to scrutinize about the underlying cloud client construction and add the batch tool's configuration in sync with it. The batch tool's maintenance cost is close to zero because we don't need to do any code changes to support the new setting. The raw file is passed, and the `CloudServiceClientBuilder` extracts both the `auth` and `timeouts` sections from the YAML file.

If you anticipate changes to happen quite often and that they will be additive, you can see that the presented approach in this section works well. Moreover, let's assume you have multiple services that integrate with the same downstream cloud client. This means when you add a new setting, you don't need to change anything in those services. It will be the client's responsibility to take care of new settings and provide those with your tools. The maintenance burden is propagated to your tools' callers, so we can argue that it is a nonideal UX in this context. Let's see how the streaming tool can handle the addition of a new cloud client setting.

6.4.2   Adding a new setting to the streaming tool

The streaming tool takes a different approach for UX and the configuration of the underlying library: it owns all its settings and exposes them under the dedicated `streaming` section. To be able to pass the new connection timeout setting, we need to add this section to the streaming tool's YAML configuration, as the following listing shows.

Listing 6.22   New timeout setting for the streaming configuration

```
streaming:
  username: u
  password: p
  maxTimeMs: 100
  connectionTimeout: 1000        Exposes the
                                 new setting as
                                 connectionTimeout
```

Because the streaming tool constructs the cloud client programmatically, the code responsible for it needs to change. For this, the `connectionTimeout` is extracted from the YAML file and passed to the `CloudServiceConfiguration`, as the following listing shows.

Listing 6.23   New timeout setting in the `StreamingServiceBuilder`

```
new CloudServiceConfiguration(
        new UsernamePasswordAuthStrategy(
            (String) streamingConfig.get("username"),
            (String) streamingConfig.get("password")),
        (Integer) streamingConfig.get("connectionTimeout"));
```

There is a maintenance cost associated with every new setting added to the cloud client. In real-world systems, adding a configuration may be more common, and such changes may be required often. The more settings added, the higher the maintenance cost associated with it. Let's analyze this configuration mechanism in this scenario when you anticipate changes that are happening quite often and are additive.

Every new setting of the underlying cloud client needs to be mapped programmatically. If you have multiple services using this library, the code in all of them needs to change. Remember, with every code change, there is an associated maintenance cost. You also need to cover this change with end-to-end tests but also execute some high-level integration or end-to-end tests. Once the new code change's quality is good enough, you need to deploy your changed application to production.

This procedure needs to be repeated for every service or tool that uses the downstream client library! The more services that are using the cloud client and that add a new setting, the more work you have. The maintenance cost of supporting the encapsulation is quite high. At this point, you may not see the benefit of this additional complexity.

In the next section, I will demonstrate a different example that allows you to justify the maintenance cost associated with this approach. First, let's sum up our findings of UX and the cost of maintenance of both solutions when a new setting is added.

6.4.3 *Comparing both solutions for UX friendliness and maintainability*

We saw that adding new settings to the underlying library caused changes in both tool's configuration mechanisms and that

- The batch service propagates changes to the end user.
- The streaming service tries to abstract away that it uses a cloud service.

With the batch service, the client's responsibility is to provide a new dedicated section with a setting that is expected by the cloud client. The most significant advantage of this solution is that it does not require any maintenance cost on our side. We don't need to change the code because the configuration file is passed directly to the cloud client builder. However, you need to remember that the cost of maintenance is propagated to the end user. All users of our services and tools will need to adopt their configuration according to the new downstream cloud client setting.

Because the streaming service abstracts away its usage of the cloud service, it needs to map the settings provided by the end users to the cloud client configuration. Adding a new setting to the cloud client also requires adding the new setting to the streaming service, which owns the new setting. The end user has no idea about the underlying construction of the cloud service. This comes with a cost. Every new setting of the downstream system needs to be exposed and mapped to the expected format for the streaming service. Because of that, every setting requires a maintenance cost: we need to change the code in the streaming service.

Table 6.1 sums up these scenarios for us. It is important to note that this table presents UX and maintenance costs from one service's perspective.

Table 6.1   Adding a new setting to client and how it impacts both tools

Tool name	Maintenance cost	UX
Batch tool	No cost	User needs to add a new setting
Streaming tool	Growing cost	User needs to add a new setting

If you are using the cloud client from *N* services, you need to multiply these costs by the *N* factor. The maintenance cost grows for every piece of software using the cloud client and encapsulating the settings.

In the next section, we will see a scenario in which the streaming tool's abstraction is worth the additional costs. The cloud client will deprecate and remove the settings.

6.5 Deprecating/removing a setting in the cloud client library

In this section, we will analyze a different scenario in which the cloud client setting is deprecated and needs to be removed. As you may remember, the cloud client uses the authentication strategy when connecting to a cloud service. Let's assume that, after some time, we see that the current `UsernamePasswordAuthStrategy` is not safe because it keeps the plain text password in the YAML configuration and in memory. This is dangerous from a security perspective. It allows for the possibility of a malicious attacker to steal the password(s) used in our code.

We decide to develop a new `UsernamePasswordHashedAuthStrategy` that uses the hashed version of the password when performing authentication. This will use the SHA-256 algorithm from the hashing class (http://mng.bz/q2aA). When it performs the request's authentication, it compares hashed versions of the password. The following listing shows the code for the new hashed authentication strategy.

> **Listing 6.24 The new `UsernamePasswordHashedAuthStrategy`**

```
public class UsernamePasswordHashedAuthStrategy implements AuthStrategy {
  private final String username;
  private final String passwordHash;
  public UsernamePasswordHashedAuthStrategy(String username, String      ⟵── Stores the password
    passwordHash) {                                                            in the hashed form
    this.username = username;
    this.passwordHash = passwordHash;
  }
  @Override
  public boolean authenticate(Request request) {
  if (request.getUsername() == null || request.getPassword() == null) {
    return false;
  }                                                                          Performs
  return request.getUsername().equals(username)                             authentication on
    && toHash(request.getPassword()).equals(passwordHash);  ⟵──            the hashed
  }                                                                          version of the
  public static String toHash(String password) {                           password
    return Hashing.sha256().hashString(password,
      StandardCharsets.UTF_8).toString();    ⟵──      Uses the SHA-256
  }                                                    algorithm to hash
}                                                      the password
```

The unique identifier of the new authentication strategy is `username-password-hashed`, as the following listing shows. Clients of the cloud configuration should use this new value instead of the old `username-password` that constructs the version with a plain text password.

Listing 6.25 Prohibiting the old authentication strategy

```
public class CloudServiceClientBuilder {
  private static final String USERNAME_PASSWORD_STRATEGY = "username-password";
  private static final String TOKEN_STRATEGY = "token";
  private static final String
  USERNAME_PASSWORD_HASHED_STRATEGY = "username-password-hashed";

  // ...
  public DefaultCloudServiceClient create(Path configFilePath) {
    // ...
    if (authConfig.get("strategy").equals(USERNAME_PASSWORD_HASHED_STRATEGY))
    {
      authStrategy =
          new UsernamePasswordHashedAuthStrategy(
              (String) authConfig.get("username"), (String)
    authConfig.get("password"));

    } else if (authConfig.get("strategy").equals(TOKEN_STRATEGY)) {
      authStrategy = new TokenAuthStrategy((String) authConfig.get("token"));
    } else if (authConfig.get("strategy").equals(USERNAME_PASSWORD_STRATEGY))
    {
      throw new UnsupportedOperationException(
          "The " + USERNAME_PASSWORD_STRATEGY + " strategy is no longer
    supported.");
    }
    return new DefaultCloudServiceClient(
        new CloudServiceConfiguration(authStrategy, (Integer)
    timeouts.get("connection")));
  }
}
```

Implements the new username-password-hashed strategy

Constructs the UsernamePassword-HashedAuthStrategy

If the username-password is specified, throws an exception

When the cloud service constructs the authentication strategy and the old username-password strategy is specified, it throws an exception denoting that it is no longer supported. This means all callers need to migrate to the new strategy if they want to use the cloud client. Let's see how this change of behavior impacts the batch tool.

6.5.1   Removing a setting from the batch tool

As we know by now, the batch tool passes the client's provided YAML file directly to the cloud client. Up to this point, all of our clients used the `username-password` or `token` strategies. Our batch service configuration will throw an exception to the client if the client specifies a deprecated `username-password` strategy. Now, all clients need to migrate to the new type if they want to use the batch tool. This substantially impacts the UX of our solution.

All clients configuring the batch tool will see the authentication problem of the underlying cloud client. We can observe this behavior in a unit test that uses the batch-service-config-timeout.yaml file with a strategy equal to `username-password`. The following listing shows the test.

Listing 6.26 Throwing an exception for unsupported auth strategy

```
@Test
public void shouldThrowIfUsingNotSupportedAuthStrategy() {
  // given
  Path path =
      Paths.get(
          Objects.requireNonNull(
                  getClass().getClassLoader().getResource("batch-service-
    config-timeout.yaml"))
              .getPath());

  // when
  assertThatThrownBy(() -> new BatchServiceBuilder().create(path))
      .isInstanceOf(UnsupportedOperationException.class)
      .hasMessageContaining("The username-password strategy is no longer
    supported.");

}
```

All clients can now observe the `UnsupportedOperationException`. This means all batch tool clients will need to migrate their YAML configuration to the new username-password-hashed! The UX of such a solution is poor. We expose the internals of a third-party library so that every change for this configuration will need to be adapted in the client's code.

Let's imagine a scenario in which multiple client tools use our batch service. We publish a new batch service that prevents end users from using the username-password strategy. Once the end users change their software to use the new batch service, they cannot deploy it without changes to their YAML configuration. Every client that leaves the authentication setting unchanged will get an exception at run time when using a new version of the batch service. For backward compatibility and to reduce UX problems, we need to provide a *hacky* workaround.

First, we will need to load the configuration file under the `configFilePath`. Then, we will scan and locate the map entry for `auth.strategy`. Once we have that entry, we will modify the configuration strategy by replacing `username-password` with `username-password-hashed`. Next, we need to extract the plain text password and hash it manually, replacing the password map entry. The following listing shows the workaround.

Listing 6.27 `BatchServiceBuilder` hacky workaround

```
// DON'T DO THIS
public BatchService create(Path configFilePath) {
    try {
      Map<String, Map<String, Object>> config =
          mapper.readValue(configFilePath.toFile(), yamlConfigType);
      Map<String, Object> batchConfig = config.get("batch");
```

The first place where the cloud service config abstraction leaks

Overrides another setting

Saves the modified configuration

```
BatchServiceConfiguration batchServiceConfiguration =
    new BatchServiceConfiguration((Integer) batchConfig.get("size"));

Map<String, Object> authConfig = config.get("auth");
if (authConfig.get("strategy").equals(USERNAME_PASSWORD_STRATEGY)) {
  authConfig.put("strategy",
    USERNAME_PASSWORD_HASHED_STRATEGY);
}
String password = (String) authConfig.get("password");
String hashedPassword = toHash(password);
authConfig.put("password", hashedPassword);
Path tempFile = Files.createTempFile(null, null);
Files.write(tempFile, mapper.writeValueAsBytes(config));

CloudServiceClient cloudServiceClient = new
CloudServiceClientBuilder().create(tempFile);
return new BatchService(batchServiceConfiguration, cloudServiceClient);
} catch (IOException e) {
throw new UncheckedIOException
    ("Problem when loading file from: " + configFilePath, e);
}
}
```

Overriding a setting may lead to hard-to-debug problems!

Another config leak

Creates a temporary file

Passes the altered config file (not the one passed by the caller)

Finally, we need to save a modified configuration to a new temporary file path and pass that file location to the CloudServiceClientBuilder. Such a solution is awful: it tweaks the original file, changes the configuration value without the user's knowledge, and may introduce bugs that are hard to debug. Besides that, we need to create a temporary file every time the client is created.

It is also important to note that the actual configuration setting names are leaking from the CloudServiceClientBuilder to the new BatchServiceBuilder hacky work-around, which introduces tight coupling between our components. The service builder that is only responsible for loading configuration sections from the YAML file suddenly needs to know the exact cloud client configuration structure and alter it.

The streaming service takes a different approach to the configuration. Let's see how the settings removal is handled by the streaming tool in the next section.

6.5.2 *Removing a setting from the streaming tool*

With the streaming tool, the internal authentication strategy used by the cloud library is abstracted away from the user. The clients of the streaming tool do not know anything about its configuration mechanism. We can transparently change the authentication strategy without user knowledge and without breaking compatibility. We can migrate without affecting our users, and the YAML configuration of the streaming service will not change at all.

In listing 6.28, we use the same username and password as passed before, passing the password as plain text. The StreamingServiceBuilder constructs the Username-PasswordHashedAuthStrategy, then passes the hashed version of the password to it.

Listing 6.28 Abstracting away the construction of the hashed strategy

```
CloudServiceConfiguration cloudServiceConfiguration =      Constructs the hashed
    new CloudServiceConfiguration(                          strategy instead of
        new UsernamePasswordHashedAuthStrategy(      ◁──    plain text
            (String) streamingConfig.get("username"),
            toHash((String) streamingConfig.get("password"))),
        (Integer) streamingConfig.get("connectionTimeout"));
```

Hashes the password before passing it to the hashed strategy ▷

This change of behavior is hidden from streaming tool users. The UX provided by this solution is better because it does not require a change in the configuration of the streaming service. The end users of the streaming service can easily use the new version of it without changing anything on their side.

The streaming service can change the cloud client library it is using without exposing this to the end users. If the team that is developing a streaming service decides to change the cloud client to a different library, it will be easy to do. The mapping of settings is already in place, so in that situation, only the mapping layer needs to be adapted to a new configuration format.

Mapping the old authentication strategy to the new `UsernamePasswordHashed-AuthStrategy` without the end user's knowledge is a good short-term solution. However, in the long term, we should migrate to the new `UsernamePasswordHashedAuthStrategy` because it provides better security for our users.

The migration step needs to be implemented at some point, but because the streaming tool encapsulates the underlying cloud configuration, the migration process is simplified. For example, we can introduce a new configuration property that carries the hashed password. If the end user provides the hashed password, we don't need to do a manual mapping from a plain text password to the hashed one. Instead of that, we can use the new `UsernamePasswordHashedAuthStrategy`.

While the migration is in progress, we should support both ways of providing passwords. It will allow the streaming tool clients to migrate at their peace without worrying about breaking the underlying cloud client's changes.

Let's now compare the UX and the maintenance cost of both solutions. The next section presents this comparison.

6.5.3 *Comparing both solutions for UX friendliness and maintainability*

We can conclude that the UX and maintenance cost when the downstream system removes or deprecates the setting differs. Let's look at the differences.

First, the streaming tool owns the whole configuration, and it can handle the migration of any downstream component more easily. If we want to remove the cloud client entirely and replace it with a different one, it will be easier with the streaming service.

The batch service passing the settings directly from its clients to the cloud client is a terrible situation in this scenario. Removing the dependent setting means all clients simultaneously need to migrate to the new value. We cannot hide it from them.

Additionally, the UX of our tool is brittle. If we wanted to handle it gracefully, we would need to create a very hacky workaround that is error prone.

The additional configuration abstraction introduced in the streaming service gives us the possibility to evolve our tools in a UX friendly way. Let's conclude this discussion with table 6.2, which provides a comparison of the two tools:

Table 6.2   Removing or deprecating a setting from the client and how it impacts both tools

Tool name	UX	Maintenance cost
Batch tool	Low; users greatly impacted	High/nonfeasible
Streaming tool	High; users not impacted	Very low

The decision regarding the maintenance cost is associated with the risk of breaking and nonbackward compatible changes of the downstream component. If the downstream cloud client library evolves in a nonbackward compatible way, the services that are using the client would need to abstract their configuration mechanism. Suppose you are developing a service, and you impact the lifecycle of the underlying library. In that case, you may be able to reduce the number of nonbackward compatible changes. You may even forbid such changes and evolve the downstream library without breaking changes. You may not need to pay additional maintenance costs associated with abstracting away its configuration mechanism in such a case.

Contrary to that, let's assume you are using a downstream library that evolves in an unpredictable way, and you don't influence this library's life cycle. This means nonbackward compatible changes are possible, and you should guard against those. In such a scenario, the additional maintenance cost may be worth the effort. You will create a much better UX tool; one that is easy to use by your clients.

In this chapter, we learned about different ways of designing our tools. We started by creating a cloud client library that was later used by two tools: streaming and batch. The former took the indirect approach to configuration. It abstracted away from the underlying library, paying some maintenance cost when the new setting was added. The latter used the cloud client config API directly without the abstraction layer. We were able to evolve the batch tool without any maintenance cost when the new setting of the underlying library was added.

The situation changed drastically when the downstream setting was deprecated and removed. The abstraction introduced in the streaming service allowed us to keep the excellent UX for our users with a small maintenance cost. However, the batch service was not able to address this change, while keeping the good UX. The little maintenance cost improved our UX in this situation. In the next chapter, we will learn about tradeoffs and mistakes when working with the date and time APIs.

Summary

- Technical decisions can impact UX.
- Adding the new setting to a downstream library can be handled with zero maintenance cost.
- Additional abstraction can allow us to evolve our tools without breaking compatibility. However, it adds a maintenance cost.
- With additional abstraction, each change if the underlying component results in additional work in our code.
- If our product is public-facing, and the UX of our users is important, it is wise not to propagate internal details of libraries we use in our code.

Working effectively
with date and time data

Dates and times occur very naturally in almost all applications, even if it's only in the timestamp of the application's log messages. Unfortunately, they often cause significant problems, either with overcomplicated code or bugs that might only be seen for two hours per year or only by users in one remote corner of the planet. It's all too easy to dismiss such bugs, but with the right set of tools you can avoid them.

The tools here come in two distinct flavors:

- *Concepts*—Help you think and write clearly about the information you're working with
- *Libraries*—Help you turn those concepts into code

Sometimes, the libraries you use will be part of the underlying platform (e.g., using the java.time libraries introduced in Java 8), or they may be third party libraries you need to install explicitly (e.g., the Noda Time library for .NET, to pick an example *entirely* at random [Well, maybe not quite so random. Jon is the primary author of Noda Time.]).

Depending on which platform and libraries you're using, there may not be a 1:1 mapping between the concepts we introduce in this chapter and the types you'll use to represent them. That's okay. It makes life *slightly* harder, but the concepts can still be applied to your project; you'll just need to be more careful about documenting your intent, whether that's through comments, naming, documentation, or a mixture of all three.

As well as talking about the concepts and how your application code can put them into practice, this chapter will give you some guidance on how to test your date- or time-related code effectively too. By the end of the chapter, you'll be in a position to design and implement date and time logic carefully as well as confidently.

Figure 7.1   A high-level requirement for an online shopping site

To try to make everything concrete, we'll use an online shopping scenario. Figure 7.1 shows a product requirement as it might initially be presented to the development team.

As we go through the chapter, we'll see how this requirement should be transformed into one that is much more detailed with clearly testable acceptance criteria. We'll then implement the requirement and write the corresponding tests. We'll start off looking at the concepts, hardly mentioning code at all.

7.1   *Concepts in date and time information*

As with so many topics, you can always dig deeper into date and time, finding more and more esoteric examples of odd behavior. If you keep digging, you may well never get back to the surface. Some platforms and libraries err in the opposite direction, trying to pretend the world is so simple that they miss really important situations. We've tailored the concepts provided in this section to achieve a happy medium: they're detailed enough to cover most business applications but without going so deep that the chapter becomes an entire book.

> **NOTE**   This does mean that if you work in particularly niche areas you'll need to look elsewhere for inspiration, but even then, the concepts here may well be enough for *most* of your application. If you're building GPS devices,

representing data in ancient history, or writing a Network Time Protocol (NTP) client, the concepts here may well be enough for *most* of your application. Keep the niche and fiddly aspects as confined as you can.

It also means that if you understand leap seconds intimately, you may object to some of the hand-waving here. I do empathize, but this is one of those areas where *absolute* accuracy would get in the way of clarity.

Where concepts are represented directly in the java.time and Noda Time libraries, the corresponding types will be listed, so you can experiment with them further, should you wish to. Let's start with some basic concepts: an instant in time, an epoch, and a duration.

7.1.1   *Machine time: Instants, epochs, and durations*

How humans handle date and time information is very culture specific. It's probably the area of software engineering that is most heavily influenced by religion, for example. While it's important to understand that cultural aspect, it's also useful to try to remove it from the equation where possible. That's why the first concepts we'll look at are the *purer* ones, which don't include any of the mess that humans tend to bring to software.

INSTANTS

Type in java.time: `java.time.Instant`. Type in Noda Time: `NodaTime.Instant`.

An instant is a universal timestamp. Two people anywhere in the world (or beyond!) can agree on what *now* means as an instant. They might look at their watches and see different local times due to time zones or disagree about which month they're in due to cultural differences, but they can still agree on an instant. You can think of an instant as a sort of *machine time* that doesn't care about puny human concepts, such as *days* or *years*.

You can think of instants as being plotted on a timeline that doesn't have any subdivisions. See figure 7.2 for an example of this concept.

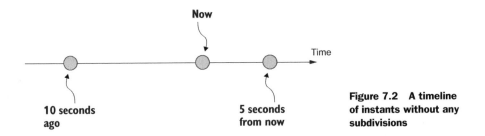

10 seconds ago   **5 seconds from now**   **Figure 7.2   A timeline of instants without any subdivisions**

Even instants would become really complex, or even impossible, if we needed to take relativity and other tricky bits of physics into account. That's where trying to achieve *absolute correctness with the physical universe* would be a mistake in almost all applications.

Instants are the natural conceptual type to use when considering *when something happened*—for example, when a database transaction is committed, or when a log entry is created. You may be wondering how instants should be represented internally. While that's an implementation detail, it's still a useful one to consider, and it requires a new concept.

EPOCHS

The timeline shown in figure 7.2 doesn't have any numbers on the axis; the points on the line are just relative to each other. The typical solution is to agree on an artificial *zero point*, known as an *epoch*, and measure everything from there. Let's add an epoch to the existing example, where the epoch was 15 seconds before *now*. At this point we can represent each instant as a number of seconds since the epoch. See figure 7.3 for a graphical representation of this, expanding figure 7.2 by adding an epoch and the relative durations from it.

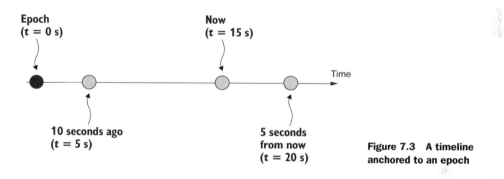

Figure 7.3 A timeline anchored to an epoch

It's important that everyone using the same representation uses the same epoch, so in some ways we've just moved the problem a little. We still need to agree on *one* instant in time, but then, we can represent every instant.

The epoch that most systems use is the *Unix epoch*, which is the instant that occurred at midnight at the start of January 1, 1970, in UTC. We haven't discussed UTC, months, or years yet; one of the problems inherent in talking about date and time is that the concepts can feel cyclical.

That's not the only commonly-used epoch, however. The .NET epoch is midnight at the start of January 1st, AD 1, although that's AD 1 in a proleptic Gregorian calendar, which refers to even *more* complexity we haven't talked about yet.

Excel and Microsoft's COM representation use epochs around the start of 1900, although those epochs become harder to discuss due to bugs in software that treats 1900 as a leap year.

In a well-encapsulated date and time library, you shouldn't need to know which epoch is used internally, although many libraries provide functions to convert between the library representation and, for example, a number of seconds since the Unix epoch. For this reason, you usually won't even see a type encapsulating the concept of an epoch in date and time libraries.

In the examples so far we've only considered amounts of time since the epoch in terms of seconds, but of course, in real life we often want far more fine-grained measures of time. Rather than always assuming a particular unit, it's useful to encapsulate the concept of *an amount of elapsed time* as a *duration*.

DURATIONS

Type in java.time: `java.time.Duration`. Type in Noda Time: `NodaTime.Duration`.

A *duration* is a measure of *elapsed* time, rather than a point *in* time. If you measure the difference between two points on the timeline, that's a duration. If you start a stopwatch, the value shown is a duration. Durations can be negative as well as positive (e.g., an instant that occurs before the epoch might be represented internally with a negative duration). Logically, the following operations are available with instants and durations:

- `Instant – Instant => Duration`
- `Duration + Duration => Duration`
- `Instant + Duration => Instant`
- `Instant – Duration => Instant`

Figure 7.4 shows these graphically. In particular,

- The result of *now – x* is a duration of 10 seconds.
- The result of 10 seconds + 5 seconds is a duration of 15 seconds.
- We can add or subtract durations to get 10 seconds before now or 5 seconds from now.

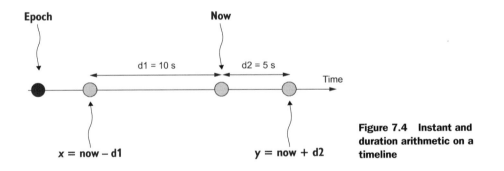

Figure 7.4 Instant and duration arithmetic on a timeline

The internal representation of a duration typically has a limit in terms of precision. Common precisions include milliseconds; microseconds; and nanoseconds, or ticks—the last of which being specific to Windows or .NET—where a tick is 100 ns.

Importantly, a duration is always absolutely fixed in terms of the elapsed time it measures. So while *1 second, 5 microseconds,* and *3 hours* are all valid durations, but *2 months* isn't because months vary in length. Whether *1 day* is a valid duration or not depends on how you understand 1 day. If you think of it as *the elapsed time between midnight one day and midnight the next day*, then it's not because that comes into time zone territory, where a day could be 23 hours or 25 hours long. However, if you think of 1 day as a synonym for 24 hours, then it *is* a valid duration.

> **NOTE** If it helps, you can think of an instant as being like a point in geometry and a duration as a vector. If you look at the operations available between instants and durations, they all map to point and vector operations.

Some libraries in the past have avoided encapsulating the concept of a duration, instead keeping numbers and units separately. That leads to function signatures like this (from `java.util.concurrent.locks.Lock`):

```
boolean tryLock(long time, TimeUnit unit)
```

While there are cases where this is useful, it generally becomes much more awkward than having a `Duration` type you can use everywhere the concept of an elapsed time is relevant.

  While instants and durations are the most important concepts in machine time (with epochs as a sort of background concept), libraries often provide additional types for convenience. The most common of these is an *interval*, which just encapsulates a pair of instants: a start and an end. Different libraries take different approaches about whether intervals can be open-ended (without a start instant or without an end instant) and whether the start instant can be later than the end instant (a sort of *negative interval*). It's worth being aware of what's available within the library you're using, but we won't go into more detail here, as it's not a fundamental concept in the same way as instant and duration.

  Machine time is useful in several situations, but it's extremely unfriendly for end users, and even developers, if you want to look at the information. If you're reading a log file, which would you rather see: 1605255526 or 2020-11-13T08:19:46Z? Computing often gets a lot more complicated when humans get involved, and that's particularly true in the area of date and time information. Let's look at how humans break time up into different concepts.

7.1.2 Civil time: Calendar systems, dates, times, and periods

If you've ever been stung by time zone bugs, you may have been surprised to see the absence of time zones in the list of concepts we're describing in this section. Don't worry, they're coming—just not yet. First, we can imagine a world without time zones and discover it's not the paradise of simplicity you might expect it to be. Let's start with a question you might expect to be straightforward: what day is it today?

CALENDAR SYSTEMS: BREAKING TIME INTO DAYS, MONTHS, AND YEARS

Types in java.time: `java.time.chrono.Chronology`, `java.time.LocalDate` and `java.time.chrono.ChronoLocalDate`. Types in Noda Time: `NodaTime.CalendarSystem` and `NodaTime.LocalDate`.

  One fairly universal aspect of human experience is the way we live on a day-to-day basis. Every civilization has the concept of day and night, and we tend to work during the day and sleep at night. It's, therefore, entirely natural to break the timeline up into days.

Next, the seasons have been historically important to a large proportion of humanity, and even though fewer of us are farmers these days, the yearly cycle still has an impact on our lives, so it's also reasonable to break the timeline up into years.

Months are more a matter of convenience, as a useful level of granularity. The lunar phase cycle of about 29.5 days probably had an impact on civilizations designing their calendar systems, but the phases of the moon have less impact on our lives than days and years do.

So a *calendar system* is a way of referring to a specific day in terms of a year, a month within that year, and a day within that month. This would all be relatively straightforward if we had a single calendar system, but that's not reality.

NOTE When we think about dates and times from a human perspective, with days, months and years, this is known as *civil time*. It's very culture-sensitive, unlike the machine time we looked at in the previous section.

So to answer the question that led into this section: as I'm writing this, it's November 20th, 2020, at least in the United Kingdom. That sounds like an unambiguous statement, but even that has an implicit assumption in it because I could also accurately say it's November 7th, 2020. How can it be both dates at the same time? It's November 20th, 2020 in the Gregorian calendar system and November 7th in the Julian calendar system. It's also the 4th day of Kislev in the year 5781 in the Hebrew calendar and the 4th day of Rabīʿ ath-Thānī 1442 in the Hijri calendar system. These are just a few of the calendar systems used around the world. Table 7.1 shows a few days leading up to today's date in all of those calendar systems.

Table 7.1   A timeline of dates in four calendar systems

Gregorian	Julian	Hebrew	Hijri
16 November 2020	3 November 2020	29 Heshvan 5781	30 Rabīʿ al-ʾAwwal 1442
17 November 2020	4 November 2020	1 Kislev 5781	1 Rabīʿ ath-Thānī 1442
18 November 2020	5 November 2020	2 Kislev 5781	2 Rabīʿ ath-Thānī 1442
19 November 2020	6 November 2020	3 Kislev 5781	3 Rabīʿ ath-Thānī 1442
20 November 2020	7 November 2020	4 Kislev 5781	4 Rabīʿ ath-Thānī 1442
21 November 2020	8 November 2020	5 Kislev 5781	5 Rabīʿ ath-Thānī 1442
22 November 2020	9 November 2020	6 Kislev 5781	6 Rabīʿ ath-Thānī 1442

Different calendar systems can have very different traits. The Gregorian and Julian calendar systems are almost identical; they only differ in terms of which years are leap years. Compare that with the Hebrew calendar system, for which the length of both Heshvan and Kislev vary year by year and where a *leap year* isn't a year with an extra day—it's a year with an extra month. (The month of Adar is split into Adar I and Adar II.) There are many calendar systems associated with Islam, which makes it quite tricky to know exactly what someone means if they simply refer to *the Islamic calendar system.*

The calendar system that has surprised me most in terms of handling it in code is the Badí calendar used in the Bahá'í faith, in which each year has 19 months of 19 days long and four or five days that come between the 18th and 19th month. Those days aren't in a month at all.

Not to mention that all of the above description includes an assumption that everyone agrees on when one day ends and the next starts—that's midnight, right? That's not correct for all calendar systems, historically. In Hebrew and Islamic calendars (among others) the boundary between days is sunset—not midnight.

I understand if all of this sounds terrifying, but we'll see in section 7.2.1 that most of the time you won't need to worry about it too much. That's the good news; the bad news is that, even sticking to the Gregorian calendar system, you need to keep on your toes. But once we've divided a timeline (again, ignoring time zones) into years, months, and days, referring to the time of day is relatively straightforward.

TIME OF DAY

Type in java.time: `java.time.LocalTime`. Type in Noda Time: `NodaTime.LocalTime`.

While there *have* been systems of timekeeping that choose different units of time, you can probably ignore them for the most part. If you want to find out more, the "Internet Time" article from Swatch (https://www.swatch.com/en-us/internet-time .html) is a good starting point.

Leaving that aside, and still ignoring time zones and leap seconds, we can probably all agree to think of a day as 24 hours, each composed of 60 minutes, each composed of 60 seconds. A second can be further subdivided into whatever units of precision you're interested in, such as milliseconds, microseconds, or nanoseconds.

It's *almost* as simple as that, leaving this as the shortest subsection in the chapter. The only tricky aspect is whether 24:00 is useful to consider as time of day, representing the *exclusive* end of the day, as opposed to 00:00 representing the *inclusive* start of the day. A value of 24:00 is not used very widely, but you may well come across situations where you need to take it into account.

To return to somewhat trickier ground, let's think about arithmetic within civil time. In machine time, this was simple: you could always add durations together, add or subtract a duration from an instant, and take the difference between two instants to obtain another duration. Everything is fairly predictable. In civil time, arithmetic can be surprising.

PERIODS: ARITHMETIC IN CIVIL TIME

Type in java.time: `java.time.Period`. Type in Noda Time: `NodaTime.Period`.

Normally, when we think of arithmetic, there's a natural right answer. If you're taking a math test as a child, and you're asked to calculate 5 + 6, the right answer is definitely 11. You'll either get a tick or a cross—not a *maybe*.

Calendar arithmetic isn't like that. At least not in the edge cases, and those edge cases are sufficiently common that you can't ignore them. If the question is "What is the date one month later than May 31st 2021?" you could reasonably answer "June 30th, 2021" or "July 1st, 2021." Figure 7.5 shows this ambiguity.

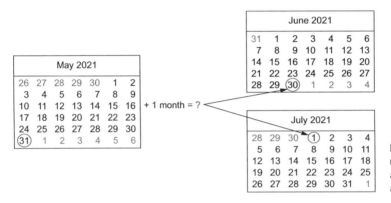

Figure 7.5   Adding a month to a date doesn't always have an obvious answer

We can still define a useful concept, however: a *period*. A period is like a vector of values for different calendrical units, such as a certain number of years, a certain number of months, etc. So *3 years, 1 month, and 2 days* would be a period. Within date and time libraries, there isn't consensus about whether periods should stop at days or go down to smaller units (e.g., hours, minutes, seconds, and subsecond units).

> **NOTE**   A duration always represents a fixed amount of elapsed time, regardless of context. Three seconds is always three seconds. The elapsed time within a period can vary with the most obvious example being 1 month, which varies based on which month it is (and in the case of February, which year).

Periods can have numbers that sound slightly nonsensical, too; it's entirely reasonable to have a period of *16 months* or *35 days*, even if those sound odd to start with. While you might reasonably normalize *16 months* to *1 year and 4 months* (if you know you're dealing with the Gregorian calendar system), you definitely *can't* normalize *35 days* into an equivalent period of *1 month and x days* because the value of *x* would depend on the length of the month when you happen to use the period.

Arithmetic purely between periods is quite straightforward: adding *2 months and 3 days* and *1 year and 2 days* gives you *1 year, 2 months and 5 days*, for example. It's a matter of opinion within date and time libraries whether subtraction always makes sense; a difference between those two periods leading to a result of *1 year, –2 months, and –1 day* can work reasonably well in terms of the code, but there isn't consensus on whether it's a meaningful and useful period. More generally, the question is whether periods with mixed signs are a good idea, given that they'd rarely come up naturally.

By and large, I'd expect the following operations to be available:

- `Date + Period => Date`
- `Date – Period => Date`
- `Date – Date => Period` (potentially specifying what units you want to use)
- `Period + Period => Period`
- `Period – Period => Period`

While purely-period arithmetic is simple, as soon as we introduce date and period arithmetic (the first two operations listed above), we end up with potential problems. Going back to the edge cases mentioned earlier, different libraries will give different results for some calculations, and different *humans* would give different answers if you ask them, too. This isn't a matter of libraries being broken (although that's always a possibility), it's a matter of there being no clear right answer. But whatever answer a library gives to any given question, it's likely that it will violate some simple expectations you might have. There are two particular aspects that surprise many people.

Firstly, addition in calendar arithmetic isn't *associative*. For example, suppose we want to add the values of *January 31, 2021, 1 month*, and *2 months*. We could bracket that in two different ways:

- (January 31, 2021 + 1 month) + 2 months
- January 31, 2021 + (1 month + 2 months)

In both java.time and Noda Time, the result of the first operation is April 28th 2021, whereas the result of the second is April 30th 2021. Here are the steps to get those results:

- (January 31, 2021 + 1 month) + 2 months
  - January 31, 2021 + 1 month => February 28, 2021
  - February 28, 2021 + 2 months => April 28, 2021
- January 31, 2021 + (1 month + 2 months)
  - 1 month + 2 months => 3 months
  - January 31, 2021 + 3 months => April 30, 2021

Other libraries might give different results, which may be consistent with each other in this case but inconsistent in other situations.

Secondly, addition of a date and a period isn't reversible. In other words, for a date d and a period p, you might like the result of (d + p) - p to always be d, but that's not going to work out. For example, whatever rules a library has, if you add a month to January 31st and then subtract a month from the result, you're not going to get back to January 31st.

If this all sounds like it wouldn't matter in the real world, consider this hypothetical situation, shown in figure 7.6: There is an election on February 28, 2022, and

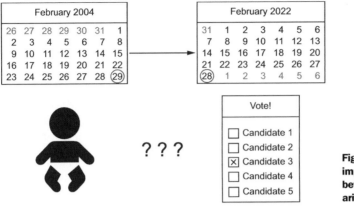

Figure 7.6   Real-world implications of choices between calendar arithmetic options

anyone who is 18 years old on election day is eligible to vote. Should someone born on February 29, 2004 be able to vote in the election?

While this example is hypothetical, such elections can happen. The United Kingdom held a general election on February 28, 1974, for example. It might be considered sensible to try to avoid creating such ambiguities, where you have control over the dates in question.

How would you express that requirement using arithmetic? Here are two options which *sound* reasonable:

- "Subtract 18 years from election day. Anyone already born on that day can vote."
- "Add 18 years to a person's birth date. They can vote if the election is on that day or later."

Both java.time and Noda Time are consistent with each other, but give different results for the different options. The first option would suggest that the person can't vote, because the person hadn't been born on February 28th 2004. The second option would suggest that the person *can* vote, because adding 18 years to February 29th 2004 returns February 28th 2022. A different library might decide to "roll over" the result to March 1st 2022.

I would personally *expect* that the second approach is the right one here, and that the result from java.time and Noda Time is the one most likely to be correct in law. But I don't know whether every country in the world would phrase its laws that way—and it's entirely possible that some countries have laws which are ambiguous or inconsistent.

None of this is intended to act as scaremongering. Instead, it's intended to encourage you to think really carefully any time you perform calendar arithmetic, and make sure everyone involved has the same expectations.

So far we've looked at machine time in terms of well-defined instants, and civil time which splits a timeline into years, months and days, but we haven't tried to map machine time onto civil time. In order to do that, we need time zones.

7.1.3   *Time zones, UTC, and offsets from UTC*

Types in java.time: `java.time.ZoneId` and `java.time.ZoneOffset`. Types in Noda Time: `NodaTime.DateTimeZone` and `NodaTime.Offset`.

You probably already know what time zones are, at least roughly. Unfortunately, there are quite a few ways in which time zones are commonly misunderstood, which we'll try to correct here. For the sake of this section, I'll pretend that the Gregorian calendar is the *only* calendar system. It's not actually hard to extend the description of time zones here to other calendar systems, but it makes it more complicated to explain.

Humans generally like to treat time in a way in which 12 noon on any given day is roughly when the sun is directly overhead. That happens at different instants in time for different places around the world. Time zones are a way of accounting for that. For example, as I'm writing this, it's 3:53 p.m. in the UK. I know that for someone in San Francisco, it's 7:53 a.m. For someone in India, it's 9:23 p.m.

A time zone essentially contains three pieces of information:

- An identifier or name
- A region of the earth's surface, which is deemed to be in that time zone
- A function that maps any instant to a civil date and time

If you imagine that everyone is wearing an accurate wristwatch, correctly configured for the time zone they're in, then everyone within a single time zone will see the same date and time at any instant in time as the result of the mapping in the time zone. Two people in different time zones *may* see the same date and time, but they may be different, and even if they see the same date and time as each other right now, they might see different values from each other a minute later.

When we introduced epochs, I mentioned that the Unix epoch was the instant represented by midnight at the start of January 1, 1970 UTC. So what is UTC? It's the null time zone, or baseline, used to describe other time zones. Strictly speaking, it's not a time zone at all (because there's no region of the earth that is designated as being within the UTC time zone), but it's very often used as if it were a time zone—and the simplest possible one. I'm introducing it here because it's a sort of stepping stone to working with real, more complex time zones.

Mapping an instant to a civil date and time using UTC is simple. You'll already know the UTC date and time represented by the epoch (such as January 1, 1970 00:00:00), and the instant is just a duration added to that epoch. In UTC, every day is 24 hours long, every hour is 60 minutes long, and so on. There are none of the annoyances of other time zones that I'll describe in a moment. You still need to deal with leap years, but that's not too hard. Instants before the epoch work in the obvious way as well; if you're dealing with the Unix epoch and the instant has a duration of –10 seconds, then that represents December 31, 1969 23:59:50, for example.

Once you've got the idea of UTC, the function that maps any instant to a civil date and time in a time zone can be thought of as equivalent to a function that maps any instant to a *UTC offset*—a value that tells you how far ahead or behind UTC that time zone is at that instant.

To give a concrete example, at the instant in time that maps to November 20, 2020, 3:53pm UTC, the UTC offset for the San Francisco time zone is –8 hours. San Francisco is said to be 8 hours behind UTC at that instant, which is why it's 7:53 a.m. there. In India, the UTC offset at that instant is 5 hours and 30 minutes, which is why it's 9:23 p.m. there.

But that mapping function from an instant to a UTC offset doesn't have to give the same results for all instants, and in most time zones it doesn't. So for example, on *June* 20, 2020 at 3:53 p.m., the UTC offset for the time zone in Francisco would be –7 hours instead, so it would have been 8:53 a.m. The UTC offset for India would still be 5 hours and 30 minutes—it's used that offset constantly since the year 1945.

While the mapping from an instant to a civil date and time is unambiguous, the reverse isn't true. Some civil date and time values are *ambiguous* (when more than one instant maps to that civil date and time), and some are *skipped* (when no instant maps to that civil date and time). For example, in the time zone for San Francisco, the offset changed from UTC-7 to UTC-8 on November 1, 2020 at 2 a.m. local time (9 a.m. UTC), when the *fall back* daylight saving change happened. That means any San Franciscans with accurate watches could have seen the following sequence of times:

- 01:59:58
- 01:59:59
- 01:00:00 ← *Fall back* happens here
- 01:00:01
- 01:00:02

That means a civil date and time of 1:45 a.m. on November 1, 2020 happened twice. Two people in San Francisco could say they were woken up by their cats at 1:45 a.m. that night and have actually woken up an hour apart.

On the other hand, on March 8th 2020 in San Francisco, the clocks went *forward* by an hour at what would have been 2 a.m. local time (10 a.m. UTC), changing from UTC-8 to UTC-7. So this time, San Franciscans would have seen this sequence of times:

- 01:59:58
- 01:59:59
- 03:00:00 ← *Spring forward* happens here
- 03:00:01
- 03:00:02

That means a civil date and time of 2:45 a.m. on March 8, 2020 didn't happen at all. Anyone in San Francisco claiming to have been woken up by their cats at 2:45 a.m. that night would have been mistaken.

Figure 7.7 shows a graph of the UTC offsets of four time zones (Europe/Moscow, Europe/Paris, America/Asuncion, and America/Los_Angeles) during 2020. America/Asuncion is the time zone observed in Paraguay, and America/Los_Angeles is the time zone observed in San Francisco. Notice how Paraguay is in the southern hemisphere, so its fall back date is in March, and its spring forward date is in October.

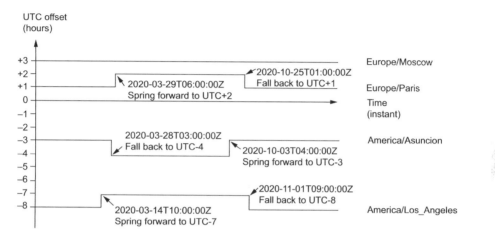

Figure 7.7   Four time zones with UTC offset plotted over time

You don't need to learn the exact details of what happens when in which time zone. (That's why we have time zone databases, after all. We'll discuss time zone databases more later.) You do need to remember that converting from an instant to a civil date and time in a particular time zone is unambiguous, but converting in the other direction has corner cases to think about.

WHAT *ISN'T* A TIME ZONE?

In the previous examples, I deliberately didn't use the terms *Pacific Standard Time* or *Pacific Daylight Time* for the time zone in San Francisco. While those are commonly used as a sort of shorthand for the UTC offset, they aren't time zones in themselves. It's more accurate to say that the time zone that includes San Francisco alternates between Pacific Standard Time and Pacific Daylight Time over time. Other time zones may also observe Pacific Standard Time sometimes as well but have different times than San Francisco for some of the time. So Pacific Standard Time, and similar descriptions, *aren't* names of time zones, in general.

> **NOTE** Annoyingly, the Windows time zone database *does* use Pacific Standard Time as the identifier for the time zone that includes San Francisco and follows the same pattern for many other time zones as well. So you can ask for the description of the time in Pacific Standard Time and receive a result of Pacific Daylight Time. I would personally recommend avoiding the Windows

time zone database when possible, instead using IANA time zones, which I'll describe later.

Given that the descriptive names for these *half time zones* aren't really time zone names, it makes sense that the abbreviations derived from them, such as *PST* and *PDT*, don't name time zones either. The abbreviations are even worse than the descriptive names though because they're more likely to be ambiguous. As one horrible example, *BST* is an abbreviation for both *British Summer Time* and *British Standard Time*—the latter being used between 1968 and 1971. Abbreviations *can* be useful to display to users, but you should avoid them for every other purpose.

Finally, UTC offsets themselves are not time zones. It's unfortunate that even ISO-8601 (the standard for textual date and time representations) gets this wrong. The value that's described as a *zone designator* in ISO-8601 only represents the UTC offset. That's important because the UTC offset at one instant in time doesn't tell you much about the UTC offset at another instant within the same time zone. Again, UTC offsets can be very useful and simpler than trying to convey an actual time zone, but it's important to distinguish the two concepts.

As an example, consider the date and time and offset 2021-06-19T14:00:00-04—in other words, June 19, 2021 at 2 p.m. local time in a time zone that is 4 hours behind UTC at that instant. What would the UTC offset be on December 19 at the same local time? In New York, it would be –5; in Asunción (the capital of Paraguay), it would be –3, even though both of them had a UTC offset of –4 in June. The original information *does* contain a UTC offset, but it *doesn't* indicate the time zone.

WHERE DOES TIME ZONE INFORMATION COME FROM?

Type in java.time: `java.time.zone.ZoneRuleProvider`. Types in Noda Time: `Noda-Time.DateTimeZoneProviders` and `NodaTime.IDateTimeZoneProvider`.

The note above mentioned the *Windows time zone database*, which is installed on all Windows machines and updated via Windows update. However, that's not the most commonly used source of time zone information. Instead, the volunteer-run database maintained at the Internet Assigned Numbers Authority (IANA; the time zone database is available at https://www.iana.org/time-zones) is used by almost every non-Windows system. Due to its long history, the IANA time zone database has a number of other names. You might hear about Olson time zones, zoneinfo, tz, or tzdb. These are all names for the same data source; different names have come and gone over time.

> **NOTE** Different development platforms take different approaches to obtaining time zone data. For example, Java uses IANA time zones by default, even when it's running on Windows. .NET uses the platform-native time zones, so will use IANA time zones when running on Linux or Windows time zones when running on Windows. .NET 6 introduced improvements here. It's worth finding out which time zone information will be used for your code, bearing in mind all the operating systems it will run on.

IANA time zones are "typically identified by continent or ocean and then by the name of the largest city within the region" (https://data.iana.org/time-zones/tz-link.html). The time zones I've been using in examples so far have been:

- San Francisco: America/Los_Angeles
- Moscow: Europe/Moscow
- Paraguay: America/Asuncion
- England: Europe/London
- India: Asia/Kolkata

Time zone rules change multiple times a year. When I talk about a rule changing, I'm not talking about the change in America/Los_Angeles from UTC-8 to UTC-7 or back again; I'm talking about changes to the rules that govern those changes. For example, the Energy Policy Act of 2005 changed the rules for when daylight saving time is observed in the United States, taking effect in 2007. Time zone rules are a political matter, decided by governments. When the group of volunteers for the IANA database becomes aware of a change to the rules (with clear documentation that it's actually been ratified by the government involved, rather than just being proposed), the change is made to the database, and it's released. Sometimes, multiple changes are batched together into a single release. The release names are based on the year of the release with a letter afterward (e.g., the first release of 2020 was 2020a, followed by 2020b, and so on).

How that change to the information reaches the computer your code is running on can vary enormously, depending on your environment. We'll revisit this aspect later on in section 7.4.4, along with the impact it can have on your code.

To recap, we've looked at three sets of concepts so far:

- *Machine time*—has instants, epochs and durations
- *Civil time*—has calendar systems, dates, periods, and times of day
- *Time zones*—UTC and UTC offsets

Other concepts can be derived from these, and good date and time libraries will often provide a really large range of types, which allow your code to express what you mean clearly and precisely. But before we start thinking too closely about code, I want to briefly point out a few things I've left out in the descriptions above.

7.1.4 Date and time concepts that hurt my head

Most of the time, I'm a stickler for accuracy in technical books. Why would you read a technical book you knew to be inaccurate? Well, sometimes being totally accurate gets in the way of being useful. I've already mentioned a couple of the aspects of date and time handling that aren't going to be covered in detail in this chapter, but there's a little bit more information here. You can skip this section entirely; it won't affect what comes later. But it can be quite nice after a hard day's work to console yourself by thinking, "Sure, I have to deal with time zone rules changing, but at least I don't have to deal with relativity." Which brings us to our first topic. . . .

RELATIVITY

In one of my favorite episodes of *Doctor Who*, "Blink," the Doctor says: "People assume that time is a strict progression of cause to effect, but actually, from a nonlinear, non-subjective viewpoint, it's more like a big ball of wibbly-wobbly, timey-wimey . . . stuff." That's roughly the level of my understanding of relativity. I understand enough to be scared of it, particularly the concept that we (humans *and* machines) experience time differently, depending on frames of reference, speed, and acceleration.

We started with the concept of an instant in time as something we can all agree on. Two people in different time zones and calendar systems would still give the same answer of *now* when considering an instant. Relativity suggests it's not that simple, and perhaps, even that the concept of *now* doesn't make much sense.

Some infrastructure (such as GPS) does need to take this into account. Business code really doesn't, fortunately.

LEAP SECONDS

Time isn't the only thing that's wibbly-wobbly. The earth's rotation is wobbly too, and it's slowing down very gradually. That means there's a slight discrepancy between "observed solar time" (which would always have the sun directly overhead at noon on the Greenwich meridian) and the time reported by an atomic clock. Leap seconds are the way of accounting for this. They're inserted into (or removed from, theoretically) the UTC timeline when they're needed to keep UTC and observed solar time close together.

The way a leap second is inserted or removed is just to change the length of the final minute at the end of either June or December. That means that while a minute usually lasts 60 seconds, it could last 61 seconds or 59 seconds instead. For example, the leap second inserted at the end of 2016 occurred at 2016-12-31 23:59:60. At the time of this writing, there haven't been any *negative leap seconds* (where a second is removed from the timeline instead of being added), but it's possible.

Different systems have different ways of either reporting leap seconds or pretending they don't exist. For example, some systems use a *leap smear*, which effectively distributes the extra second over a longer period of time. So near the time when a leap second would be inserted, a second might last a bit longer than a second. Yes, I'm aware of how ridiculous that sounds.

If all of that isn't hard enough to keep straight in your head, leap seconds aren't predictable. They're announced six months in advance, which is significantly better than some time zone changes, but even so, it means you need to think carefully in terms of the validity of any data you might be storing about the future. We'll look at this problem in more detail in section 7.4.4. Again, some infrastructure (such as NTP) needs to be very aware of leap seconds, but most other software doesn't.

WHAT'S THE TIME ON MARS?

If you think it's hard to organize a meeting with people in multiple time zones on earth, imagine a scenario in which one attendee is on Mars (where a day is 24 hours and 37 minutes long), another is on Jupiter (where a day is a little under 10 hours long), and another is on Venus (where a day is about 5,832 hours; that's longer than a Venusian *year* lasts). Once you've organized it, imagine at the end of the meeting someone saying, "Same time tomorrow?"

It has been seriously suggested that new date and time libraries should handle nonterrestrial time. I hope to have retired by the time it becomes relevant to mainstream software engineering.

CALENDAR SYSTEM TRANSITIONS

In Rome in 1582, October 4 was followed by October 15. In London in 1752, September 2 was followed by September 14. These are examples of transitioning from the Julian calendar to the Gregorian calendar—something that happened at different dates in different places.

That means people from different countries who *usually* use the same calendar system can disagree on dates. For example, the Battle of Lowestoft took place on June 13, 1665 . . . or June 3, 1665, depending on which side of the battle you were on.

One notable oddity is Sweden's transition from the Julian calendar to the Gregorian calendar. Sweden planned to do this gradually by skipping all the leap days from 1700 onward, until they were aligned with the Gregorian calendar. Unfortunately, while 1700 went as planned, Sweden was distracted by the Great Northern War (1700–1721) and forgot about the plan. It treated 1704 and 1708 as leap years, contrary to the plan, which was then abandoned. To get back to the Julian calendar system, Sweden included *two* leap days in 1712: February 29 and February 30.

Some date and time libraries attempt to handle calendar transitions like this, although I'm not sure any mainstream ones model the Swedish history. It does lead to even stranger arithmetic than normal and is generally best avoided, in my opinion.

Those are some of the odder corner cases you almost certainly don't need to worry about. In the next section, we'll look at aspects you definitely *should* consider as soon as you start planning a feature—well before you start writing the code for it.

7.2 Preparing to work with date and time information

If you came to the end of the previous section anxious to finally see code, I'm afraid I've got some bad news for you: there's not much code in this section either. I promise we'll get there, but the structure of this chapter is designed to mirror a productive approach to date and time handling; if you prepare carefully and think about the concepts first, the actual code is the easy part. Now that we have some common concepts and terminology to work with, we can think about how those concepts are applied to real-world products.

7.2.1 Limiting your scope

We've seen how the world of date and time information can get bewilderingly complicated. The good news is that you probably don't need all that complexity in your application. When you start planning either a whole application or an individual feature that uses dates and times, it's worth explicitly trying to limit the scope of your work and documenting the decisions you make.

You can probably start off by ruling out the most complex and niche aspects:

- Does your application need to deal with relativity?
- Do you need to be aware of and account for leap seconds?
- Do you need to work with dates that are sufficiently far in the past that historical calendar system changes might be relevant?

If the answer to any of these questions is yes, then you may find that you're limited in terms of the libraries you can use, and you'll *definitely* want to take even more care than usual and do plenty of research into the niche you're stuck with. I don't have much more specific advice than that, as I've never had to work in that sort of application, but I would expect that choosing appropriate types to represent product concepts is even more important than normal.

The second level of complexity to think about relates to calendar systems and time zones. Do you need to work with any calendar system other than the Gregorian calendar? Most business applications can probably just use the Gregorian calendar, but there will certainly be counterexamples, particularly if your application's audience is a religious community that pays particular attention to a specific calendar. Consumer applications are slightly more likely to need support for the preferred calendar system of the user, but you probably want to weigh up the costs and benefits of doing so before committing. (The benefits will be application specific, and the costs may well be technology specific; support for non-Gregorian calendar systems varies significantly.)

The level of complexity around time zones can vary significantly. Questions to ask yourself here include

- Does the product need to support time zones at all? Sometimes, an entire application can be built around the machine time concepts, which can simplify things a lot.
- Does the product need to interoperate with time zones specified by another system? If so, which time zone database does it use?
- Does the product need to allow users to choose time zones, or can you just rely on detecting their default time zone?
- Does the product need to work in more than a single time zone? If so, are you confident it will stay that way?
- Does the product need to keep absolutely up to date in terms of time zone rules, actively keeping track of changes, or can it just use the time zone rules that come by default with the platform or library?
- Does the product need to store any data that naturally includes time zone information, or is any time zone interaction purely for display purposes?
- How much attention do you need to pay to time zone transitions, in terms of skipped and ambiguous times? If you're writing a school timetable system, for example, it's unlikely that pupils will have lessons at the time of a transition.

Most applications that need to display date and time values to a user will need some time zone awareness, but you may well be able to make your life much simpler by not building in more flexibility than you need. There's a tradeoff here, of course: if you write your code with the assumption that you'll only ever need to work with (say) the time zone for Paris, you may well find it's quite hard to undo the impact of that assumption later on. It really can make a large difference in terms of simplicity though. One way to mitigate that risk of future requirements is to make sure everyone on the team is aware of the assumptions that are being made and reflects on when they're relying on them. Keeping a document of places in the system where the assumptions are relevant can make it much easier to backtrack later on.

This sort of scoping is usually possible before you have detailed product or feature requirements. It would be relatively rare for a product to *unexpectedly* change to needing to support multiple calendar systems, for example. (It's possible, of course. That sort of new requirement is more likely to be part of an expansion into new markets than as part of adding a new individual feature.) The developers in the team can probably work through the questions above themselves, then document and validate the results with the product owners.

> **NOTE** I'm using the term *product owners* to represent the people who are responsible for deciding what the product should do. Different companies may use different names, such as *product managers*. Depending on your exact development model, these may be people within the same company as the developers, a different company, or a mixture. They may be the developers themselves, but it's worth treating this as a role that's separate from deciding *how* a product should be implemented.

When it comes to detailed requirements, however, the product owners must be involved.

7.2.2 *Clarifying date and time requirements*

I should start this section with a warning: ensuring that the product requirements related to date and time work are clear and unambiguous is unlikely to make you popular. You're likely to be faced with many responses of: "Isn't it obvious?"—even if the obvious answer for one person is different to the obvious answer for someone else. But the effort is worth it. Once the requirements are clear, the coding is often straightforward. Without clear requirements, you may well find that each individual involved in the product has different expectations, leading to chaos.

Exactly how you decide to plan and document your requirements is up to you, of course. There's no particular required methodology. You may have a big, up-front design or you may be designing individual small features as you go in a more agile approach. It's worth being careful in the *only design what you need right now* style though; if you only need a date for a particular piece of information in the first sprint but then find you need a date and time (and maybe time zone) by the time you reach sprint four, that will make life significantly harder. Try to anticipate future natural requirements to *some* extent without going too far down the rabbit hole of planning for every possible eventuality.

There are, broadly, two kinds of decision that should be recorded as part of the requirements documentation: how you're treating each piece of date and time-related data and how you operate on them. You'll also need to consider representations for storage and transmission, but those are more implementation details than product requirements. The two kinds of decision are related, but we'll consider them separately.

To try to make everything concrete, we'll use an online shopping scenario to start with. The TL;DR of the requirement we'll look at is shown in figure 7.8: *Customers can return items within 3 months*. By the end of the scenario, we'll have a set of requirements that can be implemented and tested.

Figure 7.8 A high level requirement that needs more details

PICKING THE RIGHT CONCEPTS OR DATA TYPES

Good product requirements usually state what information is collected in a given situation and, potentially, what information is deliberately not being collected. Sometimes, this is implicit and somewhat buried within a narrative describing the user journey, but it's clearer if it's called out explicitly. It's usually easy to spot date and time-related information, but it can be harder to decide how you're going to treat that data.

As a first rule of thumb, it's worth considering the source of the data. If you're recording that "something has happened," then you should usually start off with an *instant*—the instant at which the event occurred. You may *also* want to record a time zone (or, more generally, a location) if that's going to be relevant to other operations. Recording the instant is usually straightforward—most databases and logging systems have built-in timestamps.

> **NOTE** You *may* need to consider which source of current time is important: if you capture *now* in both the database and on a separate web server, the two clocks involved may not be perfectly synchronized. Whether or not that's important will depend on your application.

If you're recording a date and time value that is provided by a *user*, that's a different matter. You're in the realm of civil time, rather than machine time, at that point— even if they're reporting when something happened. You almost certainly need to bear time zone information in mind, or at least a UTC offset. You may be tempted to convert that into an instant, but I'd encourage you to retain exactly what the user gave you—or at least a representation that is parsed but not necessarily transformed. When we look at some corner cases later on, we'll see how the approach of *just storing UTC* can go wrong, particularly when recording information about the future.

For our customer returns requirement, we obviously need to capture some information, but it's not immediately clear what that information should be, let alone what representation to use. The first question to ask of the product owner is, "Customers can return items within 3 months *of what?*" For example, it might be

- Within 3 months of the user clicking *pay*
- Within 3 months of the payment being accepted
- Within 3 months of the order being confirmed
- Within 3 months of the stock being allocated
- Within 3 months of the order being shipped
- Within 3 months of the order being received

We'll be thinking about what *3 months* means later on, but the list above shows six different instants in time. Even within the fifth bullet of *shipped*, there may be several different instants, but for simplicity, we'll assume we can agree on one of those being the relevant one.

Importantly though, these *are* all instants in time, and it would make sense to record them all within the order. Some aspects may be on a per-item basis, rather than a per-order basis, such as stock allocation or even shipping—the order may be shipped in multiple deliveries. The product owner should be considering all of these aspects in the context of *customers can return items within 3 months.*

Let's assume the product owner replies that for any given item, the customer can return that item within 3 months of it shipping. (So the returns window may vary between items, even within the same order.) Great; this is already a lot more precise.

We'll probably be recording various other instants, but we know we need to record the instant at which each item was shipped. That's still not the final solution though, and this is where you can lean on the concepts we've already discussed to provoke more questions. We know that 3 months is a period, not a duration, and you can't add a period to an instant. We're going to have to derive some other information from that instant to consider it in civil time. That means we *have* to consider calendar systems and time zones.

> **NOTE** We all know that product requirements can change. The decision of *the shipping time determines the returns window* could change, and so could the decisions we ask later on. If you keep all the raw and canonical information from the start, that allows you to change your decision later on. That means we should record *all* of the instants listed earlier . . . and store them *as* instants, even if we later derive more information from them.
>
> This is related to the earlier tip about retaining *what the user gave you*, which is important if the user specifies a date and/or time. The canonical information in that case isn't an instant as recorded by a machine clock; it's the user input.

First, we can ask the product owner what calendar system we should be using. This is likely to be a simple one: the Gregorian calendar system, regardless of the user. (If the product owner gives any other answer at that point, you should probably allow for a lot more testing time.)

Second, we can ask the product owner what time zone they're interested in. This is where it's useful to have a specific example to hand to keep things concrete. You might want to give a scenario of

- a web server in Brazil;
- storing data in a database in New York;
- placing an order for a company based in California;
- shipping items from a warehouse in Texas;
- for a customer with a billing address in Berlin, Germany; or
- shipping to an address in Sydney, Australia.

The instant at which the item is considered *shipped* will represent different local times and possibly even different *dates* in each of those places. So what's important here? One big hint: it almost certainly shouldn't be the web server or database. Just about any other answer is plausible, but products should almost *never* behave differently based on the physical location of the computers involved, unless the users are sitting in front of those computers.

Even if the product owner thinks that's a far-fetched situation, they should be able to decide what the right answer is and document that decision. It also naturally forms the starting point of an acceptance test.

Let's suppose the product owner answers that the relevant time zone is the one we're shipping to—Sydney, Australia, in this case. Fantastic. That probably doesn't mean we *need* to store any more information; we already got the location we're shipping to (from which we can derive the time zone), the instant at which the item shipped as a canonical starting point, and the *always use the Gregorian calendar* decision from earlier on. We can convert the instant into a local time at the shipping location whenever we want to. It *may* be useful to store that directly in the database, but that's an implementation detail. With that information in hand, we can move on to the rest of the questions about this feature.

ASKING QUESTIONS ABOUT BEHAVIOR

The broad statement of *customers can return items within 3 months* needs all kinds of clarifications. We've identified the starting point of that 3 months, but there's still a lot more detail required before we can start implementing anything. Of course, any product owner doing their job properly would put in a lot of that detail into the requirements naturally, but we're focusing on the date and time-related details.

Suppose the actual user journey documented is along these lines:

> *When viewing a completed order on the web site, any item that was shipped less than 3 months ago is displayed with an option to return the item. When the customer clicks on that option, they are presented with a form containing the details for the return. Once they have completed the form, the returns procedure is initiated.*

There would be a lot of detail about the returns procedure, but there are two date and time aspects that need clarifying here.

Firstly, should the 3 months apply to when the user viewed the completed order, when they clicked on the option to start the returns process, or when they submitted the returns form? Those are three different instants in time. It would be irritating for a customer if they viewed the order when it was valid to return the item, but if they then clicked on the returns option a minute later, the web site said it wasn't valid anymore. On the other hand, we don't want a loophole where a user can leave a browser window up for years and effectively have an unlimited returns period. The same question could apply for completing the returns form.

Here's one possible set of requirements with more details:

> *When viewing a completed order on the web site, any item that was shipped less than 3 months ago is displayed with an option to return the item. When the customer clicks on that option, the server checks whether the returns option was valid 5 minutes earlier and returns an error if it wasn't. That allows customers a delay of up to 5 minutes between viewing the order and starting the returns process, when we guarantee to honor the return. (It also means that if the customer waited for more than 5 minutes, but they're still within the returns period anyway, they can still proceed to the returns form.) If the check passes, a returns form is presented to the customer. The form states that it must be completed within 2 hours.*

> *When the returns form is submitted, the server checks that the returns procedure was started within the last 2 hours and returns an error if it wasn't. If the check passes, the form is submitted for processing and a confirmation screen is shown to the customer.*

This has two different kinds of time limit: one that provides a sort of grace period of 5 minutes beyond the strict *you must start the returns process by time x* and a second, which limits how long you can spend on the returns form itself.

We're now half way to a good set of requirements from a date and time perspective. There's still the gnarly bit about *less than 3 months ago*, though. We've already decided that the *starting* time of the 3 months is *the instant when the order was shipped* and that the 3 months should be oriented around the time zone of the delivery address. There's still a bit of work to do in terms of precision, however.

As we saw with the voting example earlier, arithmetic involving calendars doesn't follow the same rules as we're used to with regular math. So in this case, we need to differentiate between *taking the shipping time and adding 3 months* and *taking the current time and subtracting three months*. The product owner will also need to work out what they want to do about granularity: if something ships at 10 a.m., do they want the three months to run out at 10 a.m. three months later? That could feel a little arbitrary to customers. If it's what the product owner decides, of course, then that's the requirement. But here's the sort of requirement I would probably write if I were a product owner:

> *The option to return an item is based on the date on which the item was shipped in the time zone of the delivery address. The last date on which a return is valid is calculated by adding 3 months to the current date at the delivery location when the item is shipped. If adding 3 months to the shipping date goes beyond the end of the month, the start of the*

next month is used. (Example: if an item ships on November 30th, the last valid return date is the following March 1st—not the last day of February.) The return an item option is shown to the customer so long as the current date at the delivery location is not later than the last valid return date.

That's quite wordy, but it's unambiguous. It covers

- The granularity we're using (date—not date and time)
- The nature of the calendar arithmetic (adding to the start date)
- The nature of the check (the last date is *inclusive*)
- The time zone involved (the delivery address)
- The way in which the calendar arithmetic is resolved (roll over to the start of the next month)

That last requirement may not be the simplest one to code, depending on the library you're using, but at least it's clear and testable.

I wouldn't expect a product owner to come up with requirements like that on their own, unless they happen to have done date and time work like this before. Until you're aware of the oddities of calendar arithmetic, the potential ambiguities aren't always obvious. But that's where the development team can probe the requirements until they're precise enough. The process of going from a vague set of product requirements to a specific, unambiguous, testable set of requirements will vary, depending on how your team is set up, but it's important to get there in the end. It may require multiple rounds of asking questions involving awkward corner cases, or the development team may be able to suggest a more concrete version of the ambiguous requirements. The final step before you start writing code is to make sure you're using the right tools for the job.

7.2.3   *Using the right libraries or packages*

While it's possible to write clear, readable code using poor date and time libraries, it's an uphill struggle. Once you've got a clear set of requirements, you're in a good position to evaluate the technologies to use to implement them.

This is a landscape that changes over time. For example, at the time of writing, the `Temporal` proposal for a new set of standard objects for working with dates and times in JavaScript is only a draft, but if and when it's approved, that's likely to be an option you'd want to consider for new JavaScript projects.

We're happy to provide recommendations for Java and .NET, as these are the platforms the authors know best, and they're both quite stable in terms of options. Of course, there's always the possibility that something new will have become available between the time we write this text and the time you read it, but they're at least good starting points.

On the Java platform, if you can use the java.time package introduced in Java 8, you should do so. If, for some reason, you're stuck on Java 6 or Java 7, the ThreeTen-Backport project (https://www.threeten.org/threetenbp/) is a good alternative. The main objective is to avoid using `java.util.Date` and `java.util.Calendar`, both of which are full of traps waiting to lure the unwary developer into writing buggy code.

On .NET, our *heavily biased* recommendation is to use Noda Time (https://nodatime .org). The built-in types (`DateTime`, `DateTimeOffset`, `TimeZoneInfo`, `TimeSpan`) can certainly be used effectively, but they don't separate out the different logical concepts we looked at earlier into different types. For example, there's no type to represent a date, and the same type is used for both the duration and time of day concepts. (Note that some of this has changed since the release of .NET 6, but we won't go into detail here.) This means it's easy to write code that looks correct but effectively performs invalid operations on the logical data, such as adding half an hour to a date. The way a `DateTime` can mean *in some unspecified time zone, in the system local time zone,* or *in UTC* doesn't help either.

Beyond these specific examples though, there are more general questions you can evaluate against any given library for your platform:

- If you need to handle non-Gregorian calendar systems, does the library support those calendar systems?
- Does the library provide enough control of the time zone data it uses? (For example, if you need to work with IANA time zone IDs, it's best not to choose a library that only supports Windows time zones.)
- Does the library support all the concepts you've identified in your requirements, providing sufficient distinctions between those concepts to help your code express your intentions clearly?
- Does the library provide immutable types? While immutability as a general concept has distinct pros and cons, as we saw in chapter 4, in the context of a date and time library it's almost always a good thing.
- Do your external dependencies (e.g., databases, other libraries, network APIs, and the like) already lead in the direction of a particular library? If you need to perform conversions between different representations, is that easy to do?

Wherever possible, it's useful to try prototyping some of the date and time requirements against the candidate library, so you'll have an idea of what your final code will feel like. This can usually be done in a small console application or unit test project, isolated from any existing application code. For example, with the requirements around item returns described earlier, I'd probably write some unit tests to check the logic for whether or not to show the *return item* option. If you're evaluating multiple libraries, you may be able to have a single set of test cases that are then implemented using different libraries. Once you've got *working* code using all the libraries, you can compare the implementations for readability. Once you've documented application-wide requirements, worked with the product owner on feature-specific requirements, and chosen a good library to use, finally, you can start writing your production code.

7.3   *Implementing date and time code*

Even with all the right preparations in place, we still need to be disciplined with the code itself. It's all too easy to let things slip by taking shortcuts, and the result can be hard to disentangle.

7.3.1   *Applying concepts consistently*

If we're consistent in our use of concepts within the application, that will help avoid mistakes creeping in. That can be difficult when some pieces of information have different uses in different contexts. For example, the returns policy in our ongoing scenario revolves around an effective shipping date, but that in turn is based on an instant in time when the *it's left the warehouse* event occurred in conjunction with the time zone of the location we're shipping to. We can still be consistent, but we need to be clear which of these we mean any time there's code that deals with *when an item shipped.*

Date and time information tends to exist in three different forms:

- *In memory, while the code is executing*—Typically, this is in the form of objects from whatever date and time library you're using.
- *In network requests, while the information is being exchanged between machines*—Typically, this is textual, particularly for web applications, and the developer may be responsible for making sure both the sender and receiver use and expect the same format. However, it may also be a binary protocol, which is typically opaque, in which case we don't need to know or care what the actual bytes are.
- *In storage, such as in a JSON, CSV, or XML file or in a database*—Like network requests, we may or may not be in control of the precise format. However, we are often able to choose the data type, whether that's through SQL fields or standard text format representations.

Again, consistency is incredibly helpful here. For example, if part of the application allows a user to specify a date (without a time), then we should make sure that the information flow respects that choice to avoid any confusion later. That might be an HTTP request containing a textual value of *2020-12-20*, which is then parsed as a `java.time.LocalDate` and stored in a database in a field of type *DATE*. It's absolutely possible to write an application that works properly but uses a different date and time concept for those three layers, but it's very confusing. Of course, I've picked a really simple example there, but life doesn't always work that cleanly.

HANDLING IMPEDANCE MISMATCHES

When we're using a good date and time library for the core of our application, it's not uncommon to find that the database doesn't have the same rich set of types or that the frontend code might have a slightly different rich set of types. To continue with the example above, suppose we're able to pass the user-selected date nicely as textual date representation, we work with it in our code as a `LocalDate`, but then, we have to store it in a database whose only date and time-related data type is a timestamp. What should we do? There are multiple options here and no cut-and-dried right answer.

The first option is to convert to the concept that is provided by the database. In our case, we could decide to convert the `LocalDate` into the `Instant` of *midnight at the start of the given date in UTC*. This has the benefit that you can use other date and time-related functionality within the database and is easily used by other code, but it could lead to the impression that it would be valid to start instants that don't represent midnight UTC on any particular date.

The second option is to use a text-based field instead. For example, the date could be stored in the same way it's being transmitted from the frontend as *2020-12-20*. This makes it clearer that it's genuinely just a date, and if we use the ISO format shown in the example (year-month-day), then it's still easily sortable. On the other hand, it may well be stored less efficiently in the database and harder to use in queries.

The third option is to use a numeric field with a well-known meaning. For example, you could represent the date as *the number of days since January 1, 1970*. This may well be efficient in both storage and querying, but would require more complex code in every system that uses the database directly, and also makes it hard to understand the data with database access tools, such as SQL Server Management Studio.

> **NOTE** Try to convert incoming data into the preferred in-memory data type as early as you can, and convert outgoing data into the destination type as late as you can. This minimizes how much of your code needs to deal with an inconsistent representation. This is also somewhere that the *don't repeat yourself* (DRY) principle is important; the conversion code itself should be centralized to avoid any inconsistency in how the conversions take place.

This sort of impedance mismatch is reasonably common, but it's not the only time that effort is required in terms of converting between concepts at system boundaries.

APPLICATION-SPECIFIC CONCEPTS

Occasionally, we may find that one of the natural application concepts doesn't map cleanly to one of the standard concepts described earlier or represented in the library or database we're using. One example might be *financial quarter* with details that depend on the precise accounting scheme that the company in question uses. This sort of custom concept should be fairly rare, but it's good to be aware of the possibility of it happening and planning to handle it accordingly.

As before, consistency is important here. When the new concept is identified, it's worth encapsulating it in a fashion that feels idiomatic to the library you're using. Include whatever conversions are relevant, design appropriate textual representations, and work out how you want to represent the concept within storage systems.

There's a tradeoff to be found in terms of how early you put this into action. The earlier you work on encapsulating the new concept, the more flexibility you will have in its design, and the fewer headaches you'll have converting existing code to use the new representation. On the other hand, if you make all the decisions based on a single example of the concept's use, you may find you overfit the design to that example, resulting in a design that doesn't meet the requirements of later use cases. One way of trying to mitigate these risks is to actively look for other examples when you encounter the first one. You don't need to design every aspect of the future features that might use the data, but you can at least think about what operations you might need and any constraints.

One aspect of an effective encapsulation is to promote build testability into the design from the start. This doesn't just affect custom concepts though; it's worth thinking about testing throughout your codebase.

7.3.2   *Improving testability by avoiding defaults*

As we discussed earlier when thinking about our online shopping item return policy, it's often useful to give lots of examples within requirements documents. Those examples are then ideal candidates to turn into unit tests but only if your code can be tested in a reasonable fashion. Some libraries don't make this as easy as we might like, but this is one area where it's easy to workaround that deficiency by maintaining some discipline.

Let's look at one concrete example, where simple-looking code has a lot of hidden assumptions. (This uses classes in the java.util and java.text packages; I'm pleased to say that java.time at least addresses two of the issues here.)

```
String now = DateFormat.getDateInstance().format(new Date());
```

That one line of code hides multiple decisions because the platform designers thought it was useful to make those decisions implicit. It's also hard to test, presumably because testability wasn't high on the list of priorities when designing this:

- It uses the system clock, which means we can't test what will happen at specific instants in time.
- It converts the current instant in time into the system time zone, which makes it hard to test how code would react in different time zones.
- It uses the default calendar system of the default locale.
- It uses the date format of the default locale.

Those assumptions do make life easier if you don't need to test this code and you're writing a desktop application where the current culture and time zone may well be the ones you want to use. For any other situation, you should avoid code like this. We'll go into the string formatting more later on, but we'll start by looking at the first three aspects.

USING AN EXISTING CLOCK ABSTRACTION

Modern date and time libraries often abstract the concept of a clock already, but even if they don't, you can do so. The java.time package has a `Clock` abstract class that provides a time zone as well as a *current instant in time* service. Noda Time has the `IClock` interface with a single `GetCurrentInstant()` method. Both provide ways of obtaining instances for test purposes. Any time your code needs to know the current instant, we recommend using dependency injection to make a clock available and use that, rather than any approaches that will always use the system clock.

In case it's not obvious why this is needed for testing, let's look at an artificially simple example. Suppose we want to create a class that is able to tell whether the current instant in time is within one minute of some target instant. In real code we'd normally make the target flexible using a `Duration` parameter on construction, but we'll keep it hardcoded for simplicity for now. We can write pretty simple code that uses the system clock, as shown in the following listing.

Listing 7.1 An untestable `OneMinuteTarget` class

```
public final class OneMinuteTarget {
  private static final Duration ONE_MINUTE = Duration.ofMinutes(1);
  private final Instant minInclusive;
  private final Instant maxInclusive;

  public OneMinuteTarget(@Nonnull Instant target) {
    minInclusive = target.minus(ONE_MINUTE);
    maxInclusive = target.plus(ONE_MINUTE);
  }                                                    This line makes
                                                       the code hard
  public boolean isWithinOneMinuteOfTarget() {         to test.
    Instant now = Instant.now();              ◁─────┘
    return now.compareTo(minInclusive) >= 0 && now.compareTo(maxInclusive) <= 0;
  }
}
```

But how do we test that code? I would want to test five scenarios:

  1 The current instant is more than one minute before the target instant.
  2 The current instant is exactly one minute before the target instant.
  3 The current instant is less than a minute before and less than a minute after the target instant.
  4 The current instant is exactly one minute after the target instant.
  5 The current instant is more than one minute after the target instant.

With the code above, we can't test this cleanly. We could reasonably write code for tests 1, 3, and 5 because we can make reasonable assumptions about how quickly our tests will run, but we can't make sure the system clock itself is *exactly* one minute before or after the target instant. We can find out when the test starts executing, but we don't know how much time will pass between then and the call to `Instant.now()` within the method we're testing. If we inject a `Clock` in the constructor, however, the code becomes testable, as shown in the following listing.

Listing 7.2 A testable equivalent of listing 7.1, using `java.time.Clock`

```
public final class OneMinuteTarget {
  private static final Duration ONE_MINUTE = Duration.ofMinutes(1);
  private final Clock clock;                  ◁─┐  The clock we will consult
  private final Instant minInclusive;            whenever we need the
  private final Instant maxInclusive;            current instant
```

```
public OneMinuteTarget(@Nonnull Clock clock, @Nonnull Instant target) {
    this.clock = clock;                              ◄──┐  Retain the caller-provided
    minInclusive = target.minus(ONE_MINUTE);            │  clock for later use.
    maxInclusive = target.plus(ONE_MINUTE);
}
                                                    ┌──  Replace the untestable
public boolean isWithinOneMinuteOfTarget() {        │    static method with a
    Instant now = clock.instant();           ◄──────┘    clock method call.
    return now.compareTo(minInclusive) >= 0 && now.compareTo(maxInclusive) <= 0;
}
}
```

Now, we can easily write tests for as many different situations as we want. Parameterized tests are often useful in date and time work, as shown in the following listing.

Listing 7.3   Testing a `current-time-sensitive` class using `Clock.fixed`

```
class OneMinuteTargetTest {                     ┌─  Specify the values
    @ParameterizedTest                          │   we want to test.
    @ValueSource(ints = {-61, 61})       ◄──────┘
    void outsideTargetInterval(int secondsFromTargetToClock) {
        Instant target = Instant.ofEpochSecond(10000);    ◄──┐  Create an arbitrary
        Clock clock = Clock.fixed(                            │  target instant.
            target.plusSeconds(secondsFromTargetToClock),
            ZoneOffset.UTC);                              ◄──────
        OneMinuteTarget subject = new OneMinuteTarget(clock, target);
        assertFalse(subject.isWithinOneMinuteOfTarget());       Construct a clock
    }                                                           with time relative
                                                                to the target.
    @ParameterizedTest
    @ValueSource(ints = {-60, -30, 60})
    void withinTargetInterval(int secondsFromTargetToClock) {
        Instant target = Instant.ofEpochSecond(10000);
        Clock clock = Clock.fixed(
            target.plusSeconds(secondsFromTargetToClock),
            ZoneOffset.UTC);
        OneMinuteTarget subject = new OneMinuteTarget(clock, target);
        assertTrue(subject.isWithinOneMinuteOfTarget());
    }
}
```

Here we've used two separate methods: one to test times that are outside the target interval and another to test times that are inside the target interval. Given that the methods only differ in their parameterized values and whether they call `assertFalse` or `assertTrue`, you could choose to have a single method, which is also parameterized on the expected result. The exact design of the tests is beyond the scope of this chapter, but the important point is that it's easy to test code when you control the passage of time.

INTRODUCING YOUR OWN CLOCK ABSTRACTION

If you're using a date and time library that doesn't have a suitable abstraction already, just create your own—ideally in a library that you can reuse throughout not only this application but any other application that uses the same date and time library. It's up to you whether you keep it as a pure *what is the current instant?* abstraction (like Noda Time) or whether you include a time zone (like java.time). Typically, the code is split into three types:

- The abstract class or interface that most of your code depends on.
- A singleton implementation that uses the system clock.
- A fake implementation that allows the caller to set the instant, either on construction or afterwards. You may choose to expose this in a dedicated testing package to explicitly prevent production code from taking a dependency on it.

Just to make this concrete, imagine that `java.time` *didn't* provide a clock abstraction or that we wanted to use one that was restricted to the current instant, instead of including the time zone aspect. We could define our own `InstantClock` interface, as shown in the following listing.

Listing 7.4 Introducing our own Instant-oriented clock interface

```
public interface InstantClock {
  Instant getCurrentInstant();
}
```

Then, we can implement this with a `SystemInstantClock` singleton.

Listing 7.5 Implementing `InstantClock` with a system clock singleton

```
public final class SystemInstantClock implements InstantClock {
  private static final SystemInstantClock instance =
      new SystemInstantClock();

  private SystemInstantClock() {}        ← Prevent instantiation elsewhere.

  public static SystemInstantClock getInstance() {    ← Public method to
    return instance;                                    access the singleton
  }                                                     instance

  public Instant getCurrentInstant() {
    return Instant.now();        ← Delegate to Instant.now(),
  }                                which uses the system
}                                  clock.
```

Finally, we can create a fake for testing purposes, as shown in the following listing.

Listing 7.6 Implementing `InstantClock` with a fake for testing purposes

```
public final class FakeInstantClock implements InstantClock {
  private final Instant currentInstant;

  public FakeInstantClock(@Nonnull Instant currentInstant) {
    this.currentInstant = currentInstant;
  }
```

```
public Instant getCurrentInstant() {
  return currentInstant;
}
}
```

There are details you could definitely change here, of course. For example, you could define a static method in the interface to obtain instances of the fake and system clocks, keeping those classes themselves private within the interface. Or you could provide the FakeInstantClock with an option to automatically advance the clock by a particular duration each time the getCurrentInstant() method is called. The important aspect is how you use the clock to avoid untestable production code.

There's little commentary in the previous code because it's so simple. You might be tempted to think it's so simple that it can't provide much benefit, but the difference in testability is enormous.

> **NOTE** You may wonder why we've bothered providing a fake clock here at all. It's easy to mock a single-method interface, after all. We find that mocks are very valuable for *interaction* testing, where you care exactly when and how many times interface methods are called, but that's rarely useful for clocks. Instead, we just want to provide them with the data they should return later, and fakes are great for that. You can use a mock for that if you want, but we tend to find a dedicated fake implementation is simpler to use, and it decouples your test code from any particular mocking library.

Having removed one implicit source of information with a clock, let's do something similar for time zones.

AVOIDING IMPLICIT USE OF THE SYSTEM TIME ZONE

While support for a clock abstraction in date and time libraries is somewhat variable, I'd expect any modern date and time library to have a type representing a time zone. However, you may find there are plenty of methods that still implicitly use the system time zone, which leads to the same problems in testability. You really don't want to have to write tests that change the system time zone, run your production code, then reset the time zone back to what it was before. It's far better to just tell your code which time zone it should operate in, even if you expect it to always use the system time zone in production.

While you *can* write two overloads (either of the method in question or the constructor of the relevant type), one of which accepts a time zone and the other of which always uses the system time zone, this can lead to code that has a hidden dependency on the system time zone. By the time you're three or four levels of indirection away from that constructor or method, it may not be immediately obvious that you're doing anything that needs a time zone at all. If you're always explicit about it, you can't be surprised.

That surprise aspect is something to watch out for when calling code you aren't responsible for, too. That might be code in the date and time library itself or another external dependency. Again, it may take a little thought to work out that time zones are even involved in a particular operation or that the code might use the system time zone by default.

To go back to our returns policy example, we might have a method to compute the final return date for an item in an order. The requirements document already talks about a time zone, so it's obvious that one will be required, but that doesn't mean we need to supply it ourselves. Two pieces of information are required for the computation:

- The instant at which the item shipped from the warehouse
- The time zone of the delivery address for the item

The time zone is already determined by the context in which we'll be performing the operation, so we don't need to provide it in a method that asks for an order item's final return date.

When we come to write the code, however, it's worth thinking about simplicity of testing again. It's easy to specify those two pieces of information in a test. It may take a bit more effort to come up with a complete order containing items. We can simplify our unit tests by writing a method that only takes those two parameters and then call it with the shipping instant and the delivery time zone. We don't want to make this method fully public, but we just need it to be sufficiently visible for test purposes.

That leaves us with two methods in our `OrderItem` class: a trivial public one and a more complex internal one, as shown in the following listing. (We'll come back to the actual implementation later.)

Listing 7.7 Simplifying testing for a complex scenario

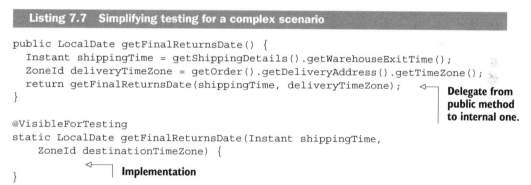

```
public LocalDate getFinalReturnsDate() {
  Instant shippingTime = getShippingDetails().getWarehouseExitTime();
  ZoneId deliveryTimeZone = getOrder().getDeliveryAddress().getTimeZone();
  return getFinalReturnsDate(shippingTime, deliveryTimeZone);   ⟵  Delegate from
}                                                                    public method
                                                                     to internal one.

@VisibleForTesting
static LocalDate getFinalReturnsDate(Instant shippingTime,
    ZoneId destinationTimeZone) {

                   ⟵    Implementation
}
```

If you wanted to put all the logic for returns in a single place, you could move the complex one there, of course, away from the `OrderItem` class. Either way, the important aspect is the method signatures:

- Within the method that will use the time zone directly, we already have one, so it's obvious which one to use.
- Anywhere you need to call that method, you have to *provide* one, so it's unlikely that we'll accidentally end up using the system time zone.

When it comes to spotting code that might use the system time zone by default, it's a good idea to keep an eye out for overloads. If you call a method that accepts a time zone in one of its overloads, but you're not providing one as an argument, check carefully which time zone will be used by default. Even if it's the one you want to use, your code will be clearer if you're explicit about it. There's one more aspect related to system defaults that's worth mentioning and that will lead us into the bigger topic of textual representations.

AVOIDING IMPLICIT LOCALE OR CULTURE ASSUMPTIONS

Internationalization, localization, and globalization (sometimes called i18n, l10n, and g11n) are huge topics, and we're not going to cover them in detail here. For the purposes of date and time work, we need to be aware that the locale of a user can affect two aspects of code: the default calendar system and the default text format used to represent dates and times.

While we've mostly replaced the system clock for testability, rather than because we expect it to do the wrong thing, the system locale is similar to the system time zone: we really don't want to assume that the locale we want to work in is the same as the locale for the system.

A lot of the time, we actually want to avoid doing anything culture specific. As we discussed earlier, most business software only needs to use the Gregorian calendar system, even if some users will talk in terms of a different calendar system in their personal life. Likewise, text formats should be irrelevant for most of our code in the same way that we perform arithmetic with numbers without considering whether they're *hex numbers* or *decimal numbers*.

We don't have much in the way of specific *coding* recommendations here. It's more a matter of knowing the libraries you're using well enough to be aware of any time that you might accidentally find yourself calling culture-sensitive methods. Here, you may want to lean on the defaults a bit more, for calendar systems at least. If the library uses the Gregorian calendar system by default, and that's all you need to support, most people will probably find the code more readable to just go with that default, rather than explicitly specifying the Gregorian calendar system everywhere. If, on the other hand, the default is to use the default calendar for the system locale, I would recommend being explicit in the call.

In terms of textual representations, there's more to consider than *just* cultural assumptions. Let's dive in.

7.3.3   *Representing date and time values in text*

Working with date and time data using a well-abstracted library that does all the difficult work for us and attempts to protect us from mistakes is great while we're working in memory, but we often need to represent date and time values as text—sometimes for diagnostic purposes (such as logging and debugging), sometimes to transmit data between different machines (such as Javascript in a web browser making a request to a server), and sometimes to display to users. It's surprisingly easy to go wrong at this point in various different ways. Like so much of this chapter, this section is more about providing questions for you to ask yourself than it is about one perfect approach that's appropriate in all situations. Let's start off with a topic that sounds almost philosophical: when we have a text representation, what does that *mean*?

AVOIDING CONFUSION BETWEEN TEXT AND TRUTH

When we see a string with some date and time information in it, it's not always clear exactly what's being represented. More worryingly, it's not always obvious that it's not clear what's being represented; we can come to incorrect conclusions simply by inferring too much.

One of the most obvious examples of this is with the `java.util.Date` class. We've already recommended against using this class, but its text representation is a useful teaching aid in terms of what *not* to do. Take this line of code:

```
System.out.println(new Date());
```

On my machine, right now, that prints out *Sun Dec 27 14:21:05 GMT 2020*. Leaving aside the fact that `Date` is clearly a misleading name and that it's implicitly using the system clock, let's see what we might infer from this.

- The value includes a not-quite-time-zone abbreviation: GMT. That suggests the value itself is time-zone aware.
- The value includes a day of week, abbreviated month name and a year. We *might* infer that the value is calendar-system aware.
- The value only goes as far as seconds. Does that mean we happened to call the `Date` constructor exactly at the turn of a second, or has it lost information? We can't easily tell.

The first of these bullet points is the most infuriating one. There are many, many Stack Overflow questions asking how to convert a `java.util.Date` to a different time zone, and I can understand why. Really, the `Date` class represents an instant in time with millisecond precision. It doesn't have an associated time zone *or* calendar system. The `toString()` method always uses the Gregorian calendar system and the system default time zone, but those aren't part of the value itself. The month and day names are not localized.

The use of the system default time zone causes a lot of confusion here, but even a more sensible `toString()` implementation could still cause confusion. Suppose instead it used an ISO-8601 representation, so the same value might be represented as *2020-12-27T14:21:05.123Z*, and you'd get the same result on any machine in the world (assuming the system clock reported the same value, of course). Unless you already *know* what's being represented, it's still unclear. We don't know the precision, and we don't know whether the *Z* means that every value will be expressed in UTC or whether the type of data being represented can include different offsets or time zones. We don't even know whether the type of data being represented could use different calendar systems.

If this all sounds like doom and gloom, please take heart. The aim isn't to discourage you from ever working with text representations—it's to encourage you to be aware of the limitations. Most importantly, you should be aware of the type of data being represented, ideally as one of the concepts listed earlier, or a combination of those concepts (such as a "date and time with a UTC offset"). What precision is available, and is this representation meant to be lossless? What do you need to know if you want to parse a value like this? Do you know the *exact* format?

One scenario to be particularly aware of is what your debugger shows you. Depending on the text format being used, it's entirely possible for the debugger to display the values of two variables as the same text representation but also show that those values aren't equal to each other. This isn't unique to working in the date and time domain—floating point numbers, and even plain strings, can suffer the same pitfalls. Just be aware that what you can see in the debugger may not be the whole truth. Having warned you about the perils of reading too much into text representations, next we'll look at some areas where conversions can creep in and cause problems without being needed at all.

AVOIDING UNNECESSARY TEXT CONVERSIONS

This sounds obvious, but it's worth avoiding conversions to or from text forms wherever you can. I've seen a lot of code converting date and time values into strings to achieve goals that aren't fundamentally text-oriented at all:

- Including the value in a database query, either directly in the SQL or as a parameter
- Converting between different representations, either between types in the same library (such as getting a LocalDate from a LocalDateTime) or between different libraries
- Deliberately losing information, such as formatting a LocalDateTime value without including the fractions of a second, then parsing again as a way of truncating to second granularity

In all of these cases, introducing text conversions has multiple downsides:

- It obscures what you're trying to achieve by doing it in a roundabout way.
- It introduces the risk of accidental loss of precision or other bugs.
- It's almost always slower than a more direct approach.

Whenever you find yourself performing a text conversion, it's worth considering whether this is inherently a text-oriented task. If it's not, consider whether there's a better approach. It may take a bit more research, but it's likely to be clearer and perform better once you've got there. Assuming we've already gone through this due diligence step and decided we really, really want to perform a text conversion, there are still a few pitfalls to avoid.

DESIGNING EFFECTIVE TEXT REPRESENTATIONS

I appreciate that it may feel like we're putting too much effort into this area. After all, it's easy to just call toString() or the equivalent on your platform and be done with it. But just taking a little bit longer to consider the desired result carefully can make a big difference.

You may well want to centralize all your text handling within any given application; decide on what you want the results to look like for each concept and each audience, document it, write the code once, then call it everywhere. That will ensure you are consistent throughout the application, which can avoid some frustrating diagnostic sessions. You still need to make sure you use the right centralized option in each case, of course, and that means being clear about the audience.

Any time you convert a date and time value into a string, you should consider what will read that string later. Most situations fall into one of three categories, as shown in figure 7.9:

- Text to display to a user
- Text to be parsed by code on another system
- Text to help a developer diagnostically

These three categories have different motivations and requirements. You might expect users and developers to be similar, but typically, developer-oriented messages (in logs and exceptions) look more like machine-readable representations.

Figure 7.9   **Different text for different audiences**

User-visible text should usually take the user's locale into account, at least in terms of preferred date format. The most obvious example of this is in the numeric date formats used. The United States uses a month/day/year format, whereas most of the rest of the world uses a day/month/year format. Beyond the ordering, different locales use different date separators, different time separators, and different longer date formats (that might include the month name, for example). It's almost never a good idea to try to achieve a precise format here; most libraries allow you to specify a general format, such as *short time format* or *long date format*, and they will then do the right thing.

The variability here means it's almost never a good idea to try to *parse* text that has been formatted for users. It's possible you'll need to do that for screen-scraping purposes, but that's just one more in a long list of reasons to try to avoid screen scraping, if possible. If you *must* parse user-visible text, try to find a way of specifying the locale to whatever is creating it. If you don't know whether 6/7/2020 is *July 6, 2020* or *June 7, 2020*, it is very hard to do the right thing without error-prone and complex heuristics.

Text that is machine-readable is a different matter, however. When you're creating text for another machine to read, you should use a standard format as far as humanly possible. For date and time values, that almost always means using an ISO-8601-compatible format. Even within ISO-8601, there are multiple formats available. For example, a date and time value half way through June 7, 2020 at 3:54:23 p.m. could be represented as *20200607T155423.500, 2020-06-07 15:54:23,5*, or multiple other variants. When choosing between these, my general recommendations are

- Where space allows, including date and time separators (dash and colon, respectively) makes values a lot easier to read. Bear in mind that colons can't appear in Windows filenames though, and they can be awkward in colon-separated paths in Unix too.
- The optional *T* between the date and time can make the value slightly harder to read, but it helps to keep the values together. This is particularly important if the context contains multiple space-separated values.
- Although the fractional-second separator can be a comma or a dot, and comma is notionally preferred in ISO-8601, the practical reality is that dot is far more prevalent.
- Specifying fractions of a second to a fixed length can be wasteful of space, but it can help readability if you end up with columns of multiple values. If you choose to use a variable length, you might want to stick to millisecond, microsecond, or nanosecond precision, using 3, 6, or 9 digits of subsecond precision, respectively. Values with (say) 4 digits after the dot or comma look a little odd.

You may be surprised to see considerations for (human) readability here. After all, these are values intended to be parsed by code. But reality is that developers are likely to end up looking at text files, JSON requests, or wherever else the text ends up. You sometimes need to balance space concerns, which affect every value with readability concerns that might only be relevant for one value in a million—but where the cost of hard-to-read data is very high.

This leads to the final category of audience: developers. Typically, a developer-oriented text representation should be culture neutral, like the machine-readable representation, but you may want to add more information that isn't *strictly* necessary. I would recommend starting off with a simple ISO-8601 representation and adding more information where necessary. For example, if you're representing a date and time and a UTC offset, you might want to include both the local time and the UTC instant, so you can compare values more easily. Occasionally, the most appropriate developer representation may have *less* information than normal. For example, you might be displaying log entries for a currently-running, short-lived app and decide not to include the date part of the instant to avoid clutter. Once you've decided how you want to represent a value in text form, the final step is writing the code to do it.

LEANING ON LIBRARIES

There's a golden rule when it comes to text handling with date and time values (and, indeed, most other text representations): don't do it yourself. All worthwhile date and time libraries have both formatting and parsing capabilities, and they're much more likely to get it right than you are because that's their job.

There's *one* exception to this, which is where you've got a representation that is sufficiently awkward that the library can't handle it directly without a bit of text manipulation first. For example, suppose you have to parse text such as *Dec 28th 2020* into a date. That's far from an ideal representation to parse, but sometimes you may not have any viable alternative. Depending on the library you're using, it may not be able to handle the ordinal part (the *th* of *28th*). In that situation, it's best to perform minimal manipulation to get the text into a parsable format, such as *Dec 28 2020*, and then use the library to parse the value as normal.

It's worth reading the text handling documentation for whatever library you're using carefully, particularly if you need to specify a custom format. Don't assume that format strings mean exactly the same thing on all platforms. Most of the date and time questions on Stack Overflow around unexplained date and time parsing problems are due to developers not paying enough attention to their format patterns, particularly around *m* and *M* (for *minutes* and *months*) or *h* and *H* (for *12-hour hour-of-day* and *24-hour hour-of-day*).

As we discussed earlier, it's generally worth centralizing at least some aspects of your date and time text handling. If you find yourself specifying the same format string in multiple places for the same purpose, it's definitely a good idea to remove that duplication. Depending on the library you're using, the centralization could consist of some mix of

- Exposing common, immutable, thread-safe formatting objects (such as `java.time.format.DateTimeFormatter` in `java.time` or `NodaTime.Text.LocalDatePattern` in Noda Time)
- Exposing methods to perform the formatting and parsing
- Exposing the format strings themselves (such as `"yyyy-MM-dd'T'HH:mm:ss'Z'"` for an ISO-8601 format for an instant in time with precision down to just a second)

The last of these is simple but not ideal in terms of type safety; you could easily end up using the wrong format string with nothing to warn you that you're trying to format a date as if it's a date and time. It's still a lot better than writing the same format string in multiple places though.

For much of this section we've assumed that we're able to design the text format ourselves, leading to a useful representation of the natural concept we're modelling. What about when that isn't the case?

PARSING TO THE CONCEPT IN THE TEXT FORMAT

Sometimes we don't get to control the format of the data we receive, and sometimes that means we have to work with some unfortunate choices. That can lead to a situation in which the semantic meaning of a value doesn't match the format used to represent it.

Let's take a somewhat extreme example. Suppose we're writing an alarm clock application, and we want to integrate with a third-party service that allows users to create alarms to be used by multiple applications. The alarms could be daily, or they could be for a specific date. Those feel like they're somewhat different values—one is just a time of day (which we would want to represent in our application as a `java.time.LocalTime`), and the other might be a date and time (`java.time.LocalDateTime`). We might expect those to have different representations in the API, but they may not. We may receive JSON like the following:

```
{
  "alarms": [
    {
      "dateTime": "2021-04-01T07:00:00",
      "type": "once",
      "label": "April Fool prank"
    },
    {
      "dateTime": "1970-01-01T06:00:00",
      "type": "daily",
      "label": "Wake up"
    }
  ]
}
```

Here the time-of-day part is represented within a full date and time, using a date of January 1, 1970 as information that can just be thrown away, as shown in figure 7.10.

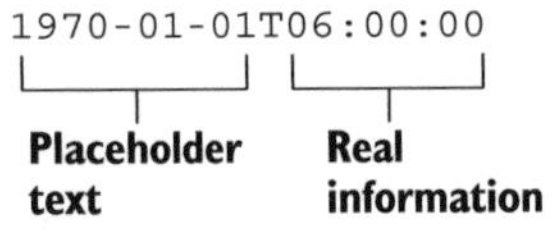

1970-01-01T06:00:00

Placeholder   Real
text   information

Figure 7.10   Text values can be a mixture of placeholder text and real information.

Assuming we want to represent the time-of-day as a `java.time.LocalTime` in our application, there are two ways we could do this:

- We could parse the value as a `LocalTime` directly with a custom format that includes a literal *1970-01-01T* before the time part.
- We could parse the value as a `LocalDateTime` and then obtain the time-of-day part of the value (which is trivial via the `toLocalTime()` method).

I would recommend using the latter approach. It separates the two operations of *converting the value from text to its natural representation* and *obtaining the representation we actually want*. It also allows us to model the JSON directly as a class should we wish to with a `dateTime` property of type `LocalDateTime`. The JSON can be parsed without worrying about how much of the `dateTime` value will be useful, and then we can convert into potentially different classes based on the `type` value. The two different conversions (one JSON to object and the other object to object) can be tested independently.

Anyone reading the code for the JSON model and looking at some sample JSON text will see a direct correspondence between the two.

That's all we're going to say about text representations of date and time values. It's one of those topics where there's always more to learn, but the guidance above should help to approach any issues you face in a productive way. Our final topic regarding actual code doesn't directly impact the behavior of the code at all as far as the computer is concerned, but it can make all the difference for humans.

7.3.4 Explaining code with comments

There are plenty of opinion pieces on the internet suggesting that commenting your code (in terms of implementation) is an admission of failure. While I can see where those views come from, they're too extreme for me. I certainly support clarifying the code using carefully considered variable names, refactoring to keep each method short and so on. But that's typically about *what* the code is doing rather than *why*. Where there are corner cases that may not be obvious to the reader, comments can be vital to explain why an apparently simpler approach hasn't been taken. This is particularly relevant in date and time work. Comments can also be helpful when writing tests, explaining the purpose of each test case. Let's go back to our getFinalReturnsDate method, implementing it and explaining the implementation at the same time, as shown in the following listing.

Listing 7.8 Providing copious comments to explain code

```
/**
 * Computes the final date on which this item can be returned in the
 * simple "click a button" workflow. This is based on the date on
 * which the item is shipped from the warehouse, from the perspective
 * of the delivery location. The returns period (currently three
 * months; see {@link #RETURNS_PERIOD}) is added to the shipping date
 * to obtain the final returns date. When adding the returns period,
 * if the day-of-month goes beyond the end of the resulting month,
 * the result should be the start of the following month.
 *
 * @param shippingTime The instant at which the item shipped from
 *     the warehouse.
 * @param destinationTimeZone The time zone where the item will be
 *     delivered.
 * @return The final date on which this item can be returned.
 */
@VisibleForTesting
static LocalDate getFinalReturnsDate(Instant shippingTime,
    ZoneId destinationTimeZone) {
  LocalDate shippingDateAtDestination =
      shippingTime.atZone(destinationTimeZone).toLocalDate();
  LocalDate candidateResult = shippingDateAtDestination.plus(RETURNS_PERIOD);
  // LocalDate.plus truncates if the day-of-month overflows. For example,
  // March 31st + 1 month is April 30th, not May 1st in java.time. Our
  // requirements say we need to move to the next day in such cases
```

```
            // instead. The simplest way of checking for this is to subtract the
            // returns period and see whether we get back to the original shipping
            // date. If we don't, we know there's been an overflow and we need
            // to add a day.
            return
                candidateResult.minus(RETURNS_PERIOD).equals(shippingDateAtDestination)
                    ? candidateResult
                    : candidateResult.plusDays(1);
        }
```

Even though this is a package-private method (and would be completely private if we didn't want to use it directly for testing), the Javadoc is useful for giving the details of exactly what this method does. The comment within the implementation explains why we're subtracting the returns period from the result: that's how we test for the overflow situation.

Obviously, tastes vary when it comes to the verbosity of comments. The comments here could be made a bit shorter, depending on what the team involved finds clearest. Maybe the Javadoc could just link to the public method declaration for example, although it wouldn't be appropriate for that to refer to the private RETURNS_PERIOD field. If we removed the Javadoc entirely, we'd still have the requirements documents to fall back on, but those won't explain why the method is implemented in the way that it is. The implementation comment is valuable information that isn't captured anywhere else, and I'd be wary of removing that entirely.

Some developers who dislike comments point to tests as a way of providing information, and I'd agree. With the right tests in place, we'd be unlikely to accidentally break the corner case around the day-of-month overflowing. But when reading code, you don't really want to have to try something different and see what breaks to understand why it's been written the way it has. Speaking of the tests, let's look at some tests for this method in the following listing.

Listing 7.9   Providing comments in tests to explain corner cases

```
public class OrderItemTest {
    private static Stream<Arguments> provideGetFinalReturnsDateArguments() {
        return Stream.of(
            // Simple case: UTC to make the date obvious, and no overflow.
            Arguments.of("2021-01-01T00:00:00Z", "Etc/UTC", "2021-04-01"),
            // America/New_York is UTC-5 in winter, so shipping time is on 2020-12-31.
            Arguments.of("2021-01-01T00:00:00Z", "America/New_York", "2021-03-31"),
            // Day-of-month overflow, example specified in requirements
            //document.
            Arguments.of("2020-11-30T12:00:00Z", "Etc/UTC", "2021-03-01"),
            // Check destination time zone usage: America/New_York moves from
            // UTC-5 to UTC-4 at 2021-03-14 07:00:00Z. First test below ships
            // on 2021-03-13, and the second ships on 2021-03-15 despite being
            // exactly 24 hours apart.
            Arguments.of("2021-03-14T04:30:00Z", "America/New_York", "2021-06-13"),
            Arguments.of("2021-03-15T04:30:00Z", "America/New_York", "2021-06-15"));
    }
```

```
@ParameterizedTest
@MethodSource("provideGetFinalReturnsDateArguments")
void getFinalReturnsDate(String shippingText, String zoneText,
    String expectedText) {
    Instant shippingInstant = Instant.parse(shippingText);
    ZoneId zoneId = ZoneId.of(zoneText);
    LocalDate expectedDate = LocalDate.parse(expectedText);
    LocalDate actualDate = OrderItem.getFinalReturnsDate(
        shippingInstant, zoneId);
    assertEquals(expectedDate, actualDate);
  }
}
```

This is a single test method with five parameterized tests. The comment above each set of arguments for the test method describes what aspect of the method the test is interested in. We could have written five different test methods with descriptive names instead, but parameterization tends to be more compact and versatile. In some test frameworks, we could provide a description for each argument list that would be reported on failure; it's worth exploring what's possible with the test framework you're using. The exact mechanism for describing the purpose of each test isn't important, but the presence of the description is.

Another point to note about these tests is that they use strings for the parameters to the test method, which are then parsed in the method. That may feel slightly odd after all the advice in this chapter to use the most appropriate data type throughout your code, but it makes the tests significantly simpler to specify in my experience. In the final section in this chapter, we'll take another look at some corner cases you might not otherwise consider.

7.4 Corner cases to specify and test

Everything in this section has been at least *mentioned* earlier, but we've collected the points here as a sort of checklist to think about. These are all areas that regular applications need to be aware of—we're not in the niche landscape of leap seconds, for example. We'll start off with the situation we've just covered in our returns date example: adding a period to a date.

7.4.1 Calendar arithmetic

If you only need to deal with the Gregorian calendar, as most applications do, you can probably just think about four ways in which calendar arithmetic can go wrong:

- Leap years causing February 29 to only occur (roughly) once every four years
- Day-of-month overflow, such as adding a month to March 31st because April 31st doesn't exist
- Expecting operations to be reversible; in general, (date + period) - period doesn't always give a result of date.
- Expecting operation simplification to work; in general, (date + period1) + period2 doesn't always give the same result as date + (period1 + period2).

Just being aware of these oddities is often enough to help you design and test for them. The voting scenario earlier is a fairly common one in that it requires careful consideration between the strategies of *adding a period to a starting date and seeing if the result is in the past* and *subtracting a period from the current date and seeing if the result is before the starting date*. Where the choice is arbitrary, I'd generally recommend performing calendar arithmetic on the fixed aspect (i.e., adding a period to a starting date), as I find it easier to think about and implement.

When it comes to leap years, as well as testing, I'd strongly recommend against ever implementing "is *x* a leap year?" logic yourself. This is something that's firmly in the realm of the date and time library, which you should trust to give the right answer. This is a more general recommendation, in fact, with leap years just being one simple specific example: if you find yourself doing anything particularly fiddly with date and time data, you should take some time to see whether the date and time library you're using already has that functionality covered.

One final part of calendar arithmetic is to consider whether you actually need to do it at all. Often, you *can* work in either instants and durations or civil dates and periods. Consider whether you're really concerned with elapsed time (i.e., suggesting a duration) or the dates that humans will care about (i.e., suggesting periods). All of the rest of the corner cases in this section are around time zones, which probably doesn't come as much of a surprise to anyone who's had to deal with them for significant pieces of code.

7.4.2   *Time zone transitions at midnight*

How would you define *midnight*? There are two obvious answers: *12 o'clock in the morning, also known as 00:00, using the 24 hour clock* or *the time when the date changes*. Those sound like the same thing, but they're not always.

Most time zones that observe daylight saving time change the clocks at 1 a.m. or 2 a.m. local time—but not all. In some cases, the change can skip the hour between 12 a.m. and 1 a.m. or fall back from 1 a.m. to 12 a.m. In that case, the second definition above always occurs exactly once, but the time of 00:00 might happen twice or not at all.

This means if you're trying to represent the whole of a day in a specific time zone, you need to find out when that particular day starts in that time zone. If you assume it will be 00:00, you could end up facing a mountain of exceptions in log files one day, after a daylight saving transition. I learned that the hard way. Check whether the date and time library you're using has a specific call that provides the date and time at the start of this date in a given time zone. If it doesn't, you'll need to check whether or not 00:00 is valid before you use it.

This is just one specific example of having to worry about ambiguous or skipped times. The solution for this case is *usually* to find the start of the day, but that's not the right approach for the general case. Let's think about that now.

7.4.3 *Handling ambiguous or skipped times*

As we saw in our earlier discussion of time zones, any given civil date and time can occur zero times, once, or twice in a specific time zone, due to changes in UTC offset. (These are almost always daylight saving time changes, but sometimes, the standard UTC offset of a time zone can change too.)

This can cause a problem either when a single date and time is specified (e.g., *wake me up at 1:30 a.m. on March 28, 2021, in London*) or when you're working with a recurring event (e.g., *perform a backup at 1:30 a.m. every day*). There's a significant difference between these two in terms of user interaction: if a single date and time is given by the user, you may reasonably be able to prompt the user with more options. If you're dealing with a recurring event, you may need to decide on the action to take on your own. In the backup example, you could decide to start the backup operation the first time that the local time is 1:30 a.m. or later, so you'd perform it at 2 a.m. if the clock skips from 1 a.m. to 2 a.m. or the earlier occurrence of 1:30 a.m. if the clock falls back in the opposite direction. That's not the only option, although it's probably the simplest to understand. What's important is that you anticipate it and make a decision in the requirements and code.

This sort of predicament is reasonably easy to test, at least if you're using a clock abstraction. It's usually worth leaving comments with details of the time zone you're using for testing purposes though, rather than expecting every developer reading the code to know exactly when each time zone has transitions. I'd also recommend using dates in the past for these tests because you, hopefully, have accurate information about the past, whereas the future can change. Let's dig into that now.

7.4.4 *Working with evolving time zone data*

Earlier, we talked about the Windows and IANA time zone databases and how they're updated multiple times per year, as countries change their time zone rules. To be absolutely clear, there isn't a database change every time a country goes from daylight saving time to standard time or vice versa. That kind of predictable change is covered by the rules. Instead, the database changes when the rules themselves change. Examples of changes include

- Countries deciding to *stop* observing daylight saving time
- Countries deciding to *start* observing daylight saving time
- Countries changing when the spring forward and fall back daylight saving time transitions occur
- Countries changing their standard UTC offset

For any individual country, changes are relatively rare (at least in general). But there are many countries in the world, so the database changes several times in a year. Often, multiple changes are batched together, so there isn't one database version per change. Before we talk about the impact of time zone changes on your code, we should pause to consider where your application gets its time zone data from.

SOURCES OF TIME ZONE DATA

The time zone data source varies based on which platform you're using and which library you're using. For example, if you're using java.time, then the Java platform you're using comes with a built-in version of the time zone database, and that can be updated using the TZUpdater tool. Other time zone rule providers can be registered using the `java.time.zone.ZoneRulesProvider` class. Many other platforms will load their time zone data from the operating system, possibly with a way of manually providing a specific version of the data.

If you're writing client-side code that runs in the browser, then the time zone data will be obtained from your users' browsers, unless you use a library that allows you to load a specific set of rules. That can lead to a situation where different users may have different versions of time zone data at the same time, which can obviously complicate matters.

It's well worth researching—and then documenting—the sources of time zone data for your application, remembering that each platform you use may have a different source. (If some of your code runs on a user's browser, some in a serverless Node function, and some in a .NET service, for example, then you need to document all of those sources separately.) How are updates to that data applied, and how much control do you have over that process? Once you've got that context, you can think about how it impacts the data in your application.

STORING DATA THAT IS SENSITIVE TO TIME ZONE CHANGES

Earlier, we talked about discussing the source of any data in your system. It's worth repeating that to limit the scope of this section, partly because that may provide an element of relief. Any timestamps recorded in your system should be recorded as instants in time, and those *don't* depend on time zones. The instant at which a database record was committed, an order was placed, or a user was deleted doesn't depend on any time zone. (It probably does depend on the accuracy of the clock on the system running the code, but that's a separate matter.) In many systems, that accounts for the bulk of date and time data.

You may well convert those instants into local times in a particular time zone elsewhere in your code, but the value that's stored as an instant doesn't need to change. That should remain your source of truth, even if other derived data is stored.

The opposite is often true for user-entered data though, particularly when that data is in the future. Here, the source of truth is the local date and time that the user entered, along with their location or time zone. I frequently see recommendations to store *all* date and time data in UTC, effectively converting everything into instants. For data that's inherently instant-based, that's fine, but it can cause problems in other situations.

The simplest example of this is if a user schedules an event in a particular location. At the time of writing, France still observes daylight savings of an hour in summer, so Paris has an offset of UTC+1 in the winter and UTC+2 in the summer. It's entirely possible—even likely—that in the near future, France will drop daylight saving time entirely and stay on UTC+2 all year round. Let's consider an example with the following timeline, where a user in France is scheduling a meeting:

- January 10, 2021: user schedules a meeting for Friday, December 1, 2023 at 9 a.m. in the gallery Le Coin des Arts in central Paris.
- September 1, 2021: the French government declares that from March 27, 2022 at 1 a.m. UTC, the local time in France will become UTC+2 permanently. (This is the currently-planned date of the spring forward—all later transitions are effectively cancelled.)
- November 27, 2023: our user looks at his schedule for the coming week in the application.

What *should* the user see? This is something that the product owner should decide, but I suspect that in almost all applications, the user would expect to see the meeting as they originally scheduled it: in Paris, on December 1 at 9 a.m. For the rest of this thought experiment, let's assume that's what we want. (It's important not to skip the question in your own application though; this isn't a one-size-fits-all situation.)

Suppose when the user schedules the meeting, the application converts the date and time to UTC, as so many developers advise. In 2021, the time zone data maps 2023-12-01T09:00 in Paris to 2023-12-01T08:00Z (where Z indicates UTC). When the user checks their calendar on November 27, 2023, the application has to perform the reverse mapping, but according to the up-to-date time zone data, it then maps 2023-12-01T08:00Z to 2023-12-01T**10**:00 in Paris, so the user is led to believe their meeting is at 10 a.m. This sequence of events is shown in figure 7.11.

My recommendation is that if you want to preserve what the user told you (the local date and time in Paris), then you should *store* what the user told you (the local time in Paris). I'm aware that sounds trite, but it goes against the often-accepted wisdom.

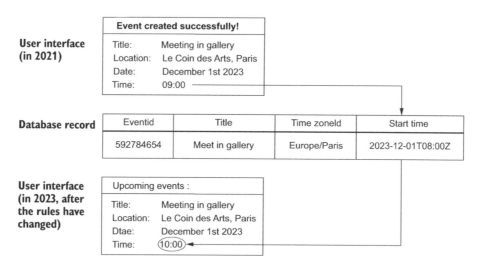

Figure 7.11   Converting to UTC for storage can have negative consequences

Now, just because you store what the user told you doesn't mean that has to be the *only* thing you store. It's often really, really useful to store UTC values because then, you can sort records in a global ordering of when things happen around the world. (For example, if you've stored UTC values, you can tell that 5 a.m. in California happens after 9 a.m. in Paris, on the same date.) This requires you to differentiate between source-of-truth data (what the user told you) and derived data (some other form of the data that is computed from the source-of-truth data to make some use cases simpler).

When you have this distinction between source-of-truth data and derived data, you can recalculate the derived data whenever you want, such as when the time zone data changes. This introduces another aspect of data, of course: the *version* of the time zone data you're using. IANA data is versioned in a simple year-based way: 2020a, 2020b, etc. Windows time zone data isn't versioned as transparently.

If this sounds like it's adding a lot of complexity to things, I agree. We're now storing the local date and time, the time zone ID, the UTC date and time, and the time zone data version, and we need to write an update process to run every time the time zone data changes. It's entirely possible that for many applications, particularly those that usually store data in the past and only occasionally data in the future, the tradeoff between effort and accuracy suggests not worrying too much about this. But it should be a conscious decision with documented reasons.

Countering the myth of *store everything in UTC*

The idea that you should store all date and time data in UTC is a very frequently-repeated myth, even among seasoned developers. Most developers don't consider the possibility of time zone rules changing. You may well hear this in your own conversations, whether in person or on social media. Please play a part in raising awareness about the problems with this approach.

In the above discussion, I've deliberately obscured source-of-truth data and derived data distinction. Did you spot it? We started talking about *in Paris* (because the gallery is in Paris), but we then stored a time zone ID. What about locations that change time zones over time? That may sound far-fetched, but new time zones *do* come into being sometimes, often because of wars. If a country is split in two due to a civil war, for example, the resulting two countries may well choose to observe different local times, so two places that *used* to be in the same time zone no longer are.

Applying the same guidance as above, we should treat the time zone ID as derived data and make sure we store the location as source-of-truth data. Then, when the mapping of location to time zone ID changes, the derived data in the database can change too. Knowing when that mapping changes may be a more nuanced process than detecting a simple change to the IANA time zone data, and the details are likely to depend on what technology you use to perform the mapping in the first place. Going back to tradeoffs, most applications may well decide that handling this sort of change is out of scope. The time zone mapping changes less often than the rules associated with each time zone.

Speaking of problems that don't happen terribly often, and at the risk of scaring you somewhat, let's combine this section with the previous one. We talked about recomputing UTC values from local values when the time zone data changed, and earlier, we talked about some options when it comes to local-to-UTC mapping in situations where the local value is skipped or ambiguous. I happily talked about prompting the user for more information if they entered a *difficult* date and time. Oh, what a simple world that is . . . one where we have the user's attention and can ask them questions. What if we're in a situation in which the user enters an unambiguous date and time *in terms of the time zone data when they enter it*, but that same date and time *becomes* skipped or ambiguous later due to time zone data changes? You then need to make a decision without the user's input. *Maybe* you could send them an email to ask them for clarification, but that's a lot of effort for a rare corner within an already-rare corner case. At least you are now aware of the challenge and can decide what's right for you.

Summary

- Working with date and time information is complex, but is manageable if you apply discipline and the right set of tools.
- Date and time data broadly falls into culture-insensitive *machine time* concepts of instants and durations, and *civil time* concepts of calendar systems, dates, times-of-day, and time zones.
- Calendar arithmetic (such as adding a month to a date) can behave in unexpected ways; it doesn't have the same properties as simple integer addition.
- Most applications don't need to deal with advanced concepts, such as leap seconds and relativity. Scoping your requirements before you start can save a lot of work.
- Date and time product requirements are often ambiguously specified. Pin down exactly how the product should behave with plenty of examples, including corner cases.
- Many developer platforms have multiple date and time libraries available. Take some time to pick one that meets all your requirements and lets you write clear, unambiguous code.
- Apply concepts consistently in your code base, converting between representations only at system boundaries.
- Use a clock abstraction to make code that uses the current date and time testable.
- Avoid implicitly depending on the system time zone or the system culture; where you want to use these, be explicit about it or inject them as dependencies.
- Date and time values can be represented as text in different ways, depending on the context. Consider the audience for the information, and design the text representation accordingly.

- It can sometimes be hard to understand why date and time code is written in a particular way. When you're satisfied that code achieves its goals in the clearest way possible, but it's not obvious why a simpler approach would fail (for example in corner cases), don't be afraid to use comments to explain the *why* of the code.
- Time zone transitions (such as for daylight saving time) lead to local date and time values that are either skipped or ambiguous. Think about (and document and test) how you want to handle problematic values like this.
- Time zone rules change over time. Consider how your application should use updated information and how that can affect existing data, particularly data that refers to the future.
- Converting local values to UTC according to time zone information prior to storage is sometimes appropriate, but it can lose information due to rules changes. Be careful, and don't assume this is a silver bullet!

Leveraging data locality and memory of your machines

This chapter covers
- Data locality in big data processing
- Optimizing join strategies with Apache Spark
- How to reduce shuffling
- Memory vs. disk usage in big data processing

With both streaming and batch processing in big data applications, we often need to use data from multiple sources to get insights and business value. The data locality pattern allows us to move computation to data. Our data can live in the database or the filesystem, and this situation is simple as long as our data fits into the disk or memory of our machines. Processing can be local and fast, but in big data applications, it is not feasible to store large amounts of data on one machine. We need to employ techniques such as partitioning to split the data into multiple machines. Once the data is on multiple physical hosts, it gets harder to gain insights from data that is distributed in locations that are reachable via the network. Joining data in such a scenario is not a trivial task and needs careful planning.

We will follow the process of joining data in such a big data scenario. Before we delve into that though, let's start our chapter by gaining understanding of the main concepts related to big data: data locality.

8.1   *What is data locality?*

Data locality plays a crucial role in processing a nontrivial amount of data. To understand why this concept solves many problems, we will look at a simple system that does not use data locality. Let's imagine we have a /getAverageAge HTTP endpoint that returns the average age of all users managed by the service. Figure 8.1 shows how we can move this data to computation.

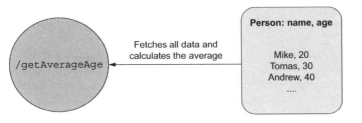

Figure 8.1   **Moving data to computation for the** /getAverageAge **HTTP endpoint**

When the client executes this HTTP call, the service fetches all the data from an underlying data store. This can be a database, file, or anything persistent. Once all the data is transferred to the service, it executes the logic of calculating an average by adding all ages for each person, counting the number of persons, and dividing the sum by the number of persons. Such a value is returned to the end user. It's important to note that only one number is returned.

We can describe this scenario as moving data to computations. There are a couple of important observations to make here. The first one is that we need to fetch all the data, which can be tens of gigabytes. As long as this data fits in the machine's memory that calculates the average, there is no problem. The problem starts when operating on big data sets that can have terabytes or petabytes of data. For such a scenario, transferring all the data to the machine may be complex or not feasible. We could, for example, use a splitting technique and process data in batches. The second important observation to make is that we will need to send and retrieve a lot of data via the network. The I/O operations are the slowest ones in data processing. It involves filesystem reads and blocking because we are transferring a substantial amount of data. There is a nonnegligible probability that some of the network packets will get lost, and we will need to retransmit parts of the data. Finally, we can see that the end user is not interested in any data besides the result or the computation, which is an average.

One of the pros of this solution is its simplicity from the programming perspective, assuming the amount of data we want to process fits in machine memory. Those observations and drawbacks are the main reasons why processing in such a scenario is inverted, and we are moving computations to data.

8.1.1 Moving computations to data

At this point, we know that sending data to computations has a lot of drawbacks, and this may not be feasible for big data sets. Let's solve the same problem presented in the previous section by using a data locality technique.

In this scenario, the end user sees the same /getAverageAge HTTP endpoint responsible for calculating an average. The underlying processing changes a lot. The calculation of an average is simple logic, but still, it involves some coding. We need to extract the age field from every person, add this data, and divide by the count. Big data processing frameworks expose an API that allows engineers to code such transformations and concatenation easily.

Let's assume that we want to use the Java language to code this logic (however, it can be any other language). The logic responsible for such a computation is created in the service, but we need a way to transfer it to the machine that has the actual data. Figure 8.2 illustrates the processing of moving this data.

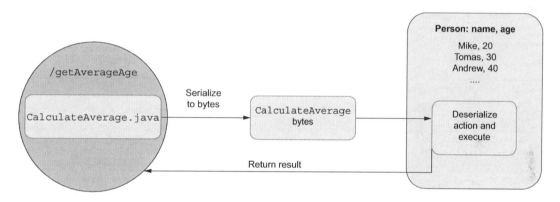

Figure 8.2 Moving computation to data and returning a result

The first step that needs to be done is to serialize the CalculateAverage.java file to bytes. We need this form of representation to be able to send the data easily via a network. The data node (a machine that stores data) needs to have a running process responsible for retrieving the serialized logic.

Next, we transform the bytes (deserialize them) into a form that can be executed on the data node. Most big data frameworks, such as Apache Spark or Hadoop, provide a mechanism for serializing and deserializing the logic. Once the logic is deserialized, it is executed on the data node itself. From the calculated average function's perspective, the logic operates on the data that resides on the local filesystem. There is no need to send any person's data to the service that exposes the HTTP endpoint. When the logic calculates the average successfully, only the resulting number is transferred to the service. The service then returns the data to the end user.

Again, there are important observations to make in this scenario. First, the amount of data we need to transform via a network is small. We need to transform only the serialized function and the resulting number. Because the network and I/O is a bottleneck in such processing, this solution performs substantially better: we turned the processing that was I/O bound into processing that is CPU bound. If we have to speed up the average calculation, we can, for example, increase the number of cores on the data node. For this use case (moving the data to computation), it's harder to speed up the processing because increasing network throughput is not always feasible.

The solution that uses data locality is more complex because we need logic for serializing processing. Such logic may get complicated for more advanced processing. Also, we need a dedicated process that runs on the data node. This process needs to be able to deserialize the data and execute the logic. Fortunately, both steps are implemented and provided by big data frameworks, such as Apache Spark.

Some readers may notice that the same data locality pattern is applied for databases. If you want to calculate the average, you issue a query (e.g., with SQL) that is transferred to a database. Next, the database deserializes the query and executes the logic that uses data locality. These solutions are similar, but big data frameworks give you more flexibility. You can execute the logic on data nodes that contain all kinds of data: Avro, JSON, Parquet, and any other format. You are not tied to a database-specific execution engine.

8.1.2 Scaling processing using data locality

Data locality plays a crucial role in big data processing because it allows us to scale and parallelize the processing easily. Imagine a scenario in which our data stored on the data node doubled. Thus, the total amount of data does not fit the disk space of one node. We cannot store all the data on one physical machine, so we decide to split it into two machines (how the data is split will be covered in the next section).

If we used the technique of moving data to computations, the amount of data we need to transfer via the network would double. It will slow the processing substantially and get even worse if we have more than two data nodes. Figure 8.3 shows how our data would look after splitting our data on two machines.

Scaling and parallelizing the processing while using data locality is fairly easy to achieve. Instead of sending the serialized processing to one data node, we send it to two data nodes. Each of the data nodes will have the process responsible for deserialization of logic and running the processing. Once the processing is complete, the resulting data is sent to the service that coalesces it and returns it to end users.

At this point, we know the benefits of data locality. Next, we need to understand how to split big data into N data nodes. This is essential to understand if we want to operate on big data and gain business value. We will discuss this in the next section.

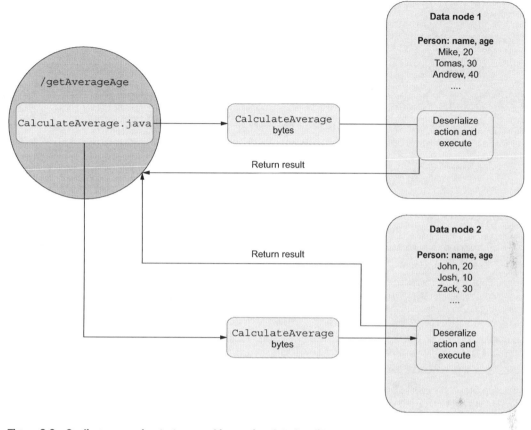

Figure 8.3 Scaling processing to two machines using data locality

8.2   *Data partitioning and splitting data*

In the previous section, we saw that scaling big data processing is easier if we can use the data locality technique. In real-world big data applications, the amount of data we need to store and process can be often counted in the hundreds of terabytes or peta-bytes. It is not feasible to store such an amount of data on one physical node. We need a way to split that data into *N* data nodes. The technique for splitting the data we'll look at in this section is called *data partitioning*, but there are many techniques to par-tition your data.

For online processing sources (like a database), you can pick some ID (for instance, user ID), and store a range of users on a dedicated node. For example, assuming that you have 1,000 user IDs and 5 data nodes, the first node can store IDs from 0 to 200, the second node can store data from 201 to 400, and so on.

When picking the partitioning scheme, you need to be careful not to introduce data skew. Such a situation can occur when most of the data is produced by an ID or a group of IDs that belong to the same data node. For example, let's assume that the user ID 10 is responsible for 80% of our traffic and generates 80% of the data. Therefore, this means that 80% of the data is stored on the first data node, so our partitioning will not be optimal. In the worst case, this user's amount of data may be too big to store on the given data node. It is important to note that for online processing, partitioning is optimized for reading or writing data access patterns.

8.2.1   Offline big data partitioning

We will focus now on the offline big data processing partitioning. For big data systems, we often need to store the historical data (cold data) for an indefinite amount of time. It is crucial to store the data for as long as we can. When the data is produced, we may not be aware of the business value that it can bring.

For example, we may save all user's request data with all the HTTP headers, but when the data is saved, there may be no use case for these HTTP headers. In the future, however, we may decide to build a tool that profiles our users by the type of device (e.g., Android, iOS, etc.) they use. Such information is propagated in the HTTP headers. We can execute our new profiling logic based on the historical data because we stored it in the raw data. It is important to note here that the data was not needed for a long time.

Now, suppose we need to store a lot of information and save it for later. Thus, our storage needs to contain a lot of data stored in cold storage. In big data applications, this often means data is saved to a Hadoop distributed filesystem (HDFS). This also means the data should be partitioned in a fairly generic way. We cannot optimize for read patterns because we cannot anticipate how those read patterns will look.

For these reasons, the most common data partitioning scheme for big data offline processing is based on dates. Let's assume we have a system that saves user's data on the /users filesystem path and clickstream data in the /clicks filesystem path. We will analyze the first data set that stores the user's data. We assume that the number of records we store is equal to 10 billion. We started collecting the data in the year 2017, and it's been collected since then.

The partitioning scheme that we pick is based on the date. It means that our partition identifier starts with the year, so for example, we will have 2017, 2018, 2019, and 2020 partitions. If we have smaller data requirements, partitioning by year may be enough. In such a scenario, the filesystem path for our user's data would be /users/2017, /users/2018, and so on (as figure 8.4 illustrates), and it will be analogical for clicks: /clicks/2017, /clicks/2018, and so on.

By using this partitioning, the user's data will have four partitions. This means we can split the data into up to four physical data nodes. The first node will store the data for the year 2017, the second node for 2018, and so forth. Nothing prevents us from keeping all of those partitions on the same physical node. We may be OK with storing the data on one physical node, as long as we have enough disk space. Once the disk space runs out, we can create a new physical node and move some of the partitions to the new node.

In practice, such a partitioning scheme is too coarse-grained. Having one big partition for all data in one year is hard from both a read and write perspective. When you

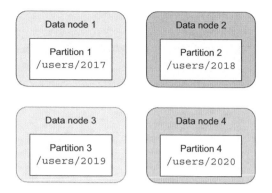

Figure 8.4 Four data partitions for a partitioning scheme based on the date

read such data and are interested only in events from a particular date, you need to scan the whole year's data! This is not only time-consuming, it's inefficient. It is also problematic from the writing perspective because if your disk space runs out, there is no easy way to split the data further. You won't be able to perform a successful write.

Because of that reason, offline big data systems tend to partition the data in a more fine-grained fashion. The data is partitioned by year, month, and day. For example, if you are writing data for January 2, 2020, you can save the event in a `/users/2020/ 01/02` partition. Such partitioning gives you a lot of flexibility on the read side as well. If you want to analyze events for a specific day, you can directly read the data from the partition. If you want to perform some higher-level analysis (for example, analyze the whole month's data), you can read all the partitions within a given month. The same pattern applies if you want to analyze a whole year's worth of data. To sum up, our 10 billion records will be partitioned, as figure 8.5 demonstrates.

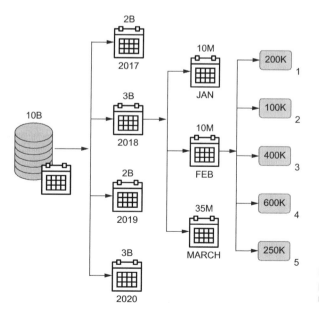

Figure 8.5 Date-based data partitioning by year, then by month, then by day

You can see that the initial 10 billion records are partitioned into year, month, and, finally, a specific day of the month. In the end, each day's partition contains 100,000 records. Such an amount of data can easily fit into the disk space for one machine. It also means that we have 365 or 366 partitions per year. The upper number of data nodes on which we can partition the data is equal to the number of days times the number of years we store the data. If your one-day data does not fit into one machine disk space, you can easily partition your data further by hours, minutes, seconds, and so on.

8.2.2   Partitioning vs. sharding

Assuming we have our data partitioned by the date, we can split that data into multiple nodes. In such a scenario, we put a subset of all partition keys in a physical node.

Say our user's data is partitioned into N partitions (logical shards). Let's assume our partition granularity is one month. In that case, the data for the year 2020 has 12 partitions that can be split horizontally into N physical nodes (physical shards). It is important to note that N is less than or equal to 12. In other words, the maximum level of physical shards is 12. This architecture pattern is called *sharding*.

Now, let's assume we have three physical nodes. In that case, we can say our user's data for the year 2020 is partitioned into 12 partitions. Next, the data is assigned to three shards (nodes). Each of the nodes stores four partitions for the year 2020 (12 partitions ÷ 3 nodes = 4 partitions per node), as figure 8.6 shows.

In the figure, the physical shard is the same as the physical node. The partition keys (logical shards) are distributed evenly to physical shards. In case a new node is added to a cluster, each physical shard needs to reassign one of its logical shards to a new physical node.

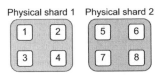

Figure 8.6   Sharding for 3 physical nodes and 12 partitions

There are a variety of algorithms for shard assignments. These also need to handle shard redistribution in case of adding or removing a node (failure or scaling down). This technique is used by most big data technologies and data stores, such as HDFS, Cassandra, Kafka, Elastic, and others, and the details how they perform sharding vary depending on the implementation.

8.2.3   Partitioning algorithms

The previously described technique is called *range partitioning*, where data is divided into ranges based on the dates when data was produced. Depending on the read pattern, we may decide to partition data differently.

Let's assume we want to fetch all events saved for a specific user ID. Assuming we have a range partitioning, this is tough to achieve. To retrieve all users for a given ID, we need to scan all partitions that may live on different physical nodes and then filter the data that we need. We won't be able to use the data locality. All partitions must be scanned because we don't know upfront when the specific user_id action was executed. It can be in any date's partition.

Let's assume that we need to partition our data based on the user_id. We want to distribute *N* keys into *M* physical nodes evenly. The proven technique for achieving this would be the hash partitioning algorithm. First, we need to hash the user_id using some hashing algorithm (e.g., MurmurHash), which returns a number. Next, we need to execute a modulo, *M*, operation on that number (*M* is a number of nodes). This will assure us that *N* partitions keys will be evenly split into *M* nodes. Ideally, every node should contain $N \div M$ partitions. We can skip the hash operation and execute modulo directly on the user ID, as long as the ID is a number. However, to make this algorithm work for any type of partition key (e.g., for a String), we apply the hashing to transform the nonnumber value into a numeric one. Figure 8.7 depicts this usage.

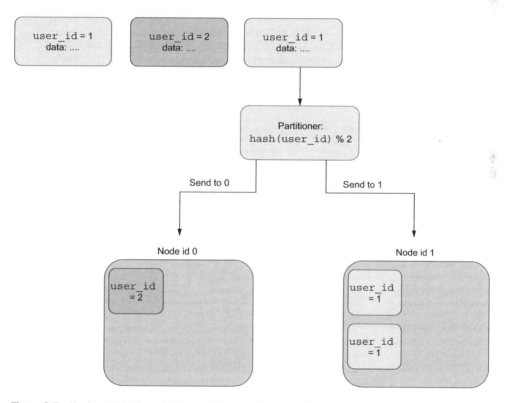

Figure 8.7 Hash partitioning used to partition our data based on the user_id

In our example, we have two nodes (*M* = 2). Let's assume that node's IDs are 0 and 1. When the first event for user_id 1 arrives, we apply a hash function on this ID, and then we do modulo 2 on the result. For the user_id 1, the result will be 1. As a result, this event will be sent to a node ID 1 and saved there. When another event, but this time for user_id 2, arrives, our partitioning algorithm assigns it to node 0 and saves it there. Next, another event for user_id 1 arrives. Our partitioning determines that it should land on node ID 1.

Because of this behavior, there is a guarantee that every event for user_id 1 will be stored in the same node. Due to that, we can easily apply operations by user_id that use data locality. The data for this user is already on the same node. By using this algorithm, all N users_id will be split evenly into two nodes.

The presented solution shows an excellent example for understanding the partitioning but has a couple shortcomings. The main problem with this approach is when we decide to add a new node to a cluster. The same problem is when one of the nodes is removed (on purpose or by failure).

Let's consider a situation where we add a new node (see figure 8.8). Suddenly, our partitioning algorithm changes because we need to execute modulo 3 (the number of nodes).

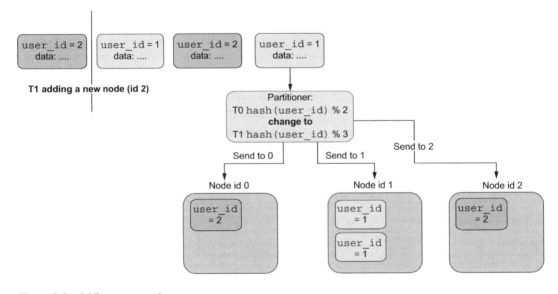

Figure 8.8   Adding a new node

Let's assume that the first three events are sent when we have two data nodes (so the partition's assignment is the same as in the previous example). This is our state $T0$ (time 0). Next, at the time $T1$, a new node is added to the cluster. It changes the partition's assignment because suddenly, we need to calculate modulo 3. When the user_id 2 arrives, the new partitioning algorithm calculates a partition for this ID to be equal to 2. This results in sending this new event to a new node. It is clear to see that we are losing our data locality. The events for the same user id (2) are now on two physical nodes. Our partitioning is broken from the perspective of what we wanted to achieve.

How do we alleviate this problem? We could transfer all events for user_id = 2 to a new node that is an ID owner. However, with our naive way of calculating a partition assignment based on the number of nodes, the number of such operations will be substantial. It will involve a lot of data movement that is costly. Let's calculate that for 10 event IDs. When calculating modulo 2 for these, the IDs 1, 3, 5, 7, and 9 will land on node ID 1, and the values 2, 4, 6, 8, and 10 will land on node ID 0.

How does this change if we add a new node (modulo 3)? The IDs 3, 6, and 9 will land on node 0. Ids 1, 4, 7, and 10 will land on node 1, and the rest of the IDs (2, 5, and 8) will land on node 2. Only IDs 3, 6, and 9 have the same physical node location. The rest of the IDs (70% of the data) need redistribution.

In a real-world cluster, this effect will be multiplied by the number of nodes. The more nodes we have, the more data movement we may need. When our nodes store a lot of data, such a redistribution process may not be feasible in a sane amount of time. What's worse, this may impact the online application that saves data to such a data store.

To reduce this effect, we may consider using a consistent hashing algorithm (http://mng.bz/Yg9B). This solves our problem by introducing virtual slots that are assigned to M nodes. When a new node is added, only a small portion of virtual slots needs redistribution. Different variants of this algorithm are used in many production systems.

Now that we know about data locality principles and know how to partition the data, let's try to solve the problem of joining data sets from multiple partitions residing on different physical machines. The next section presents a solution for this problem.

8.3 *Join big data sets from multiple partitions*

We will dive into three separate business use cases that require different join strategies. Each of those strategies uses the data locality at some level. We will analyze those use cases conceptually without delving into implementation details yet. Those will be covered in the next section.

Let's start by understanding the structure of stored data. As you remember, we divided our data into partitions based on dates, and we have two data sources. The first data source stores the user's data. Each partition (for example, users/2020/04/01), contains N files with N number of users rows. The data can be stored in any format: textual or binary.

For example, if we pick the binary AVRO format, a batch of records will be serialized to this format and saved to a file on the HDFS. One partition can contain N files. Each of those files will contain its part of the data for the given partition. Typically, one file will occupy at most the maximum block size of the filesystem. For the HDFS, this value is equal to 128 MB.

If, for example, we have 200 MB data for `users/2020/04/01`, we will have two files: `users_part1.avro` and `users_part2.avro`, as figure 8.9 shows. Each of those files will contain the user's data. Let's assume that each user has multiple values (e.g., age and name). Most importantly, the users have a `user_id` identifier that identifies a user uniquely. We will use that field when performing a join operation with other data sets.

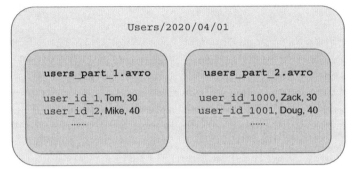

Figure 8.9   User's partition data

The same situation happens for the clicks partition. We will have *N* files within a partition responsible for a specific date. For example, `clicks/2020/01/20` might contain files with rows for this given partition. For our join use case, it is important to note that the clicks data contains the `user_id` field as well. It allows us to correlate clicks with a specific user from the user's data set. We will use this relationship when performing joins on those two big data sets.

8.3.1   Joining data within the same physical machine

The first business use case we need to solve is joining clicks and user data for the same date. In other words, we need to get all clicks for the user's visit within a given day.

This is a common business use case: joining data generated by different systems for the same user IDs. We can imagine that the user's data contains information about the payments, transactions, and other things users do. It could be collected by services responsible for making payments and finalizing users' actions. On the other hand, the clicks data contains less strict information; each click on the website is collected and saved by the clicks service. This information can be used to track the usage patterns and activity of a given user. Our goal is to correlate the clicks with the actual users' actions. Does the click lead to a specific transaction? Did users click a lot of times but abandon the product and not make the purchase? By joining this data, we can infer more meaning from it and provide a business value for our company.

For example, let's assume we need to join the users and clicks data for the whole year 2020. We can parallelize the processing to a maximum factor of 366 (days). The reason for this is we have that many partitions for this year. Our process needs to go through all rows for a given user's partition, find the corresponding data in the clicks partition, and join the data using the user_id identifier.

Let's assume the same physical machine carries the same data for the same date partition for both users and clicks data. For example, when we join the data for 2020/01/01, the data for both clicks and users will be local to a process. We will be able to use data locality. There is no need to fetch data from a remote location. Every piece of data needed for performing joins is present on the data node.

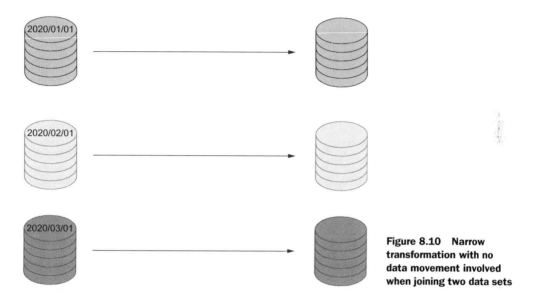

Figure 8.10   Narrow transformation with no data movement involved when joining two data sets

Let's assume all partitions for a specific month live on the same physical data node. When we perform a join for January 2020, clicks for the month's first day are present locally. The user's data is also present locally. Joining the data in the big data ecosystem can be described as *transforming* two data sets into one final data set. When such a transformation does not require any data movement, we call this a narrow transformation. In other words, we can transform our data (perform a join) fully, using data locality. Next, we will look at a business use case that requires a join operation involving data movement.

8.3.2   Joining that requires data movement

The next business use case we need to solve requires joining data between partitions (figure 8.11). Let's assume we need to find all unique users for the year 2020. This means we need to join data from all month's partitions using user_id. Once we join the data, we need to keep only one value per user's ID, removing the duplicates. The final user ID is returned.

It's important to note that we need to process all user events for every user's partition. For example, let's consider a case for joining data for user_id 1. First, we need to

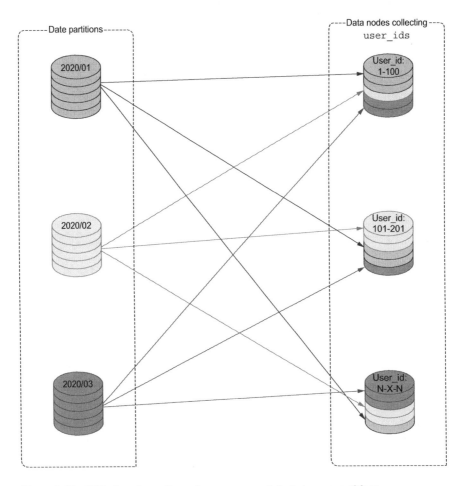

Figure 8.11   Wide transformation, where we move data between partitions

filter the users with this ID on every data node. All days partitions for 2020/01 can execute the filtering logic using data locality. This operation needs to be executed on every date partition. Once we filter the data, it needs to be sent to a data node that processes the given user_id 1. We still have the assumption that each month's data resides on the dedicated data node. This means that data from all 12 months for the year 2020 need to be sent to a data node that performs a join operation for our user ID. In reality, every data node will process a range of IDs.

Our join logic requires substantial data movement at the second stage. Although we are using data locality at the filter stage, the second stage requires network usage. Such a transformation that requires data movement is called *wide transformation*. The process of exchanging the data between data nodes is called *data shuffling*. The more data shuffling our big data processing has, the slower it is. As you may remember from the data locality chapter, operations that require substantial network usage are far from optimal.

Some optimizations can reduce the data shuffling when performing joins. However, they strongly depend on the business use case and data characteristics. When you join the data, it's often the case that one of the data sets is smaller, while the other is huge. In such a case, we can implement a hybrid solution that uses data locality as much as it can. On the other hand, the data also requires shuffling, but this can be reduced to a minimum.

8.3.3   *Optimizing join leveraging broadcasting*

Let's now consider a use case that allows us to implement a useful join optimization. Our business use case states that we need to get only clicks for one month of user's data.

This is needed because we want to find a correlation between one of the user's clients and the user's data change that happened recently. By *recent*, we mean the current day of processing.

Such a process runs every day to match the clicks for the current day for all users. We will run the join process for users within the current year. To demonstrate the optimization, we will make one additional change to our initial example. It turns out that clicks and user's data take up too much disk space, and we need to move both data sources to a separate physical machine. This means there is no more data locality between users and clicks. All operations that require joining these data sources require data movement.

There is one important observation we should focus on. The clicks data we need to join has only one day of data, meaning that the size of this data set is relatively small. The user's data we need to join, however, is relatively huge. We need a whole month of user data to fulfill our business use case. This gives us a scenario in which one data set is orders of magnitude smaller than the other dataset needed to perform a join.

When doing joins, our main goal is to reduce data shuffling, leveraging data locality as much as possible. We can achieve both of these goals by sending the smaller data set (clicks) to a data node that contains the larger data set (users), so in this scenario, we retrieve those clicks and propagate them to all the data nodes that carry the 2020 year's user data (figure 8.12). Remember, we have a dedicated physical machine for each month. This means that we need to propagate the clicks data to 12 machines.

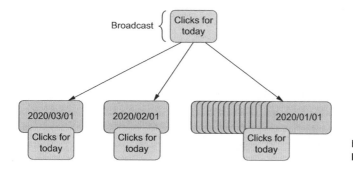

Figure 8.12   Using broadcast with joins

The clicks for today's data set is broadcast to all data nodes that contain the user's data. Thus, it is called a *broadcast data set*. The network consumption (data shuffling) is required only to send the smaller data set to nodes where the bigger data set resides. Because the join process runs locally on the machines with the user's data, the process will examine all days' partitions for 2020/01 and join the data with clicks for today. The same operation is repeated for all months in the year 2020.

With this technique, we can leverage the user's data set data locality. Only a small portion of clicks data needs to be sent over the network. There is one important caveat here we need to be careful about though. This optimization technique only works properly as long as the smaller data set can fit into data node memory. Once the data is in memory, we can access it orders of magnitude faster than data on disk or data that needs to be transferred via the network. The next section describes the tradeoffs between big data processing that utilizes memory (e.g., Apache Spark) versus an older disk-based approach (e.g., Hadoop).

Note that, although we use Spark, the techniques described are common to most big data processing frameworks. Regardless of the API that big data frameworks expose, they tend to implement the MapReduce paradigm underneath. Therefore, the optimization we discuss next can be applied to all of those frameworks. Let's see how that impacts our join operation's performance.

8.4   Data processing: Memory vs. disk

So far, we have learned how we can leverage data locality in joins. This allows us to reduce our processing time by lowering the amount of data that needs to be sent over the network. However, even if we have the data local to our processing, we need to load that data into the big data framework that performs the join.

Let's elaborate more on the example given in the previous section. As you remember, we joined the smaller data set (i.e., clicks) with the larger one (i.e., users). The clicks data set was sent over the network to the node that does the processing and that contains the user's data. Next, it was kept in the data node's memory.

8.4.1   Using disk-based processing

Let's now consider what will happen with the user's data. We are assuming that the user's data does not fit into the machine's memory, so it needs to be accessed from the disk as the processing progresses. We can solve this problem in two ways.

The first solution reads segments of files lazily. Let's assume that the user's data takes 100 GB, split into 1,000 parts. Each of those parts has 100 MB and has a dedicated file. When the join process finishes the first chunk of the file, it writes the result into an intermediate file. Then, it continues the processing by loading the next part of the data, performing another join, and saving it again. This process is repeated until all data is processed, as figure 8.13 shows.

This is, in fact, how the standard MapReduce Hadoop-based big data processing works. Hadoop processing is built around access to the disk, and it's the filesystem.

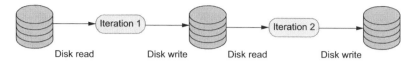

Figure 8.13   Disk-based big data processing

The main integration point between stages in big data processing is a file. Every stage that produces results saves those results into an HDFS (file system). The next Hadoop task takes the data and processes it.

Such an approach has a couple pros. It allows engineers to write their processing independently. Every processing stage produces immutable results that shouldn't be modified. Each stage in the processing takes the path to the filesystem as an input. Then, it produces files in a different location as output. Unfortunately, disk-based big data processing has one huge con—it's incredibly slow.

8.4.2   Why do we need MapReduce?

The main idea behind MapReduce is data locality. To understand why we need the map and reduce phases and how it leverages the data locality, let's explain how the famous word count problem can be solved. We will solve it using the MapReduce paradigm and try to understand why it is the best solution for big data sets.

Let's assume we have N text files split into M data nodes in our cluster. Each text file is a big data set and occupies N GB. Our task is to calculate the occurrences of every word in every text file. What's important is that all the data sets (M nodes × N GB per file) cannot fit the memory in one machine. Therefore, we need to distribute our processing somehow.

Let's focus on the first stage of our processing that is local with data locality. All operations are executed in the context of a node where the data originates. Figure 8.14 shows the first stage in this process.

In this scenario, we have three data nodes. On the left side of figure 8.14, we can see that each of the nodes has a big data file with some text in it. Each of those files is so big that it is not possible to send all of those to one node and do our calculations there. First, we split the text file into N words. For each word, the map phase creates a key-value pair: the key is a word, and the value is the number of occurrences of the given word. At the first stage of processing, the value is always equal to 1.

At first glance, this stage seems naive and unneeded. However, the main point of doing this is to create a partition key for every record. Our *partition key* is just a word for which we do a word count. All pairs with the same partition key will eventually be sent to the same data node. We will get back to this shortly.

Once our data is partitioned, we can execute a local reduce. This means that all pairs with the same key (word) will be coalesced and reduced to a new pair, where the key is

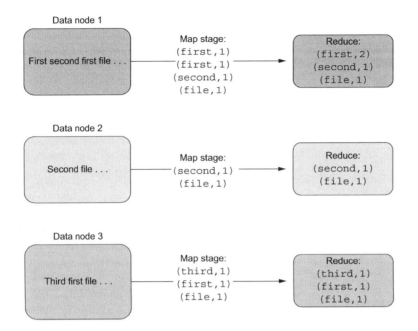

Figure 8.14   Word count: First phase on a local machine using data locality

the same as before. However, the count will change for some of our words. The reduce operation on data node 1 reduces two occurrences of the pairs (first, 1) to one occurrence (first, 2). This is the first stage of our word count, which is executed locally on each node. Once we reduce all pairs locally, we are ready to execute the second stage.

The second stage (figure 8.15) involves moving data over a network (data shuffling). According to the partitioning algorithm, the data is distributed into N nodes. What's important here is that the data for the same partition key (word) always lands in the same data node.

We can see that the first data node processes pairs for the partition key we've named first: all pairs with this partition key must be sent to the first data node. The (first, 2) pair stays on the same data node, so it does not involve data shuffling. However, the third data node has a (first, 1) pair to send over the network to a first data node. Once the data movement completes, the last reduce step can be executed.

What's important at this stage of processing is that we can be sure all the data for the same partition key is on the same data node. Therefore, we can execute yet another reduce that uses data locality. The reduce operations can be executed in parallel per partition key, speeding up our computations.

Finally, as shown in figure 8.16, the results of our processing produces one pair for every analyzed word. The result can be saved to a filesystem, database, queue, etc., for further processing.

It is important to note that this solution will have problems in case of data skew. Let's assume we have one partition key that contains most of the data we need to

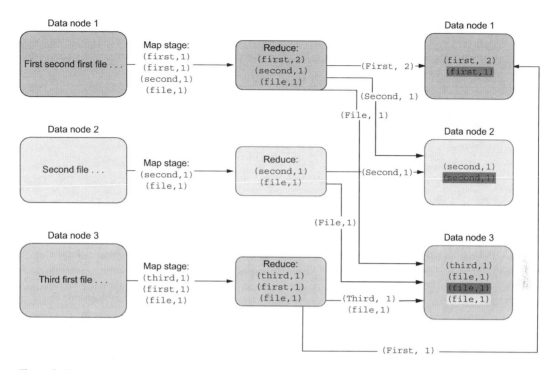

Figure 8.15   Word count: Second phase with data shuffling

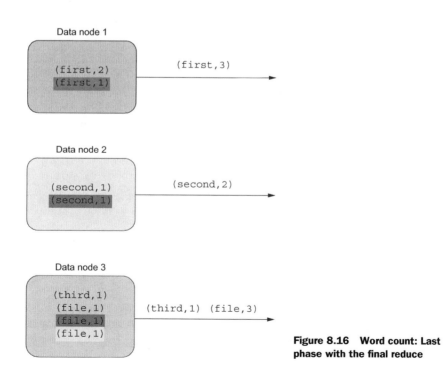

Figure 8.16   Word count: Last phase with the final reduce

process. In such a situation, we would send all of this data to the same data node. If this data does not fit this data node disk space/memory, we won't be able to reduce the data for this particular partition key. Yet again, the partitioning of our data and its distribution turns out to be very important.

The MapReduce solution has a lot of complexities compared to approaches that work in a one-node scenario. However, when we execute our processing in the context of big data (meaning that it is impossible to fit all data to one node), we need to live with these complexities if we want to solve our problems.

Let's now calculate how slow the disk-based MapReduce is compared to processing that's based on memory access. We will also compare MapReduce to the data that needs to be fetched via the network and see why data locality is so essential.

8.4.3   *Calculating access times*

Let's say we need to process 100 GB of data, and the data is split into 1,000 files. We want to calculate the time required to send 100 GB of data over the network (data shuffling). Next, we want to calculate the same for reading data from disk (both HDD and SSD). Finally, we will compare results to a situation where the data is in memory.

We expect that RAM access times will be the fastest. (The SSD is a bit slower, whereas the HDD is orders of magnitude slower.) If you don't want to dig into the math behind this, feel free to skip this section.

We will use well-proven numbers for our calculations (http://mng.bz/GGov). They may be a little outdated, but the order of magnitude between these numbers is still relevant. Once the data is in main memory, it can be accessed fast: read 1 MB sequentially from memory: 250,000 ns 250 μs.

We need to remember that, for the memory use case, we need to load the data upfront—but only once. Comparing this to disk (both SSD and HDD), the difference is huge: read 1 MB sequentially from SSD: 1,000,000 ns 1,000 μs (1 ms ~1 GB ÷ sec SSD, 4X memory). Read 1 MB sequentially from disk: 20,000,000 ns 20,000 μs (20 ms 80x memory, 20X SSD).

Finally, the network read, including request and response, is: send packet CA -> Netherlands -> CA: 150,000,000 ns 150,000 μs 150 ms.

Of course, our data center shouldn't send the data between continents when doing big data processing. However, even in a local data center, sending data over the network will be a couple of times slower than accessing local data from disk. For the network data, the difference becomes enormous.

Let's calculate the total time that our big data processing should be dedicated to loading the data, depending on the approach where the data lives. Operating on 100 GB of the data that already lives in the RAM takes: 250,000 ns × 1000 (MB) × 100 (GB) = 25,000,000,000 ns = 25 s.

For SSD disk it is: 1,000,000 ns × 1000 (MB) × 100 (GB) = 100,000,000,000 ns = 100 s. And finally, for HDD disk it is: 20,000,000 ns × 1000 (MB) × 100 (GB) = 2,000,000,000,000 ns = 2000 s = ~33 min.

We can see that, even if we were able to use an SSD disk for all big data, the data loading is four times slower than operating on RAM. In reality, when we need to store terabytes of data, we will store it on the standard HDD because it's more cost efficient. In that case, the processing based on the HDD disk is 80 times slower! When writing this, the HDD cost per GB is $0.050, whereas the price per GB for SSD is twice that much: $0.10. We can, thus, conclude that storing the SSD data is 100% more expensive than storing the data on HDD. Table 8.1 sums up our findings.

Table 8.1   Disk vs. memory read access

Resource type	Size (GB)	Time (seconds)	Time (minutes)
RAM	100	25	0.25
SSD disk	100	100	~1.66
HDD disk	100	2000	~33

We saw that Hadoop big data processing is based on disk access. Because of this slowness, and because memory has gotten cheaper, the new approach based on memory access is now more popular. We will look at this approach next.

8.4.4   *RAM-based processing*

As the RAM gets cheaper, the new big data processing tools started changing their architecture to use it fully. It is not uncommon to see a cluster of processing nodes that has terabytes of RAM. This allows engineers to create data pipelines that fetch as much data as possible into memory. Once the data is there, big data processing can access it substantially faster than the disk-based approach. One of the most well-known and production-proven big data processing frameworks is Apache Spark, which uses memory as the main integration point between processing stages (figure 8.17).

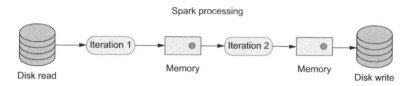

Figure 8.17   RAM-based big data processing with Apache Spark

The entry point for big data processing requires loading the data from some filesystem. Assuming data locality, this requires loading data from the local disk. With RAM-based processing, the data is loaded into the machine's memory. When the current stage of processing finishes, the results are not written to disk (contrary to Hadoop-based big data processing). The data stays in the memory of the node that does the processing. When the next stage of processing (transformation, join) starts, it doesn't need to load the disk data again. The cost of loading disk data is removed for subsequent stages. Only the first stage needs to load this data. When the final processing stage produces results, they can be saved to disk to make them persistent.

When calculating disk versus memory times, we saw that even in the best case (using SSD), Hadoop-based processing is four times slower. When using Spark-based processing, we need to pay this cost only two times—the first time when the data is loaded and the second time when the results are persisted to disk. The same processing flow that involves only two iterations over data (transformation) requires two times disk reads and two times disk writes. In the best case of using SSD everywhere, Hadoop-based processing will be eight times slower than Spark-based processing because Hadoop-based SSD: $100 \text{ s} \times 2$ reads $+ 100 \text{ s} \times 2$ writes $= 400 \text{ s}$; and Spark-based: $25 \text{ s} \times 1$ read $+ 25 \text{ s} \times 1$ write $= 50 \text{ s}$. Then, $400 \div 50 = 8$.

In practice, writing to disk is often slower than reading from it. Because of this, the differences between Spark and Hadoop will get even higher. Also, real-world big data pipelines tend to have more stages than only two iterations (transformations). There could be pipelines that involve 10 or more stages before the end result is produced. For such a big data pipeline, we would need to multiply our calculations by the number of stages.

It's easy to notice that the more stages we have, the more significant the difference between RAM and disk-based processing will be. Lastly, as I mentioned earlier, the HDD disk is still used because of its cost efficiency. Let's calculate the total processing time for disk-based processing that uses HDD disks underneath: Hadoop-based HDD: 33 minutes seconds $\times 2$ reads $+ 33 \text{ min} \times 2$ writes $= 132 \text{ min} = 2 \text{ h}$ and 12 min. You can see that the difference between RAM-based and HDD-based processing is huge. It is 50 seconds versus more than 2 hours!

I hope those numbers convince you that when creating modern big data processing pipelines, you should consider building them based on memory-based tools, such as Apache Spark. In the next section, we will implement our join using Apache Spark.

8.5   *Implement joins using Apache Spark*

Before we start implementing our logic, let's take a look at the Apache Spark basics. It is a Scala-based library for big data processing that allows us to store intermediate memory results. As I mentioned earlier, there are situations in which it is not possible to store all data in RAM. Spark allows us to specify what to do in such cases.

Spark also provides the `StorageLevel` setting that allows us to state if the data should be kept in memory only or spilled up to disk if the memory is full. If we pick the former, the process will fail fast, signaling that there is not enough memory. We can consider splitting our data to fit it into a machine's memory. If we pick the latter, the data is stored on disk without the process failing. Our processing will finish, but it will take a lot more time to complete. From this, we can see that Spark lets us create memory-based processing. What about data locality?

To understand how data locality can be achieved using Spark, we need to take a look at its architecture, as illustrated in Figure 8.18.

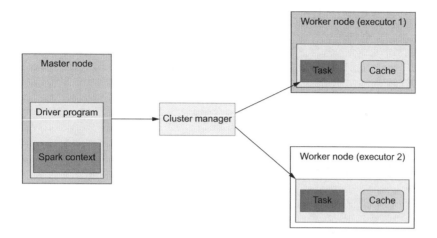

Figure 8.18 Spark's architecture

Spark works in a master-worker architecture. Each one of the Spark processes works on nodes that contain data that we want to process. Assuming we have three data nodes, two of them will be Spark executors and one the Spark master. The spark master is a special process that is responsible for coordinating our processing and sending the computation to data.

In this section, the program we will write using Spark is submitted to a master node. The master node serializes the program (similarly to what we learned in the first section) and sends the program to executor nodes. The executor nodes run on the data nodes, which contain the data we want to process. We can then build the processing that uses data locality. In this case, the executor processes its local data in the partitions that are stored on this node. The second executor processes the partitions that are stored on the second node.

If we map this to our clicks with the users join example, the executor will process data for some part of the users. The second executor lives on the node where the rest of the users are stored. The cache component on the Spark executors is our RAM. The processing data is fetched from disk or via the network and stored in RAM.

The smaller clicks data set taking part in the join process is sent to all executors. The driver component on the master node fetches the clicks data from the data node that contains those clicks. It is important to note that the driver process needs to have enough memory to store the clicks data. Next, the clicks data is sent to all executors. This is stored in the cache (RAM). Thus, the memory available to these processes also needs to be big enough to hold the data.

8.5.1 Implementing a join without broadcast

Let's start with the use case in which we want to join the clicks and users data, but we will not make any assumptions about the size of both data sets. We will use a simple join operation without any optimizations. Next, we will analyze the execution plan, which will show us how the Spark engine interprets and executes that.

The code examples in this section are written in Scala because it allows us to create fluent and readable Big data processing. Also, Scala is Spark's native language. The following listing shows the simple data model for our example.

Listing 8.1   Data model

```
case class UserData(userId: String, data: String)

case class Click(userId: String, url: String)
```

Both of the users and clicks data sets contain the user ID that we will use to join the data. The user has a *data* field associated with it. The click is executed in the context of a specific *url*. This field is therefore present in its data model.

For this, we will use the Spark Dataset API (http://mng.bz/zQKB), which allows us to use SQL-like syntax. It is a higher-level API that encapsulates RDD (http://mng.bz/0wpN).

To test the data, we will mock the clicks and user data. In real-world applications, you will load the data from the filesystem using readers. The following listing shows how to read the Avro data (http://mng.bz/KBQj) from some HDFS path.

Listing 8.2   Reading Avro data

```
val usersDF = spark.read.format("avro").load("users/2020/10/10/users.avro")
```

For the sake of simplicity, let's now mock the two data sets. The following listing shows how this is done.

Listing 8.3   Mocking the users and clicks data sets

```
import spark.sqlContext.implicits._
val userData =
  spark.sparkContext.makeRDD(List(
    UserData("a", "1"),
    UserData("b", "2"),
    UserData("d", "200")
  )).toDS()

val clicks =
  spark.sparkContext.makeRDD(List(
    Click("a", "www.page1"),
    Click("b", "www.page2"),
    Click("c", "www.page3")
  )).toDS()
```

Here, we are filling the userData with the rows for the IDs a, b, and d. Finally, the RDD is transformed to a Dataset using the toDS() function, as listing 8.3 demonstrates. We want to operate on the data set because it provides a better API and optimizations atop of the RDD API.

The actual join logic is simple but hides a lot of information. In the following listing, we join the user data with the clicks data.

Listing 8.4 Joining without assumptions

```
val res: Dataset[(UserData, Click)]
  = userData.joinWith(clicks, userData("userId") === clicks("userId"), "inner")
```

We are joining the userData with clicks. The join is performed on the userId field from both the user data and clicks data sets using an inner join. Because of that, when we execute the query we will have two results, as the following listing shows.

Listing 8.5 Two results from the inner join

```
res.show()
assert(res.count() == 2)

+-----+-------------+
|  _1|          _2|
+-----+-------------+
|[b,2]|[b,www.page2]|
|[a,1]|[a,www.page1]|
+-----+-------------+
```

Notice that the result is presented in a table. The left side contains the user's data, and the right side contains the clicks data. The user data for userId d is not included because it does not have a matching click. The same situation happens for the click data with userId c.

The join hides a lot of complexity underneath. We can reason about this by extracting the actual physical plan of the query. This shows us what join strategy was picked. To extract the physical plan, execute the explain() method, as the following listing shows. The method returns a detailed physical plan.

Listing 8.6 Getting the physical plan of the query

```
res.explain()
== Physical Plan ==
*SortMergeJoin [_1#10.userId], [_2#11.userId], Inner
:- *Sort [_1#10.userId ASC], false, 0
:  +- Exchange hashpartitioning(_1#10.userId, 200)
:     +- *Project [struct(userId#2, data#3) AS _1#10]
:        +- Scan ExistingRDD[userId#2,data#3]
+- *Sort [_2#11.userId ASC], false, 0
   +- Exchange hashpartitioning(_2#11.userId, 200)
      +- *Project [struct(userId#7, url#8) AS _2#11]
         +- Scan ExistingRDD[userId#7,url#8]
```

We can see that both data sets are treated in the same way. First, both are sorted in ascending order. Once the data is sorted, the hash partitioning algorithm is used. There are no assumptions about the data. This plan corresponds to the use case that requires data shuffling. One of the data sets will need to be transferred to the executor that contains other parts of the data.

Because the data is sorted, the Spark query engine can apply some optimizations, such as moving only some range of the data. The optimizations are intelligent, and sometimes, they may behave better than the optimization that we impose on the query engine. Still, it is essential to measure your solution and compare it with another one. It may turn out that your custom hand-crafted optimization performs worse than the standard Spark query optimizer logic. Let's now take a look at a join plan that uses the broadcast technique we discussed in section 8.3.3.

8.5.2   *Implementing a join with broadcast*

Next, let's implement the joining behavior that broadcasts one of the data sets (we will do it for clicks) to all data nodes. To achieve that, we need to modify our join logic by wrapping the data set we want to broadcast into the `broadcast()` function. We will do this for the clicks data set. Let's take a look at the full test suite in the following listing.

Listing 8.7   Joining with broadcast

```
test("Should inner join two DS whereas one of them is broadcast") {
  import spark.sqlContext.implicits._
  val userData =
    spark.sparkContext.makeRDD(List(
      UserData("a", "1"),
      UserData("b", "2"),
      UserData("d", "200")
    )).toDS()

  val clicks =
    spark.sparkContext.makeRDD(List(
      Click("a", "www.page1"),
      Click("b", "www.page2"),
      Click("c", "www.page3")
    )).toDS()

  //when
  val res: Dataset[(UserData, Click)]
  = userData.joinWith(broadcast(clicks), userData("userId") ===
   clicks("userId"), "inner")

  //then
  res.explain()
  res.show()
  assert(res.count() == 2)
```

The data returned by this query is the same as the previous one because we didn't change any logic. What is interesting for us is the physical query plan. Let's take a look at it in the following listing.

Listing 8.8 Viewing the physical query plan with broadcast

```
* == Physical Plan ==
* *BroadcastHashJoin [_1#234.userId], [_2#235.userId], Inner, BuildRight
* :- *Project [struct(userId#225, data#226) AS _1#234]
* :   +- Scan ExistingRDD[userId#225,data#226]
* +- BroadcastExchange HashedRelationBroadcastMode(List(input[0,
struct<userId:string,url:string>, false].userId))
* +- *Project [struct(userId#230, url#231) AS _2#235]
* +- Scan ExistingRDD[userId#230,url#231]
```

Did you notice that the physical plan changed substantially? First, the data isn't sorted anymore. The Spark execution engine removed this step because we didn't need to send parts of one of the data sets. Therefore, it doesn't need to be split. The Broadcast-Exchange step is responsible for sending the clicks data to all data nodes. Once this data is present on all data nodes, Spark executes the Scan step that uses the hash to find the matching data.

Achieving those results is one part of the story. In real life, you should measure both solutions. As I mentioned before, it may turn out that the standard Spark query engine will perform better.

When broadcasting your data to data nodes, you need assurance that this data fits your machine's RAM. If the data you are broadcasting grows in an uncontrolled manner, you should strongly reconsider using the broadcast strategy. In the next chapter, we'll look at strategies for picking third-party libraries used in our code.

Summary

- Moving data to computations is easier but expensive. It becomes infeasible for big data sets. This happens because we need to move too much data via the network.
- Data locality can be fully leveraged by sending computations to data. It is more complex, but it is worth the effort for big data sets because we don't need to move so much data. Therefore, our processing will be substantially faster.
- Processing that uses data locality can be parallelized and scaled more easily than processing without data locality.
- In the big data ecosystem, we need to split data into multiple machines by using partitioning.
- Offline and online data partitioning provides us with different characteristics. Online partitioning can optimize for query patterns, although offline partitioning needs to be more generic because we often don't know the access pattern up front.
- Offline partitioning based on dates is commonly used and gives us more flexibility.
- Some types of joins can use full data locality if we perform the joins on the same physical machine. Other types of joins that require wider data need data shuffling.
- We can reduce data shuffling by reducing the partitions needed for our join operations.

- If we can make assumptions about the data, we can use a broadcast join strategy.
- Disk-based big data processing is more mature but provides worse performance than RAM-based processing. Hadoop implements the former strategy; Spark uses the latter.
- We can use Apache Spark API to implement joins.
- Analyzing physical plans allows us to reason about the query. For example, we can use the broadcasting technique and then see how it is used by the query execution engine.
- We should know our data to analyze the tradeoffs of different joining strategies.

Third-party libraries: Libraries you use become your code

This chapter covers

- Taking responsibility for the libraries you import
- Analyzing third-party libraries for testability, stability, and scalability
- Making decisions about reimplementing logic vs. importing code you don't own

When building our software systems, we have time and budget limitations. Because of those limitations, it is not feasible to write every piece of code that your software uses. Almost every application needs to interact with the underlying operating system, filesystem, and external I/O. For those interactions, we usually don't reimplement the logic. We pick the libraries that are already present and provide that functionality for us. We call those libraries *third party* because our team or company does not create them. They could be developed by an open source community or other companies specializing in a specific part of the system's design. For example, when sending data to an external HTTP system, we often pick an existing HTTP client implementation.

When we choose an existing third-party library and use it in our codebase, we take full responsibility for this piece of software—the software we didn't develop and produce. Our end users don't care if we picked one library over another. They don't know if we implemented a specific part of the code or used a code created by someone else. As long as our system works as expected, there is no problem. When a failure happens, users will notice that, however. The failure can be caused by a bug in the third-party software. That means we didn't test the third-party code well enough or had a false assumption about it.

In this chapter, you will learn how to pick a robust third-party library for your application. You will learn about the most common mistakes and how to validate your assumptions about the code you don't own.

9.1 *Importing a library and taking full responsibility for its settings: Beware of the defaults*

Some libraries and frameworks, such as Spring (https://spring.io/), favor convention over configuration. Such a pattern allows potential users to start using a specific library right away without any necessary configuration. It trades off explicit settings for the simplicity of UX. As long as an engineer is aware of this tradeoff and its limitations, there is no real danger.

The prototyping and experimentation phase is a lot easier and faster when using software components that do not require a substantial configuration upfront. Those frameworks are built using best practices and patterns, and they should be good enough for you as long as you are aware of their drawbacks and problems.

> **NOTE** Those framework and library concepts are often used interchangeably. A framework provides a skeleton for building an application, but the actual logic is implemented in the application. You need to provide the logic to the framework somehow: it can be an inheritance, composition, listeners, etc. (e.g., a dependency injection framework). On the other hand, a library already implements some logic, and we only call it from our code. It can be, for example, an HTTP client library providing the way to call HTTP services.

The fact that the majority of all configuration is based on convention has some drawbacks as well. When we use a third-party library, it's tempting not to dig deeper into all its configuration options. If we leave the defaults unset, we rely on the configuration that is shipped within a library. The values that become defaults are usually picked logically, based on some research. However, even if the defaults are a good fit, in most contexts they may not be good enough for your use case.

Let's consider a simple scenario where we want to use a third-party library that is responsible for HTTP calls. We will pick the OkHttp library (https://square.github .io/okhttp/) for demonstration purposes. We want to query the data that is available under the /data endpoint of the service. For testing, we will mock this HTTP endpoint using the WireMock library (http://wiremock.org/). We will stub the /data endpoint that returns the OK status code and some entity's body data. The following listing shows this code.

Listing 9.1   Mocking the HTTP service

```
private static WireMockServer wireMockServer;
private static final int PORT = 9999;
private static String HOST;

@BeforeAll
public static void setup() {
  wireMockServer = new WireMockServer(options().port(PORT));    ⟵── Starts the WireMock server on a dedicated PORT
  wireMockServer.start();
  HOST = String.format("http://localhost:%s", PORT);    ⟵── Saves the location to a HOST variable
  wireMockServer.stubFor(
          get(urlEqualTo("/data"))
          .willReturn(aResponse()          Mocks the HTTP response
          .withStatus(200)                 with status code 200 and
          .withBody("some-data")));    ⟵── some data
}
```

The OkHttp client logic for querying the service and getting the response is straightforward. In listing 9.2, we build the URL based on the HOST variable. Next, we will build the OkHttp client using the builder and executing the call. Finally, we will assert that the response is 200, and the content matches that stubbed by WireMock.

Listing 9.2   Building the HTTP client with defaults

```
@Test
public void shouldExecuteGetRequestsWithDefaults() throws IOException {
  Request request = new Request.Builder().url(HOST + "/data").build();

  OkHttpClient client = new OkHttpClient.Builder().build();
  Call call = client.newCall(request);
  Response response = call.execute();

  assertThat(response.code()).isEqualTo(200);
  assertThat(response.body().string()).isEqualTo("some-data");
}
```

Note that the HTTP client is created as a builder, but no explicit setting is specified. The code looks simple, and it's fast to start development using it. Unfortunately, it shouldn't be used in production in this form. Remember that once you import the third-party library to your codebase, you need to start treating it as your own code. Because this section focuses on the defaults, let's see which settings may be problematic.

When analyzing the third-party library settings, you need to understand their main configurations. In the context of every HTTP client, timeouts play a crucial role. It impacts the performance and SLA of your service. For example, if your service SLA is 100 ms, and you are executing the call to other services to fulfill the request, the other call must complete faster than your service SLA. Choosing a proper timeout is crucial if you want to keep your SLA.

High timeouts are also dangerous in the microservices architecture. To deliver business functionality in this architecture, there is often a need to make multiple network calls. For example, one microservice may need to call multiple others. Some of those others may need to contact the following microservices and so on. In such a scenario, when one of the services hangs on the request processing, it may cause cascading failure to other services that are calling it. The higher the timeout is, the longer it may take to process a single request, then there is a higher probability of cascading failure. Such a failure may be worse than breaking your SLA because it involves a risk that the system will crash and stop working.

Let's see how our client will behave if we query an endpoint that takes a long time to execute. We will test it for 5 seconds (5,000 milliseconds). We can simulate the scenario in WireMock by using the `withFixedDelay()` method, as the following listing shows.

Listing 9.3   Emulating a slow endpoint

```
wireMockServer.stubFor(
        get(urlEqualTo("/slow-data"))
                .willReturn(aResponse()
                        .withStatus(200)
                        .withBody("some-data")
                        .withFixedDelay(5000)));
```

The new endpoint can be queried using the /slow-data URL. We will execute the query using the same logic, but we will measure the time it takes to execute the HTTP requests, as the following listing shows.

Listing 9.4   Measuring an HTTP client's request time

```
Request request = new Request.Builder()                          Executes a
                    .url(HOST + "/slow-data").build();           request for
                                                                 the /slow-data
OkHttpClient client = new OkHttpClient.Builder().build();        endpoint
Call call = client.newCall(request);

long start = System.currentTimeMillis();                         Measures the total
Response response = call.execute();                              execution time
long totalTime = System.currentTimeMillis() - start;

assertThat(totalTime).isGreaterThanOrEqualTo(5000);             Validates that the request
assertThat(response.code()).isEqualTo(200);                     took at least 5,000 ms
assertThat(response.body().string()).isEqualTo("some-data");
```

Did you notice that the request took at least 5,000 milliseconds? That happens because the WireMock HTTP server introduces that kind of delay. If our code that needs to fulfill the request within 100 ms calls this endpoint, it will be slow enough to break the SLA.

Instead of seeing a response in 100 ms (whether the response is success or failure), our clients will be blocked on the wait for 5,000 ms. It also means that the thread that executes these requests may be blocked for that long. One thread that is supposed to execute ~50 requests (5000 ÷ 100 ms) will be blocked. Thus, this thread won't serve any other request for that amount of time, impacting the overall performance of our service. This problem may not appear if only one thread waits too long. However, we will start noticing performance problems if all or the majority of allocated threads are blocked for too long.

It turns out that the default timeout settings cause this situation. Our client should fail the request if we need to wait for more than our service's SLA (100 ms). If the request is failed, the client can retry it instead of waiting for the 5,000 ms for any response. If you look at the read timeout of the OkHTTP (http://mng.bz/9KP7), you will notice it's set to 10 seconds by default!

> **NOTE** Checking the defaults is important not only for third-party libraries but also for the standard development toolkits (SDKs). For example, when using the HttpClient that ships with the Java JDK (http://mng.bz/jylr), the default timeout is set to infinite!

This means every HTTP request can block the caller's execution for up to 10 seconds. Such a situation is far from ideal. In a real-world system, you should configure the timeouts according to your SLA.

We are assuming our code must execute the call to a slow-data endpoint with up to 100 ms. We are also assuming that the service that we are calling has a defined SLA in the 99 percentile equal to 100 ms. This means that 99 out of 100 requests will be executed within 100 ms. There could be some outliers that take longer to execute. We can simulate such an outlier that takes 5,000 ms to execute.

Let's execute the HTTP request once again, but this time let's provide an explicit setting for the read timeout instead of relying on the default. Note the `readTimeout()` method in the following listing, which is used to specify the timeout.

> **Listing 9.5   Executing an HTTP request with an explicit timeout**

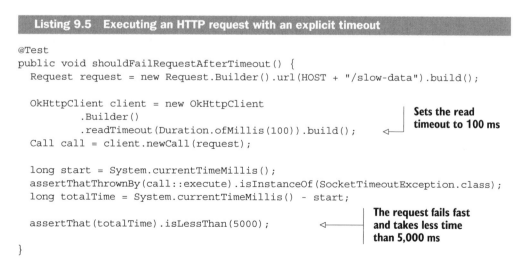

```
@Test
public void shouldFailRequestAfterTimeout() {
  Request request = new Request.Builder().url(HOST + "/slow-data").build();

  OkHttpClient client = new OkHttpClient                         Sets the read
        .Builder()                                               timeout to 100 ms
        .readTimeout(Duration.ofMillis(100)).build();       ◁
  Call call = client.newCall(request);

  long start = System.currentTimeMillis();
  assertThatThrownBy(call::execute).isInstanceOf(SocketTimeoutException.class);
  long totalTime = System.currentTimeMillis() - start;
                                                             The request fails fast
  assertThat(totalTime).isLessThan(5000);           ◁       and takes less time
                                                             than 5,000 ms
}
```

Calling the execute method triggers the actual HTTP request. The request will fail after around 100 ms because this is the new timeout that we specified with read-Timeout(). After this time, an exception is propagated to the caller. Therefore, the SLA of our service is not impacted. Next, the request can be retried (if it's idempotent), or we can save the information about the failure. Most importantly, the HTTP service's slow response does not block the thread for a long time. Thus, it will not impact the performance of our service.

When you import any third-party library, you should be aware of its settings and parameters. Implicit settings can be suitable for prototyping, but explicit and well-tuned settings for your context are must-haves for production systems. In the next section, we will look at concurrency models and the scalability of libraries that we may use in our codebase.

9.2 *Concurrency models and scalability*

We are adding third-party libraries to our codebase because we want to order them to do some job. This means we need to call the API, wait for the execution, and (optionally) get the result. This simple flow hides some complexity regarding the processing execution model. When we call code we don't own, we need to be careful about its concurrency model.

The first scenario that we will consider is quite simple. We have a program that works in a sequential, blocking manner. Figure 9.1 illustrates this program.

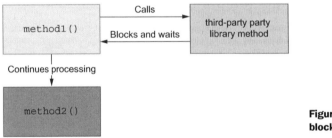

Figure 9.1   A program with a blocking call from our codebase

In our program, method1() executes a third-party library method. The latter method is blocking, meaning the method1() caller thread will block until the third-party library method returns. Once this method returns, the caller flow continues, and it progresses by calling method2().

The situation gets more complicated when we have an async, nonblocking processing flow. Some web frameworks (such as Node.js, Netty, Vert.x, and more) base their processing on the event-loop model (figure 9.2).

When operating in this context, every request or piece of work that needs to be processed is put in to a queue. For example, when the web server needs to process an HTTP request, the worker thread that accepts the request does not do the actual

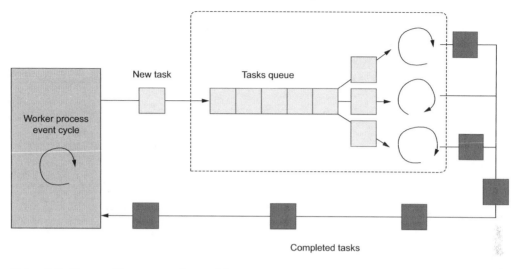

Figure 9.2 The event-loop processing model

processing. It puts the data that needs to be processed in the queue. Next, the thread from the thread pool responsible for processing takes the queue's data and does the actual processing. When you execute any method call from code that cannot block, you need to be careful about calling the code you don't own (figure 9.3).

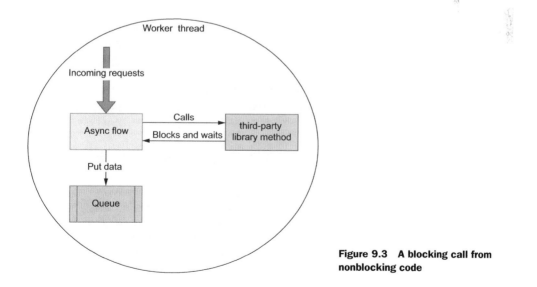

Figure 9.3 A blocking call from nonblocking code

In such a scenario, everything is executed within the same worker thread. The async flow accepts the data and can do some preprocessing such as deserializing it from bytes. Next, it puts the data information in to a queue. This operation must be fast and nonblocking to not stall the processing of incoming requests. If we call the code that we don't own from such a code, we risk blocking the main processing. Therefore, we will be degrading the overall performance of our application.

For those reasons, we must know the execution of the code that we call. Does it block? Is it async or sync? Next, let's see how to use a third-party library that offers both models.

9.2.1   *Using async and sync APIs*

Let's consider a situation where we are integrating with a third-party library to save and load an entity. The API is blocking, meaning that we should not call it from the async code. The following listing shows the code for this scenario.

Listing 9.6   Blocking API

```
public interface EntityService {
  Entity load();
  void save(Entity entity);
}
```

The caller thread will block whether it calls the load or save method, but this is problematic and limits the ways you can use this API. For example, it will be hard to plug this blocking processing into an async code you already have. Also, your application threading model may not allow any blocking (e.g., when using Vert.*x*).

What can we do if we still want to leverage the third-party library, even if it is blocking? The easiest and most obvious way is to create a wrapper around the blocking code, as listing 9.7 shows. The wrapper delegates the actual processing to the external library, and it provides the methods that can be used in an async way. Both methods can return the CompletableFuture entity, a promise that will be fulfilled in the future. The async code that does not allow blocking calls only the nonblocking versions of those methods.

Listing 9.7   Wrapping a blocking call into async

```
public CompletableFuture<Entity> load() {
  return CompletableFuture.supplyAsync(entityService::load, executor);
}

public CompletableFuture<Void> save(Entity entity) {
  return CompletableFuture.runAsync(() -> entityService.save(entity), executor);
}
```

Note that the load() method returns the promise of Entity, which can be fulfilled at any time. The caller can chain async operations without blocking the caller's thread.

At first sight, it seems that the solution is easy. However, wrapping the blocking code into async is not always simple. We need to execute the async actions in a separate thread. For that purpose, we need to create a dedicated thread pool that this code will use. The thread pool needs to be monitored and fine-tuned. We need to pick the proper number of threads and also a queue for incoming operations, as the following listing shows.

Listing 9.8 Creating an executor

```
public WrapIntoAsync(EntityService entityService) {
  this.entityService = entityService;
  executor = new ThreadPoolExecutor(1, 10, 100, TimeUnit.SECONDS, new
    LinkedBlockingDeque<>(100));
}
```
◁— **Takes corePoolSize, maximumPoolSize, keepAliveTimeout and tasks queue**

Finding the optimal configuration for the code we don't own may not be an easy task. We need to learn about its expected traffic and conduct performance tests. Also, if the library is written in a blocking way, its performance may be worse than the code that is written in an async way. Wrapping the blocking code may only postpone the scalability problem without solving it.

If performance is crucial, and there is no existing third-party library that does the job in an async way, you may consider implementing parts of it on your own. Let's consider a situation where we are picking an external library that provides the async API out of the box. The following listing shows how our entity service API would look.

Listing 9.9 Creating an async API

```
public interface EntityServiceAsync {
  CompletableFuture<Entity> load();

  CompletableFuture<Void> save(Entity entity);
}
```

All methods of this component are returning a promise, denoting that the processing is async. It means that the internals of the library that we are integrating with is written in an async way. We don't need to implement any translation layer from the sync to the async world with such an approach. This often means that the thread pool that we use for performing this async task is encapsulated within the library. It may be already fine-tuned for most of our use cases. However, as you may remember from the first section of this chapter, you need to be aware of the defaults.

The fact that a thread pool is encapsulated within the library does not mean it does not create threads. The code is called from our application. The threads created internally for the purpose of the library we are calling will still occupy resources in our application. If you have a blocking, synchronous flow in your application, it is easier to call the async code than when the flow is async and needs to call the blocking code.

The only thing you need to do is get the underlying value from returned CompletableFuture. You also need to be aware that this is blocking, so passing a reasonable timeout to that action is advised. However, if your application flow is already blocking, it won't be problematic for you. The following listing shows this approach.

Listing 9.10   A nonblocking to blocking flow

```
public class AsyncToSync {
  private final EntityServiceAsync entityServiceAsync;

  public AsyncToSync(EntityServiceAsync entityServiceAsync) {
    this.entityServiceAsync = entityServiceAsync;          The translated
  }                                                        method
                                                           returns the
  Entity load() throws InterruptedException, ExecutionException,   Entity.
    TimeoutException {
    return entityServiceAsync.load().get(100, TimeUnit.MILLISECONDS);
  }                           Blocks the async call, getting the value
}
```

If you choose to pick a library that exposes async or sync API, it is often more reasonable to choose the async version. Even if your application flow is blocking today, you may want to convert your application to asynchronous processing to increase its scalability and performance.

If you are already using a library that provides the asynchronous APIs, it will be easier to migrate to the new flow. However, if you are using a library that was written in a blocking way, the migration won't be as simple. You will need to provide a translation layer and manage the thread pool. Moreover, the code that was not written as an async call in the first place is often implemented differently. Wrapping the calls into a promise API would provide a fast workaround.

A library's performance that is written in an async way from the beginning will often be better than the blocking version. You may observe this, especially if your whole processing flow is async. Let's now look at how our application's scalability may be limited by the library that is not written in a way that can scale out.

9.2.2   Distributed scalability

When your application is executed in a distributed environment, it is crucial to understand the scalability of the third-party libraries you want to use. Let's consider a library that provides scheduling capabilities for our application (similar to the cron job). Its primary responsibility is to check whether the task should be executed and to run it when a time threshold is met.

The third-party library needs a persistence layer to store its tasks. Every task has a date and time when it should be executed. Once it is executed, the scheduling library updates its status. It could be *Success*, *Failed*, or *None*, if the task is not yet processed. Figure 9.4 shows the scheduling library.

The tasks that are due to be executed are stored in the database and fetched by the application at some interval. When developing such a feature, we may be tempted to start thinking and designing for a one node use case. Our integration tests may validate

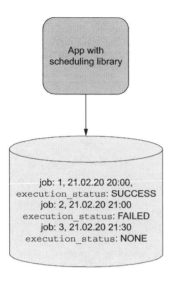

job: 1, 21.02.20 20:00,
execution_status: SUCCESS
job: 2, 21.02.20 21:00
execution_status: FAILED
job: 3, 21.02.20 21:30
execution_status: NONE

Figure 9.4 Application with a scheduling library

the behavior of the scheduling library with the embedded database. However, we may not observe any problem when data is queried from the database in such a case.

The situation can radically change when we operate in a distributed context. The application that needs scheduling capabilities can be deployed to multiple nodes, and the same scheduling task cannot be duplicated. This means that when our application is deployed to multiple nodes, they need to agree on which of those nodes should process each of those tasks. In other words, the same task cannot be processed by more than one node.

Such a requirement means that the state of jobs needs to be globally synchronized or partitioned. If the scheduling library we picked does not have a proper scalability logic implemented, we risk severe performance, or even correctness, problems.

Let's assume we want to deploy our application to three nodes. Each of those nodes has a scheduling library, as figure 9.5 illustrates.

If the scheduling library we use is not implemented in a way that can scale, all of those nodes will contend for the job record in the database, as demonstrated in figure 9.5. The correctness of those changes could be achieved via using transitions or a global lock on a specific record. But both of those solutions may impact the performance of our library substantially.

This problem can be addressed if the scheduling library supports partitioning. For example, the first node could be responsible for tasks in a given minute range, the other node for a different time period, and so on. What's important is that the library we use should be designed in a way that can scale out. Often, this is a nontrivial task and requires careful planning and engineering. Not all libraries are designed to work in such a context. Therefore, when picking a library we know will be executed in a distributed environment (on multiple nodes), we should analyze it carefully to determine whether it can run in a distributed context.

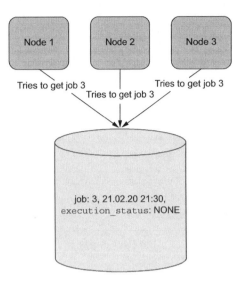

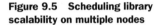

**Figure 9.5   Scheduling library
scalability on multiple nodes**

Another solution for the scheduling library that we may apply is the leader–followers architecture. In this approach, all schedule requests are executed by a leader. In the background, the replicas will synchronize their databases with the leader. However, they will not execute any actual logic. If the leader node crashes, one of the follower nodes will become the new leader and will start executing cron jobs. However, the scheduling library needs to be designed to work in a multinode context up-front.

Understanding the scalability model and knowing if it requires a global state allows us to scale our application without the hard to fix problems. When the library is not designed to work in a distributed environment, we are risking scalability and correctness problems. Such problems may often appear when we deploy our applications to *N* nodes, where *N* is a higher than usual number of nodes. Such situations often happen when we have a surge in traffic to our application. What's worse, most often, you will see a surge in traffic when there is a high business opportunity for your product. It can happen, for example, during holidays. This is not a time when we want to learn that our application relies on a library that does not scale.

Once again, the code that we use becomes our code, and this will be obvious to our customers when they notice an outage. In the next section, we will look at the testability of third-party libraries to mitigate these concerns.

9.3   *Testability*

When picking a library with code that we didn't design and develop, we should always have limited trust in it. We should assume almost nothing. However, when we pick a proven and widely used library, the quality and correctness are often good enough. In those cases, testing will likely validate our assumptions about the library, rather than its correctness. The best form of experimenting and validating a third-party library that we consider to use in our code is via testing. However, testing code that we don't influence is a bit different than testing our own code. The main reason for this is we cannot change this code easily, if at all.

When we want to test a component from our codebase, and it turns out that our code does not allow us to impact some behavior, this is relatively easy to change. For example, if our code initializes an internal component without giving the caller the possibility to inject the fake or mock value, we can refactor the code without huge problems. On the other hand, when we use a third-party library, impacting the code-base may be hard or not feasible. Even if we submit the change, the time from change to deployment can be substantial. Because of that, before choosing a third-party library, we should validate its testability.

Let's start from the first checkpoint on our testability list. This is: does the third-party library provide a testing library that allows us to test it?

9.3.1 *Testing library*

When importing a library that provides some complex capabilities, we should be able to test its code reasonably easy, and testing should be straightforward. Let's consider a situation where we want to implement reactive processing in our application. For that purpose, we need to choose between a couple libraries that provide this functionality.

We start by implementing a processing skeleton that serves as a prototype for more advanced logic (see listing 9.11). We want to sum all incoming numbers within a 10 second window. The logic operates on a stream, meaning that as the events arrive, they are windowed, and then processing continues.

Listing 9.11 Reactive processing

```
public static Flux<Integer> sumElementsWithinTimeWindow(Flux<Integer> flux) {
  return flux
        .window(Duration.ofSeconds(10))
        .flatMap(window -> window.reduce(Integer::sum));
}
```

This reactive processing is concise and looks clear. This aspect of the library is very positive. However, we should also consider its testability and validate how easy it is to test the defined processing. Let's start with a naive approach when we write the testing logic from scratch. This example will demonstrate a couple of problems and will highlight the need for a dedicated testing library.

Let's construct a stream of three values: 1, 2, 3, as listing 9.12 shows. Next, we sleep for 10 seconds before we validate the windowing logic. Note that using the `Thread.sleep()` method in a test is a bad pattern, but shortly, we will see how to improve this. Finally, we assert that the resulting value is equal to 6.

Listing 9.12 Testing reactive processing: A native approach

```
// given
Flux<Integer> data = Flux.fromIterable(Arrays.asList(1, 2, 3));
Thread.sleep(10_000);
```

```
// when
Flux<Integer> result = sumElementsWithinTimeWindow(data);

// then
assertThat(result.blockFirst()).isEqualTo(6);
```

Unfortunately, our logic has a couple problems. First, we are using a thread sleep that increases the time needed for this unit test. In a real-world system, we would need to test a lot more processing and scenarios. This increases the time needed for all unit tests to an unacceptable threshold. Second, using this testing approach is hard to validate in more complex scenarios. For example, how do we verify that the value after 10 seconds is not taken into account? We would need to emit another value, wait some more time, and then validate the results. By examining this simple use case, we can see that using even a well-written library without the testing infrastructure would be painful and sometimes not feasible.

Fortunately, the library we are using in this chapter provides a testing library. For the reactive testing code, we'll use the reactor-test library (http://mng.bz/8lPz). This allows us to simplify the tests and enable the testing of more advanced scenarios.

For our test, we will use a `TestPublisher` class that allows us to provide data to the reactive flow (see listing 9.13). It will also allow us to simulate delays without actually causing any slowdown in the overall test execution time. There is no sleep needed, so our tests will finish almost instantaneously. This `TestPublisher` is passed to a `Step-Verifier`. Both of those classes are provided by the reactive testing library that is compatible with the reactive production library.

> **Listing 9.13   Testing reactive processing using a testing library**

```
final TestPublisher<Integer> testPublisher = TestPublisher.create();

Flux<Integer> result = sumElementsWithinTimeWindow(testPublisher.flux());

StepVerifier.create(result)
    .then(() -> testPublisher.emit(1, 2, 3))
    .thenAwait(Duration.ofSeconds(10))
    .then(() -> testPublisher.emit(4))
    .expectNext(6)
    .verifyComplete();
```

The `StepVerifier` class allows us to emit values, await for a specific time without blocking, and emit values again. For our test scenario, we emit 1, 2, 3 values, once again. However, after emitting those values, we simulate a delay of 10 seconds, which is equal to a time window span. After the delay, we emit another value. Finally, we assert that the first produced value is equal to 6. This means the value emitted after the window span was not included in the first window.

Using this approach, we can test any scenario we need to think about. Also, the fact that we are testing the delay does not mean that the unit test takes longer. Our tests will be fast, so we will be able to create many unit tests to cover the logic that is implemented using a reactive library.

> **TIP** Many of the libraries out there provide a testing library for our use. Often, this is a sign of high quality and easier development.

Let's now take a look at the second aspect of testability for third-party libraries. This is how to inject fakes or mocks.

9.3.2 *Testing with fakes (test double) and mocks*

The other important aspect that we should focus on when considering using a third-party library is the ability to inject a user-provided object for the purpose of testing. The object can be a mock that allows us to simulate and validate a specific behavior. It can also be a fake object (test double) that allows us to provide data or context to a tested code. Often, libraries hide too many internals from the callers guarding against potential overuse by the user. However, this can make the library hard to test.

If you can take a look at the library's codebase, look for the new instance creation. If there is no way to inject the alternative implementation for testing purposes, it may signal future testing problems. If we are using a proprietary library that does not expose its source code, it may be impossible to analyze the code. In such cases, experimenting via tests and validating our assumptions gets even more important. The reason for this is that we cannot look into its source code.

We will now look at the testability of a third-party library, whether it provides the possibility to inject the caller's provided test double or not. Let's assume we want to pick a third-party library that provides cache functionality to our app. One of the most important use cases of a cache is the possibility to evict old entries. Eviction can be based on either the size of the cache or the amount of time the entry was in the cache. It can also be based on both conditions. When evaluating a new library, we should test the expected behavior to validate our assumptions about it.

We'll start our experiments by building a simple cache that takes a key and returns it to the uppercase version. The production system will have a more complicated cache loader behavior, but the more straightforward example presented here is good enough for us.

We want to validate the behavior of the library based on our assumptions. In the following listing, we construct a new cache with an expiration after write equal to DEFAULT_EVICTION_TIME. The CacheLoader gets the value for a user's provided key.

Listing 9.14 Initial cache use

```
public class CacheComponent {
  public static final Duration DEFAULT_EVICTION_TIME = Duration.ofSeconds(5);
  public final LoadingCache<String, String> cache;

  public CacheComponent() {
    cache =
```

```
            CacheBuilder.newBuilder()
                .expireAfterWrite(DEFAULT_EVICTION_TIME)
                .recordStats()
                .build(
                    new CacheLoader<String, String>() {
                      @Override
                      public String load(@Nullable String key) throws Exception {
                        return key.toUpperCase();
                      }
                    });
    }

    public String get(String key) throws ExecutionException {
      return cache.get(key);
    }
}
```

The logic seems straightforward, but still, we need to test our assumptions about its behavior. We didn't write the code for this library, so it can surprise us.

We want to test the eviction strategy of the underlying cache. To test it, we need to simulate a delay between the insertion of the cache's element and validation of the eviction process. Because of that, we need to wait for a time equal to the eviction time. For the use case, it was equal to 5 seconds. However, in a real-world system, the eviction time can be substantially longer (even hours or days). The following listing shows an initial, naive approach of testing that requires the use of the `Thread.sleep()`, which also requires a wait equal to `DEFAULT_EVICTION_TIME`.

Listing 9.15   Testing without injection

```
// given
CacheComponent cacheComponent = new CacheComponent();

// when
String value = cacheComponent.get("key");

// then
assertThat(value).isEqualTo("KEY");

// when
Thread.sleep(CacheComponent.DEFAULT_EVICTION_TIME.toMillis());

// then
assertThat(cacheComponent.get("key")).isEqualTo("KEY");
assertThat(cacheComponent.cache.stats().evictionCount()).isEqualTo(1);
```

Note that the eviction is done on the load (the `get` method) operation. To trigger this, we need to call the accessor method. This is one of the things that may surprise us and doesn't align with our assumptions about this library. Without the proper unit test, we would not be able to catch that behavior. As I mentioned, if our component's eviction time is too high, it may not be feasible to test our cache component. At this point, we need to think about, and possibly look at, the source code of the third-party library to find the component that influences the testing behavior.

After a quick investigation, we find that the LoadingCache, when doing a get operation, uses a ticker to find if the value should be evicted or not. The following listing provides the evidence.

Listing 9.16 Investigating the Cache library testability

```
V get (K key, int hash, CacheLoader<? super K, V> loader) throws
    ExecutionException {
...
long now = this.map.ticker.read();
...
}
```

Indeed, this listing shows that the third-party cache library we are using encapsulates the time logic in a ticker component. The last thing we need to do to improve our unit test for this library is to check if the user can inject this component. This allows us to provide a fake implementation and influence the milliseconds returned by it. By doing so, we can simulate time progression without the need for waiting. Fortunately, the LoadingCache builder has a method for providing such a component from the outside, as the following listing shows.

Listing 9.17 Injecting a user-provided component

```
public CacheBuilder<K, V> ticker(Ticker ticker) {
    Preconditions.checkState(this.ticker == null);
    this.ticker = (Ticker)Preconditions.checkNotNull(ticker);
    return this;
}
```

We can use this method in our unit test, passing a user-provided ticker via the builder. The first step is to implement the Ticker interface the cache builder accepts. The fact that this interface is well-designed and simple makes it easier to create a fake for it. If the third-party component allows you to inject your own implementation but requires you to implement an interface or extend a class with lots of methods, the fake behavior may be harder to achieve. We would need to know a lot about its internal components, state, and the methods that we need to fake.

In listing 9.18, the FakeTicker uses AtomicLong for returning nanoseconds. It is important to use a proper unit, as defined by the third-party library contract. This fake allows us to advance a time on any unit in the future or in the past.

Listing 9.18 Improving testability with a user-provided fake

```
public class FakeTicker extends Ticker {
  private final AtomicLong nanos = new AtomicLong();

  public FakeTicker advance(long nanoseconds) {
    nanos.addAndGet(nanoseconds);
```

```
    return this;
  }

  public FakeTicker advance(Duration duration) {
    return advance(duration.toNanos());
  }

  @Override
  public long read() {
    return nanos.get();
  }
}
```

Because we can use the FakeTicker in our tests, we no longer need to use Thread
.sleep(), so our unit tests can be fast and cover a lot of use cases. We can use this new
mechanism (as the following listing shows) to validate a wider range of our assumptions about this library.

Listing 9.19   Improved test with fake

```
// given
FakeTicker fakeTicker = new FakeTicker();
CacheComponent cacheComponent = new CacheComponent(fakeTicker);

// when
String value = cacheComponent.get("key");

// then
assertThat(value).isEqualTo("KEY");

// when
fakeTicker.advance(CacheComponent.DEFAULT_EVICTION_TIME);

// then
assertThat(cacheComponent.get("key")).isEqualTo("KEY");
assertThat(cacheComponent.cache.stats().evictionCount()).isEqualTo(1);
```

Our test improves substantially. We can simulate the time movement using the
advance() method. Even if our eviction time were days long, our unit test would finish instantaneously.

Imagine a scenario in which the third-party library we're validating does not
expose the ability to inject the internally used Ticker component. In that case, we
wouldn't be able to validate some of our assumptions. If we decide to choose this
library, it will be problematic because we won't be able to test some of its behaviors.
For that reason, we will probably select a different library.

Almost every third-party library we may use has some internal state. If the library
allows us to inject a different implementation, that is a significant advantage of a
library regarding its testability.

> **NOTE** If the third-party library we are testing has some hard-to-test dependencies, we may consider using Mockito, Spock, or other testing frameworks. They may simplify the testing of some of those edge cases.

Up to this point, we looked at unit testing third-party libraries. Let's now look at the possibilities to perform integration testing of third-party code. It may also impact our decision about choosing one library over another.

9.3.3 *Integration testing toolkit*

Once we are sure the third-party library we plan to use provides a way to unit test it, we can focus on the next layer: integration tests. Suppose the library we are importing provides functionality that can be isolated from other components. In that case, it may be enough for us to unit test it and rely on integration tests that do not need to know about the actual implementation. The idea behind integration tests is they should test higher-level components without worrying too much about lower-level details. However, we tend to build our applications based on frameworks that provide a lot of functionalities. In the JVM world, we can use Spring, Dropwizard, Quarkus, OSGi, or Akka, to name a few. Such frameworks may have multiple dependent components providing an API layer (HTTP), a data-access layer, a dependency injection framework, and so forth.

It is also worth noting that those components can have their own lifecycle. Starting an application with a given framework should be relatively easy, but we still need to create proper components and inject them. Moreover, sometimes the configuration of our application may differ for integration tests versus the normal application run. For example, we may have a different connection string to a database, different usernames, different passwords, and so on.

When we start building an application based on some framework, we should assert that the framework allows us to easily spin up the application in the integration tests. For example, the Spring framework allows us to start the application in integration tests via an @SpringBootTest annotation (http://mng.bz/ExPd) and SpringRunner (http://mng.bz/NxPn), as the following listing shows.

Listing 9.20 Spring integration test

```
@RunWith(SpringRunner.class)
@SpringBootTest(webEnvironment = SpringBootTest.WebEnvironment.RANDOM_PORT)
@ActiveProfiles("integration")
public class PaymentServiceIntegrationTest {

  @Value("${local.server.port}")        ⟵┐  Injects the
  private int port;                            │  assigned port

  private String createTestUrl() {
    return "http://localhost:" + port + suffix;
  }
}
```

```
// ...
}
```

The Spring framework provides a couple of options to run our tests. In listing 9.20, we use testing from a Spring Boot library with all required annotations. If your application is based on this framework, the `@SpringBootTest` will find all components and start them using a proper lifecycle. We don't need to worry about the actual starting procedure. Moreover, if you want to test the HTTP API, it will spin up the embedded HTTP web server with a free port. The port will be injected once the server is running. (We don't need to worry about picking a free port either. It will be taken care of by the Spring testing library.) Finally, we can execute normal HTTP requests to a localhost endpoint created by the `createTestUrl()` method.

Also note that we can activate different profiles for our integration tests. This is useful when we want to have a different configuration of components initialized for integration tests. When using the Spring testing library, the possibility for picking different profiles in test executions is built-in and provided for us.

Starting an HTTP embedded server and exposing HTTP endpoints may not sound too problematic. However, in real life, our applications tend to be more involved. We will have data access layers with repositories, integration with other services, and many other components. If the framework provides an integration testing library, we can experiment and reason about the library faster and more easily. In the next section, we will focus on the problem of too many dependencies in third-party libraries that can seriously impact our application.

9.4   *Dependencies of third-party libraries*

Every library or framework we import and use in our code is written by engineers who may need to make a similar decision: should we implement a small part of the logic ourselves or use another library that provides that functionality for us? It is obvious that when we import a library that provides, for example, HTTP client functionality, it should not rely on yet another library providing the same functionality. The situation is a bit different when engineers who create a library are not working on its core functionality. For example, the HTTP client library may provide out-of-the box JSON serialization and deserialization capabilities, as figure 9.6 shows.

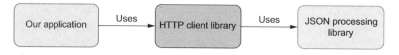

Figure 9.6   HTTP client with JSON processing

JSON processing is not a trivial task, and the designers of the HTTP client library may not be experts in that. Because of that reason, perhaps they chose to use other third-party libraries to provide this functionality. It is a reasonable decision, but it creates a couple of problems for our application.

The situation gets complicated if our application needs to use JSON processing capabilities in our logic, unrelated to the HTTP client library. We need to remember that every class that is shipped with the HTTP client (including their dependencies) will be visible to our application's code. Because of that, we can use the JSON processing library via transitive dependency that the HTTP client library uses. However, this is a bad idea for a couple reasons.

Mainly, we will tightly couple our application code to the library used by the third-party library. The HTTP client library may decide to change the JSON processing library in the future. In that case, our code will have problems because this library will no longer expose the original JSON library and its classes.

9.4.1 Avoiding version conflicts

The other (better) solution is to create a direct dependency from our application to a JSON processing library that we want to use (see figure 9.7). Unfortunately, this also has a problem because we might have a version clash between two JSON libraries. This will happen if the HTTP client and our application use a different version of the JSON library.

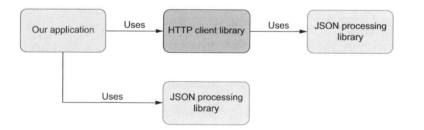

Figure 9.7 Our application uses HTTP and JSON libraries directly

For our example, it is important to note that real-world applications often depend on many third-party dependencies. Each of those dependencies may bring its own dependencies. It may get unmanageable pretty fast. We may have multiple versions of multiple libraries used in our one and only app.

All the classes the JSON library provides are exposed under the com.fasterxml .jackson package. For example, if we want, we can use the com.fasterxml.jackson .databind.ObjectMapper. This means both versions of this class, one from the HTTP client and one from our application, are accessible via this package. For that reason, a build tool needs to pick one of those classes. This may create a variety of problems like method not found, method signature changed, and similar, as we'll discuss in chapter 12.

> **Semantic versioning and compatibility**
>
> Most libraries have adopted semantic versioning with a version string consisting of three parts: major, minor, and patch. Any breaking change should be indicated by a change to the major part of the version string. We'll look at this in much greater detail in chapter 12, but the impact here is that if the complete set of dependencies only uses the same major version for the JSON library, we should be able to just use the latest of those versions everywhere. If there are multiple major versions involved, we need them to be effectively independent dependencies.

Fortunately, this problem can be solved in the third-party library that we import. This technique is called *shading*. We will explain it based on the HTTP library client example. Let's consider a situation where the JSON library that it uses is a FasterXml Jackson (https://github.com/FasterXML/jackson).

If the HTTP client use the shading technique for its JSON dependency, it can rewrite all the package names and put them under a different prefix. For example, the HTTP client may expose all its classes under the com.http.client. In that case, after shading, all the JSON library classes from the HTTP client library will be accessible under the com.http.client.com.fasterxml.jackson package name.

This technique allows the HTTP client to *hide* the JSON processing library classes from our application. They are still reachable, but we would still be able to use the independent Jackson version in our application. We would not need to worry about the dependencies brought by the third-party HTTP client library.

The shading technique is powerful, but it requires substantial maintenance overhead from the third-party libraries' engineers. The shading process that rewrites the classes would need to be done for every third-party library it needs to hide. This is done during the build phase of a library. Therefore, it complicates the build process because it may require defining shading behavior for multiple libraries. In case the third-party library that is shaded changes its package scheme, we would need to adapt the shading plug-in configuration.

When evaluating a library we are considering, we should examine all the library's dependencies. If it uses the shading technique, it means it hides its third-party dependencies from our application. By doing so, it will not pollute our application. Therefore, this may be a significant advantage over other competitive libraries that provide the same functionality but do not hide its third-party dependencies (those that do not use shading). It can also signal that the third-party library we are using is well-designed and carefully thought out.

9.4.2   *Too many dependencies*

We need to be aware that almost every library needs to use other libraries to provide noncore functionality. Because of that, we should examine the number of libraries it brings. There is a big difference between importing other libraries for hard-to-write, complex functionality and for simple tasks that can be easily achieved and implemented from scratch.

We need to remember that every library that we import impacts our application. It is often not feasible for library creators to perform shading for all dependencies, as it requires too much time and effort.

Every dependency that is imported into our application influences our target application. The most common method of deploying an application is by building a self-contained package (fat jar, also known as uber-jar) that contains all the required dependencies, as figure 9.8 illustrates.

Assuming that our application code takes 20 MB, we still need to package the Java runtime environment and all third-party libraries we are using. The target file will be a self-contained runnable application. In our example, it will take 120 MB.

When an application is deployed as a fat jar, it allows running the application straightforwardly, everywhere, without any external dependencies. This is getting even more popular in containerized environments (e.g., Kubernetes and Docker).

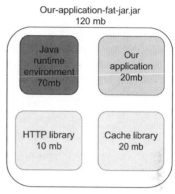

Figure 9.8   The makeup of a fat jar

It means that the produced file with our application will grow for every dependency it has. If it includes all third-party dependencies and dependencies used by those third-party libraries. For that reason, we should seriously take into account the number of dependencies our application has. The fewer the dependencies there are, the smaller our app will be. The smaller our app is, the faster it will start, and also, it will be easier to deploy and manage.

The runtime overhead will also be lower because the built application needs to be loaded in the machine's RAM that runs it. This is gaining more attention, as the serverless approach is getting more popular. In the serverless environment, applications have a limited environment (e.g., CPU and RAM). Also, the startup time in the serverless environment is highly important.

In the Java ecosystem, the Maven-shade-plugin (https://maven.apache.org/plugins/maven-shade-plugin/) simplifies the build process of the fat jar. It also provides a way to perform shading using the renaming technique. In the next section, we will consider how to choose third-party code in your application, along with options for how you use it.

9.5   Choosing and maintaining third-party dependencies

Choosing a library our code will use always introduces some coupling between our code and the third-party library. We can hide the third-party library behind an abstraction layer and expose methods called from our code, but this requires some maintenance overhead. Yet, it is feasible. Libraries we use have their own development lifecycle.

9.5.1   *First impressions*

When we first consider adopting a library and including it as part of our application, there are various aspects to check fairly quickly before doing a deep dive to determine technical suitability. This is generally easier to do if the library is open source, but most of the following questions should still be answerable for commercial libraries. Of course, the aspects covered in the previous sections should be considered in detail too.

- *How stable is the library?* If it doesn't yet have a stable release, are you convinced it will have one before you need to ship your own code?
- *Is the library under active development?* If the library solves a well-constrained problem, it may be OK if it's effectively done and doesn't required any updates for a while, but it's worth ensuring that it hasn't been abandoned.
- *Is the library popular in the rest of the community?* It's a lot easier to get help if there's an active ecosystem, and that's typically a good indicator of the quality of the code as well.
- *What does the team behind the library look like?* A library authored by multiple people, possibly backed by a large company that uses it themselves, is less of a risk than the hobby project of a single developer.
- *Is the library clearly documented?* Look for API reference documentation, conceptual documentation, and tutorials or quick-starts.

While these are reasonable indicators, they're definitely not simple yes or no answers. Large enterprises can still walk away from libraries they've developed for years, lone developers can diligently maintain projects for decades, and sometimes you can make do with quite sparse documentation. These are all just aspects to consider consciously. Let's look in a bit more detail at some more aspects, starting with options for how you adopt the third-party code within your codebase.

9.5.2   *Different approaches to reusing code*

Up to this point, we can see that picking a library is not a trivial task. We need to consider many factors, such as their configuration, concurrency, scalability models, testability, number of dependencies, development lifecycle, and versioning. If the task you are expecting the library to do is complex, and you plan to use a variety of its features, using the third-party library will justify all those tradeoffs and maintenance costs. However, if, for example, you need a particular and small feature, such as properly formatting a string or having more utility methods on collections, you may consider implementing a specific method in your codebase. The third-party library method you would like to use, on the one hand, may simplify your code a little bit. However, it will bring all the maintenance problems and complexity to your codebase.

Depending on the license of the third-party library you are considering, you may be able to copy the needed method into your codebase, add the unit test for it, and take full ownership of this code. It will allow you to use existing production-proven code without the need to import the library with all its APIs and methods. This may be a rational solution if you need to use small parts of the third-party library. Of course, it has its disadvantages because you need to be responsible for its bug fixes. However, if the code that you are porting is small and you understand it fully, there shouldn't be many problems with it.

You can also fork the original library and develop needed functionalities if it's impossible or hard to change the original code. This also comes with many maintenance problems. For example, you need to keep the fork up to date to include the bug fixes from the original codebase. Also, after some time, both code versions may diverge, making it impossible or hard to keep them consistent.

9.5.3 Vendor lock-in

It is important to be aware that, regardless of the popularity of the given library and the company that backs it, the solution we use may be deprecated and, finally, removed—whether it is some cloud service that gets replaced with a better version or proprietary software we bought, but the company behind it was acquired, and the product changed. Also, a third-party open source library might be popular, so we choose it to use in our application. However, after some time, a new library is developed. The new one solves the same problem faster and more cleanly, so people start migrating to this new solution. The solution we used has lost its traction and, after some time, is in maintenance mode—no longer developed.

Architectures evolve, new patterns are created, and software gets deprecated. When we start using a new library or service, we should be aware that there may be a need to migrate to a new solution in the future. The probability of such an event is not the same for all software components we use. We should hide the integration points with those libraries (or services) behind an abstraction layer if we know that this probability is high. Then when there's a need to switch the implementation, the change will not propagate to a lot of places in our code. Instead, it will be encapsulated within the abstraction, and a code change will be needed only there.

When starting with a new library, we should observe how it impacts our application and architecture. The more invasive the integration is, the harder it will be to change the vendor in the future. It is hard (or impossible) to hide every possible library and service integration point behind abstraction in the real world. Some level of vendor lock-in is also hard to alleviate, but we may strive to minimize it by picking libraries that do not require tight coupling with our applications.

9.5.4 Licensing

When deciding on using the code from another library, you need to consider its license. For example, let's suppose you want to use a library that has a GNU General

Public License. If you're going to use its code in your project, you may need to make your project source code public as well. This may be a blocker for many internal projects for which you don't want to expose your code. Decisions about licensing are complicated, and the cost of a mistake could be high. For that reason, if you have any doubts about it, I recommend consulting with a legal department that can give you proper guidelines for your questions.

9.5.5   *Libraries vs. frameworks*

Often, when starting out with a library in our codebase, we can abstract it away without a substantial cost. For example, all calls to the HTTP service using a specific library can be hidden in our custom service class. Next, all the interaction between the HTTP library and our application code can be done via this service class and not directly via the HTTP library. However, we need to be careful not to leak anything specific to a library that we are using, including exceptions (as we learned in chapter 3) and configurations (as we learned in chapter 6). Once we do that, it is easier to change the decision later. We can switch a library for another implementation without a considerable cost. We can also decide to implement it ourselves and remove the dependency on this library.

The situation changes a lot when we are using frameworks. Frameworks tend to impact the code of our applications substantially. Some frameworks are invasive and require us to use their constructs throughout our application. We can easily see that by looking at our codebase imports. The more framework imports are in our codebase, the more tightly coupled it is to our application. It is significantly more difficult to change the framework to something else during the lifecycle of our application compared to a library. Due to that fact, we should be more careful and do a thorough investigation before choosing a framework for our application (compared to the choice of a library).

9.5.6   *Security and updates*

The last, but not least, aspect we will focus on is the security impact of third-party libraries on our software. As we know, every piece of software can contain bugs. Those bugs not only impact correctness and performance but also the overall security of our application. For that reason, we should perform security tests before deploying a new release of our application. Our codebase's automatic security scan can also find issues, but we cannot forget that the libraries we use become our code.

Every third-party dependency we use evolves and can also contain its security vulnerabilities. When a new security vulnerability is found in the third-party library, it should be treated by the library's authors with top priority. Most often, it results in a new version being published soon after the vulnerability is found. Once it is fixed, we should update the offending library in our codebase as quickly as possible. The longer we wait, the more time there is for the potential attacker to exploit that vulnerability.

How can we find out if the third-party dependency had a security problem? We can, for example, check a variety of websites with security vulnerabilities (e.g., https://www.cvedetails.com/) and look for the library we use. These sites contain updates regarding security problems of different products and libraries. However, checking the website manually can be tedious and time-consuming. Fortunately, we can automate security checks that scan all third-party libraries and notify us when there is a problem. Some of those tools (e.g., https://dependabot.com/) can even automatically upgrade the version of the offending library and submit a change (e.g., a pull request using Git) to our codebase.

Security updates are the most important thing to consider, but it's worth keeping an eye on other updates for the library. If there's a new major version, you may want to plan to investigate how much has changed and consider upgrading sometime in the near future, particularly if the older version only has a limited support lifetime.

Minor versions should be easier to adopt if the library follows semantic versioning properly, and you may find that some of your code can be simplified due to new features. It's also worth checking out which bugs have been fixed in new releases, too. Sometimes you may find your application has been suffering from a problem without you even being aware of it.

9.5.7 *Decision checklist*

If you need to use a third-party library with more of its functionalities (or the solution with copying code is not possible), consider following the checklist of things to validate from this chapter. This checklist may alleviate a lot of your application's problems in the future.

- *Configurability and its defaults*—Can we provide (and override) all critical settings?
- *Concurrency model, scalability, and performance*—Does it provide an async API if our applications workflow is async as well?
- *Distributed context*—Can it be safely run in a distributed context (multi-node)?
- *Investigating reliability*—Are we choosing a framework or a library? If it's a framework, we need to do a more thorough investigation.
- *Testing via unit and integration tests to check assumptions about the library*—How hard it is to test the code that uses this library? Does the library provide its own testing toolkit?
- *Dependencies*—What does the library depend on? Is it self-contained and isolated? Or does it download a lot of external dependencies, impacting the size and complexity of your app?
- *Versioning*—Does the library follow semantic versioning? Is it evolving in a backward-compatible way?
- *Maintenance*—Is it popular and actively maintained?
- *Integration*—How invasive is the integration with this library? How much do we risk being locked into a single vendor?

- *Licensing*—Is the license of the third-party library that you are using allowing the usage in your context?
- *Security and updates*—Is it frequently upgrading the downstream components to address their security vulnerabilities?

Summary

- The majority of libraries we use need some configuration. Beware of the defaults that may impact your production code.
- Convention over configuration simplifies the prototyping and development phase but may hide some problems that will manifest in the production traffic.
- Our application should use third-party libraries that provide a similar concurrency model. This allows us to create applications that have better performance.
- In Java, it is easier to use the async API in the sync context rather than wrapping the async API in a sync abstraction, which is straightforward. Creating an async wrapper around sync API adds substantial complexity to our application.
- Picking a library with the synchronous design may limit our scalability in the future if we choose to change the execution model.
- Third-party libraries' scalability may differ substantially between a one node use case and the distributed system with N nodes. We should validate our assumptions about the library's scalability models that we consider using before it will be too costly to change.
- We should validate our assumptions about the code we don't own via testing.
- Testability of the third-party library we want to use should be essential when choosing one over another. This also manifests the overall quality of the code that we want to use.
- Unit and integration testing toolkits that ship with libraries allow us to test the code much more easily and quickly.
- Every third-party dependency brings its own dependencies. We should be aware of them and examine them before importing the code into our application.
- The size of our application gets more critical in containerized and serverless environments. The smaller the application is, the faster it can be deployed.
- We should keep the third-party libraries up to date to leverage all bug, security, and performance fixes of those libraries. Semantic versioning should be implemented by any library we use. It will simplify the update process.
- Semantic versioning gives us a lot of information about the cycle and development activity of third-party libraries. When the major version changes, it gives us information that upgrading won't be simple. However, when a minor or patch version changes, the upgrade should be straightforward.

Consistency and atomicity in distributed systems

10

This chapter covers

- Traffic flow between microservices deployed to N nodes and a distributed database
- Applications that work correctly in a one-node scenario and evolving them to work properly on N nodes
- Differences between atomicity and consistency in your application's environment

If we want our application to scale and run in a distributed environment, we need to design our code for that. Having a consistent view of the system is important and relatively easy to achieve if our application is deployed to one node and uses a standard database that works in a primary–secondary architecture. In such a context, a database transaction guarantees the atomicity of our operations. However, in reality, our applications need to be scalable and elastic.

Depending on our traffic patterns, we want to be able to deploy our services to N nodes. Once we deploy the application to N nodes, we may notice scalability problems on the lower layer—the database. In such a case, there is often a need to migrate the data layer to a distributed database. By doing so, we are able to distribute the incoming traffic handling to *N* microservices, which, in turn, distribute the traffic to *M* database nodes. In such an environment, our code needs to be designed in an entirely different way. This chapter focuses on the decisions and changes we need to perform to make our application logic consistent and atomic in such a distributed environment.

Let's start by understanding a simple architecture with multiple services, where each service is deployed to only one node. We'll learn and understand the traffic characteristics in such a context. Next, we will gradually progress to more complex architectures and see how our system design assumptions evolve.

10.1 At-least-once delivery of data sources

It is tempting to have a simplified view of our application deployed to one node that uses a nondistributed, standard SQL database. However, it is important to realize that even if our service has a straightforward deployment model and is not designed for scalability, it can (and probably will) operate in a distributed environment. The reason for that is if our system provides some business functionality, there is a high probability that it needs to call a different service. Every time we call an external service, a network call is performed. This means our service needs to execute a request that reaches out via the network and waits for the response.

10.1.1 Traffic between one-node services

Let's assume that our application A, which is deployed to one node, needs to perform a call to a mail service. When the service receives the request, it sends an email to the end user. In this case, we are operating in a distributed environment.

It's important to remember that every network request can fail (see figure 10.1). The failure can be caused by an error from the service we are calling.

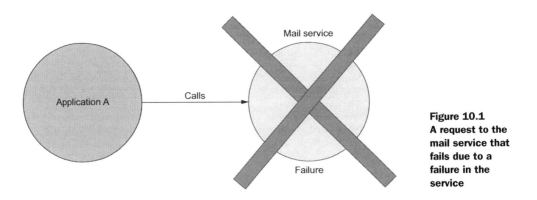

Figure 10.1
A request to the mail service that fails due to a failure in the service

At first glance, this is a simple situation. However, this is not simple to reason about from the caller's perspective (application A). In reality, application A may be an e-commerce service, a marketing automation service, a payment confirmation service, or others. The mail service's failure may happen after or before it sends an email. If there is a failure when sending an email, and the mail service is able to respond reasonably (with a status code denoting there is a maintenance break, for example), application A can conclude that the email was not sent. However, if application A gets a generic error without reason, we cannot safely assume that the mail was not already delivered.

This situation can get even more complicated when considering a network failure. There could be a situation in which we call the mail service, which results in a successfully sent email. The mail service responds to application A with a status denoting that everything went well. However, we need to remember that the request and response are sent via a network. As mentioned, every network call can fail for an arbitrary number of reasons. For example, some routers, switches, or hubs that are on the network path may break. There could also be a network partition preventing the package delivery (of the response), as figure 10.2 illustrates.

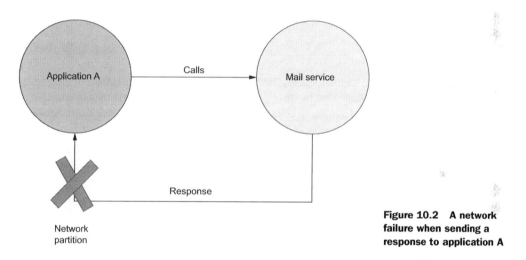

Figure 10.2   A network failure when sending a response to application A

When there is a network failure, the caller of application A cannot reason about the outcome of the operation. Application A will observe a timeout, denoting that the response was not sent within some time-bound limit. For that reason, the caller ends up in an inconsistent state: it does not have a complete view of the system. The mail may or may not have been sent.

10.1.2 *Retrying an application's call*

When application A does not receive a successful response, it may retry the initial request as one solution for this problem. If there was a temporary network partition, there's a high probability the retry will succeed. In that case, the caller application has a (mostly) consistent view of the system again.

However, in our system's architecture, retries are problematic. It can happen that we need to retry more than once. In such a situation, there is a chance that the mail service will send more than one duplicated email, as figure 10.3 shows. Let's consider a situation in which the first request fails, then the retry fails, and the request is retried yet again. In such a case, there is a possibility that the given email will be sent up to three times! The reason for this is that we don't know if the previous call (before the retries) failed before or after the mail was sent.

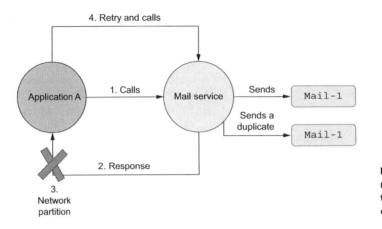

Figure 10.3 Retrying a request from application A that end ups with duplicate emails

Let's explain all the steps in figure 10.3. At the first stage of processing, application A sends a request to the mail service called via some protocol. Next, the mail service successfully sends the email. After it sends the email, it returns a response to the caller (application A). Unfortunately, during the response, there is a network partition. From application A's perspective, this will be observed as a failure. The caller application doesn't get the response and fails with the timeout. If the caller decides to retry in such a situation, it will call the mail service again. From the mail service's perspective, the retry is just another request that needs to be handled. For that reason, it sends the same email again. This time, the response is delivered to the caller application A successfully, so there is no retry. Unfortunately, the email was sent twice.

In real-world systems' architectures, we may need to integrate with more than one external service. Retries for sending email in this case may not be problematic, although it may result in sending emails to a customer's spam folder. We may have more significant problems if, for example, our system needs to make a payment. Making a payment is also an external call, and retrying a payment is problematic because we may debit the user's account twice (or more).

When we retry an operation to the mail service, it will offer an at-least-once delivery semantically. If application A retries the operation until it succeeds, the mail will be delivered once or more. There could be a duplicated delivery, but there is no way that there will be no delivery at all (besides some critical failure of the whole mail service). We will discuss the different delivery semantics in detail in the next chapter. For the purpose of this chapter, we only need to know that our architecture works in an at-least-once delivery approach, resulting in duplicates at the mail service side when application A sends retries.

10.1.3 *Producing data and idempotency*

Retrying an operation that has side effects is usually not safe. That's the case in our current architecture. But how do we decide if a retry operation is safe or not? The idempotency characteristic of the system answers this question. An operation is *idempotent* if it results in the same outcome, regardless of the number of invocations.

For example, getting information from a database is idempotent (assuming that the underlying data hasn't changed between attempts). All get operations, such as getting the data from an HTTP endpoint, should also be idempotent. If our service needs to retrieve data from a different service, it may retry the get operation multiple times. This is assuming that none of the get operation executions modify any state. It is safe to get the value, retrying as many times as needed.

As another example, deleting the record for a given ID is also idempotent. It gives the same outcome, regardless of the number of times it is executed. If we remove an entry with a specific ID and retry it, that is idempotent. Let's assume the entry was removed by the first operation. If there is a retry of removing an element that was already removed, it does nothing. Regardless of the number of invocations, the outcome is the same.

On the other hand, producing data is most often a nonidempotent operation. Sending mail is not idempotent. When we issue a sent operation, the mail is sent. In the architecture presented in the previous section, this is a side effect that cannot be rolled back. Retrying such an operation results in another send, so this is yet another side effect.

It is worth noting that some producing actions can be idempotent. If we properly design our business entities, this operation may be idempotent. For example, let's assume a situation in which we have a cart service that sends the events with the user's products status on an e-commerce site. These events can be consumed by other services interested in the cart state.

In this section, we will design an event in two ways: one will be idempotent and one will be nonidempotent. The most straightforward approach is to send an event denoting that a product was added to a cart each time an item is added. For example, if the user adds a new book A to a cart, a new event with quantity one is sent. Next, the users add the same book to the cart again, so quantity two is sent as figure 10.4 depicts.

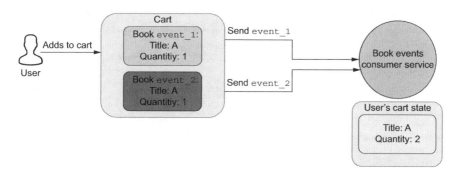

Figure 10.4   Nonidempotent entities that produce data in a shopping cart for a book service

The book event's consumer service builds its own view of the cart's state, based on the sent events. Such an event-based architecture is often used to build a system that follows the command query responsibility segregation (CQRS) pattern. This allows independent scaling of the writes (the cart service) and the read parts of our system. For our scenario, the events from the cart service are sent to some queue, and multiple independent consumer services can consume those events. Every service can build its database model optimizing it for its read traffic. Moreover, adding more read-side services does not impact the write performance of cart service. (We will look at this pattern more in depth in the following section.)

The problem with the presented business model is that it is not idempotent. If the cart service needs to retry the send for any cart event, there will be a duplicate state delivered to the book events consumer service. Because the consumer service needs to recreate the cart view based on events, it will increment the quantity of the item in the cart in case of one duplicated event. The resulting quantity will be equal to 3. The view will then be inconsistent and broken. It is clear to see that such a business model is nonidempotent. How can we rework it to be idempotent?

Instead of sending an event with every modification, the cart service can send an event with a full view of its cart. With this improved architecture, every time the new item is added to a user's cart, the new aggregated event is sent to an external service. The first time the user adds book A to a cart, the event with quantity one is sent. However, the second time book A is sent, a new event will contain a quantity equal to two. Because of that, all cart event consumer services will get the full view of the cart. They will not need to recreate the local view that can become inconsistent in case of retry. The cart service can now retry send of such an event without the danger of introducing an inconsistent state.

There is one more caveat we need to be careful about. In the case of a retry, the cart service can still emit a duplicate. Because the cart's full state is propagated, the more recent event sent to the customers can override the older cart state for the user. However, in the case of a retry, the ordering of events may get mixed, as figure 10.5 shows.

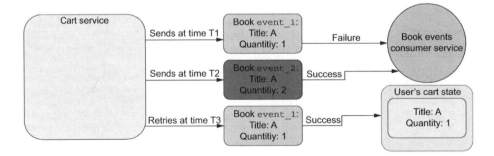

Figure 10.5   Out-of-order retry

Let's assume that the first operation at time $T1$ fails and the retry operation is scheduled to be executed after some time. In the meantime, the later operation at time $T2$

successfully finishes. Then, the scheduled retry operation is executed at time *T*3, and it will override the state propagated by book event_1. The event's customer service will end up with an inconsistent state. Because of that, we need to be careful when doing retries for the same user. This problem can be solved by ordering the events at the customer side or ordering the event's send at the cart service side. We should also not mix the ordering by retries.

Usually, we don't need to have a global ordering of events: the cart is created and owned by a specific user. Every user has a unique ID. Therefore, we can propagate the user_id of the user to which the cart belongs. By having that information, we only need to order events for this specific ID. If the cart events are ordered within a user_id, the services that consume events can recreate the cart per user_id without worrying about overriding behavior. We can say that cart data is partitioned by user_id, and that ordering is guaranteed within a partition. The queue frameworks that are widely used (e.g., Apache Kafka and Pulsar) provide a way to achieve an order within a partition.

Propagating the full state of a view also has some drawbacks. If the state gets bigger, we need to transfer more data over the network every time the event is sent. It also means that the serialization and deserialization logic will need to perform more work. However, in a real systems, the idempotency of such a business model often justifies those tradeoffs.

As we can see from this example, making the non-get operations idempotent is complex, fragile, and sometimes even impossible. The problems will be multiplied when we operate in a distributed architecture, such as CQRS, with many components.

10.1.4 Understanding Command Query Responsibility Segregation (CQRS)

To understand CQRS more, let's assume we need to build two services that consume users' cart data. The existing cart service is responsible for writing the user's event to a persistent queue. This is the writing model commands (C) of our architecture. On the other hand, we may have *N* services consuming the users' events asynchronously (sometime in the future). For that, let's assume we have two services: a user profile service and a relational analysis service, as figure 10.6 shows.

The first user profile service needs to optimize its read model for faster data retrieval via the user_id. We may pick some distributed database and use the user_id as a partition key. Next, the customers of the user profile can then query the service via user_id, using the read-optimized data model. The other relational analysis service data model is optimized for totally different use cases. It also reads the users' data, but it builds a different read model optimized for offline analysis, and it allows different query patterns optimized for batch queries. It may, for example, save those events to a distributed file system, such as HDFS. Both user profile and relational analysis services are the Query (Q) part of our CQRS architecture.

This architecture gives us a couple essential benefits. First, the data producers and consumers are decoupled from each other. Second, the service that produces the events does not need to guess all possible future uses for its data. It saves the events in the data

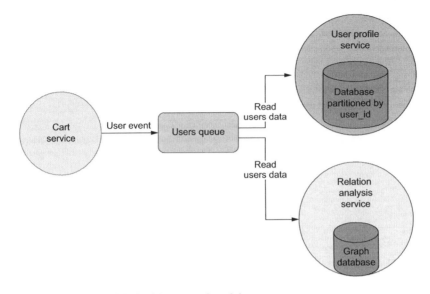

Figure 10.6   Using CQRS with two read models

store that is optimized for writing. The consumer's responsibility is to fetch this data and transform it into its database model optimized for the specific use case. Teams developing consuming services can work independently, creating a business value based on the commonly available data. When using CQRS, the data is a first-class citizen. Consumer services can consume different sources of data and use them for their own purpose.

However, this pattern has a lot of drawbacks. First, the data will be duplicated in N places. The more read model services we need, the more duplication there will be. Also, this architecture requires a lot of data movement. There will be many requests sent from both write model services (to save the initial data) and read model services. Any of those requests can fail, so all the problems discussed previously (such as retries, at-least-once-delivery, network partition, and idempotency of operation) will influence the state of our system. In fact, they will be even more apparent: the more services we have, the more things may go wrong. An out-of-sync state can occur between reading model services if we are not guarding against such problems properly. One nonidempotent duplicate sent to one of the two services can make the state of the whole system diverge.

How do we design a fault-tolerant system (meaning that it retries the failed actions) that works in a distributed environment (in reality, this is almost every production system) and assure ourselves that we have a consistent view of the system? The well-proven pattern for this is a deduplication logic implemented on the consumer side. When a service that performs a nonidempotent action (one that cannot be retried) implements deduplication logic, it effectively changes its behavior to be idempotent for all callers. In the next section, we'll implement deduplication logic in a library.

10.2 *A naive implementation of a deduplication library*

We will try to make the mail service send out idempotent. This can be achieved by implementing a deduplication logic in the mail service. When a new request arrives at this service, it checks if it was delivered before. If the request was not delivered, it means that it's not a duplicate, and it can safely process the request.

It is important to note that every event needs to have a unique identifier to make deduplication work. The caller service (application A) will generate the UUID that uniquely identifies each request. When the request is sent again, the same UUID is used. By using this information, the mail service, which receives an event, can validate whether it was received previously. If we have an architecture where a request (or event) can travel through multiple services, all of those services can use the same unique ID of that request. Usually, the unique ID is generated at the producer side (the first service that executes a request or event) and can be used for deduplication along the way by multiple services.

The information about whether or not the ID was processed must be persistent. Because of that, the ID needs to be saved in the database that provides the persistence. The database is a new component that needs to be used by our system. There is a good chance your service uses some database already, so adding a new dedicated table for deduplication may be straightforward. Figure 10.7 shows the deduplication logic.

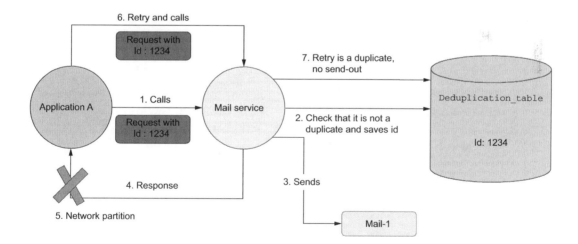

Figure 10.7 Deduplication logic in the mail service

Let's consider the same situation that caused mail duplicates. The first request in figure 10.7 with ID 1234 (in real life, it will be a UUID) is sent. When the request arrives at the mail service, it first checks if the request with the given ID was processed. It does that by executing a database query. If there was not a processed event with the given

ID, it adds that record to the database. Then, it continues processing by sending the mail to the end user. Next, the mail service sends information (at step 4) that the data was correctly processed, and unfortunately, the network partition happens (step 5).

Application A does not know if the mail was sent or not, so it retries the request with the same ID. When the retried request arrives at the mail service, it checks whether it is a duplicate. If the request was already processed, it does not process this request.

The solution looks robust, but it has one problem. What happens if there is a failure after the mail service saves the ID of processed request information but before actually sending the mail? Let's consider this situation now, as demonstrated in figure 10.8.

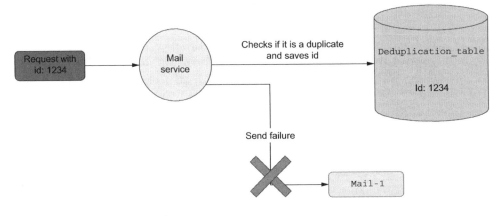

Figure 10.8   Partial failure send out

If our deduplication service checks and saves the ID of the event before the sending, we are risking a partial failure. It is possible that after the request is marked as processed, the mail sent process fails. A response with failure will be sent to the caller application. The caller application will retry as expected with the same request id. However, the mail service has the given ID marked as already processed. Therefore, the request will not be processed, and the mail will not be sent. The most straightforward approach for implementing this would be to split the deduplication service into two stages and to insert the mail send action between those stages. Figure 10.9 shows this process.

First, the new approach will try to get the record from a database for a given ID. When the ID is not present, it should execute any action provided by the caller. For our use case, it will be the mail sent action. Once the send finishes successfully (returned without exception), we can insert a new record with the request id. Listing 10.1 shows the code for such logic.

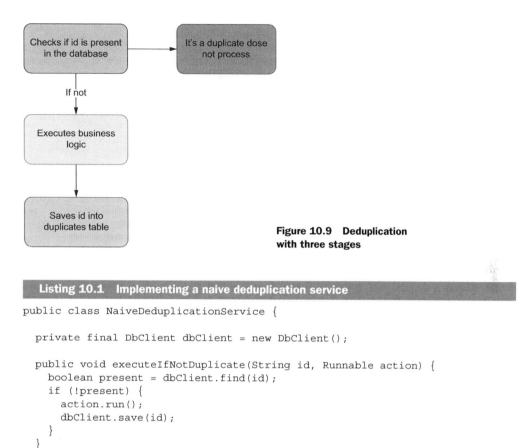

Figure 10.9 Deduplication with three stages

Listing 10.1 Implementing a naive deduplication service

```
public class NaiveDeduplicationService {

  private final DbClient dbClient = new DbClient();

  public void executeIfNotDuplicate(String id, Runnable action) {
    boolean present = dbClient.find(id);
    if (!present) {
      action.run();
      dbClient.save(id);
    }
  }
}
```

The DbClient is responsible for the interaction with an underlying database backend. The provided Runnable is our mail send process. The dbClient.find(id) call is the first stage of our processing. This tries to find if the record is present in the database. If it is not present, the actual processing is executed. The last stage saves a new ID record to the database. If the record for an ID is present in the database, such a request is ignored.

The provided solution seems to behave properly for both failure scenarios we are discussing. When there is a network partition after the successful mail send, the request id is already persisted in the database (it is after the dbClient.save() method call). In this case, retrying requests will be caught as a duplication.

The second scenario we are considering (when there is a failure during the mail send) will fail the Runnable processing. This will, in turn, cause no save of request-id to the database. When retrying the request, it will be properly reprocessed because the request id is not saved.

However, we need to remember that our mail service operates in a distributed environment. Because this is an inherently concurrent environment, the discussed solution will not provide idempotency for all use cases. Let's consider why the solution is not atomic and how we can do it in an atomic way.

10.3 Common mistakes when implementing deduplication in distributed systems

Let's consider our naive implementation from the previous section in two contexts. The first context assumes that the mail service and application A, which sends the data to it, are deployed to only one node. The second one adds some complexity: the mail service will be deployed to multiple nodes. The latter use case is more realistic because it's how services are deployed in the microservices architecture, which is fault-tolerant and scalable. Having more than one node gives us fault tolerance because, in case one node fails, another node (or nodes) will start handling its traffic. We will analyze how this context affects the consistency of our deduplication logic.

10.3.1 One node context

Let's see how our deduplication logic performs in the context of one application A service and one mail service. Both services are deployed to only one node. Figure 10.10 illustrates this context.

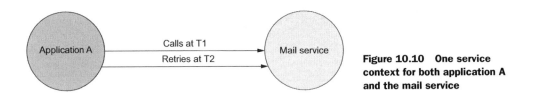

Figure 10.10   One service context for both application A and the mail service

Let's analyze a retry for a given unique ID. The first call executed by application A is executed at time 1 ($T1$). We will assume that it fails, and the retry is executed after it fails at time 2 ($T2$). Again, we will assume there is a happens-previously relationship before the first request and the retry action. In this case, our current deduplication logic is not atomic. It is split into three stages:

- *Stage 1*—Searches for the request-id in the database
- *Stage 2*—Executes the mail service logic if the request-id is not found
- *Stage 3*—Saves the request-id in the database

For simplicity, we'll consider the only failure at stage 2, but in a real-world application, the failure can happen at any stage. This makes it even more tricky and complex to analyze. Our analysis focuses on the main functionality of this component: preventing duplicate email sends.

If the first request ($T1$) fails at stage 2, the response is returned to the caller's application. Because request fails at stage 2, the stage 3 action is not executed. The retry at $T2$ will be executed, and the mail send action succeeds. There is no possibility for a duplicate send in that case, even if our `executeIfNotDuplicate()` method, as shown in the following listing, is not atomic.

Listing 10.2 Blocking email send actions

```
public void executeIfNotDuplicate(String id, Runnable action) {
  boolean present = dbClient.find(id);
  if (!present) {
    action.run();
    dbClient.save(id);              Blocks send actions
  }                                 for N seconds.
}
```

Let's consider what happens if the email send action executes for a long time. In the listing, the email send action is blocking, and it involves yet another remote call (sending an actual email). This call can block the processing of our code. It can also fail during the response because of the network partition; this is the same situation as in section 10.1.2, but this time it's applied to the mail external network call.

As we know from chapter 9, every network request should have configured a reasonable timeout to prevent the blocking of threads and resources. Let's assume that application A defines the timeout as equal to 10 seconds, but the mail service sends out blocks for twice as long (20 seconds). In such a situation, the request at $T1$ fails after 10 seconds. However, it does not mean that the mail send fails. It may succeed but only after 10 seconds more. Figure 10.11 shows this depiction.

Both requests will interleave. From the perspective of application A, the first request at $T1$ fails (times out). However, the main action is blocked for 20 seconds, and after that time, it will succeed. Next, the application will just save its `request-id` to a database. Unfortunately, in the meantime, application A retries the request at $T2$ because it observed a failure. The retried request will arrive at a mail service before it saves its `request-id` from $T1$ as an already-processed request. Due to that fact, $T2$ is treated as a new, nonduplicated request. This causes an email to be sent. In the meantime, the request at $T1$ completes and also causes the mail to be sent. Because the duplicate was sent, our nonatomic deduplication service causes an inconsistency in our system.

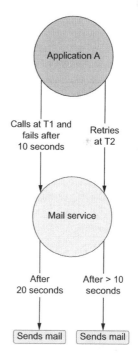

Figure 10.11   One service context with a duplicate send

This is only one of the failure scenarios that can cause a duplicate in the one node context. However, when designing a robust component, even one use case where the requirements are broken should be enough to consider changing a design. Before we do that, let's analyze the same scenario in a multi-node context.

10.3.2 *Multiple nodes context*

Let's analyze the consistency and correctness of our deduplication logic in the multi-node context by looking at a situation in which the mail service is deployed to multiple nodes. It is common to deploy a service to more physical machines (nodes) to increase its overall performance and fault tolerance.

When the mail service is deployed to multiple nodes, its API is exposed via Load Balancer. Every service is reachable via its IP address. We will assume this offers dynamic scalability, meaning that new mail service instances can be added or removed, depending on the traffic. Because of this, the mail service instance IPs are hidden from application A. The request executed by application A is sent to a load balancing service. The load balancing service captures the request and redirects it to a specific backend for the mail service.

The actual implementation of load balancing is abstracted away from the application A service. When the new mail service is deployed, it registers itself with the load balancing service. From that point, the load balancing service routes the traffic to the newly added node. Figure 10.12 illustrates the load balancer's role in a multi-node context.

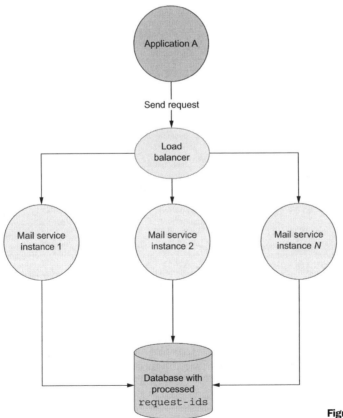

Figure 10.12   One service context

In this scenario, the mail service must be stateless; it should be able to process any arriving request. All needed state, including the table with the already processed `request-ids`, is kept in a separate database. For the simplicity of our analysis, we will assume that the database is not distributed and keeps all its state on one node (it can be a primary–secondary architecture if you like). In a real-life application, however, the scalable application (which achieves that by adding or removing nodes) should probably use a distributed database, so the `request-id` data is partitioned into N nodes. This also allows the data layer to scale horizontally by adding or removing nodes. However, the failure scenarios we are discussing will be present when using both (distributed and nondistributed) database types.

Let's assume our load balancer component works simply by doing a round-robin on a request to an underlying backend for the mail service. The first request will be routed to mail service 1, the second request to mail service 2, and so on. Note that load balancing algorithms widely use the round-robin strategy because it's simple to implement and easy to understand. It also tends to perform well for a lot of use cases. There are other load balancing algorithms that, for example, can take the latency of the nodes into account. One of the most widely used is the power of two choices algorithm (http://mng.bz/DxPR). The specific algorithm used by the load balancing service, however, does not influence our analysis.

Unfortunately, our current deduplication logic will not work correctly in such an environment. Let's consider a scenario when application A retries a request in the multi-node context, as figure 10.13 shows.

In step 1, application A sends the request for a mail send. The request flows through the load balancer and, in step 2, is routed to the first mail service backend. In step 3, the mail service checks whether the `request-id` is in the database. It is not, so it continues processing. Unfortunately, this step results in a timeout that is returned to application A in step 4. Application A issues a retry in step 5, and this retry request is routed to a second mail backend in step 6. In step 7, the mail service checks whether the request id was processed already. If it turns out it was not processed, it continues with the send. In the meantime, the first mail service backend completes the mail send request and, in step 8, saves the request id to a database. Then, in step 9, the second backend finishes its execution and saves the request id to the database, overriding the previous save operation that the first mailing backend issued. This also means that both mail service instances didn't observe a duplicate when our deduplication logic started and resulted in a duplicate execution of logic that sends the actual email.

In a real-life scenario, the situation may get even worse. Application A triggers the mail send based on some logic. It may turn out that the logic is triggered by yet another external call from another service. This is not uncommon in microservices architecture (especially event based). The business flow may span multiple services. Also, assuming that our applications are stateless, application A may also receive duplicated requests. For that reason, our deduplication logic is not atomic and may result

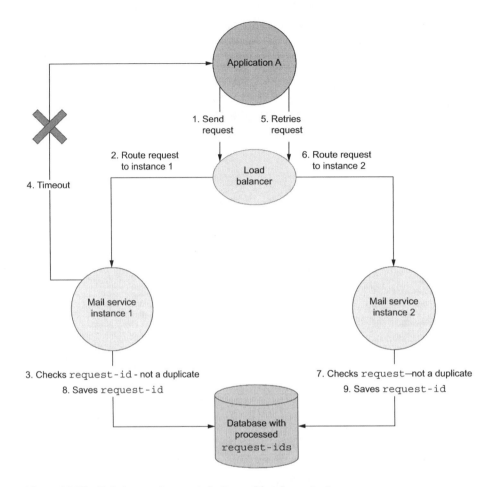

Figure 10.13   Retrying send requests in the multi-node context

in more mail duplication. A consistent view of our system will be strongly impacted because it's possible there will be a lot of duplicates. At this point of our analysis, it is clear to see that our deduplication logic needs improvement. Let's next see how to make it atomic in single- and multi-node contexts.

10.4   *Making your logic atomic to prevent race conditions*

Let's recap our current deduplication logic. We have three stages:

- *Stage 1*—Searches for the `request-id` in the database
- *Stage 2*—Executes the mail service logic if the `request-id` is found
- *Stage 3*—Saves the `request-id` in the database

It is worth noting that all discussed failure scenarios will break our system's consistency, regardless of whether we have stage 2 in our logic or not. Let's simplify our example and assume that our deduplication logic has only stage 1 and stage 3. Our deduplication logic will look like this now:

- *Stage 1*—Searches for the `request-id` in the database
- *Stage 2*—Saves the `request-id` in the database

There is still a possibility to send a duplicate email because both calls to retrieve and save the data from or to the database can also fail because those are remote calls executed in a distributed system. There could also be a network partition when a successful response from the database is sent via a deduplication logic.

All failure scenarios that we discussed in the context of application A apply to database calls as well. For example, when calling the save `request-id` operation (stage 3), the operation may throw an exception denoting a timeout. As we know, a timeout does not give the caller a lot of information. There could be a situation in which the client-side timeout is triggered, but the operation on the server side is still executing. From application A's perspective, this means the action fails, returning an error to the client. The retry may happen before the `request-id` is inserted into a table by service instance 1. Therefore, the request will be routed to the second service instance. This situation is almost the same as discussed in the previous section. Figure 10.14 shows how this can lead to a race condition.

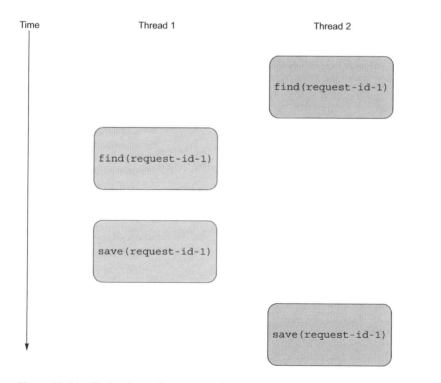

Figure 10.14 Find and save in two operations yielding a race condition

The find and save action can interleave, making the system inconsistent. For example, the find operation on one thread (or node) can be executed after it is executed on another node. The find operation can take an arbitrary amount of time. Therefore, we cannot make any strong assumptions here. For both find calls, it will return false, so the logic continues, and finally, a save will be called twice. Because of that, our deduplication logic does not work correctly.

To achieve the atomicity of our deduplication logic, we need to reduce the number of stages required to only one stage. We also need to check whether the given request is a duplicate and save the `request-id` in one operation. This should be one external call without any intermediate steps. Every time the process needs to retrieve a value, do some action, and save another value, there is a potential for a race condition.

This is true when executed in a multithreaded environment. We can synchronize all calls to our deduplication component, but that would mean this component's concurrency level is equal to one. In other words, the service processes only one request at a time. Such a solution is unusable in real-life applications that need to handle *N* requests per second. The more requests the system needs to handle, the higher the contention and number of threads will be. This increases the likelihood of intermediate failures that will make our deduplication logic inconsistent sooner rather than later.

Fortunately, most distributed databases that will be used the most often in a horizontally scaling architecture expose a way to perform our task in a single atomic operation. (The standard SQL database also allows us to execute atomic operations.)

We need to execute a save action that inserts a new record only if it is not present. Moreover, it needs to return a Boolean, denoting if the insert was successful or not. Such an operation gives us all the information that we need to implement a robust deduplication logic. This is called an *upsert*; the save action inserts a value only if it is not present and returns the outcome. Figure 10.15 illustrates this concept. You need to find out if your database of choice exposes such a method. Upsert should be atomic, meaning that the database should execute it as a single operation.

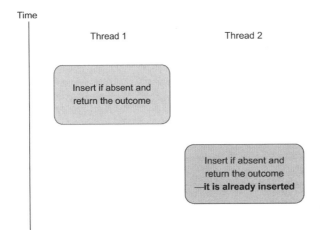

Figure 10.15   **Atomic upsert that inserts a value only if it is not present and returns the outcome**

Because upsert is atomic, there is no way for a race condition between two interleaving operations. All logic is executed at the database side, and the outcome is returned to the caller.

Let's see now how the implementation of deduplication service changes when using an upsert. Most importantly, the DbClient will expose a method that allows us to insert data if missing and return the outcome. The following listing shows this method.

Listing 10.3   Using upsert for deduplication

```
public boolean findAndInsertIfNeeded(String id);
```

We need to ensure that the implementation we use is atomic. This should try to insert an entry with a given ID. If the entry is already present in the database, it returns false. If the insert is performed, it returns true (the upsert operation). The following listing shows the new isDuplicated() method that returns true or false, depending on whether the given ID is a duplicate.

Listing 10.4   Implementing atomic deduplication logic

```
@Override
public boolean isDuplicate(String id) {
  boolean wasInserted = dbClient.findAndInsertIfNeeded(id);
  if (wasInserted) {
    return false;
  } else {
    return true;
  }
}
```

When findAndInsertIfNeeded() returns true, it denotes that the given ID was inserted in the database. This means that it was not previously present there. What is important is that this method will insert the given ID into the database. We don't need to implement stage 2, which was needed before. When the method findAndInsertIfNeeded() returns false, the ID is a duplicate. It also means the upsert didn't insert a new ID because the value was already present.

Our logic is atomic now and, therefore, is not prone to a race condition. We need to note that using an atomic operation that both inserts and checks if a value is present does not allow us to execute a custom action between those stages. However, we saw that such an approach was faulty. Currently, the deduplication logic is responsible only for finding duplicates. It does not try to assure that the request was successfully executed in an end-to-end fashion. The new deduplication logic has one functionality, and it performs that in an atomic and correct way.

When using this new deduplication component in the mail service without another mechanism that checks the correctness of sending mail, we are risking a chance that mail will not be delivered. Let's consider a situation where the deduplication logic marks the request as processed at the time when the request arrives at the mail system. If the failure of processing happens after that, the application request retry does not take effect because this request is marked as already processed.

On the other hand, if the duplicate is marked after successful processing, there is no mechanism preventing duplicate send again. Due to that fact, we should use atomic deduplication at the entry to a system. However, we should use it with other mechanisms that verify the system's correctness, such as transaction logs or rollback (removal) of the processed ID in case of a failure. All of those techniques have their complexities and tradeoffs and should be analyzed separately.

The example presented in this chapter demonstrates that executing and reasoning about the actions in a distributed system is challenging and complex. If you can design your processing to be idempotent, your system will be more fault-tolerant and robust. However, not every processing service can be idempotent, and we need to design a mechanism that guards our system against retrying an action that should not be retriable. If you don't want to design a complex deduplication logic, every request failure will be critical from your application's perspective because you are not able to retry. Only manual action by the system administrator can reconcile the data. This is not ideal if you want to make your system fault tolerant and reliable.

For that reason, we may decide to implement mechanisms, such as deduplication with retries, to address those problems. However, we need to be careful because implementing such mechanisms in a distributed system may generate different characteristics than what we expected. Implementing a system that is supposed to be consistent but works differently is dangerous. We may risk introducing hard-to-debug errors and losing money when executing duplicate transactions. For those reasons, we should analyze all incoming and outgoing traffic in the context of correctness and delivery semantics. In the next chapter, we will dive deeper into delivery semantics and data flow between our applications.

Summary

- If your application executes any network call, you are operating in a distributed systems environment. Remember that every network call can fail.
- Every external call can fail for a variety of reasons, such as network failure or the actual target application failure, but we can analyze and reason about those failures.
- Retry mechanisms allow us to design fault-tolerant applications.
- Idempotent operations allow us to retry actions without worrying about duplication.
- We can design our business domain to be more idempotency friendly. The more operations that are idempotent, the more autonomous and fault tolerant our system will be.
- Besides idempotency, we need to be careful about the ordering of requests. We can analyze the impact of idempotency on the retry strategies used in our application.

- When implementing a logic that operates in a distributed context (such as a deduplication library), we need to analyze edge cases and failure scenarios carefully.
- It is complex and sometimes not possible to have atomicity in our system if the processing that is supposed to be atomic is split into N stages. We can rework the nonatomic solution into an atomic one by using the correct database operations.
- When splitting an action that should be consistent into N remote calls, we risk losing our system's consistency.
- All systems have guarantees that we can use from our code. If the interaction between them requires an external call, every one of those calls can fail.
- When using a system designed to work in a distributed environment, chances are great that the problem we want to solve is already solved. For example, a lot of atomic operations that may be hard to achieve at first sight can be implemented using the upsert method. This improves the consistency of our system.

Delivery semantics in distributed systems

11

This chapter covers
- Publish–subscribe and producer–consumer models in data-intensive applications
- Delivery guarantees and their impact on resilience and fault tolerance
- Building fault-tolerant systems leveraging delivery semantics

In the previous chapter, we learned about fault tolerance, retries, and idempotence of operations in the context of a relatively straightforward system architecture. In real life, our systems consist of multiple components responsible for different parts of our business domain and infrastructure. For example, we may have a service that is responsible for collecting metrics. Another service may be responsible for collection logs and so on. Besides that, we need applications that provide the primary business use cases of our domain. This can be a payment service or a database that is responsible for persistence. In those architectures, services need to connect with each other to be able to exchange information.

The more components our system has, the more points where failure can occur. Every network request can fail, and we need to decide if an action should be retried or not. If we want to create a fault-tolerant architecture, we need to build handling failure into the system. Then, every component needs to provide precise delivery semantics when producing the data. On the other hand, consumption of data should also follow expected delivery semantics.

In this chapter, we will learn how to build such architectures, allowing us to create loosely coupled and fault-tolerant systems. We call this architecture *event driven*. We will use Apache Kafka as the main component in our system. This will allow us to learn about delivery semantics: at-most-once, (effectively) exactly once, and at-least-once, in practice. Finally, we will build fault tolerance into a system, leveraging a system that offers expected delivery guarantees. Let's start by understanding event-driven architectures of data-intensive applications and their pros and cons.

11.1 Architecture of event-driven applications

Why do we need to be concerned about implementing a system that follows an event-driven architecture? Let's start with a simple design and see how it evolves in the context of tight coupling and fault tolerance. Then, we will see how it can be improved by reworking our architecture to be event-driven.

Suppose we have two frontend applications. We can think of both as separate microservices that run on different nodes. They both produce metrics that need to be sent to a metrics server responsible for persisting metric values. Figure 11.1 shows this scenario.

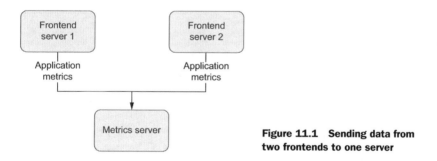

Figure 11.1 Sending data from two frontends to one server

It also means there are direct connections between our frontend service 1 and the frontend service 2 to the metrics service. This is a standard request–response process. The frontend service sends a request (it can be HTTP or another protocol), waits for the response, and finishes. In reality, sending the metrics may be an intensive task, so each of the frontend services will need to have a pool of threads that will send the requests.

There will be two times the number of frontend service connections to keep from the metrics service perspective. In case of a metrics service failure, both frontend services won't be able to send any data. This may mean that failure of the metrics service will cascade to all of its clients. Fault tolerance in such a solution is not ideal, as the metrics service becomes a single point of failure.

In reality, this may get a lot more complicated. We may need to have *N* different metrics services with each specialized for a given use case. For example, we may have a metrics service that exposes a UI dashboard. For offline metrics analytics, we may have a different service that processes the data. The most critical metrics may need to be sent to yet another metrics service that is specialized for on-call purposes.

Moreover, our architecture may grow in the number of services that need to be monitored. Besides our frontend services, we may have databases that need special monitoring. If our business provides value for our users, we may need to handle our users' payments and accounts. All of those services need to send the metrics data, as figure 11.2 demonstrates.

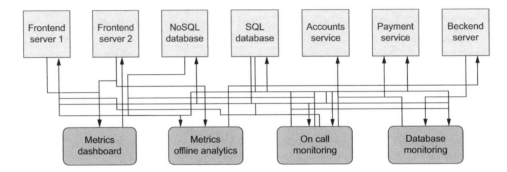

Figure 11.2   Multiple services, multiple metrics

With the current architecture, such a situation causes an explosion of connections between services. Each of the metrics producer service needs to send data to *N* metrics services. In case of failure in a metrics service, all of those producer services will fail as well. Every connection is direct, and our architecture is tightly coupled. It's hard to keep the SLA if the producer service needs to send data via an unreliable medium (network) in a synchronous way. Fortunately, the event-driven architecture solves these problems, providing decoupling and fault tolerance.

In this section, we introduce a new component in an improved approach that provides an indirection layer between producer and consumer applications. We can call this a publish–subscribe (pub–sub) system or event queue. The event queue is the only integration point between producer and consumer applications.

For example, when a service needs to send a metric, it no longer sends it directly to the target metrics service. Let's assume it's necessary to send a single metric to the metrics dashboard, metrics offline analytics, and on-call monitoring services, as figure 11.3 shows.

In the previous solution, the frontend service needed to connect to three different services (dashboard, offline analytics, and on-call monitoring). Failure of any of those services will propagate to the caller service.

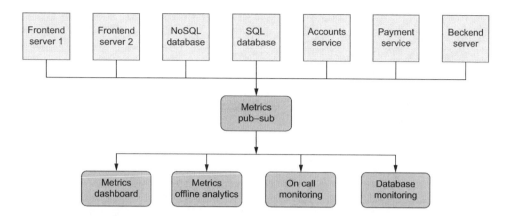

Figure 11.3 Event-driven architecture with an indirection layer between producer and consumer apps

Currently, the frontend service is connected to only one component: the pub–sub system. All consumer applications that are interested in the specific metric produced by the frontend service will subscribe to events emitted to the queue. Once the emitted event is there, all consumer services will get this event.

It is important to note that our architecture shifted from synchronous to asynchronous; there is no direct connection between producer and consumer applications. In case of a failure of any of the metrics services, the frontend (producer) application is not impacted. The events are still emitted to a queue (this is our metrics pub–sub system). The queue can persist the events for a finite (or infinite) time and resume sending to the metrics application when it is back online.

By using this mechanism, we built fault tolerance into our system. However, to implement such a mechanism, we need to properly understand the delivery semantics and implement both producer and consumer logic. We will learn how to do that later in this chapter. For now, some readers may notice that the current architecture has a new problem. The queue component is a single point of failure in our system. In case of its failure, our system won't be able to operate.

That is true; fortunately, the production-proven queue systems, such as Apache Kafka or Pulsar, are implemented in a way that allows incredibly high SLA and availability. In fact, depending on our use case, we may tweak those systems to favor availability or consistency. The availability can be improved by increasing the number of servers (Kafka brokers) and/or the replication factor of topics. The more brokers we have, the more failures we can tolerate. If your data is replicated to N brokers (where $N > 1$), and there is a failure of one of the Kafka servers, the system may still be available. This is because the other broker can start handling the traffic in case of failure in the first broker.

The other solution we can implement to improve our system's fault tolerance, availability, and loose coupling is to deploy and maintain N-independent queues. In such a setup, we might have a dedicated queue that is responsible for metrics, another that is responsible for logging, and yet another that collects tracking events from our applications as figure 11.4 shows.

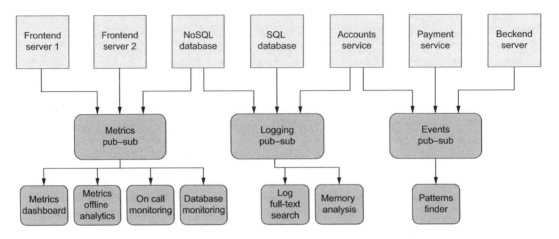

Figure 11.4   Multiple independent pub–sub systems designed to avoid a single point of failure

In such a setup, we no longer have a single point of failure. The eventual failure of one of the queue systems does not impact clients of the other systems. For example, in case of a failure of the events pub–sub, the caller applications are still able to send metrics and logging, as each pub–sub deployment can be configured differently. If, for example, the metrics collection is critical to our architecture, we can tweak the system to be more available. We can do this by investing more money into infrastructure, deploying more servers and keeping the copy of data in more locations. On the other hand, we may decide that collecting tracking data is not so critical and trade the possibility of some unavailable data for cost. (We spent less money on the events pub–sub, but we are tolerating some data loss.) By splitting the queue functionality into *N*-independent systems, we can have the best of both worlds—loose coupling, asynchronously fault-tolerant systems, and no single point of failure.

In case of a failure of the events pub–sub, the caller application may decide to buffer (or not) send events for some small amount of time. Such a pattern is called a *circuit breaker*. Therefore, our architecture will still be operational. Before we start to understand delivery semantics in such an event-driven architecture, let's start by understanding the basics of Apache Kafka.

11.2 Producer and consumer applications based on Apache Kafka

Before we start analyzing delivery guarantees from the consumer and producer side, let's understand Apache Kafka architecture's basics. The main construct used by both producer and consumer sides is a *topic*. The topic is a distributed, append-only data structure. The distribution is achieved via the topic's partitioning. A topic can be split into *N* partitions; the more partitions it has, the more distributed processing it will have. Let's assume we have a topic with `topicName` and four partitions (figure 11.5). Partitions are numbered from 0 upward.

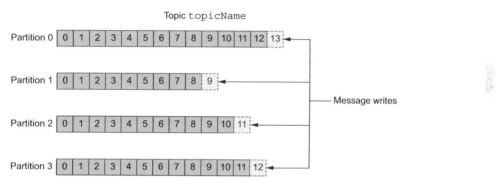

Figure 11.5   Topic structure as a distributed, append-only log

Each partition has its own offset that identifies precisely one record in the append-only structure. When the producers send a new record to a topic, the producer first calculates the partition to which the record should be routed. Each record consists of a key–value pair.

The key determines the partitioning for a given record. It can, for example, contain only the `user_id`. When partitioned by `user_id`, Kafka guarantees that all events for a single user are sent to the same partition. Because of that, the ordering of events for a specific `user_id` will be kept. In real pub–sub systems, we can have a lot of topics. One topic can have account data, another can have information about payment, and so forth.

When the producer writes its message, it appends it to the end of the given partition. For example, if the partitioning algorithm determines that the event should be sent to partition 0, it will be appended to the end of this log. The offset of the new record will be equal to 13. It's worth noting that we may end up in a situation where one partition processes too much data in the case of partition *skew*. This means the key we are using for partitioning is too narrow. We may decide to add additional data to a Kafka key to improve the partition's distribution.

11.2.1 *Looking at the Kafka consumer side*

The producer is decoupled from the consumer, and the data-consuming part is done in an asynchronous way. The consumer is a process that reads the data from a Kafka topic. As you may remember, topics are partitioned. Due to that, the consumer needs to know about all partitions for a given topic. We may have a single consumer that reads the data from all partitions. However, in real life, our applications are structured to be more parallelizable.

Let's assume that we have a topic with four partitions again. We have an application that needs to fetch data from those four partitions. In such a setup, depending on the performance requirement, we may deploy up to four consumers. Each consumer will be responsible for reading the events from a single partition. In case we have more consumers than partitions, the additional consumers will be idle. That's because all topic's partitions are already assigned to a consumer.

Let's assume a bit more complex situation. Our topic still has four partitions, but we don't need to have four consumer applications (see figure 11.6). After our performance tests, it turns out that three consumer processes are enough for our throughput.

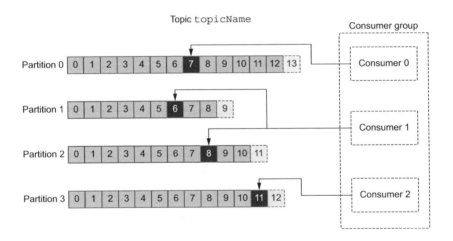

Figure 11.6   Assignment for a consumer group with multiple consumers

Such a situation is totally feasible. In this setup, one of the consumer processes (consumer 1) gets two partitions. On the other hand, consumer 0 and consumer 2 process a single partition. Consumer 1 will process both partitions 1 and 2. Please also note that the assignment of partitions to consumers may be different in a real-life use case. However, in the discussed scenario, every consumer will have at least one partition assigned.

It is important to note that the additional partition processing cannot be distributed among N nodes. This would break the ordering guarantees within a partition. Multiple consumers would get the same partition key events, and there will be no way to assure the ordering in such a setup. Therefore, such a situation is not possible in Apache Kafka.

The described solution (four partitions and three consumers) is problematic because one of the consumers will process twice as many events as the other consumers. For that reason, in a real-life setup, we should consider picking an even number of consumers. If we have four partitions, creating two consumers results in two consumers that process the same amount of traffic. If we need higher throughput, we may decide to have four consumers.

> **NOTE** It is important to pick the number of partitions upfront when creating a topic. Thus, you should be careful to select a number that is backed by performance tests and empirical data.

Let's assume it turns out that we picked a number of partitions that are too low for processing our traffic. In this case, we would need to create a new topic with more partitions and migrate the old topic to the new one. This operation is resource intensive and time-consuming, however.

One of the most important benefits of using Apache Kafka is the ability to deploy N-independent consumer applications. Every application is called a consumer group in Kafka. Each of those consumer groups can have N consumers. This allows for the use case described in the pub–sub section.

We may have multiple applications consuming the same topic. Each application can consume the data from the same topic independently at its own pace. For example, if the metrics dashboard application (which has a dedicated `customer_group`) does not have high throughput requirements, it can run on one physical node with one Kafka consumer process. On the other hand, the on-call monitoring application may be more critical and performance sensitive. This consumer group can have N consumers that will process the data faster.

11.2.2 Understanding the Kafka brokers setup

Let's finally analyze the full setup of Apache Kafka deployed to N brokers. We will look at the simplest use case, where Kafka is deployed to two physical machines. Each of those machines has one Kafka broker. We will analyze a topic called T that has two partitions. It means the producer and consumer sides' maximum parallelism is equal to two (number of partitions). Besides that, the topic T replication factor is set to two, so every event is (eventually) saved to both brokers.

We assume the described setup has only one producer and one consumer. We can have up to two producers and up to two times the number of consumers per each consumer group in practice. However, simplifying the setup to one producer and one consumer allows us to reason about the Kafka broker setup easily. Figure 11.7 shows the setup for our use case.

The topic T has two partitions. Each of those partitions is replicated to both brokers because this topic's replication factor is set to 2. If it is set to 1, each partition is

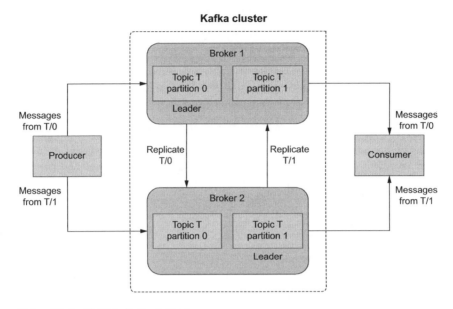

Figure 11.7   Multiple Kafka brokers

kept on only one broker. The partition works in a leader–follower model. Only one broker is a leader for a given partition. In our setup, broker 1 is the leader for topic T, partition 0, and broker 2 is the leader for topic T, partition 1.

We need to remember that the higher the replication factor is, the more resources our cluster needs. For example, when the replication factor is set to 2, we need twice as much disk capacity compared to a replication factor set to 1. The reason for this is that the data needs to be saved to two physical locations. For a replication factor equal to 3, we need three times as much disk space. Also, saving data to more brokers requires more network traffic and more CPU consumption. When replicating data, it needs to be sent to more brokers via the network.

When the producer sends the data to a topic's partition, it sends it to a leader for this given partition. Next, the data is replicated to a follower broker that stores the data in case of a crash. If broker 1 crashes, broker 2 can start serving a leadership role for this partition. The consumer process needs to keep a list of leaders for all topic's partitions. Because of that, it can consume the data from a proper partition. In case of a broker failure, the rebalancing process updates the consumer's leaders for all partitions. Now that we understand how Kafka works, let's analyze the producer's delivery semantics.

11.3   *The producer logic*

Let's start by looking at the Kafka producer logic. Apache Kafka's producer (http://mng.bz/lad2) will be our main entry point for sending data to a Kafka topic. The Kafka producer can be configured with a variety of settings (http://mng.bz/BxP1). However, there are three required settings we need to specify.

The first setting is a list of Kafka brokers called *bootstrap-servers*. These should contain a list of the Kafka brokers in a cluster. The producer uses them to determine where the events should be sent. In addition, every Kafka record has a key–value pair. We need to specify serializers for both of these. Serializers provide the logic to transform a Java object (e.g., `String`) to an array of bytes sent to the Kafka topic. The following listing shows an example Kafka producer configuration that uses the Spring Kafka library (http://mng.bz/dojo).

Listing 11.1 Creating a Kafka producer configuration

```
@Configuration
public class SenderConfig {

  @Value("${kafka.bootstrap-servers}")
  private String bootstrapServers;

  @Bean
  public Map<String, Object> producerConfigs() {
    Map<String, Object> props = new HashMap<>();
    props.put(ProducerConfig.BOOTSTRAP_SERVERS_CONFIG, bootstrapServers);
    props.put(ProducerConfig.KEY_SERIALIZER_CLASS_CONFIG,
      IntegerSerializer.class);
    props.put(ProducerConfig.VALUE_SERIALIZER_CLASS_CONFIG,
      StringSerializer.class);           ◁─┐  The map of
    return props;                            Kafka's producer
  }                                          settings

  @Bean
  public ProducerFactory<Integer, String> producerFactory() {
    return new DefaultKafkaProducerFactory<>(producerConfigs());
  }

  @Bean
  public Producer<Integer, String> producer() {        The Producer
    return producerFactory().createProducer();   ◁─┤  processes an Integer
  }                                                    key and String value.

  @Bean
  public KafkaTemplate<Integer, String> kafkaTemplate() {
    return new KafkaTemplate<>(producerFactory());
  }
                                        The Sender is a Spring
  @Bean                                 abstraction atop of a
  public Sender sender() {              raw Kafka producer.
    return new Sender();       ◁─┘
  }
}
```

The producer logic uses the previously created `Producer` to send data to a Kafka topic. Because the logic is asynchronous, the `Producer`'s action is nonblocking, which returns a `Future`. It is worth pointing out that it is safe to share one instance of the `Producer` between multiple threads to send data to multiple topics. The `Producer` takes the topic, partition key, and actual value as arguments. Based on the partition key, it will route the request to the appropriate topic's partition, as the following listing shows.

Listing 11.2   Creating the Kafka producer

Returns a Future

The Producer accepts the topic, partition key, and actual data to send.

Passes the ProducerRecord directly to the Kafka producer

Executes the async callback once the record is successfully sent

```
@Autowired private Producer<Integer, String> producer;

public Future<RecordMetadata> sendAsync
  (String topic, String data, Integer partitionKey) {
  LOGGER.info("sending data='{}' to topic='{}'", data, topic);
  try {
    return producer.send(
      new ProducerRecord<>(topic, partitionKey, data),
      (recordMetadata, e) -> {
        if (e != null) {
          LOGGER.error("error while sending data:" + data, e);
        }
      });
  } finally {
    producer.flush();
  }
}
```

The send operation is asynchronous, and we can register a callback that is executed when the send finishes. Our callback checks whether the exception is not null. If it is not null, there was a failure with the send.

This simple `send()` logic hides a lot of complexity. Let's recap the logic by analyzing the diagram in figure 11.8 with the producer's flow.

First, a `ProducerRecord` is created. It contains a topic, key, and value. We can provide the partition, and if it is not, it is calculated from the key value. If we don't provide the key (it's null), messages are distributed using the round-robin algorithm. Next, the data is serialized to a byte array. Then, the partitioner determines the partition to which the record should be sent.

It is important to note that the records are batched on the producer side per the topic's partition. It means that one batch can contain *N* records for the same partition. When the send finishes successfully, it returns the metadata for every sent record. It contains, for example, an offset within a partition where the data was sent. If there is a failure, the send is retried. The retries parameter (http://mng.bz/VlXy) configures this. If there are more retries, the batch of records is retried. If there are no more retries, an exception is propagated to a caller.

It's worth noting that retrying a batch for a given partition may break the ordering guarantees within a partition. If the first request fails and is scheduled for a retry, the second request may succeed before the scheduled retry. In that case, the batches will

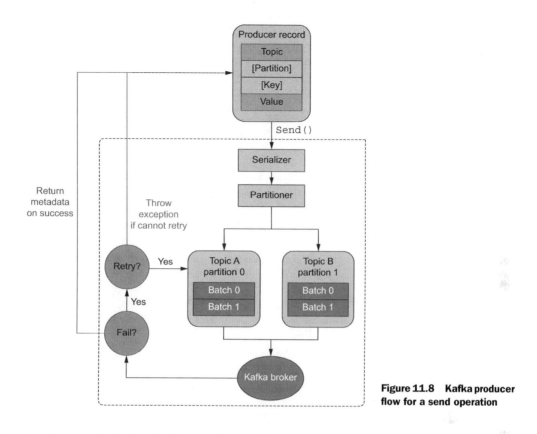

Figure 11.8   Kafka producer flow for a send operation

interleave (a behavior similar to what we discussed in the previous chapter). This results in out-of-order events within a partition.

If the retries behavior is enabled (and it's enabled by default), there is a possibility of duplication. The producer that works in this mode offers at-least-once delivery guarantees—the same record can be sent once or more times. If we want our producer's logic to be fault tolerant and robust, retries play a crucial role.

11.3.1 Choosing consistency vs. availability for the producer

The other important tradeoff we need to make on the producer side is to choose the consistency of data versus its availability. Let's assume we have a cluster with two brokers and topic A is replicated to both brokers. For simplicity, let's assume that topic A has only one partition (the behavior will be the same for *N* partitions). When the producer sends the data to this topic, we have three options regarding the brokers' number of acknowledged responses (http://mng.bz/xvQd). Each of these options offers different consistency and availability characteristics. Let's start by inspecting the acks parameter set to all, as figure 11.9 displays.

If the topic is created with a replication factor equal to 2, the record needs to be successfully saved and acknowledged by all brokers (in our use case, 2). For our topic

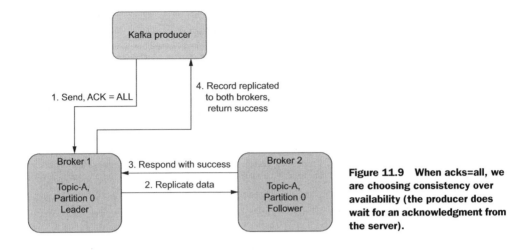

Figure 11.9   When acks=all, we are choosing consistency over availability (the producer does wait for an acknowledgment from the server).

A and partition 0, broker 1 is the leader. The producer sends the data to this broker. Because the `acks` parameter is set to `all`, the leader propagates the record to broker 2 (the follower). Once the data is successfully saved on the follower, the leader gets the response from its return success to the producer.

If one broker fails, the data will be consistent. This guarantees that the same data for topic 1 is on both brokers. However, in this case (one broker failing), the replication factor that is set to 2 cannot be fulfilled. When this happens, our system will not be available. We've sacrificed the consistency of our data over the availability of the whole system.

In a real-life setup, we should have more brokers. If we had three brokers and the replication factor is set to 2, one broker's failure will not make our system unavailable. As long as two brokers are up, we can successfully send the data.

Picking the number of brokers and replication factor of topics is dependent on your use case. To determine that, first find the maximum number of requests per second (also the MB/s) that your cluster needs to handle. Once you have that information, you can performance test one broker to find its maximum throughput. You can also use resources available online (e.g., http://mng.bz/Axwo), but beware that your maximum throughput may differ depending on the type of machine that you use. Disk speed, number of CPUs and RAM size all influence the throughput.

Once you have the maximum throughput per broker, you can calculate the number of brokers that you need for your traffic. However, for high availability and consistency in your Kafka system, you should increase your topic's replication factor. The replication factor depends on your individual needs and should be picked carefully. The more replicated the topic is, the more throughput your cluster needs to handle. For example, when setting the replication factor to 2, your network traffic will double. Because the two Kafka brokers need to store the data, you would need twice as much disk space.

NOTE Creating a production-ready Kafka cluster is a complex topic, so I advise you to do more experiments and reading to find your optimal setup.

Let's consider a situation in which the acks parameter is set to 1. In such a case, the producer waits for only one broker (leader) acknowledgment of the saved data. Figure 11.10 depicts this configuration.

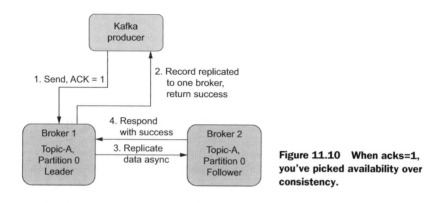

Figure 11.10 When acks=1, you've picked availability over consistency.

In this scenario, the data is still replicated to the number of brokers equal to a replication factor of topic A. However, the replication process is done in an asynchronous way. Once the leader successfully saves the producer record, it immediately returns success to the caller.

In the background, the data is synced to the follower. However, there is a possibility that the failure can happen before the follower saves the data. In such a scenario, the data is not replicated to the second broker. Because the producer waits for only one acknowledgment, it does not know that there is a background failure. If broker 1 fails and broker 2 doesn't have all topic A data up to date, we risk losing the data. On the other hand, even if only one broker is functioning in the cluster, the producer still sends the data to topic A. In this scenario, we traded the availability of topic A over its consistency.

There is a third value that can be passed to the acks parameter. We can set it to 0. In this case, the producer does not wait for any acknowledgment from the Kafka broker. This is a fire-and-forget situation and has limited production use cases. There is a high possibility of losing your data without even noticing.

Now that we understand the producer side, let's delve into the Kafka consumer side. We will implement consuming logic with different delivery semantics.

11.4 *Consumer code and different delivery semantics*

Once the data is successfully saved into the topic's append-only log, the Kafka consumer code can fetch it. Because we can configure a retention time for the topics, events with the oldest offsets are removed after this time. The retention time can be infinite, meaning the old events won't be removed at all. Let's start by looking at an example consumer's code.

When configuring the consumer, we also need to pass a list of Kafka brokers. As you may recall, the producer part needs to use a serializer to transform the object into an array of bytes. The consumer needs to do a contrary transformation: from bytes to objects. Therefore, we need to provide the key–value deserializer classes. Every consumer works within a consumer group, so we also need to pass the group ID this consumer will use.

It is important to be aware that the Kafka topic's offsets are tracked by the specific consumer group. This means that when the consumer fetches the batch of events from a topic, it should commit the offset, denoting that the events were properly processed. In case of a failure, another consumer from this consumer group can resume processing from the last committed offset.

The way we commit and resume processing impacts the delivery semantics provided by our consumer application. Let's start with the simplest case, where the Kafka consumer commits the offsets automatically for us. We can achieve this by setting the enable.auto.commit (http://mng.bz/ZzgR) to true, as the following listing shows.

> **Listing 11.3   Configuring the Kafka consumer**

```
@Bean
public Map<String, Object> consumerConfigs() {
  Map<String, Object> props = new HashMap<>();

  props.put(ConsumerConfig.BOOTSTRAP_SERVERS_CONFIG, bootstrapServers);
  props.put(ConsumerConfig.KEY_DESERIALIZER_CLASS_CONFIG,
      IntegerDeserializer.class);
  props.put(ConsumerConfig.VALUE_DESERIALIZER_CLASS_CONFIG,
      StringDeserializer.class);
  props.put(ConsumerConfig.GROUP_ID_CONFIG, "receiver");
  props.put(ConsumerConfig.ENABLE_AUTO_COMMIT_CONFIG, "true");
  return props;
}
```

We can use this configuration to construct a Kafka consumer. The consumer can work for *N* topics, and it can be shared between threads. We only need to remember to subscribe to a topic we want to consume, as the next listing shows.

> **Listing 11.4   Creating a Kafka consumer with autocommit**

```
public KafkaConsumerAutoCommit(Map<String, Object> properties, String topic) {
  consumer = new KafkaConsumer<>(properties);
  consumer.subscribe(Collections.singletonList(topic));    ◁─┐  The consumer
}                                                             │  receives events
                                                              │  from the
public void startConsuming() {                                │  subscribed topic.
  try {
```

```
  while (true) {
    ConsumerRecords<Integer, String> records =
    consumer.poll(Duration.ofMillis(100));
    for (ConsumerRecord<Integer, String> record : records) {
      LOGGER.debug(
        "topic = {}, partition = {}, offset = {}, key = {}, value = {}",
        record.topic(),
        record.partition(),
        record.offset(),
        record.key(),
        record.value());
      logicProcessing(record);
    }
  }
} finally {
  consumer.close();
}
}
```

Iterates over the processing in a while loop

Polls all records available, waiting at most 100 ms

Returns a batch that can contain records for all subscribed topics

The startConsuming() method invokes the consumer's poll() method in a loop and waits 100 ms for the result. This method returns a batch of records that should be processed. Every record contains keys and values as well as tracking information, such as topic and partition. The offset() method returns the exact offset of the specific record in the given topic's partition. Finally, we iterate over a batch of records and process each of those.

When a consumer is working in autocommit mode, it commits the offsets in the background every *N* ms, as specified by the auto.commit.interval.ms setting (http://mng.bz/REnZ), which is 5 s by default.

Imagine our application processes 100 events per second, as figure 11.11 illustrates. Let's assume they arrive in five batches. In such a scenario, the offset is committed after 500 events are processed. If an application fails before 5 s, the offset is not committed. The last known offset for this processing is then equal to 0.

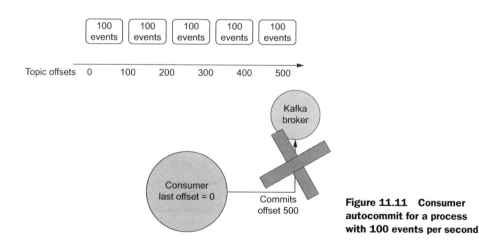

Figure 11.11 Consumer autocommit for a process with 100 events per second

If another consumer in this consumer group resumes processing due to a failure, it observes that the last committed offset is equal to 0. It will poll 500 events that the previously failed consumer may have already processed, meaning that there is a possibility of processing 500 duplicated events. This is a case of at-least-once-delivery semantics. Our consumer can receive the event once in case of a successful commit. However, if the commit is unsuccessful, another consumer reprocesses the data.

11.4.1 Committing a consumer manually

We can improve the previous situation by using manual commits. First, we need to disable the autocommit behavior by setting it to false, as the following listing demonstrates:

Listing 11.5 **Disabling autocommit**

```
props.put(ConsumerConfig.ENABLE_AUTO_COMMIT_CONFIG, "false");
```

From that point, the consumer no longer commits offsets automatically. It becomes our responsibility. The most important decision we need to make now is whether we should commit offsets at the entry to our system or after processing. If we want to keep the at-least-once delivery semantic, we should commit the offset after the processing logic. By doing this, we can be sure the message is marked as committed after it was successfully processed. The following listing shows this process.

Listing 11.6 **Synchronous commit**

```
public void startConsuming() {
  try {
    while (true) {
      ConsumerRecords<Integer, String> records =
      consumer.poll(Duration.ofMillis(100));
      for (ConsumerRecord<Integer, String> record : records) {
        logicProcessing(record);
        try {
          consumer.commitSync();          ◁──┐ The only difference in
        } catch (CommitFailedException e) {    │ this consuming code is
          LOGGER.error("commit failed", e);     │ a manual commit.
        }
      }
    }
  } finally {
    consumer.close();
  }
}
```

In listing 11.6, we use the `commit()` method to achieve our goal. It commits offsets for all partitions assigned to this specific consumer. It is important to note that the `commit()` method is blocking. This means that the processing will not progress until offsets are committed. Although this provides safety, the overall performance of the new solution may be impacted, so the `commit()` operation may be costly.

If cost is an issue, we may decide to use the `commitAsync()` method that does not block the processing thread. However, when committing in an asynchronous way, we need to be careful about error handling because exceptions are not propagated to the main caller thread. The following listing shows the implementation of `commitAsync()`.

Listing 11.7   Committing asynchronously

```
consumer.commitAsync(
        (offsets, exception) -> {
            if (exception != null) LOGGER.error(
    "Commit failed for offsets {}", offsets, exception);
        });
```

Sometimes we may observe that an async commit fails, but the commit for the subsequent batch of events passes. In such a scenario, our system is not impacted because the correct offset committed by the subsequent action was saved.

Let's consider a situation in which we want to commit offsets before the logic processes the events. In such a case, a failure in the processing logic goes unnoticed by the Kafka broker. The offset is already committed, so when the consumer logic resumes its processing, the previous batch won't be reprocessed.

If the `logicProcessing()` method doesn't finish successfully, some events aren't processed. In this case, there is a risk of losing events. Such a system will have at-most-once delivery guarantees. The same event will be processed once (but there is also a possibility that it will be processed zero times).

11.4.2   Restarting from the earliest or latest offsets

There is a second aspect that influences the delivery guarantees of our consumer applications. Let's consider a scenario in which we have a topic with 10 records (and therefore 10 offsets). Our customer application fetches all the records from the batch. The batch can contain from 1 to 10 events and commits an offset equal to N, which can be any number from 0 to 10 and equals the number of events in a batch. Unfortunately, during the commit phase our application crashes. In that case, we don't know how many events the consumer application processed. This can be influenced by many factors, such as consumer pool timeout, batch size, and so forth. When the app restarts, we have two ways to resume processing.

In such a scenario, both strategies to resume processing are controlled by the auto.offset.reset strategy (http://mng.bz/2jqg). When setting it to the earliest, resuming processing of events will start from the last committed offset for the topic's partitions (if it is present). If the offset is not present, reprocessing all events starts from the beginning. Figure 11.12 illustrates this strategy.

In this situation, the consumer application may get duplicates. This is because a crash of the consumer logic may happen at any time during processing of subsequent records. In fact, we may get up to 20 duplicates if we have one restart (2×10 events). This offset reset strategy offers the at-least-once delivery semantics.

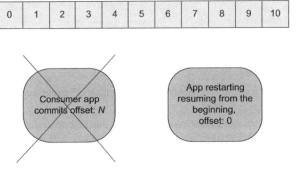

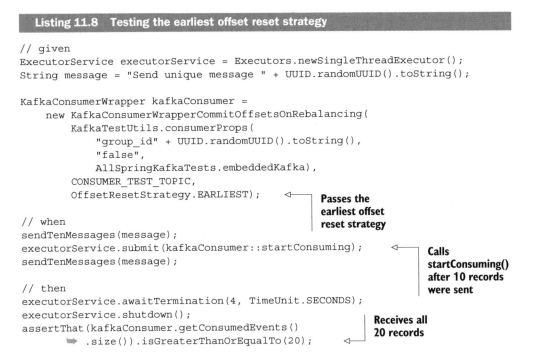

Figure 11.12   Restarting
from the earliest offset

We can observe this strategy in an integration test. In this test, we pass the OffsetReset-
Strategy.EARLIEST to the Kafka consumer, as the following listing shows.

Listing 11.8   Testing the earliest offset reset strategy

```
// given
ExecutorService executorService = Executors.newSingleThreadExecutor();
String message = "Send unique message " + UUID.randomUUID().toString();

KafkaConsumerWrapper kafkaConsumer =
    new KafkaConsumerWrapperCommitOffsetsOnRebalancing(
        KafkaTestUtils.consumerProps(
            "group_id" + UUID.randomUUID().toString(),
            "false",
            AllSpringKafkaTests.embeddedKafka),
        CONSUMER_TEST_TOPIC,
        OffsetResetStrategy.EARLIEST);        ⟵──┐ Passes the
                                                   earliest offset
// when                                            reset strategy
sendTenMessages(message);
executorService.submit(kafkaConsumer::startConsuming);   ⟵──┐ Calls
sendTenMessages(message);                                      startConsuming()
                                                               after 10 records
// then                                                        were sent
executorService.awaitTermination(4, TimeUnit.SECONDS);
executorService.shutdown();                            ┌ Receives all
assertThat(kafkaConsumer.getConsumedEvents()           │ 20 records
    ⇨ .size()).isGreaterThanOrEqualTo(20);     ⟵──────┘
```

After sending 10 events, starting the consumer, and sending 10 events again, we can
validate the number of events received. Here the consumer receives all 20 events the
producer published before the consumer was created.

   The other strategy we can choose is the latest offset. With this strategy, resuming
processing after failure when there is no offset for a given topic starts from the latest
offset on this topic. For our scenario, our app will start from offset 10 or later. The
later situation occurs if the producer appends new events. Figure 11.13 shows this
strategy.

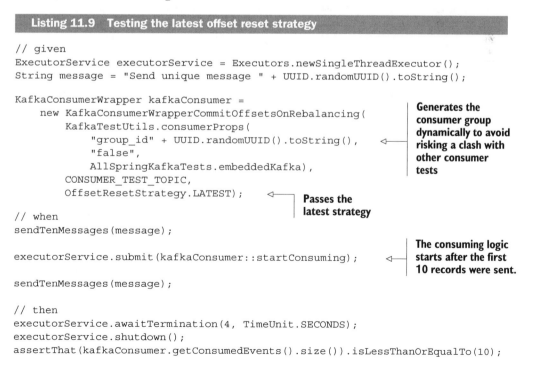

Figure 11.13 Restarting from the latest offset

In this scenario, the application may lose some events that were delivered before the crash. They may be delivered but not processed. In this scenario, we won't get duplicates, but we may also lose events. Using the latest offset strategy offsets the at-most-once delivery guarantee.

The testing logic is similar to the previous example. First, we'll create the Kafka consumer with OffsetResetStrategy.LATEST, as listing 11.9 shows. We don't need to pass this parameter because it's a default in Kafka; we pass it here to be explicit and clear. The consumer is created for a random group ID (to start from a nonexisting offset), and the offsets are not committed automatically. Next, we'll send 10 messages to a Kafka topic. After the messages are sent, we can start the Kafka consumer. Once it is started, the next 10 messages are sent.

Listing 11.9 Testing the latest offset reset strategy

```
// given
ExecutorService executorService = Executors.newSingleThreadExecutor();
String message = "Send unique message " + UUID.randomUUID().toString();

KafkaConsumerWrapper kafkaConsumer =
    new KafkaConsumerWrapperCommitOffsetsOnRebalancing(
        KafkaTestUtils.consumerProps(
            "group_id" + UUID.randomUUID().toString(),    ⟵  Generates the
            "false",                                           consumer group
            AllSpringKafkaTests.embeddedKafka),                dynamically to avoid
        CONSUMER_TEST_TOPIC,                                   risking a clash with
        OffsetResetStrategy.LATEST);    ⟵                      other consumer
// when                                  Passes the            tests
sendTenMessages(message);               latest strategy

executorService.submit(kafkaConsumer::startConsuming);   ⟵  The consuming logic
                                                             starts after the first
sendTenMessages(message);                                    10 records were sent.

// then
executorService.awaitTermination(4, TimeUnit.SECONDS);
executorService.shutdown();
assertThat(kafkaConsumer.getConsumedEvents().size()).isLessThanOrEqualTo(10);
```

You may have observed that the Kafka consumer fetched our 10 events. The events that were published before the consumer started are not taken into account by this consumer.

The integration test is similar to the previous one. Both situations have their pros and cons and their own use cases. If we have a latency-specific domain that needs to react to recent events, we may be OK with resuming from the latest offset. For example, an alert system may not be interested in events that were delivered minutes ago. Reacting to the outdated data doesn't give us much value. On the other hand, if we have a system that needs to offer correctness, we should process all the events and guard against duplicates. For example, if a payment system crashes, we need to resume the processing from the point it crashed and process all pending payments.

11.4.3 *(Effectively) exactly-once semantic*

Building a system that offers an exactly-once guarantee is hard. Up to this point, we saw two possible delivery semantics: at-least-once and at-most-once. If our system logic is nonidempotent, and we cannot lose any event, we need a form of exactly once.

In practice, systems that offer effectively exactly-once are often built atop the at-least-once delivery semantics. As we learned in the previous chapter, implementing the deduplication logic may offer us a form of effective exactly-once semantics. We say *effective* because, at some layer, the events can be duplicated. For example, they may be duplicated by the retry logic on the producer side. In that case, those duplicates are hidden from the system that is expecting exactly-once delivery.

Apache Kafka builds an effective exactly-once semantics by implementing a form of distributed transactions. In the Kafka architecture, we can have duplicates at both producer and consumer levels. By default, the producer retries requests that were not successfully performed. The consumer can also get duplicates in case of restarts because of the committing offset behavior described in the section 11.4.

To alleviate that problem, Apache Kafka implements transactions. The transaction starts on the producer side before a new event is sent to a Kafka topic. It uses the `transactional_id` (http://mng.bz/1jPX) to provide effectively exactly-once semantics within a transaction. Every record gets a transaction ID. In the case of a failed send, the operation is rolled back, so Kafka guarantees the given record won't be present in the Kafka topic. We may decide to retry again with a different transaction. However, the transaction only spans the logic within that given Kafka producer. If the service production logic is based on an external event (received from another Kafka cluster or from HTTP), we may still get a duplicate.

The event that triggers the producer send can be delivered with at-least-once guarantee semantics (see figure 11.14). If the system that uses Kafka transactions does not guard against such duplicates, those events are treated by the producer as two independent events.

Let's assume that the client application does not implement transactions and offers at-least-once delivery semantics. It can retry a request in case of failure. The application that based its logic on this client event uses Kafka producer transactions to

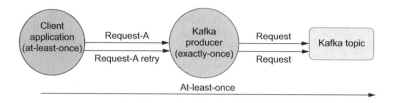

Figure 11.14 Exactly once in at-least-once context

provide an effectively exactly-once semantic. It is important to note that this does not guard against duplicates.

From the perspective of the Kafka producer application, both requests are different. If a deduplication mechanism is not implemented, there is no way to determine if those requests are duplicates. Next, the requests are both delivered using transactions, and both are delivered in the effectively exactly-once guarantee. However, from the logical perspective of the system, the same event was sent to Kafka twice (both events are duplicates). Therefore, it is logically an at-least-once delivery guarantee.

It is clear to see that effectively exactly-once semantics can work but only if all components that create the business flow of your application offer this semantic. In practice, we may have N stages of processing, communicating, and exchanging data via a pub–sub system, HTTP protocol, or something else. This would mean the whole pipeline needs to be enclosed in one transaction. Such a solution may be fragile and not fault tolerant. In case of a failure in any of the stages, our business flow might not be able to progress without the operator's manual intervention to fix the broken transaction.

If you want to use the effectively exactly-once semantic in your application, you should be careful about your system's performance and availability. The decision about whether to use this mechanism should be backed by substantial performance and chaos tests of your solution. In the next section, we will see how we can use Kafka's delivery semantics to improve our system's fault tolerance.

11.5 Leveraging delivery guarantees to provide fault tolerance

Let's consider a scenario in which we have two systems that work in an event-based way, and the only integration point between those is a Kafka topic. Let's say our checkout service produces a payment event using Kafka's asynchronous producer logic. Then, our billing service consumes the data from the topic and processes it, as figure 11.15 shows.

Figure 11.15 Billing and checkout service that work as event-based processes

Let's assume that the checkout service sends 50 requests per second on average. The billing service SLA guarantees it can process up to 100 requests per second, as figure 11.16 shows. Now consider a situation in which the billing service fails or stops during the deployment of a new version. The billing service cannot consume events from the Kafka topic during that time. The decoupling between those two services gives us fault tolerance at the checkout service level.

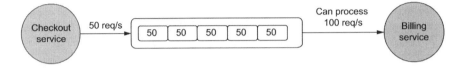

Figure 11.16   Buffering events in the Kafka topic

The payment events can still be produced even if the billing service does not work. However, those events will persist in the Kafka topic. Let's assume that the billing service is restarted and starts operating normally after 5 seconds. During that time, the checkout service sends 250 events to the Kafka topic (50 req/s × 5 s). Those events are buffered and persisted in the Kafka topic. The consumer application can resume processing buffered events when it's back online.

It is important to note that the resuming of processing from the latest processed event can be done if the billing service works in at-least-once delivery guarantees. It means the consumer needs to commit offsets properly (after the successfully processed logic), and the reset offset strategy should be set to the earliest. The 250 events that are buffered in the topic need to be consumed alongside the regular traffic from the checkout service; otherwise, the billing service will not be able to keep up with the incoming traffic.

As we know, the billing service can process 100 requests per second. Besides that, it needs to consume 50 events per second during its regular work. In this scenario, the billing service will need an additional 2.5 seconds to process the buffered events. During that time, we may observe a processing latency of 2.5 s or more. This is because the billing service needs to process the buffered events before it starts processing the incoming traffic, but the checkout service producer is still emitting events. After some time, all buffered events will be consumed, and the whole business flow of our two applications will continue processing with its typical latency and traffic.

The same solution can apply with an unexpected surge of traffic. Let's assume a situation when the checkout service starts producing its 200 events per second. The billing service won't be able to keep up with this traffic because it offers the 100 req/s SLA. However, as long as this situation is transient, the additional events will be buffered in the Kafka topic. When the traffic goes back to normal, the billing service will be able to process the additional traffic and, after some time, return to its regular traffic.

We can build this fault tolerance into our systems as long as we have a pub–sub architecture and a component that can buffer the traffic. Besides that, we need to be able to reason about the delivery guarantees of those components. We then need to pick the proper delivery semantic according to our needs.

The second aspect that is crucial for this solution is the consumer's ability to process additional traffic. If the SLA of the consumer is not substantially higher than the producer, the time for resuming the processing will be long. The consumer needs to be able to process the buffered traffic alongside its normal incoming traffic. Otherwise, it won't be able to keep up with the traffic once there was a partial failure. Let's now sum up what we learned in this chapter.

Summary

- The pub–sub architecture allows us to create loosely coupled, asynchronous systems, improving fault tolerance with proper delivery guarantees.
- An event queue provides the capabilities to create event-driven architectures. The more services communicate with each other, the more gain we will get from this architecture.
- We can reason about and control delivery semantics at both the producer and the consumer sides.
- We can fine-tune consistency versus availability in distributed systems.
- We can implement our consumer code with Kafka's at-least-once and at-most-once delivery guarantees:
  - Fine-grained commits can reduce the number of duplicates in the at-least-once guarantee on the consumer side.
  - At-most-once imposes a risk of not processing all the events in case of a failure.
- When splitting a queue functionality into *N*-independent systems, our systems can be both loosely coupled and asynchronously fault-tolerant with no single point of failure.
- The effective exactly-once is possible when using transactions. However, it starts getting more complex or nonfeasible when we have more complex architectures with more services in the pipeline.

Managing versioning and compatibility

12

This chapter covers

- Thinking about versioning in the abstract
- Planning versioning strategies for libraries
- Designing APIs for evolution
- Working effectively with storage schemas

There are a few topics that are almost guaranteed to cause groans from experienced engineers. If you bring up localization, merge conflicts, or time zones in conversation, be prepared for a frosty reception. Versioning falls into that category too. It's a fact of life, but many of us put off working out how we'll handle it for far too long—partly because it can feel like a waste of time. You'll hear very few positive comments when a product, library or API gets versioning *right*, but it can be a major source of complaints when it's done *badly*.

In this chapter we'll offer some perspectives on versioning that can help you design an appropriate versioning strategy for the product you're working on. We'll provide some concrete guidance and suggestions, but ultimately, it will be up to you to balance competing concerns and technical challenges.

The most specific piece of advice is easy to give right from the start, however; don't close your eyes and hope that versioning will turn out to be unnecessary.

Unless you're really expecting to throw code away almost immediately, you should plan for how it will evolve and what consequences there might be. Let's review what we mean by versioning and why it exists at all before diving into specific details of libraries, network APIs (such as web services), and data storage.

12.1 *Versioning in the abstract*

Things change. If you're looking for a life where you never need to deal with new challenges or requirements, software is probably not a good fit for you. That change comes in many forms; the most obvious, perhaps, is the changing set of requirements for any particular piece of code, but the reality is that almost every aspect of what we use (hardware, operating system, developer platform, programming language, deployment model—you name it) changes over time. All of that change leads to complexity and unpredictability.

Versioning attempts to tame that complexity, communicating expectations between different people and systems. Different versioning schemes are adapted to different requirements and expectations, and in this section, we'll look at what they have in common and what distinguishes them.

12.1.1 *Properties of versions*

Versions are applied to lots of different entities: applications, libraries, protocols, books, programming languages, and more. Different versioning schemes have different properties though, and it's worth thinking about the axes on which versions can vary.

MEMORABILITY

Many versioning schemes are designed to be memorable and readable; it's easy to remember that you're using, for example, Ubuntu 20.04 or that you're reading the first edition of this book. A few versioning schemes are really *unmemorable*—most obviously, git hashes. Somehow I doubt I'd ever remember af257385d785f597fc8be67c84f2cf714fbe4203 correctly, and even just remembering af25738 (the leading seven characters, as displayed by GitHub, Bitbucket, and the like) is going to be somewhat taxing if you need to remember several commits.

IMMUTABILITY

Often (but not always), versions we depend on in software are quite precise and immutable. If someone depends on the exact version 3.0.4 of the NodaTime NuGet package from the nuget.org feed, that package will always consist of the exact same bytes. The package feed prevents an existing version being overwritten.

Git hashes are more intrinsically immutable: the hash is derived from the content, so if the content changes, the hash *must* change (barring the astronomically unlikely event of a hash collision).

That's a really useful property to help software systems to be predictable. It's generally less human-friendly though—when describing which operating system they're using, you're more likely to get an answer of *Windows 10* than *Windows 10 build 19042.867*. Immutability and memorability aren't diametrically opposite, but there's a certain amount of tension between them, as immutable version numbers typically consist of more detailed information.

IMPLICIT RELATIONSHIPS BETWEEN VERSIONS

Many versioning systems try to convey important information within a very small amount of data (the text of the version number). We'll look at the most obvious example of that in section 12.1.3 when we consider semantic versioning, but there are plenty of other examples. Visual Studio uses year-based marketing versions: Visual Studio 2019 is clearly later than Visual Studio 2017, for example.

Some versions don't convey any kind of ordering or relationships between each other. Again, the obvious example here is git hashes. If I give you two git hashes, without access to the repository itself, you can't tell whether one is in the history of another, whether they're independent branches, or whether they even come from the same repository.

Finally, some versioning schemes sound like they give information, but you need to be really careful. Which would you expect to come first: the Xbox or the Xbox One? And when would you expect the Xbox 360? Likewise, the .NET version history is *interesting* but not necessarily a model you'd want to follow.

When designing your own versioning schemes, or picking from existing ones, consider what information you're trying to convey and what information the consumer of your versioning scheme might infer without you wanting them to.

An important part of the information that many versioning schemes try to provide within the version text is a guarantee of *compatibility* (or a suggestion of incompatibility). Let's look at what we mean by compatibility.

12.1.2 *Backward and forward compatibility*

Broadly speaking, the topic of compatibility is interested in the question of what happens when code that's aware of one version of something has to work with a different version. That's a deliberately fuzzy description because the concept can be applied in so many different ways.

Backward compatibility is the property where a new version can work with information from an old version. *Forward compatibility* is the property where an old version can work with information from a new version.

Concrete examples of these concepts include

- As a language, Java maintains *backward compatibility*. Code written in Java 7 can be compiled with a Java 17 compiler. It does not maintain *forward compatibility*; code written in Java 17 may well use features that would cause a compilation error using a Java 7 compiler.
- Libraries are usually written with backward compatibility in mind; code written against NodaTime version 2.3 will still work with NodaTime version 2.4. We'll look at library versioning in a lot more detail in section 12.2. Patch versions within semantic versioning provide forward compatibility, as we'll see in the next section.

- Web services usually maintain backward compatibility; a JSON-encoded web service request written against the service definition on January 10, 2021 should still work on April 1, 2021, even if the service definition has changed. The calling code may need to consider how to handle expected data in the response, however (which comes back to data compatibility). We'll look at network API versioning in more detail in section 12.3.
- Some data formats, such as Google Protocol Buffers and Apache Avro, are designed to enable both backward and forward compatibility, allowing old code to work with newer data stores without losing data written by new code. We'll look at data versioning in section 12.4.

In some situations, the terms backward and forward end up being more confusing than helpful and can lead to people talking past each other in meetings. I find it useful to talk in terms of specific examples; instead of talking about *a later version of the client*, give some specific version numbers. They don't have to be the actual version numbers for software you've released or are planning to release, they can just be hypothetical. But making the situation concrete can help avoid confusion. Just like the *given then when* pattern of acceptance testing, these scenarios start by defining characteristics of particular versions, envisage a particular set of interactions, and then try to play out the results. We'll see some examples of this over the course of the chapter.

12.1.3 *Semantic versioning*

Semantic versioning (commonly known as SemVer) has become the most common approach to versioning within the library ecosystems for most platforms—at least in theory. Full adherence to semantic versioning is variable to say the least, and we'll see some good reasons for that in section 12.2.4.

RULES FOR STABLE VERSIONS

A version number following semantic versioning always has three integer parts: major, minor, and patch. In Figure 12.1, the major number is 2, the minor number is 13, and the patch number is 4.

Major 〜⌄ 2.13.4 ▾〜 Patch

Minor   **Figure 12.1   Example of a semantic version**

The basic rules of semantic versioning (when applied to the same entity, such as a library) are

- If two versions have different major numbers, there are no guarantees of compatibility at all. For example, versions 2.13.4 and 3.0.2 could be entirely incompatible.

- If two versions have the same major number but different minor numbers, then the version with the larger minor number must be backward compatible with the version with the smaller minor number. For example, version 2.13.4 must be backward compatible with 2.5.3.
- If two versions have the same major and minor numbers, they must be backward and forward compatible with each other. For example, versions 2.13.4 and 2.13.1 must be compatible in both directions.

These rules are designed to allow efficient communication of when consumers can change which version they're using:

- If you change major versions, all bets are off. Proceed with care, perform rigorous testing, and allow plenty of time for the upgrade.
- If you upgrade from one minor version to a later one, everything *should* be okay. (Sometimes that expectation can be confounded, despite best intentions, as we'll see later.)
- If you upgrade *or downgrade* between patch versions in the same minor version, everything should be okay. The caveat here is that patch versions usually exist to fix bugs, and it's possible you were depending on that buggy behavior. (You might have a workaround that's broken by the bug being fixed, for example.) It should be fine to downgrade again afterward.

When discussing particular versions, it's common to use *x* or *y* as placeholders for any number. For example, you might say that 1.3.x must be backward compatible with 1.2.y.

SPECIFYING UNSTABLE VERSIONS

Semantic versioning also provides two mechanisms for specifying unstable versions. The first is to use a major number of 0 for initial development. The normal expectations of semantic versioning do not apply when the major number is 0; version 0.2.0 can be entirely incompatible with version 0.1.0, for example. There isn't even any need for patch level version number changes (e.g., 0.1.0 to 0.1.1) to maintain compatibility.

The second way of indicating an unstable version number is to use a prerelease label. In this case, the regular semantic version has a suffix of a hyphen followed by a dot-separated sequence of identifiers.

Major.minor.patch   Pre-release label

Figure 12.2   Example of a semantic version with a prerelease label

In figure 12.2, the major.minor.patch part of the version is 1.4.5, but there's also a prerelease label of beta.1. A prerelease label can have as many dot-separated identifiers as you wish, but typically, they have between one and three identifiers. Each identifier must consist of characters that are either alphanumeric ASCII or hyphens.

While there are no guarantees of compatibility with prereleases, typically, the version indicates a movement toward the version indicated by the major.minor.patch part, which would suggest compatibility with other versions. For example, a version of 1.5.0-alpha.1 would usually be backward-compatible with 1.4.x.

Choosing between 0.x.y or prerelease labels

While the use of 0.x.y version numbers has been historically common, it does come with a significant downside; it only really works for the first stable version (1.0.0). If your initial sequence of version numbers is 0.8.0, 0.9.0, 1.0, then you might be tempted to try to use 1.8, 1.9, 2.0 for the second major version. In most cases that would violate semantic versioning rules because the purpose of going to 2.0 is usually to introduce incompatible changes.

I would recommend using prerelease labels from the very first public release. You can then be consistent between the release sequence for the first major version (e.g., 1.0.0-alpha.1, 1.0.0-beta.1, 1.0.0-beta.2, 1.0.0) and for the second major version (e.g., 2.0.0-alpha.1, 2.0.0-alpha.2, 2.0.0-beta.1, 2.0.0). I would reserve 0.x.y for very early prototyping—or avoid such version numbers entirely.

BUILD METADATA

Semantic versioning also allows *build metadata* to be specified after either a stable or prerelease version with a + suffix. The build metadata consists of a dot-separated sequence of identifiers, similar to prerelease labels. Build metadata is intended to be purely informational. For example, you might include a timestamp or a commit hash in the build metadata.

In figure 12.3, the major.minor.patch part of the version is 1.2.3, the prerelease label is beta.1, and the build metadata part is 20210321.af25738. That build metadata happens to be a date and a commit hash, but semantic versioning doesn't attach any significance to that.

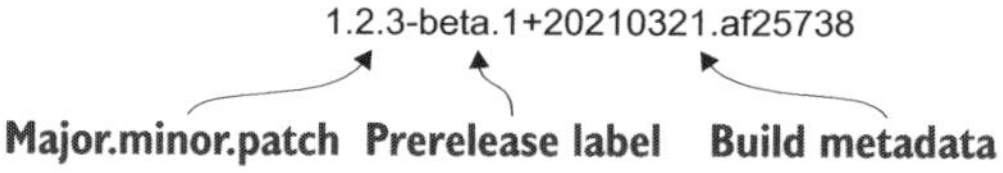

1.2.3-beta.1+20210321.af25738

Major.minor.patch Prerelease label   Build metadata

Figure 12.3 Example of a semantic version with a prerelease label and build metadata

VERSION PRECEDENCE

Semantic versioning specifies *precedence* between versions, to be used by tooling to determine compatibility, where possible, and suggested upgrades. In general, they work as you'd expect them to:

- 1.2.3 precedes 2.0.0
- 1.2.3 precedes 1.3.0
- 1.2.3 precedes 1.2.4
- 1.3.0-alpha.5 precedes 1.3.0-beta.1

- 1.3.0-beta.8 precedes 1.3.0-beta.10 (note the numerical comparison)
- 1.3.0-beta.2 precedes 1.3.0

The exhaustive and precise precedence rules are beyond the scope of this book, but they are specified at https://semver.org. Finally for this section, let's move from the precisely-specified world of semantic versioning to the other extreme: marketing.

12.1.4 Marketing versions

Semantic versioning is designed to convey technical information in a compact way. It's not designed to entice customers to buy new things. That's what marketing versions are for. The only reason to mention them in this chapter at all is to highlight the difference between marketing versioning and semantic versioning.

In many cases, there's no need for a marketing version at all. They're usually reserved for products, rather than libraries, protocols, file formats, or schemas. Where there *is* a need for a marketing version, there's often a more technical version number as well, primarily used for support purposes. That's typically more precise and long-winded and may or may not relate to semantic versioning. It may even sound quite contradictory to the marketing version; you might release *Awesome Game* with a final technical version number of 2.3.1 but then release *Awesome Game 2* with an initial technical version number of 1.0.0.

The main lesson here is that these are different versioning schemes that serve very different purposes. Try not to confuse the two, either when you're looking at someone else's versions or when you're designing your own versioning schemes.

So far, we've only looked at versioning in the abstract, although semantic versioning is *primarily* applied to libraries. We'll dig into library versioning in more detail in the next section.

12.2 Versioning for libraries

For many developers, libraries are by far the most important domain for versioning. That said, if you only *consume* libraries, you're in a relatively simple situation—or at least, you might be. Working with multiple versions of multiple libraries is inherently complex and can be immensely frustrating. Even if all the developers of all the libraries you use are following the conventions for your platform (typically, SemVer), that's no guarantee that you'll escape incompatibility issues. However, you have relatively few decisions to make.

Most of this section is devoted to developers who are *publishing* libraries. That involves far more decisions, many of which are balancing acts based on educated guesswork. Even the concept of publishing a library has nuance to it; there are different considerations for publishing a library to a package manager, such as Maven Central or NuGet, versus publishing it to a company-internal artifact repository or simply updating the library source code to be consumed by other source code.

There are no easy solutions, but the guidance here should help you ask the right questions for your context and reach the *least-worst* available answers. Given that a lot of library versioning is about compatibility, let's start by thinking about what that means.

12.2.1 *Source, binary, and semantic compatibility*

In this section, we'll address one overall situation: we want to publish a new version of a library, and we need to know whether it's backward compatible with an old version of the same library. We'll assume we don't know anything about code that is consuming our library and turn each example into a sort of challenge: can we come up with some *hypothetical* consumer code that would be broken by our change? We can then consider the nature of that breakage.

> **NOTE** Any time the text in this section refers to consumer code, that means code within an application (or another library) that depends on the library we're talking about. Often that means it is calling functions provided by the library, but that's not always the case. The consumer code *might* just be implementing an interface provided by the library, for example.

Spoiler alert: for almost every change you can imagine, it's possible to come up with consumer code that would be broken by that change. As an extreme example, consumer code could take a hash of your library and throw an exception if it wasn't exactly as expected. You couldn't modify the library *at all* without breaking that consumer.

Fortunately, most consumer code is more reasonable than that, but you may still discover cases in which a change will break consumer code in a possible but very obscure situation. Should you consider that to be a breaking change, accepting the associated costs for other consumers, or deem that obscure case to be out of scope? That's the sort of decision you'll need to make once you've worked out what code could be broken by any particular change.

For compiled languages, there are three kinds of compatibility you should consider: source compatibility, binary compatibility, and semantic compatibility. The concept of binary compatibility doesn't generally apply to languages that aren't compiled ahead of time, where the library is published as source code, effectively. This is the case for JavaScript libraries, such as React and jQuery, for example. All of the examples below are provided in Java, but rules for compatibility are highly language specific; the aim is really to demonstrate the thought process rather than focus on the particular changes shown.

Most examples show library code, both before and after the change, and some consumer code that uses the library. Let's start with source compatibility.

SOURCE COMPATIBILITY

One library version has *source compatibility* (or is *source compatible*) with an older version if consumer source code that works against the earlier version also works with the later version. In Java, that includes recompiling the consumer code against the newer library. Let's start with an obvious example of an incompatible change: renaming a method, even just by changing the case of a single letter, as shown in the following listing.

Listing 12.1   Changing a method name

Library before
```
public static User getByID(int userId) {
    …
}
```

Library after
```
public static User getById(int userId) {
    …
}
```

Consumer code
```
int userId = request.getUserId();
User user = User.getByID(userId);
```

After the change in the library, the consumer code fails to compile with an error of *cannot find symbol* for User.getByID. Renaming *anything* public (such as a package, field, interface, class, or method) is a breaking change. But not every breaking change is that obvious. Consider changing a parameter from one type to a supertype—for example, String to Object, as shown in the following listing.

Listing 12.2   Changing a parameter type (source compatibility)

Library before
```
public void displayData(String data) {
    …
}
```

Library after
```
public void displayData(Object data) {
    …
}
```

Any code *calling* the method should still be fine. Even a method reference conversion in the consumer code should still work. But consumer code can do more than call the method.

Consumer code
```
public class ConsumerClass extends LibraryClass {
    @Override
    public void displayData(String data) {
        …
    }
}
```

That's fine with the original code but fails with a compilation error with the modified library code. Now, if the class containing the method had been marked as final, that would have prevented subclassing, so *maybe* this change would have been source compatible in that case. You should generally be wary of any situation where the public API surface is being changed, and you're not quite sure whether it's compatible or not.

> **NOTE** Although we've been looking at examples in Java, the broad concept of compatibility applies to other languages. It's important *not* to assume that a change that is source or binary compatible in one language is also compatible in another. For example, renaming a method parameter is a backward compatible change in Java but not in C#, due to the *named arguments* feature of C#. To add even more complexity, the rules about what changes are backward-compatible can change over time. (For example, C# didn't always have named arguments, and Java might gain that feature in the future.)

In most cases adding something new is considered a compatible change, even though it can often *theoretically* break consumer source code by introducing naming collisions. One important counterexample to this is adding methods to interfaces; unless you provide a default method implementation, that's a breaking change, as any consumer declaring they implement the interface now *won't* be fully implementing it. The same goes for adding an abstract method to an existing abstract class.

So far, we've considered the situation in which the library is modified, and then the consumer code is recompiled. What happens if we can't recompile the consumer code? Compatibility in this situation is called *binary compatibility*.

BINARY COMPATIBILITY

Before diving into details of what changes might be binary compatible or not, it's worth mentioning why it's important. After all, we're generally happy to recompile our applications when we need to, right? While that's fine at an application level, it's typically less feasible for other dependencies. We'll look at the complexities involved in dependency graphs in section 12.2.2, but imagine the following situation:

- Your application depends on LibraryA and LibraryB
- LibraryA *also* depends on LibraryB

This situation is shown graphically in figure 12.4, where each arrow represents a dependency. If LibraryB makes a change that is only backward compatible after recompilation, you'd need to use a recompiled version of LibraryA as well, and that could be tricky.

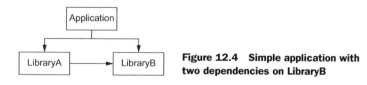

Figure 12.4   Simple application with two dependencies on LibraryB

Binary compatibility can be harder to reason about than source compatibility because it involves a layer of abstraction developers can usually ignore. Most Java developers don't need to know the bytecode generated for any particular piece of code, for example. Fortunately, for Java specifically, the language specification has a whole section on what changes are and are not binary compatible. Don't expect every language to have that level of documentation though!

Some examples of binary incompatible changes are obvious: removing or renaming methods or types is obviously going to cause problems. In other cases it's less clear. Let's revisit our earlier example of changing the type of a method parameter from `String` to `Object`. Ignoring the override problem we noted earlier, source compatibility is achievable because there's an implicit conversion from `String` to `Object`. That's a conversion that the compiler knows about though. At execution time, the JVM expects the method signature to stay the same. Let's look at a concrete example.

> **Listing 12.3 Changing a parameter type (binary compatibility)**

Library before
```
public void displayData(String data) {
    ...
}
```

Library after
```
public void displayData(Object data) {
    ...
}
```

Consumer code
```
public class Program {
    public static void main(String[] args) {
        new LibraryClass().displayData("Hello");
    }
}
```

If we try to run the consumer code that was compiled against the original library code, recompiling *just* the modified library code, an error is thrown at execution time:

```
java.lang.NoSuchMethodError: 'void LibraryClass.displayData(java.lang.String)'
```

There are two aspects that make binary incompatibility particularly nasty:

- *You only see the problem at execution time.* Developers working with compiled languages are used to the compiler catching this kind of problem (the method you expected not being present) at compile time.
- *You'll only see the problem if execution goes down a code path that makes the JVM look for the missing method.* This is particularly worrying, as the code paths that aren't typically tested quite as thoroughly are the ones involving error handling, leading to a double whammy of errors.

As we've seen, some API surface changes can be source compatible but binary incompatible. Changes like adding a new class can be binary compatible but technically source incompatible (due to naming collisions). Other changes are either source and binary compatible or source and binary incompatible.

All of this has, so far, just been about the public API though; we haven't worried about the implementation details. But there's a difference between *the code compiles and all the methods are found* and *everything works as it did before*. The final kind of compatibility we'll consider is *semantic compatibility*.

SEMANTIC COMPATIBILITY

Binary compatibility is fairly cut-and-dried. Source compatibility has a bit more nuance; you need to decide whether you'll count the possibility of naming collisions as a breaking change, for example. It's still usually clear though. Semantic compatibility is around the *behavior* of the code, and you simply don't know what people will depend on. This is expressed in Hyrum's Law (after Google software engineer Hyrum Wright; see https://www.hyrumslaw.com/):

> With a sufficient number of users of an API,
> it does not matter what you promise in the contract:
> all observable behaviors of your system
> will be depended on by somebody.

Taking this to one extreme, every release of a library would have a new SemVer major version. At the other extreme, we could take a stance of, "If you don't like the new behavior, don't use the library" and treat any change that didn't affect the public API surface as a nonbreaking change. Of course, neither extreme is a sensible position.

Most implementation changes you'll want to make don't change the behavior in huge ways, of course. There are three classes of change that are worth looking out for though:

- Parameter validation
- Inheritance
- Performance changes

Parameter validation changes generally fall into two subcategories. Either an expected-to-be-invalid input was accidentally permitted and you want to tighten up the validation to reject it (as a bug fix), or you want to allow previously-rejected input (as a feature). As an example of the latter case, consider this simple `Person` class that captures a person's legal name and their *casual* name (whether that's a nickname, an abbreviated form, or something else). Initially, both forms are required, as shown in the following listing.

Listing 12.4 Initial `Person` class with two nonnullable parameters

```
public class Person {
    private final String legalName;
    private final String casualName;
    public Person(String legalName, String casualName) {
        this.legalName = Objects.requireNonNull(legalName);
```

```
        this.casualName = Objects.requireNonNull(casualName);    ◁──┐
    }                                                                  Throw an exception if
}                                                                      casualName is null.
```

Now, suppose we find that in practice, most users don't want to specify a separate casual name. They end up passing the same value in for both the legal name and the casual name, and occasionally, that makes the code more convoluted. We could change the library to allow null, defaulting to using the same value for both fields.

Listing 12.5   `Person` **class constructor change to permit null casual name**

```
public class Person {
    private final String legalName;                               Allow casualName
    private final String casualName;                              to be null, using
    public Person(String legalName, String casualName) {          legalName if it is.
        this.legalName = Objects.requireNonNull(legalName);
        this.casualName = casualName == null ? casualName : legalName;    ◁──┘
    }
}
```

In some senses, that's a compatible change. But if any consumer was relying on the validation of the `casualName` parameter, they're now broken. More alarmingly, they may be *silently* broken. Consider the following consumer method, which happens to print to the screen but could easily be creating HTML for a web page or similar:

```
public static void createUser(String legalName, String casualName) {
    Person person = new Person(legalName, casualName);
    System.out.println("Welcome, " + casualName);    ◁──┐ Expect casualName
    ...    ◁──┐                                             to be validated as
}                Use Person for                            nonnull by here.
                 further operations.
```

This code will now print *Welcome, null* if the `casualName` parameter to the `createUser` method is null, instead of throwing an exception, as it did previously. The parameter may be used in other places in the method, propagating a null value, where it wasn't previously expected. This code could itself be in a library, documented to validate `casualName` and relying on the `Person` constructor to perform that validation.

In this case, an alternative and backward compatible approach would be to add a constructor accepting only one name (which is then used for both the legal name and the casual name). If you find yourself considering loosening (or tightening) validation, adding an alternative path (whether that's via an overload or a new method) can help to avoid silently breaking changes.

Inheritance can cause semantic changes when what might look like an implementation detail is effectively exposed because methods can be overridden. Listing 12.6 shows `Player` and `Position` classes that might appear in the source code for a game.

Listing 12.6 Initial `Player` and `Position` classes

```
public final class Position {
    private final int x;
    private final int y;
    public Position(int x, int y) {
        this.x = x;
        this.y = y;
    }
    ...
}
public class Player {
    private Position position;
    public void moveTo(int x, int y) {              Delegate to the
        moveTo(new Position(x, y));       ◁────     Position-accepting
    }                                               method.
    public void moveTo(Position position) {
        this.position = position;    ◁──┐
    }                                   │   Real change is in the
    ...                                 │   Position-accepting
}                                       │   method.
```

Suppose a subclass of `Player` wants to limit the player's movement to a particular bounded area. It can do so by just overriding the `moveTo(Position)` method, determining the bounded position, and then calling `super.moveTo(actualPosition)` to finish the operation. However, the author of the `Player` class might decide they want to avoid creating `Position` objects all the time, instead dealing with the x and y values directly. They expect to make a backward-compatible change by simply swapping the delegation in the `moveTo` methods, as shown in listing 12.7.

Listing 12.7 Modified `Player` class with swapped overload delegation

```
public class Player {
    private int x;                      Coordinates are stored
    private int y;                      directly as integers.
    public void moveTo(int x, int y) {
        this.x = x;                     Coordinate-wise method
        this.y = y;                     becomes main implementation.
    }
    public void moveTo(Position position) {           Delegate to the
        moveTo(position.getX(), position.getY());  ◁──┤ coordinate-wise
    }                                                 │ method.
}
```

At this point, the subclass only behaves correctly if the `moveTo(Position)` overload is called. That will still limit the input and call the implementation in `Player`, which will then delegate to the `moveTo(int, int)` overload. But if a user calls `moveTo(int, int)` directly, the limiting code will be bypassed.

If the `Player` class or the `moveTo` methods were final, this would be fine. But inheritance and the possibility of some methods being inherited effectively exposes the implementation detail of which overload calls the other.

This example leads on to the final category of semantic change that is worth considering carefully: performance. (Whether this is truly semantic or not is arguable. It's an observable behavior change, even though the behavior isn't as simple as *inputs and outputs*.) To continue with the `Player` class, we noted that the original change was to avoid creating lots of `Position` objects. However, depending on how the class is used, it could have the opposite effect. Suppose our `Player` class has accessors for both the position and the components of the position. These could be implemented in two ways, as shown in the following listing.

Listing 12.8   Position accessors within `Player`

Accessors before

```
public int getPositionX() {
    return position.getX();
}
public int getPositionY() {
    return position.getY();
}
public Position getPosition() {
    return position;
}
```

Accessors after

```
public int getPositionX() {
    return x;
}
public int getPositionY() {
    return y;
}
public Position getPosition() {
    return new Position(x, y);
}
```

Does the `Player` class have better performance before or after the change? That entirely depends on how it's used. Code that has calls `moveTo(int, int)`, `getPositionX()`, and `getPositionY()` will definitely see fewer allocations, but code that calls `getPosition()` will see more allocations. Effectively, the best way to use the library has changed: a previously allocation-efficient usage pattern has become inefficient, and vice versa. If the library is intended to be performance sensitive, you may well wish to consider that to be breaking, as calling code needs to change.

So now that you can evaluate the extent to which any given change is backward compatible or not, does that mean we're done? You *might* come to the conclusion that all we need to do for our library is follow the rules of semantic versioning based on the results of checking each change. You might say to yourself, "When we want to make a breaking change, that's fine. We'll just bump the major version, and all our consumers will be aware of what that means." If every application only ever consumed libraries with no further dependencies, it really would be that simple. Making a breaking change would put *some* burden on consumers (checking that the breaking change doesn't affect their code or making any necessary changes), but it wouldn't be a huge deal.

Unfortunately, life doesn't work that way. Let's take a look at what happens when lots of libraries are involved, using sprawling dependency graphs.

12.2.2 *Dependency graphs and diamond dependencies*

I should warn you that this topic can be quite alarming. Sometimes, after looking at a particularly large dependency graph, I'm astonished that we manage to rely so heavily on software working and continuing to work as it evolves. The problems in this section are very real, and anyone who has had to battle with dependency collisions will come away with scars to prove it. Yet, somehow, we seem to manage most of the time. The duct tape just about manages to hold everything together.

> **NOTE** This section includes a bunch of version numbers for libraries as examples. We're going to assume that all the libraries in question follow semantic versioning. If there are libraries anywhere in the dependency graph that *don't* follow semantic versioning, that doesn't fundamentally change the topic—it just makes it much, much harder to reason about.

So far we've considered examples in which an application depends on a single library, and we haven't considered any dependencies that single library might have. Now, we'll consider situations in which an application depends on multiple libraries, and each of which may have multiple dependencies that may, in turn, have multiple dependencies. We'll show these as directed graphs, where each node in the graph represents a single library (across all versions), and each arrow in the graph represents a dependency relationship and is labeled with the version of that dependency.

> **NOTE** Some tools (including Maven) represent dependencies using trees instead of graphs. Each node of the tree consists of an artifact and its version number, instead of the edge within a graph showing the dependency version. Both forms represent the same amount of information, but I find it easier to spot diamond dependencies when using graphs.

If all of that sounds complicated and mathematical, don't worry: it's quite easy to understand pictorially. (The problem with large dependency graphs isn't an easy problem to solve, but understanding the graph itself shouldn't be too bad.)

Let's take a hypothetical example. We have an application that needs to read some JSON files, and it also uses a message queue and a database. As it happens, the message queue library also has JSON functionality. The dependencies might be something like the following:

- Application depends on JsonLib version 1.2.0.
- Application depends on MQLib version 2.1.2.
- Application depends on DbLib version 3.5.0.
- MQLib depends on JsonLib version 1.1.5.

From the perspective of the application, the last of these is a *transitive dependency*. It's an indirect dependency, which is only present because the application depends on MQLib. Transitive dependencies can include libraries that the main application doesn't depend on directly.

The graph for this set of dependencies could be represented in figure 12.5.

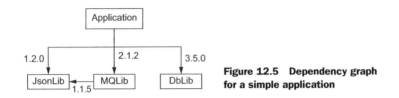

Figure 12.5   **Dependency graph for a simple application**

Although this hypothetical example is much simpler than many real applications, where the total set of dependencies can run into hundreds or thousands of libraries, it still contains a potential problem, due to JsonLib: one consumer of JsonLib (the application) expects to use version 1.2.0, whereas the other consumer (MQLib) expects to use version 1.1.5. This is one example of a *diamond dependency* problem. The origin of the name *diamond dependency* is when the two consumers of the common library are themselves libraries. Suppose the application didn't depend on JsonLib at all, but DbLib did. We would end up with the situation shown in figure 12.6, which is more obviously diamond shaped.

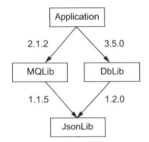

Figure 12.6   **Dependency graph with a classic diamond dependency**

Both of these are diamond dependencies, really. Depending on your language and package manager, direct dependencies from the application may have slightly different rules applied to them, but the main problem we'll be looking at in this section is the same either way.

> **Transitive dependency complexity**
>
> For the sake of simplicity, we've ignored one aspect of the dependency graphs here: typically, different versions of libraries will have different transitive dependencies. So JsonLib 1.1.5 might depend on CommonLib 1.2.0, but JsonLib 1.2.0 might depend on CommonLib 1.3.0.

The key question is: what version of JsonLib is used? Do we have to use a single version at all?

SHARED VS. ISOLATED DEPENDENCIES

Different platforms, languages, and library/package managers have different approaches to dependencies. These different approaches have different benefits and drawbacks, and each approach will also have its own specific details. The most important initial categorization is whether the dependencies are *shared* across the whole application or *isolated.*

If a dependency is shared, the whole application uses a single version of the library. If a dependency is isolated, each dependency has its own separate copy of the library, including any library-wide state.

Shared dependencies are generally more efficient than isolated dependencies and can be more convenient too:

- Multiple copies of the code take up more memory (and potentially more disk space for deployment) and can incur more optimization costs (such as each copy of the bytecode being JIT-compiled separately).
- Any singletons of expensive-to-initialize resources or caches provide their efficiency benefits across the whole application.
- Objects can be passed between different components in the application transparently.

There are two big drawbacks, however:

- If the shared state isn't designed carefully, components can interfere with each other in unexpected ways. (For example, if two components each expect to be the only user of a library-wide cache, their assumptions could be violated by each other.)
- If different components expect different and incompatible versions of the same library, no single shared version will satisfy both.

The aspect of objects being passed between different components is particularly important. In the classic diamond dependency shown in figure 12.6, suppose the three libraries have the following classes and methods:

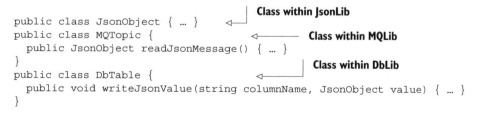

```
public class JsonObject { … }          ⊲──┐  Class within JsonLib
public class MQTopic {                  ⊲──────── Class within MQLib
  public JsonObject readJsonMessage() { … }
}                                          ┐  Class within DbLib
public class DbTable {                  ⊲──┘
  public void writeJsonValue(string columnName, JsonObject value) { … }
}
```

That's potentially really convenient for the application: it can read a `JsonObject` from a message queue and write it into the database without having to perform any conversions. That only works when the `JsonObject` types in the two method signatures (the return type of readJsonMessage and the second parameter of writeJsonValue) are actually the same type or at least compatible types.

> **NOTE** In statically typed languages, such as Java and C#, different types that happen to have the same name but come from different libraries are typically regarded as incompatible types. In dynamically typed languages, the semantics are usually somewhat looser. Isolated dependencies don't prohibit this sort of object passing as much in dynamically typed languages as they do in statically typed languages. This doesn't solve the problem of different incompatible library versions, however. It may even complicate things more, as object passing may work in one direction but not in the other within the same major version if the component creating the object uses an earlier minor version than the component consuming the object.

If the dependency of one component is used as a purely internal implementation detail (so objects from the dependency are never returned or accepted by the components public API), then isolating that dependency can be a very robust approach, aside from the potential inefficiencies mentioned earlier.

The choice between shared or isolated dependencies doesn't have to be the same throughout an application. For example, the Maven package management system offers the option of creating a *fat jar*, containing all the dependencies of a library in an isolated way. This could be used for one library with others sharing dependencies.

THE PAIN OF MAJOR VERSIONS

With the background context of shared and isolated dependencies in place, we can consider the implications of incompatible versions of libraries. Let's update our original dependency graph to require incompatible versions of JsonLib, indicated by different major version numbers (see figure 12.7).

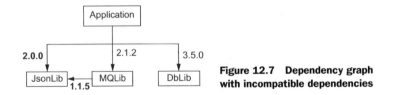

Figure 12.7 **Dependency graph with incompatible dependencies**

Now, the application depends on JsonLib version 2.0.0, whereas MQLib still depends on JsonLib version 1.1.5. Is that a problem? Maybe . . .

If the application uses isolated dependencies, it may be fine. If the application is written in a dynamically typed language and JsonLib objects are being passed between the application and MQLib, it could cause some new incompatibilities, but it should otherwise work.

If the application uses shared dependencies, the first question is which version will be shared between the two. There are three possibilities here:

- Both the application and MQLib use 2.0.0.
- Both the application and MQLib use 1.1.5.
- The dependency manager rejects the dependency graph as invalid, as there's no single version that can *expect* to be compatible.

The most likely option here is the first. Is that okay? Well, that depends on what breaking changes occurred between version 1.1.5 and 2.0 of JsonLib. It's entirely possible that MQLib doesn't use anything that's been broken, in which case all is well. That's a reasonable argument for dependency managers *not* failing hard on dependency graphs like this. The problem is, it can be very hard to know whether a breaking change *does* affect you or not, particularly if the potential for breakage is within another library. Even if tooling can help you detect that nothing is broken in terms of binary or source compatibility, it can't tell you about semantic compatibility. (This is not to discount the value of tooling that can check whether a combination of library versions will work together in terms of all the required members being present. Where such tooling is available, we recommend its use. Just do not expect it to spot every possible kind of breakage.)

> **NOTE** Different languages and package managers may make different decisions. It's worth taking the time to learn the rules and conventions of the context you're working in, as both a library producer and a library consumer.

The more intertwined dependencies the application uses, the greater the likelihood there will be this sort of major version inconsistency somewhere. Likewise, the more dependencies that are involved for any one library, the greater the likelihood there is that the inconsistency will cause genuine breakage. This is particularly true for very commonly-used libraries, such as Apache Commons libraries in Java or Newtonsoft.Json in .NET. (Despite being at version 13.0.1 at the time of writing, Newtonsoft.Json has a very good track record of backward compatibility.)

Even if everything works out, a library publishing a new major version has a significant cost. Any other library that depends on it and wants to upgrade to the new major version would need to carefully consider whether that would require a major version bump on *their* part too, as it could break anyone depending on the older version. (How dependency versions affect the versioning options of the code with the dependency is a whole can of worms in its own right.) Any application that depends on the library may need to make code changes to adopt the new version and may well need to contend with diamond dependencies and an inconsistent dependency graph.

> **NOTE** As a library author, you need to be aware of the costs to the whole ecosystem and think carefully before taking a breaking change.

I don't want to suggest you should never make a breaking change. Designing the API of a library is very much a chicken-and-egg situation: you often can't be confident in your decisions or learn from your mistakes until you've got users who are invested in your library. At that point, fixing the mistakes requires breaking those same users.

However, you can still set yourself up for a better chance of success by putting in some thought from the start.

12.2.3 *Techniques for handling breaking changes*

This section is a bit of a grab bag of ideas, which you can dip into in any order. The general takeaway is to be deliberate about versioning.

KNOW YOUR CONTEXT: LANGUAGE, PLATFORM, AND COMMUNITY

This chapter is full of caveats that language-specific details matter. As an example, remember that renaming a parameter in Java isn't a breaking change, but it is in C#. These contextual details go well beyond what counts as a breaking change. They also include how package managers resolve dependency graphs, community expectations, and even what techniques are available to avoid breaking changes.

As an example, *default methods* in Java and *default interface implementations* in C# both allow you to add new methods to an interface without taking a breaking change—at least if you are in a position to provide a reasonable default implementation. (If there isn't really a sensible default implementation, providing a no-op implementation can give the illusion of this being a nonbreaking change, while actually breaking any code that calls the default method.) That can influence your design in terms of whether you provide interfaces or abstract classes within your library. While versioning is obviously not the *only* factor that should influence your library design, it's important to bear in mind the impact of the options available in terms of future versions of the library.

Another example where this can be important is in constructor and method parameters: if you find yourself with a list of parameters that keeps expanding each time you want to add a new feature, consider whether those parameters could be encapsulated into their own type to provide more flexibility.

Again, the precise design patterns you use will depend heavily on the language you're coding in and may be further constrained by the platforms you target. (Default interface implementations in C# aren't available in older versions of .NET, for example.)

LIMIT YOUR PUBLIC API SURFACE

If you accidentally declare a public class called `Costumer` instead of `Customer` and release a version of the library with that present, fixing the typo would be a breaking change. On the other hand, if you'd kept that class internal to your library to start with, you could rename it in a new patch version, and no users would be any the wiser.

Every public class, method, property, or interface in your library is a potential headache in the future. On the other hand, if you didn't make anything public, your users wouldn't be able to use your code at all, so there's a tradeoff.

> **NOTE** Often, it's possible to provide quite a restrictive API surface initially—for example, with default options. Once users have been able to explore the basic functionality, you're likely to receive useful feedback for what additional flexibility is required. That can avoid locking the library into a specific design, which doesn't meet the needs of users and can't evolve to do so in a compatible way.

One aspect of limiting your public API surface isn't as obvious as not making classes public unless users need them. We saw earlier that changing implementation details of how one method calls another within the same class can be a breaking change when inheritance is permitted but can be changed more flexibly when those methods can't be overridden.

> **NOTE** Sometimes, there are practical reasons why you need to expose more of an API surface than you would really like to, and then you want to be able to make breaking changes in those API surfaces. If you make it clear that regular users shouldn't touch these types—for example, by putting them in a package or namespace ending with *internal* or similar—that's a practical approach, even if it's not ideal.
>
> Likewise, sometimes you may wish to expose functionality within a generally-stable release, where just part of the API surface is still unstable. The Guava library has an annotation of `@Beta` for precisely this purpose. It's not ideal—it can be easy to miss annotations and names—but sometimes, the benefits are worth the risks.

Inheritance can be a wonderful tool, but it has sharp edges that can be difficult to reason about. I favor Josh Bloch's guidance: "Design for inheritance, or prohibit it." Where you *do* design for inheritance, and where one overridable method will call another, it's worth documenting that it's no longer an implementation detail—it's effectively part of the public contract.

BE CAUTIOUS WITH YOUR OWN DEPENDENCIES

In the previous section we saw how version changes can ripple through an ecosystem. The more shared dependencies your library takes on, the more your users will be impacted by changes to those dependencies. This is not a general encouragement to reinvent the wheel, of course. It's wonderful to be able to use reliable, well-tested third-party components. You just need to be aware of the impact of taking on those dependencies.

If you want to change your decision later (e.g., moving from one JSON parsing library to another), then that can be a breaking change, and it certainly will be if you use any of the types of the dependency within your public API. Changing a dependency in a tool or application is generally easier than changing a dependency in a library.

It's well worth looking at the history of a project before deciding to use it as a dependency in a library. How much of the dependency code are you using? What's their versioning policy? How responsive are they to bug reports and feature requests? Is the project in good health?

If you isolate your dependencies, this ripple effect is much more limited, but there can still be an impact, so it's best to think carefully before adding a new dependency. By all means, depend on other libraries, but do so deliberately and with an appreciation of the potential ongoing costs involved for both you and your library's consumers.

DECIDE WHAT YOU CONSIDER TO BE BREAKING

In section 12.2.1 we saw how *breaking* isn't always a binary attribute of any given change. Some changes are very obviously breaking for anyone using that piece of code; others will only break customers who are using your library in an unusual way.

When you're considering making a change and need to evaluate whether it would count as breaking or not, try to work out the most likely consumer code that would be broken by it. If a consumer would have to use some particularly obscure language feature for it to cause them problems, it's probably best to only increase the minor version instead.

> **NOTE** It can be tempting to take an approach of *when in doubt, assume the change is breaking*. That sounds like a cautious approach, but it's actually a very expensive one due to the propagation of new major versions. Occasionally, you may want to make a change, which is *clearly* breaking in theory but which you have solid evidence to believe won't actually break any users. In that case, the best course of action may well be to make the change and just bump the minor version. If you decide to violate SemVer like this, don't try to hide it—instead, make your reasons for doing so public and transparent.

One gray area we haven't discussed yet in terms of breaking changes is deprecation. Most languages have the notion of deprecating a class or a method, which normally leads to a warning. Does introducing a new warning count as breaking a consumer? What if they have *treat warnings as errors* turned on in their build? Personally, I view this as an active decision on the consumer's part: they wanted to be alerted to breaking changes, and we're just alerting them ahead of time. As we'll see shortly, deprecation can be a powerful tool for helping users to migrate to new versions.

All of these decisions involve judgement calls. While tooling can advise you about breaking changes in some cases, that tooling is built with judgement calls built in, such as deeming *adding a new class* to be a nonbreaking change, even though it *could* cause a naming collision. (It's very unlikely to be able to advise you about semantic breaking changes, too.) Where possible, it's good to document what *your* library deems to be a breaking change to avoid surprising consumers.

BE CONSIDERATE WHEN BUMPING MAJOR VERSIONS

Finally, how should you handle a breaking change when it inevitably happens? Firstly, I'd advise keeping a document of all the breaking changes you want to make from the start. Every major version is costly, so it's worth batching the changes together, so you don't break users more often than you really need to. Again, there's no hard-and-fast rule about how often it's reasonable to release a new major version, and it will depend on your library and your users. The more users you have—and in particular, the more libraries you have depending on yours—the more painful any major version bump will be.

Next, it's worth being as clear as you can in documentation. Ideally, you'll have a version history document anyway, but that's particularly important for major version changes. Document every breaking change you're aware of, even subtle ones, and ideally, write up a migration guide to help users.

Speaking of migration, in some cases there are ways you can help users transition more easily using a minor version as a bridging release. I'll use NodaTime as a concrete example here. In NodaTime 1.0 to 1.3, the `IClock` interface was declared, as shown in the following listing.

Listing 12.9 `IClock` **interface in NodaTime 1.0–1.3**

```
public interface IClock
{
    Instant Now { get; }
}
```

This was a mistake; it's too similar to `DateTime.Now` that returns a system-local time, and it really shouldn't be a property. We fixed that in NodaTime 2.0, as shown in the following listing.

Listing 12.10 `IClock` **interface in NodaTime 2.0**

```
public interface IClock
{
    Instant GetCurrentInstant();
}
```

If we'd just done that, it would have provided users with no indication of what was wrong or how to fix it. Instead, shortly *after* releasing 2.0.0 we released 1.4.0, which made the `Now` property obsolete but introduced an extension method, as shown in the following listing.

Listing 12.11 `IClock` **migration encouragement in NodaTime 1.4**

```
public interface IClock
{
    [Obsolete("Use the GetCurrentInstant() extension [...]")]
    Instant Now { get; }          ◁────  Existing uses of IClock.Now
}                                         are marked as obsolete.
public static class ClockExtensions
{
    public static Instant GetCurrentInstant(   Extension method to look
        this IClock clock) => clock.Now;       like the 2.0 IClock method
}
```

Version 1.4.0 was entirely source and binary compatible with 1.3.0, barring the warnings. If a user wanted to ignore the warnings, that was fine. Alternatively, they could start transforming their code to get it ready for the transition to 2.0.0. Some changes couldn't be handled this way, but most could.

This may not be the right process for all libraries, but every library author can attempt the same goal of minimizing the cost of breaking changes. Maybe you provide tools to migrate config files or even rewrite source code. Maybe you provide analysis tools. Maybe all you've got is documentation, but it's really clear and goes through a worked example. Empathy is a wonderful thing: if you were consuming this library and were faced with the major version bump, what would *you* want to see? Our final subject on the topic of library versioning is on a slightly different tangent but addresses a scenario that faces a significant proportion of developers: internal-only libraries.

12.2.4   *Managing internal-only libraries*

Every company I've worked at has had slightly different practices around how internal libraries are versioned. Even the term *internal* may mean different things to different people: if your product is an application that is broken up into several libraries, but you don't expect anyone else to use them, and you always upgrade the whole system in one go, are those libraries internal or not? They almost certainly don't need to follow the same rules as regular libraries.

Likewise, you may have genuinely internal libraries where the binaries themselves never reach customer machines—they just power your web site or network API, for example. Do those internal libraries even have *versions*, as such? What are the rules for making breaking changes to those libraries?

> **NOTE**   Questions about whether a particular change will break anyone become more concrete when you can find all the code that uses it. If your overall codebase is tens of millions of lines of code, it can still be a daunting and, potentially, infeasible exercise. Still, you're in a much stronger position than an Open Source library where there is often no way of telling how it's used.

Even when it's feasible to make breaking changes fairly freely—for example, leaving a note saying, "When the payments team update to the next version of their library, they'll need to change their code"—I'd generally encourage a more measured approach, if possible. Aim to evolve the consumer code and the library code together, so everything will always keep working but the classes or methods you want to remove (or break) are gradually less widely used, so eventually you can remove them with no impact. Even then, I'd suggest having a sort of *cooling off period* before removing anything, so if any recent changes need to be rolled back, you're still in a good position.

Sometimes, this gradual approach won't be feasible or will be more effort than it's worth, it's analogous to data schema migrations, where sometimes, the cost of a small amount of downtime is lower than the cost and risk of an online migration. It's context-sensitive though: some systems have regular maintenance windows, and others are extremely sensitive to even small amounts of downtime.

One thing is for sure: making any change is much, much harder if your internal systems don't have a clear versioning strategy. Maybe that's *live at head*, where all components build against the latest versions of all other components. Maybe it's independently versioned modules in an internal package manager. Maybe it's a hybrid approach with some core versioned modules and common source control for other components. Whatever has been chosen, everyone on the team needs to understand the system and the implications of how changes to your code can affect colleagues.

> **NOTE** As we mentioned at the start of this section, companies vary significantly in their practices. Sometimes, teams are set up to be as independent as possible from one another—potentially, even with independent source control systems and limited visibility. That definitely affects how easy it is to safely evolve internal systems via breaking changes, while being more feasible than with a system that's fully open to the public. It's worth taking the time to consider—and then document—what kind of process can be used to make this sort of change without breaking other teams or compromising other aspects of the company's engineering culture.

We're now going to shift gears significantly, changing the source of complexity from *lots of libraries all running in the same application* to *lots of clients all calling the same network API*. There are definitely some common concerns between the two, but they require different ways of thinking.

12.3 Versioning for network APIs

Before we start discussing network API versioning, we should probably define what we mean by *network API*. While there can be all kinds of variations, we'll set the scope to *a request–response service accessed over a network*. There can be variations, such as webhook APIs, where it's the service that makes the request to the user's code, rather than vice versa, but it will be simpler to limit the discussion to the case where the user makes a request, and the service issues a response. I've personally had the most experience with plain HTTP services using JSON for the data and gRPC services using Protocol Buffers, but the questions you should ask yourself are broadly applicable across all kinds of services. (Protocol Buffers are Google's binary serialization format, which were initially internal but then made public in 2008. We'll look at them in more detail in section 12.4.) The answers may be very different though, so it's worth being conscious of any bias you may have towards reusing answers from a different context.

12.3.1 The context of network API calls

When we publish a library, we generally have very little information about how it's used, beyond what the users decide to tell us via bug reports, feature requests, questions on Stack Overflow, and the like. We generally expect it to be used in a single ecosystem—for example, I haven't had any questions about how the NodaTime library interoperates with Perl. The ecosystem may be fairly large and diverse, covering multiple languages, but we shouldn't have to deal with too many shocks.

With network APIs (at least ones we host ourselves), we have much more information in terms of how the API is used directly because we can see the incoming requests. But we usually have no idea of the context in which that API call is being made. That flexibility is one of the powerful features of network APIs, but it also makes it hard to reason about the impact of changes.

While Figure 12.8 shows a diversity of contexts in terms of the kinds of application and device that may be making requests, there's further diversity within that. You could receive requests from applications written in multiple different programming languages—some handcrafting those requests and others using dedicated client libraries. There could even be multiple client libraries targeting the same platform.

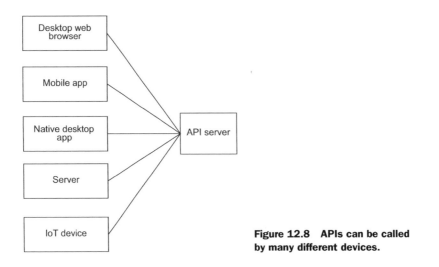

Figure 12.8   APIs can be called by many different devices.

Assumptions about client libraries

Client libraries can make the lives of your users much simpler, but they can also be hard to do well, particularly if you need to scale to target multiple languages and multiple APIs. Beyond a certain size, you're likely to need to generate at least large parts of the libraries, either with existing tooling for an API description format, such as OpenAPI, or your own code generator. This introduces further complexity in terms of compatibility: there are some changes you might want to make in the API, which are compatible in terms of the requests and responses but may generate incompatible new libraries. It's up to you to decide whether that's acceptable (via a new major version of the libraries) or not.

Even if you provide client libraries, you should avoid assuming that all requests will be generated via client libraries, unless this is enforced in some way (such as the library providing cryptographic signatures). Most APIs do not need this and, generally, feel less friendly than an API which is easy to experiment with using tools such as Postman (https://www.postman.com/).

When discussing libraries and dependency graphs, we considered applications, which depended on libraries, which each depended on a different version of a common dependency. There's no direct equivalent in network APIs, but there are similar concerns around a mixture of old and new versions being in play:

- While deploying across services, both old and new servers will be running at the same time. Modern services should generally be designed with no downtime required when updating the servers to a new version.
- The same data may be accessed by two clients—one of which is only aware of an old version, and the other of which is aware of the new version.

We'll go into more detail about the implications of this shortly, but it's worth starting to get into the mindset of considering a broad spectrum of clients and an eventually-consistent set of servers. Before that though, let's explore goals from a customer perspective.

12.3.2 *Customer-friendly clarity*

As with so many things, when you start thinking about versioning for APIs, it's tempting to dive straight into technical solutions and strategies. But without explicitly determining the requirements beforehand, you can either come up with a simple strategy that doesn't satisfy anyone or a complex strategy that is too hard to understand. (Or, worse, a complex strategy that is hard to understand, doesn't meet customer needs, and is hard to extract yourself from.)

Questions you should probably ask yourself include

- Is your API designed to be used typically from a particular context? (While, in general, APIs are *available* in multiple contexts, you may design things differently for an API where 99% of the clients are in other servers, versus an API where 99% of the clients are IoT devices that may never be updated and may be very sensitive to the size of responses.) This is reminiscent of the traffic patterns described in chapter 5 and application of the Pareto principle.
- Do you have a clear communication channel with all users to warn them of any upcoming changes that require attention?
- Do you expect to collaborate with customers on the API surface, leading to some API versions which have looser stability requirements?
- How rapidly do you expect the API to evolve, and how quickly do you expect customers to want to update to the latest-and-greatest version?
- How long are you willing to support old versions, and does that meet customer expectations?
- Are you able to keep track of the usage of your API in terms of versions, client libraries, and individual elements, such as RPCs?

Some of these are questions it makes sense to answer even for simple standalone libraries, but network APIs involve more ongoing interaction. As an example, if a user wants to keep on using a library long after the supplier has dropped support for it, they can probably do so (at their own risk, of course). With a network API, if the supplier turns off the endpoints that were serving the API, that user is immediately impacted.

> **NOTE** All of the above questions can impact your versioning strategy, but one thing is constant: customers appreciate clear and comprehensive documentation about versioning. This provides confidence to the business side of their organization about how safe it is to rely on your API and confidence to the developer side of their organization about how to plan their client code. Like most documentation, this is an area that is, unfortunately, often neglected, but the public-facing documentation should be considered one of the deliverables of your versioning strategy.

With that background, we'll look at two broad approaches that are frequently used.

12.3.3 *Common versioning strategies*

Different organizations have come up with many different approaches to versioning over the years. The most common approach seems to be: *let's hope this isn't actually a problem and make it up as we go along.* That's definitely not one I'd recommend though.

There are two more deliberate approaches that can still go horribly wrong and can still be painful to implement well but at least have a decent chance of success. I tend to think of them as *client-controlled versioning* and *server-controlled versioning.* Those are both somewhat woolly terms, but they're described in more detail below.

In both cases, though, the client specifies a version of some form when making a request. Exactly *how* that is specified doesn't do much to affect the rest of the decision-making. For example, in an HTTP request the version could be present as

- A header
- A query parameter
- Part of the path in the URL

With other protocols, it might appear in other places. There will be pros and cons to the choice of where you ask the client to specify a version, but the details are beyond the scope of this book. Instead, we're going to focus on how that version number affects the API. Let's start with the situation in which the client can be quite specific about the API version they're prepared to handle.

CLIENT-CONTROLLED VERSIONING

With client-controlled versioning, the version specified by the client determines the *precise* API surface that code knows about. For example

- The client shouldn't specify a request field that isn't in that version, even if the field appears in a different version.
- The server shouldn't respond with a field that isn't in the client-requested version.
- The server shouldn't modify resources in a way that assumes knowledge of fields that aren't present in the client-requested version.

To make various examples concrete, let's imagine a very simple API that revolves around a `Person` resource, which, in version 1.0, has fields `id` and `name`. (This is really staggeringly simplified, so we're able to focus on just the versioning. There are all kinds of other concerns, such as the nature of IDs, who gets to create the IDs. See Manning's *API Design Patterns* by J. J. Geewax for much more detail on general API design [Manning, 2021].) In version 1.1, we introduce a new field: `occupation`. Our API has methods of `CreatePerson` and `UpdatePerson` (where the request is the person resource) and `GetPerson` (where the request is the ID of the person to fetch). Table 12.1 shows some sample requests and responses with client-controlled versioning. These first examples only involve the `CreatePerson` and `GetPerson` methods; we'll look at `UpdatePerson` shortly.

Table 12.1 Sample API requests and responses with client-controlled versioning

Client request	Server response	Notes
Version: `1.0` Method: `CreatePerson` Body: `id=1, name="Jane"`	`OK`	
Version: `1.1` Method: `CreatePerson` Body: `id=2, name="Erik",` `occupation="Accountant"`	`OK`	Occupation can be specified in a version 1.1 request.
Version: `1.0` Method: `GetPerson` Body: `id=2`	`OK` `id=2, name="Erik"`	Although the resource has an occupation, it's not returned in a version 1.0 response.
Version: `1.0` Method: `CreatePerson` Body: `id=3, name="Kara",` `occupation="Engineer"`	`Bad request`	Occupation can't be specified in a version 1.0 request.

The format of the version number itself is flexible. It's useful to separate the major number and minor number in a SemVer-like way, but it's usually not worth including a patch number, as SemVer patch differences are about implementation (or comments), rather than API. The minor version can be a regular incrementing integer (creating versions of 1.0, 1.1, 1.2, etc.), but it can also be useful to make it an 8-digit date, leading to version sequences, such as 1.20200619, 1.20201201, 1.20210504. The date-based versions take longer to read but provide useful information without having to consult a complete version history.

Cost and value of patch numbers

For some niche APIs where absolute API stability is crucial, you could include patch numbers, where a client requesting a specific version will get the same behavior consistently even if that behavior is incorrect. For example, a prime number API could have

(continued)

version 1.2.0, which incorrectly claims that 1 is a prime number, and that could be fixed (with no API surface changes) in 1.2.1. Clients specifying a version of 1.2.0 would still get the incorrect result. This means having to maintain every implementation, which is a complex business. Most APIs don't need this level of absolute consistency.

Client-controlled versioning can be costly to implement, as the server needs to be aware of all of the different versions that have ever been published, or at least all the versions you still want to support. Turning down an old version number will break all existing clients of that version. The exact nature of how the clients will be broken depends on how you communicate errors—both for requested versions which have never been valid, and for versions which were valid but are no longer supported. How you do so is beyond the scope of this chapter but should be included in your design from the start.

One downside of client-controlled versioning is that the implementation needs to store details of every minor version, so it knows how to validate the request and which fields to include in the response. As the request is propagated through the system, the client-specified version number will need to be propagated too. It's worth automating this process of validating requests and removing fields that shouldn't be in the client-specified version right from the start.

In theory, client-controlled versioning allows APIs to evolve rapidly without breaking clients. For example, if you make a spelling mistake in a field name in version 1.0, you can just launch a 2.0 with the spelling mistake fixed and transform both requests into an internal request format, which is then processed in a version-neutral way. The internal response format can then be transformed back into the version-specific response format. While that's fine for the existing 1.0 users while they're using 1.0, it still comes at a cost when they want to upgrade to 2.0 in terms of making code changes.

> **NOTE** The major version number is only really present for humans; as each minor version is effectively independent, neither the server code nor the client code needs to care that 1.0 to 1.1 is a backward-compatible change, but 1.1 to 2.0 is a breaking change. Humans care when they update their application to use the new version—they know whether to expect to need to modify the code due to breaking changes.

Client-controlled versioning has a useful side effect in terms of read–modify–write cycles, which comes from the final bullet point listed at the beginning of the current section. Let's revisit our API with a `Person` resource, which in version 1.0 has fields `id` and `name`. In version 1.1, we introduce a new field of `occupation`. Our API might have an `UpdatePerson` method, accepting a `Person`, which basically sets all of the fields of that request to the values in the request. If a field isn't present, it's cleared.

Without considering the fields that the client knows about, this can have dangerous consequences. Consider the simplified code in the following listing for updating a person's name.

Listing 12.12   Simple code to update a name

```
public void updateName(String id, String newName) {
    Person person = client.getPerson(id);
    person.setName(newName);
    client.updatePerson(person);
}
```

That seems harmless enough, but what if the client only knows about version 1.0, and the person being updated has an occupation that was set by another client? Table 12.2 shows a sequence of requests that loses information in our example API if the server has not implemented versioning correctly.

Table 12.2   Read–modify–write implemented incorrectly and losing data

Client request	Server response	Notes
Version: `1.1` Method: `CreatePerson` Body: `id=2, name="Erik",` `occupation="Accountant"`	`OK`	
Version: `1.0` Method: `GetPerson` Body: `id=2`	`OK` `id=2, name="Erik"`	The occupation isn't returned because the 1.0 client wouldn't understand it.
Version: `1.0` Method: `UpdatePerson` Body: `id=2, name="Eric"`	`OK`	The 1.0 client provides all the fields it knows about.
Version: `1.1` Method: `GetPerson` Body: `id=2`	`OK` `id=2, name="Eric"`	The occupation has been lost!

In this example, the server is at fault for its handling of the `UpdatePerson` method. Although the method is expected to receive a complete resource, it can only be complete from the perspective of what the client understands. Just because the client hasn't specified an occupation doesn't mean the client wants to remove any existing occupation; it means the client isn't aware of the concept of an occupation in the `Person` resource.

Fortunately, the server can be smarter than this. It can take into account that the client has specified version 1.0 and knows to only update the fields that were present in that version. That in itself can lead to some tricky decisions if new fields are added that ought to be validated against the existing fields, but in many cases it's good enough. With a well-implemented server, the client can issue full updates without worrying that it will trample on data it isn't even aware of. This ignores the need for concurrency validation, which is a different aspect of avoiding data loss. But the two causes of data loss are effectively orthogonal, and concurrency isn't particularly related to API versioning (it's more about *resource* versioning). Implementing this server-side is not always simple but can usually be done in a reasonably generic automated way.

Let's now look at server-controlled versioning. It doesn't quite give servers a free hand, but it certainly provides more leeway.

SERVER-CONTROLLED VERSIONING

In server-controlled versioning, there's no concept of minor numbers. The API can only evolve in a backward-compatible way within the same major version, and clients should just ignore any response information they get back that they don't understand.

In server-controlled versioning, there should still be a major version number, specified by the client. That might be specified in a URL, the IP address, or a header, but it has to be somewhere. Without *that* level of negotiation, it would be impossible to ever create any breaking changes without breaking existing clients.

Server-controlled versioning feels rather more dynamic and less precise than client-controlled versioning. It's typically easier for servers to implement because they only need to maintain as many implementations as there are major versions, instead of ensuring that every minor version is supported separately. The same approach of adapting requests and responses to and from an internal format works for server-controlled versioning; there are just fewer adapters involved.

The fact that the server can respond with more information than expected can be an issue for some clients. For example, if an IoT device were to request information on a book, expecting to get just a few hundred bytes of summary information, but instead, the API started also including a sample in the form of the first chapter that could cause the device to run out of memory, while processing the response. It's not an insoluble problem, and there are API patterns to limit the information returned where a client knows it's only interested in specific parts, but it's worth bearing in mind.

The read–modify–write cycle we considered earlier is more of a problem in server-controlled versioning, as the server doesn't have any way of knowing what set of fields the client is aware of. Update methods accepting a whole resource and unconditionally copying fields can easily lose data, so a patch-based approach is preferred, where the API is designed to accept a list of fields that should be updated, along with the data for those fields. We'll change our example API to have a `PatchPerson` method, which accepts the resource but also a list of fields. Table 12.3 shows a similar sequence of events as those shown in table 12.2 but using server-controlled versioning. The information about whether the client was written against version 1.0 or 1.1 isn't part of the request anymore, and there may not even be a specific version 1.1; it's just the v1 API at the time of code generation.

Table 12.3 Read–modify–write using patch semantics

Client request	Server response	Notes
Version: 1 (client 1.1) Method: CreatePerson Body: id=2, name="Erik", occupation="Accountant"	OK	
Version: 1 Method: GetPerson Body: id=2	OK id=2, name="Erik", occupation="Accountant"	The occupation is returned because only the major version is specified. The client can discard information it doesn't understand.

Version: 1
Method: PatchPerson
Body:
  resource={id=2, name="Eric"}
  fields="name"
	OK	The client specifies the fields it wants to modify. (That may be all the ones it's aware of or just a subset.)

Version: 1 Method: GetPerson Body: id=2	OK id=2, name="Eric", occupation="Accountant"	The occupation is still present because only the specified fields were modified.

An API using client-controlled versioning can still provide patch semantics as well for the sake of efficiency; it just doesn't *have* to in order to avoid losing data because it has the extra information about which fields the client should be aware of. In an API using server-controlled versioning, patch semantics are critical for all but the simplest cases.

Preserving unknown fields

Some serialization formats are able to preserve unknown fields when parsing a response and reproduce the same information if that response data is used in another request. Protocol Buffers supports this behavior, for example. It can still be brittle, however: if the response data is deserialized into some other object model, then the unknown fields are likely to be lost at *that* point. Being explicit about which fields you want to modify is still the more robust approach.

These two approaches to versioning are both completely valid. They have different implications for client library versioning, documentation, server-side implementation, and even the design of the API itself, as we've seen for resource updates. It's up to you to decide which strategy makes the most sense for you, which could be something else entirely, although I'd recommend thinking very carefully before venturing too far from either of these schemes.

There are a few additional considerations that have roughly the same implications across both of these strategies. These end up bleeding into implementation considerations for data storage, which we'll move onto as the final section of the chapter.

12.3.4   *Further versioning considerations*

A complete analysis of every possible aspect of network API versioning is beyond the scope of this book, and would indeed be a reasonably-sized book in its own right. However, there are some final areas that are worth mentioning briefly, mostly to prompt you to think about them further in your own API-specific context.

PRERELEASE VERSIONING

API design is hard. It's often underappreciated; after all, the API surface contains no logic in itself. You might expect the implementation to be the hard part. While that's the case for some APIs, for many, the design is the part that requires a mixture of engineering and artistry. You're unlikely to know exactly how the API will be used (and, indeed, that's part of the joy of API work), which means you're designing with very incomplete information. Combine that with the restrictions on API iteration due to compatibility concerns, and it's a miracle if you get it right. That's where prereleases come in.

By providing potential users of your API with an early version of it—or an early version of a new feature being added to an existing API—you can get feedback before it's too late to change the final API surface. While you *can* always release a new major version of the API to correct any problems, it will make you unpopular with users who then need to change their code. Figure 12.9 shows how prerelease iterations can work—both before and after the first stable API release.

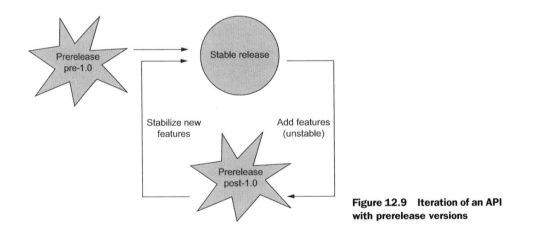

Figure 12.9   Iteration of an API with prerelease versions

Table 12.4 shows a hypothetical sequence of releases for an API. The form of the version string here isn't intended to be prescriptive; all the earlier discussions around client-controlled versus server-controlled versioning are still relevant. The table is intended to give a flavor of how you can use customer feedback to improve your API design without breaking customers who require stability.

Table 12.4 Possible API release sequence

Version	Release date	Notes
1.0-alpha.1	2023-01-10	First draft of the API for customer feedback. Some parts may not be implemented or may perform awfully.
1.0-beta.1	2023-02-15	Changes based on alpha feedback, and better implementation—but still no guarantees on the stability of the API surface or availability of the service.
1.0-beta.2	2023-02-25	Some breaking changes based on feedback from 1.0-beta.1. This could be announced as a release candidate if we're confident enough.
1.0	2023-04-05	First stable release with guarantees of API surface stability and service availability.
1.1-beta.1	2023-04-08	Prerelease for two new features (*X* and *Y*).
1.1-beta.2	2023-05-05	Update based on feedback from 1.1-beta.1; feature *X* has breaking changes in the API surface.
1.1	2023-05-30	Stable release containing feature *Y* but not feature *X*, as customer feedback suggests there's still more work to do.
1.2-beta.1	2023-05-30	Simultaneous release with 1.1, so customers trying feature *X* (which is still unstable) can use a wider stable API surface, including feature *Y*. Introduces feature *Z*.
1.3	2023-07-14	Stable release containing features *X* and *Z*. No need for a simultaneous beta release, as there are no outstanding unstable features. (In a large API, this may never happen. It's fine for there always to be some unstable features.)

Prerelease API versions aren't just regular API versions given to a select set of customers. They come with different expectations, both in terms of the API surface and the stability and performance of the implementation. It's important to make sure that customers share those expectations, so no one is surprised.

Again, there are different ways of handling prereleases, but questions you should answer for yourself are

- How are prereleases gated, so customers don't accidentally use features that aren't stable?
- Should each request indicate that it expects to use prerelease functionality?
- Do you run prerelease API versions completely independently of stable versions, or can one API server handle both kinds of traffic?
- What guarantees, if any, do you provide to customers about the stability and availability of the API? For example, if each request indicates the preview API version that is being used, how long do you have to keep each version running for? Can you make breaking changes abruptly, or do you have a short deprecation period?

- How do you make prereleases available to customers, and are there client libraries for them?
- How do you document prereleases?
- Are all your prereleases publicly visible, are they all private, or do you have some of each?
- Do you need customer-specific prereleases?
- What internal tools and processes are needed to support the answers to all of these questions?

If you try to bolt prereleases onto a versioning strategy that has been developed without considering them, you're likely to have a hard time and leave some rough edges for customers. Even if you don't implement prereleases from the start, it's worth planning for them.

SERVER DEPLOYMENT

This may sound like a statement of the obvious, but it's very likely you'll have multiple servers for your API. (Indeed, we'd be worried if that weren't the case for any API that's intended for production use.) That means that at any one time, there can be a mixture of API versions in production. Depending on the versioning strategy and how the client-specific version is expressed within a request, you *could* potentially route public requests based on the version, but it's usually simpler to make sure that all servers can handle all requests for the currently-published version, then make sure you only make details of the updated API public once the deployment is complete.

Deployment rollout may well be a sequence of steps something like this:

- Deploy to a set of canary servers.
- Monitor those canary servers for errors.
- Run any tests for new API features against those canary servers.
- Deploy to the remainder of the servers (potentially across several hours or even multiple days, depending on the size of the server set).
- Run any tests for new API features against a random selection of servers.
- Publish new API details.

You'll need to be prepared to roll back at any point, which means considering what will happen to any resources modified with new API changes during testing. If you need to roll back *after* making the new API public, you may need to handle a larger (and more sensitive) set of resources, which have new fields populated—along with communicating the rollback to clients, of course.

CROSS-VERSION RESOURCE HANDLING

We've talked about using major versions (sparingly!) to allow an API to make breaking changes occasionally. Most APIs work with persistent resources, and *usually*, you'll want clients using different major versions to be able to access the same resources. There are exceptions to this, of course: you may decide to retire some resources when moving from v1 to v2, and it's certainly reasonable that some resource types may only be available in later major versions. But most resources in v1 should be accessible via v2, and without some kind of gate that means once a resource has been accessed by a v2 client, v1 clients can no longer access it.

This has implications for how resources are addressed; the resource identifier itself should not include an API version number. It also comes with restrictions when it comes to how you design new major versions and how they're implemented. While you might *want* to start with a clean slate for v2, the need to still serve v1 clients means that complete conceptual rewrites are tricky. It's worth being consciously aware that this is not about how developers of v1 clients migrate to v2, although that's also a factor to consider. It's more about the implications for server-side implementation. You may have only a handful of customers on v1, and they may never want to migrate to v2 (so you don't need to worry about the upgrade path), but if they need to access the same resources as v2 clients, you may find grand ideas are frustrated. This doesn't mean that ground-up redesigns are impossible; it just means they come with significantly more implementation cost than you might expect.

Some of that cost may well be determined by the functionality within the storage system you're using. This brings us to the last section in this chapter: designing data storage in a version-flexible way.

12.4 Versioning for data storage

We live in an era of big data. In decades past, it would have been safe to assume that most of this data would be stored in SQL databases, and there are countless articles and book chapters dedicated to evolving SQL schema. In this section we'll discuss data evolution in a more general sense. We'll use Protocol Buffers as the format for the examples, but the lessons aren't specific to that format. There are plenty of other formats available, such as Avro and Thrift—each with their own subtleties around versioning. This section does not try to replace the format-specific documentation, but it suggests areas of documentation you'll want to pay particular attention to, whichever format you choose to use. This applies to SQL as well, although the choices may well be specific to the SQL variant you're using too.

Although this section is dedicated to storage, many of the formats we're talking about can also be used for network APIs, and format-specific considerations about breaking changes are relevant when you're considering how you design and version your API. The previous section was deliberately agnostic on that front, staying at a higher level, but once you've designed your high-level API versioning strategy, the details in this section are relevant in day-to-day work. Let's start with a very brief tutorial on Protocol Buffers—just enough to explain the rest of the section.

12.4.1 A brief introduction to Protocol Buffers

Protocol Buffers (also known as protobuf) are a serialization format invented at and used extensively within Google but increasingly used in the wider ecosystem, particularly with the gRPC RPC Framework. Protocol Buffers are designed primarily for efficient binary storage but now also support a JSON representation.

Protobuf schema files are known as protos, conventionally using a .proto file extension. These should be stored in source control and treated as carefully as any other source artifact. They consist of some options at the start of the file, and a sequence of elements to define the schema:

- *Messages*—The main part of most proto files and are roughly similar to defining a type within most programming languages. A message consists of fields and can also include nested messages and enums.
- *Enums*—Define named integer mappings.
- *Services*—Used to define RPCs. While gRPC and Protocol Buffers are very often used together, it's entirely possible to design an RPC framework using Protocol Buffers but not gRPC or to use gRPC with non-protobuf data. We won't look at services in detail here.

Each field within a message has three main aspects to it:

- *Type*—Can be one of the primitive types (integers, floating point numbers, byte strings, or text strings), an enum, or a message. The type can also indicate a *repeated* field, which is effectively a list.
- *Name*—Used in generated code and when encoding messages as JSON.
- *Number*—Used in the binary serialization format.

There are some additional concepts within Protocol Buffers, such as extensions, one-ofs, maps, and optional fields. (A *oneof* is a set of fields, where only one field within the oneof can be set at a time.) More information is available in the documentation at https://developers.google.com/protocol-buffers, but the details are beyond the scope of this chapter, which focuses on the more general considerations of compatibility.

Typically, protobuf schemas are run through the protobuf compiler tool (protoc) to generate code used in libraries and applications. While it's theoretically possible to write code that uses the binary serialization format directly, it's very rare to not use a schema. (In some languages, it's also possible to write the code for the data model and annotate it to indicate protobuf field numbers and types).

Let's take a brief example of what a proto file for part of a role-playing game might look like, just to make things more concrete. We want to represent a character the user is able to control, including the character's name, profession, health information, and what they're carrying (their inventory). The following listing shows what the proto schema might look like for that to enable us to store the data.

> **Listing 12.13   Sample proto schema for a role-playing game character**

```
syntax = "proto3";
message Character {
  string name = 1;
  bytes icon_png = 2;
  Profession profession = 3;
  repeated Item inventory = 4;
  // The maximum number of slots available before the
```

```
    // inventory is full.
    int32 inventory_slots = 5;
    int32 health = 5;
    int32 max_health = 6;
}
message Item {
    string name = 1;
    // How many slots this takes up in the inventory.
    int32 slots = 2;
}
enum Profession {
    PROFESSION_UNKNOWN = 0;
    MAGE = 1;
    THIEF = 2;
    WARRIOR = 3;
}
```

We won't go into much more detail than that, but we'll use this proto to discuss potential changes over time and their impact. Just to reiterate, this section is not intended to be a reference for every detail of protocol buffers; it's intended to show the kind of detail you need to be aware of for whichever storage format you use. We'll start by considering what kind of change can cause problems.

12.4.2 What is a breaking change?

Just as Hyrum's law suggests that any code change can break someone, any storage schema change that is detectable could cause a problem if users are working with the data in a particularly brittle way. But when it comes to schema changes for internal storage, any given change can be breaking in some subset of scenarios—none of which you may care about. It's a little like source compatibility and binary compatibility but with far more variation to consider than just those two aspects.

For example

- Protobuf has multiple types representing signed 32-bit integers, which have different serialization formats. Changing a field type from `int32` to `sint32` will change the meaning of any stored data but won't change the API of generated code.
- Changing a field name from `health` to `hit_points` won't affect the stored data at all but will be a breaking change in generated code for all users.
- The Java and C# code generators for protobuf apply Camel-casing to field names when generating methods and properties. This means that changing a field name from `inventory_slots` to `inventorySlots` won't affect the stored data or the generated code for Java and C# but will affect the generated code for most other languages.
- Adding a value to an enum (e.g., a new profession of `ARCHER`) won't cause any build failures or storage failures, but all code that tries to use a character's profession needs to either take specific action with the new value or handle it in a generic (i.e., *I don't know what this value means, but I'll just preserve it*) way.

- Removing a field will break any code that still tries to use it but won't otherwise cause any problems, even if the field is still present in stored data.
- Adding a field shouldn't break any code, even if you have a mixture of old code and new code deployed at the same time with the old code reading data containing the new field.

The last of these examples depends on the way protocol buffers handle unknown fields, which we've mentioned in the context of API responses. We'll look at that in a little more detail shortly.

I should note that all of the above statements assume we're only storing data using the binary protobuf representation. If we also store data using the JSON format, changing the name of a field will break the stored data as well: in the JSON format, the field number is ignored, but the JSON property name is derived from the field name. If you're working with a data format that has multiple representations, you need to take account of that when considering any changes.

If your storage is entirely internal, so you can find and change all the code that uses it in a controlled way, you may find that making breaking changes in terms of code generation is feasible and, potentially, even simple. It very much depends on the versioning strategy you're using for your internal code. Making changes that break the storage format is a much more difficult business and not to be taken on lightly. Typically, this is achievable via data migration, but that requires considerable planning. Let's look at an example.

12.4.3 *Migrating data within a storage system*

It's important to start off by recognizing there are many different kinds of data migration. Sometimes it can be from one system to a radically different system and other times it can be to a different schema in the same system, for example. We're going to look at the case in which we're making a change to an existing schema in a way that would be a breaking change if we did it in a single step.

Let's suppose we want to change how we handle the icon we display for a character to allow for multiple sizes and uses. We might want a large icon when displaying a single character's profile but a small icon when displaying a list of characters, for example. Currently, we just have a single field called icon_png. While we could just add more fields to the Character message, that can become hard to manage after a while and also makes it harder to reuse any logic for icon handling if we have similar situations for other entities (e.g., items or locations). Instead, we want to introduce an IconCollection message to improve opportunities for reuse both in the schema and in code.

NOTE The approach of doing the simplest thing that works can be very helpful when prototyping, but it can be dangerous when applied to aspects that are hard to change later, such as data storage. It's impossible to envisage every possible scenario, and there are downsides involved in introducing more flexibility than you'll ever need, but often, when you specify a primitive field in a schema, it's worth at least *considering* whether introducing a message is worthwhile, even if that message starts off with just a single field in it.

Our IconCollection message could end up being quite complex, but we'll keep it simple here.

Listing 12.14 Sample proto for an icon collection

```
message IconCollection {
  message Icon {
    bytes data_png = 1;
    int32 width = 2;
    int32 height = 3;
  }
  repeated Icon icons = 1;
}
```

Our eventual aim is to replace the current bytes icon_png = 2 field in the Character message with this new one: IconCollection icons = 7. We want to be able to do this without breaking any of our current clients in the process. Note that the field number is different; that's critical to enabling the data migration.

We now need to take a sequence of steps to migrate the data:

1   Write a plan with the rest of these steps, and make sure all stakeholders are happy with it.

2   Add the new IconCollection message to the schema and the icons field in Character.

3   Modify all server code that reads from the existing icon_png field:
   – If the Character.icons field is present and the repeated field within it has at least one element, use the first element.
   – Otherwise, use the old icon_png field.

4   Modify all server code that writes to the existing field:
   – Set the Character.icons field to a new IconCollection message with a single element in the repeated field.
   – Set the old icon_png field to the new icon data as well.

5   Deploy the new server code.

6   Wait until we're confident that we won't need to roll the deployment back.

7   Run a migration tool that checks every Character in the system. If the icon_png field is populated, but the icons field isn't, copy the data into a new Icon-Collection in the icons field.

8   Modify all server code to remove any reference to the icon_png field.

9   Deploy the new server code.

10 Wait until we're confident we won't need to roll the deployment back.

11 Run a migration tool that checks every character in the system and clears the icon_png field if it's populated (so we don't have stale data serving no purpose).

12 Replace the icon_png field with a reserved 2 line in the schema.

The final step ensures that we never accidentally reuse field number 2 later. While in many cases it would be harmless to do so, it's an extra safety measure just in case we later find some old data we forgot to migrate—we don't want to misinterpret the old icon data as something else.

Figure 12.10 shows the steps above graphically. The left column of text describes the state of the schema and stored data at each step, and the right column of text describes the changes required to get there. Each step must be taken carefully with a

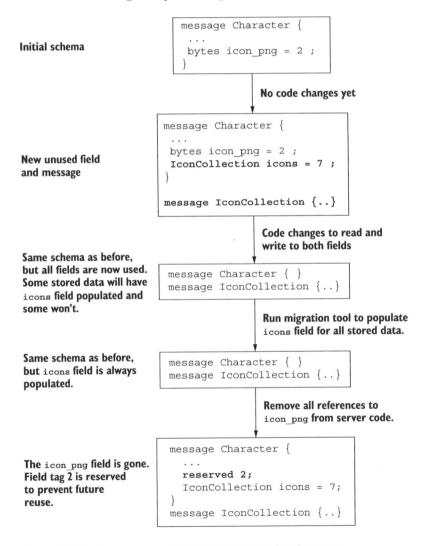

Figure 12.10 Graphical representation of storage migration steps

suitable pause before the next step to avoid having to roll back. There should be a plan for rolling back if absolutely necessary, but it should be avoided if possible.

At this point, all the code has moved to the new field, and we can start implementing new features, which may in turn require multiple careful steps as we move from *there's only ever one icon* to *there may be multiple icons per character*. The steps for waiting until we're confident we won't need to roll back a deployment are crucial. Data migration like this can only work if we know what code is accessing the data. It's inevitable that we'll need to tread carefully, so two different code versions can work on the same data storage concurrently. (This is assuming that downtime is unacceptable. If you can take down the system completely for migration, lots of things become simpler. That's rarely an option in modern systems.) Reasoning about three or more different code versions accessing the same data becomes much trickier, and it's almost always better to just take the process slowly and steadily. In our example, we had three different server versions in total:

- The original version that only knew about `icon_png`
- The migration version that knew about `icon_png` and `icons` and ensures they're consistent
- The final version that only knows about `icons`

If all three versions of these had been running at the same time, then any icon changes stored by the first code version wouldn't have been seen by the third code version, and vice versa. It's also important that we're aware of all the code that might be accessing the data: if it turned out there was one service that didn't get the memo around the new field, that could cause significant problems after the migration was theoretically complete. That's why the very first step is to agree a plan with all the stakeholders.

The steps listed above are reasonably common, but more complex migrations may well have many more steps or more *bulky* steps, perhaps migrating multiple fields at a time. Every migration comes with elements of risk and cost, and when considering a complex migration, you should consider the costs and risks associated with splitting the migration into multiple smaller migrations (e.g., more steps and taking a longer time overall) versus the costs and risks of doing it in as few steps as possible (where each step has more risk associated with it and needs more careful validation).

One of the key assumptions in the migration steps above is that the original code is able to safely read a `Character` message that contains the `icons` field, despite that field not being present in the schema when the original code was deployed. Let's look at what that means for how you write code.

12.4.4 Expecting the unexpected

Let's be honest: none of us are very good at predicting the future. We don't want this section to be misinterpreted as either a suggestion that you massively overengineer your code to be ready for *any* new requirement that might be thrown at you or a recommendation to nail down requirements for the next ten years before you write the first line of code. Neither of those approaches will work. Instead, we'd like to suggest that we can design software and data schema that have a certain amount of natural flexibility with an eye to the future without it adding too much complexity to the implementation of our current requirements. We've already looked at one way in which we can plan for the future by using open-ended schema representations, starting off with a single-field message instead of just using a primitive field.

> **NOTE** Our `Character` message contains several other primitive fields. Should we have created an `Inventory` message instead of keeping the contents of the inventory and the number of inventory slots available as separate fields? What about the health-related fields? Usually, multiple fields addressing the same concern are at least a hint toward encapsulation—just as they are in code. There are no hard and fast rules though, and the tipping point in a storage schema can be different than the equivalent in code.

Even that approach assumes our code is able to handle new fields being added though. Modern big data formats are typically designed around that expectation, but you'll need to find out *exactly* what is supported in the format you're using. In particular, it may well constrain you in terms of transformations into different representations. In protobuf, *unknown fields* (fields that are received as part of parsing data, but weren't known about when the code was generated from the original schema) are preserved in the binary representation but can't then be represented in a textual representation, such as JSON, because the field names aren't part of the binary serialization format.

Storage–format–provided cloning operations may preserve data, but what happens if you've got manually written code to transform one schema message into another? If you don't know the meaning of a particular piece of data, it's very hard to know how it should participate in a transformation. Whenever you write transformation code, it's worth bearing in mind the impact that has on your ability to introduce a new field, and whenever you introduce a new field, you should consider the transformations that are already being performed on that message.

ADDING ENUM VALUES

While adding a field generally doesn't interfere with existing logic, so long as that logic is able to propagate the new value without understanding it, enums can be slightly harder to reason about.

It's easy to think of an enum as a set of all known values for a particular context, but we sometimes forget that *all known values* really means *all known values at the time we generated the code* (or the equivalent). It's all the values your code happens to know about, but they may not be all the values that will *ever* be known about.

Some enums are obviously fixed; if you're writing an app for traditional card games, it would be entirely reasonable to have a `Suit` enum with values of HEARTS, CLUBS, DIAMONDS, SPADES. Those are easy to work with, and it's reasonable to write code that fails with an exception if it's given a value that isn't one of those.

Some enums are obviously designed to be extended, such as our `Profession` enum in the role-playing game. If you have code that definitely needs to be able to handle *every* profession, you need to make sure that's updated and deployed before it will ever come into contact with a new profession, and that's worth noting as you discover the requirement. Other code may well be able to ignore enum values it doesn't understand, so long as they're still preserved. (In Protocol Buffers, unknown enum values *are* preserved in terms of their numeric value, when deserializing and serializing using the binary format.)

Finally, some enums might feel like they're fixed but turn out to need extending later on. For example, you might have an enum of all the states within the USA. That enum has been stable for a very long time, but it's possible that you'll need to react to new values being added (or even removed) at some point. You probably don't need to have a detailed plan for this, but it's worth thinking just far enough to convince yourself that such a change won't require a complete rewrite of your application.

The subtleties involved in versioning enums might make you reconsider the use of enums at all in some cases. In particular, where there's an industry standard string representation for the kind of value you're considering, such as a MIME type or an ISO-3166 country code, it's often better just to store the string value instead.

In the last few pages, we've been considering storage representations under the assumption that you have control over all the code that interacts with the stored data. Let's take a moment to consider that assumption.

12.4.5 Separating API and storage representations

Some common best practices take a little while to get to grips with but then make your day-to-day life simple, and you rarely give them a second thought. I'm afraid the key piece of advice from this section isn't one of those. It introduces day-to-day repetition and tedious coding (or complex infrastructure), and it's generally annoying. However, the benefits are overwhelming when you need to evolve your system.

KEEP YOUR NETWORK API SCHEMA AND YOUR STORAGE SCHEMA SEPARATE

It's very common to create a system that stores data and also has a network API that accepts and returns the data being stored. Almost every system with an API has some element like this, unless it's purely about transient information, such as "the current time."

Once you've carefully designed your storage schema, it's very tempting to just publish that as your network API schema as well, assuming you're using the same overall data format for both aspects. Store exactly what you receive, send back exactly what you've stored, and life is simple. In some cases it's a reasonable first prototype, before you need to start caring about stability. Unfortunately, it achieves great initial velocity at the cost of long-term flexibility.

If you compare the recommendations in this chapter around network API versioning and storage versioning, they're quite different because they deal with different contexts. With network APIs, you usually have to assume that, at any one time, there will be clients using the API schema as it was published at multiple points in time, and making a breaking change to that schema has an enormous cost. While you can encourage customers to change their code to accommodate changes, you have very little control over the timescale without becoming actively hostile. (It's technically possible to give customers a very short time in which to migrate to a new major version, but it's likely to lose you customers, particularly if you do this frequently. *Technically possible* and *practically possible* are quite different here.) Long-lived systems tend to benefit from the ability to evolve their storage schema, and it's worth recognizing that and building it into the design from the start.

The exact way in which you separate the two schemas will depend on the storage format you're using and what tooling is available to work with it. At its core, separating the API schema from the storage scheme requires two kinds of transformation:

- How do you transform your storage schema into your API schema?
- How do you transform data between the two schemas?

Notice how I've deliberately started with the storage schema here: that will almost always be the real source of truth. There will always be a relationship between the storage schema and the API schema, but it may be hard to express that in a machine-readable way. It's particularly difficult to do that early in a system's life, when you don't have much time to invest in tooling, and you don't have much understanding of what transformations you'll need anyway.

MANUAL TRANSFORMATIONS

The simplest way of *transforming* a storage schema into a network API schema is to copy, paste, and edit. You may not even need to edit much to start with, beyond potentially changing a package name or namespace. When you make changes to the storage schema, you can copy and paste those changes straight into the network API schema too—so long as you think while you're doing it.

Transforming the data at execution time (e.g., transforming the data in a request, so it can be stored or transforming a resource fetched from storage into a response) can be more laborious. The technically simplest option is usually to just create a method to perform the conversion in each direction for each schema type. This is tedious, laborious, and error prone. It's fairly easy to make a change to the storage API and copy it to the network API but forget to make the change in the conversion methods. Still, that should usually be picked up quickly in API integration tests. (Comprehensive API integration tests are vital for all kinds of reasons—well beyond versioning.)

If all of this sounds like a terrible idea and leaves a bad taste in the mouth, I completely understand. It's grungy work that no one wants to do. It does have its benefits though. If you can keep the discipline of *thinking* while you make the cascading changes beyond the original storage schema change, you may end up spotting problems or opportunities. Sometimes the most appropriate storage representation of a new feature isn't the most appropriate API representation. As an example, there may be benefits to using an enum in the storage schema (to keep a concrete set of currently-supported values), while using a string in the network API to keep things more open for future changes. You may use different levels of granularity and denormalization, too. Remember the different contexts of these schemas and give yourself the *option* to make different decisions. As your schema grows larger and you get more confident in the transformations you need to perform, you may want to consider automating some of the work.

AUTOMATED TRANSFORMATIONS

If manually maintaining separate API and storage schemas becomes too monotonous to bear, you should look at the tooling options available. While there may be some tools available off the shelf, you may find you need to write the tools you need yourself. That provides a greater degree of flexibility, but of course, there is more code to maintain.

I would be wary of automating until you already have significant experience doing the same steps manually. That helps you to discover corner cases and oddities in the relatively simple environment of just editing files. If you're expecting to automate the transformation later on, it's worth noting down these corner cases, how you've resolved them, and why as you go along. That will help to guide the automation process and provide a good set of test cases.

When designing the automation tools, in my experience it's also useful to provide yourself with escape hatches along the way: if a particular aspect of your schema is significantly different between the storage and API representations, it may well be simpler to manually craft that part and opt it out of the automation, rather than trying to add features to the tooling, until it can do absolutely anything but is too complicated to use and maintain for simple tasks.

Finally, on the topic of schema transformation, I'd advise a careful manual review of the output of the tooling, at least for the first several schema changes. Once you've reached the stage where the tooling hasn't thrown up any surprises for a long time, then you can start removing reviews from the process.

Data transformation is trickier to review but generally easier to test. Again, the tooling that comes with whatever storage format you use may well provide a good starting point. For example, the Protocol Buffers libraries provide a reflection API, which allows dynamic access to message data and is a great starting point for automating transformations. The places where you need escape hatches for schema transformations are likely to need manual code for the data transformation, so again, it's worth considering how you'll add that manual code while you're designing the automation—even if you don't need to do anything special immediately.

You may be worried about the performance implications of transforming the data, particularly when I mentioned the word *reflection* in the previous paragraph. As ever with performance issues, it's definitely worth measuring the cost involved and comparing the impact of manual versus automated transformations, but in my experience, this rarely becomes a significant cost in terms of the overall time taken per API call. The impact is more likely to be felt in terms of memory and CPU usage; again, careful benchmarking is the key to wise decision-making.

With so many aspects of your day-to-day work depending on your choice of storage format, it's clearly a significant decision. Let's review some of the questions you should ask yourself as part of that decision.

12.4.6 *Evaluating storage formats*

It's not the place of this book to recommend any one specific storage format or technology. There are lots of inputs into the decisions around what storage to use, many of which are unrelated to versioning, but as the focus of this chapter is compatibility, the list below provides some questions you should investigate when you're evaluating different storage options.

- Does it support schemas of some form, even if it also supports schemaless storage?
- Does it provide out-of-the-box support for schema evolution? For example, Apache Avro has been designed with this in mind from the start and has compatibility rules and tooling to enforce them.
- How does it handle unexpected values, such as fields or enum values that weren't present in the schema used by the client?
- How would you include schema changes into your build process? It may be helpful to go through a few planning exercises, including writing up a sequence of steps for a hypothetical data migration.
- If you plan on using generated code, does this affect your internal code versioning strategy? What would your policy be on schema changes that didn't break storage but did break existing code?
- Do you want to use the same format for both storage and API representation? If so, ask yourself some follow-up questions:
  - Is there tooling—or at least support for you to write your own tools—for schema transformation?
  - Is there tooling or support for data transformation between different schemas?
  - How does this fit in with your planned API versioning strategy?

It's worth reflecting on the fact that this list of questions isn't a checklist of yes or no answers. Many storage technologies will have enough features to support whatever you want to do; these questions are intended to help you evaluate how easy or painful they'll make those tasks. Don't forget that when you're evaluating the storage options for a system, you're not trying to determine the best storage format in the world: you're choosing the one that is most appropriate for your system, in your context.

Summary

- Versioning is all about how something changes over time. Version numbers communicate important information about those changes in a compact form.
- Backward and forward compatibility describe how new and old pieces of code and information can interoperate with each other.

- Semantic Versioning encodes compatibility information into a major.minor.patch format:
  - A breaking change prompts a new major version.
  - A backward-compatible change prompts a new minor version.
  - A backward- and forward-compatible change prompts a new patch version.
  - Additional information, such as prerelease status and build metadata, can be included after the major.minor.patch number.
- Compatibility in library code has different forms of compatibility to consider, primarily divided into source compatibility (i.e., will existing code build against the new version?), binary compatibility (i.e., will existing binaries run against the new version?), and semantic compatibility (i.e., will existing code behave the same way?).
- Dependency graphs can introduce diamond dependencies, where different parts of the same application expect different versions of the same dependency. Breaking changes between versions of the dependency may make it infeasible to find a complete set of dependencies to run the application successfully.
- Major versions ripple through an ecosystem via dependency graphs; popular libraries should expect to make breaking changes via new major versions very, very rarely.
- Internal code can generally absorb breaking changes more easily than public code, but you still need to take care and plan for rollbacks.
- API versioning is generally more complex than library versioning, and there are multiple approaches:
  - Client-controlled versioning allows the client to provide a very specific version, and responses should never include more information.
  - Server-controlled versioning allows the client to provide a major version, and responses may include more information than the client understands.
- Prerelease versions can be used to allow users to experiment with a planned change before you commit to it. It should be very clear that this is not a stable API surface.
- Different storage formats have different characteristics around schema evolution.
- Designing code to anticipate changes in the storage schema can be challenging, but it's worth considering from the start.
- Separating your API schema from your storage schema provides much more flexibility, although it incurs additional costs, either in terms of manual chores or potentially-complex automation.
- While you may not be able to predict every kind of versioning change you'll ever need, time spent planning a versioning strategy from the start pays off in the long run.

13

Keeping up to date with trends vs. cost of maintenance of your code

This chapter covers

- Dependency injection frameworks
- Reactive programming and processing data
- Functional programming in your code
- Lazy versus eager evaluation

With software engineering, new libraries or concepts emerge regularly (indeed, almost every week). As soon as you adapt your application or architecture to a brand new shiny framework or pattern, another one is developed and popularized. We have microservices, reactive programming, serverless applications, and so on. Each of those patterns offers many benefits, such as loose coupling, better performance, or less resource consumption. However, each of those patterns and libraries comes with its own complexities.

For example, let's assume that we decide to change our whole application processing from thread per request to the asynchronous reactive pattern. If our decision is mainly based on programming trends and popularity, we might have problems. It may turn out that the time investment, and the new model does not suit our application processing model.

Before picking a new framework or pattern that promises to solve a lot of problems, we should first understand and measure whether we have those problems. If the new framework we are using in our application solves some complex problem, it also has additional complexity hidden somewhere. Let's assume it turns out that the main problem the given framework solves is not our primary stumbling block. In that case, we would use a solution that increases the complexity of our application and not see the new solution's benefits. For this reason, we should carefully investigate the pros and cons of a new approach and its framework before we start using it. It's possible that the additional complexity and costs associated with a migration to a new framework are not justified in our context.

This chapter will show us some of the well-known and proven solutions for better software engineering, such as dependency injection and reactive programming. We will analyze when it's worth following software engineering trends and whether to use them. We will also see when it's better to wait and choose a simpler, less-trendy solution. Let's start with the proven dependency injection pattern and frameworks that implement it.

13.1 When to use dependency injection frameworks

The main idea behind a dependency injection (DI) framework is straightforward. Our components, such as services, data access layers, or configurations, should not construct their own dependencies. Instead, all dependencies needed by the specific component should be injected from the *outside*, but the outside is not well defined. This can be any caller that provides an implementation, and the injection can be done at any level.

Let's assume we have a method that needs to perform an operation using component A. We can easily inject this component via the method argument that the following listing shows.

Listing 13.1 Injection via a method argument

```
public void doProcessing(ComponentA componentA){
    // processing
}
```

The caller injects the component. The doProcessing() method does not know anything about the origin of the ComponentA because it is provided from the outside, and the doProcessing() method does not create a new instance of it internally. However, this can make testing such a method a lot easier.

We can pass a mock (or alternate implementation) to a method and test everything explicitly. If ComponentA is instead created in the doProcessing() method internally, it would be harder to test this method. We wouldn't be able to alter the implementation for our testing purpose. For example, the default implementation of the ComponentA may need to connect to a live API of another service. If we can inject a stub of this component, we can easily stub the call to a live API with some fake data.

The other benefit of this injection is that the doProcessing() method does not need to be concerned about the lifecycle of ComponentA. The creation and deletion of this component are outsourced and can be handled by the caller.

The argument injection is a valid technique. However, in object-oriented programming languages, we tend to construct more complex objects that use other objects. For that reason, injecting components in every method call is not an ideal solution. Passing components to every method call makes our code verbose and hard to read.

The solution for this situation is to inject components at a higher level using constructor injection. When using this technique, the caller provides all dependent components when constructing a new instance of the object. It then assigns those components to fields. Finally, all methods on the object will use the previously injected components via field reference.

13.1.1 *Do-it-yourself (DIY) dependency injection*

Let's look at an example for setting up dependency injection, as figure 13.1 shows. We'll assume that our application consists of four components:

- DbConfiguration contains the database configuration.
- InventoryConfiguration contains the inventory configuration.
- InventoryDb is the data access layer that has a dependency on DbConfiguration.
- InventoryService, the main entry point for our application, has a dependency on InventoryDb and InventoryConfiguration.

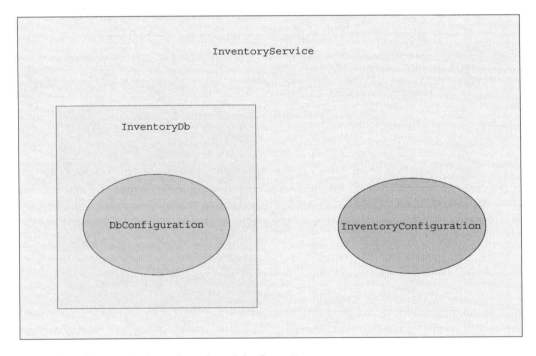

Figure 13.1   Components in our dependency injection pattern

Because we want to build our application using the dependency injection pattern, we cannot create a new instance of any of those components in any other component. In our app, we would also like to use the constructor dependency injection. This means that we need to have a dedicated place where the services and configurations are created and injected when that's needed. And after we create a graph of dependencies, we want to call the prepareInventory() method on the InventoryService.

For this scenario, we create an Application class, which is the entry point for our app. All the dependencies will be created there and injected where needed. The following listing shows the process for creating our Application class with dependency injection.

Listing 13.2 DIY dependency injection

```
public class Application {

  public static void main(String[] args) {
    // construct dependencies
    DbConfiguration dbConfiguration = loadDbConfig();
    InventoryConfiguration inventoryConfiguration = loadInventoryConfig();
    InventoryDb inventoryDb = new InventoryDb(dbConfiguration);
    InventoryService inventoryService = new InventoryService(inventoryDb,
    inventoryConfiguration);
    inventoryService.prepareInventory();
  }
}
```

Note that all the services and configurations are created in this one dedicated place. None of the components initialize any other component internally, so we can quickly test any of those classes in isolation. For example, if we want to test the Inventory-Service in isolation, we can inject any InventoryDb and InventoryConfiguration when constructing it in our test. Also, the lifecycle of all the components is in one place. For example, we can easily close or stop any service once our application finishes processing after the prepareInventory() call.

Let's assume we need to inject a specialized implementation of the InventoryDb. The following listing shows how to set this up.

Listing 13.3 Creating a specialized service

```
public class SpecializedInventoryDb extends InventoryDb {
  public SpecializedInventoryDb(DbConfiguration dbConfiguration) {
    super(dbConfiguration);
  }
}
```

Then, we can easily create a different object in our main method, where all our components are initialized. The following listing shows this change.

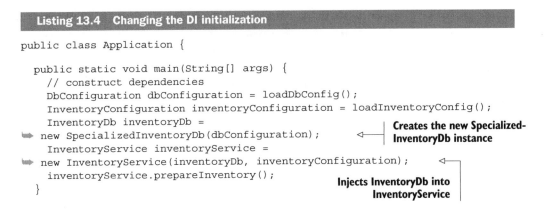

Listing 13.4   Changing the DI initialization

```
public class Application {

  public static void main(String[] args) {
    // construct dependencies
    DbConfiguration dbConfiguration = loadDbConfig();
    InventoryConfiguration inventoryConfiguration = loadInventoryConfig();
    InventoryDb inventoryDb =
      new SpecializedInventoryDb(dbConfiguration);           ← Creates the new Specialized-
    InventoryService inventoryService =                        InventoryDb instance
      new InventoryService(inventoryDb, inventoryConfiguration);   ←
      inventoryService.prepareInventory();
  }                                                Injects InventoryDb into
                                                     InventoryService
```

The DIY DI solution is straightforward; however, it has some missing features. For example, let's assume that the InventoryService is not thread-safe, but our application uses multiple threads. In that case, we should create an instance of the InventoryService for each thread (or per request if that's not possible). Our DIY DI solution does not provide this functionality. For that reason, let's assume we decide to use one of the dependency injection frameworks instead of implementing this functionality ourselves.

13.1.2 *Using a dependency injection framework*

There are a few production-proven dependency injection frameworks, such as Spring, Dropwizard, and Guice. Let's assume we pick the Spring framework because it's the most popular and allows us to construct a service per request.

The dependency injection framework uses a DI container to manage the lifecycle of all its components. Spring calls those components *beans*. The DI container allows us to register a new bean on the bean producer side. It also allows us to get the bean from the container on the consumer side. A lot is going on between producing and consuming the bean.

We can pick a different scope per bean (http://mng.bz/0w86). It can be created once per the application lifetime (the singleton pattern). This can be per request, per session, and so forth. The DI framework can also add additional logic before the bean methods are called. For example, it can intercept the calls (using a proxy) and log the parameters. The number of supported features is substantial.

Let's rework our application to use this Spring DI framework. First, both configuration classes will be annotated with the @Configuration annotation (http://mng .bz/KBJ0), as the following listing shows.

Listing 13.5   Implementing a Spring DI @Configuration

```
@Configuration
public class DbConfiguration {}

@Configuration
public class InventoryConfiguration {}
```

Next, `InventoryDb` registers itself as an `@Service` annotation (http://mng.bz/9Kx1). The following listing shows this implementation.

Listing 13.6   Creating a Spring DI @Service

```
@Service
public class InventoryDb {
  private final DbConfiguration dbConfiguration;

  @Autowired
  public InventoryDb(DbConfiguration dbConfiguration) {
    this.dbConfiguration = dbConfiguration;
  }
}
```

In listing 13.6, note that `InventoryDb` provides both producer and consumer. The `InventoryDb` also needs to have the `DbConfiguration` injected before it is constructed as a component. The `@Autowired` annotation tells Spring it needs to inject the dependent component before creating it. The DI framework handles the initialization ordering of all its components.

Finally, `InventoryService` is registered as `@Service`. This specifies its scope is equal to the `request`. Every time a new request arrives, a new instance of the `Inventory-Service` is created and injected. The DI framework also handles this, as the next listing demonstrates.

Listing 13.7   Defining a service with custom scope

```
@Service
@Scope("request")
public class InventoryService {

  private final InventoryDb inventoryDb;
  private final InventoryConfiguration inventoryConfiguration;

  @Autowired
  public InventoryService(InventoryDb inventoryDb, InventoryConfiguration
      inventoryConfiguration) {
    this.inventoryDb = inventoryDb;
    this.inventoryConfiguration = inventoryConfiguration;
  }

  public void prepareInventory() {
    System.out.println("Preparing inventory");
  }
}
```

Let's look at how our `Application` class (the previous entry point where all components were initialized) changed. First, we get rid of all logic regarding creating new instances. We can still create new instances of those classes manually; however, when doing so, they won't be managed by the Spring DI. Because of that, we would have two mechanisms for creating components. That's not ideal and is error-prone because we are relying on Spring DI exclusively. The following listing shows the changed `Application` class.

Listing 13.8 The changed Spring DI application

```
@SpringBootApplication
public class Application {
    @Autowired private InventoryService inventoryService;      ◁— Automatically injects
                                                                    the InventoryService
                                                                    by the Spring DI
  public static void main(String[] args) {
    SpringApplication.run(Application.class, args);
  }                                          Once everything is constructed,
                                             invokes prepareInventory()
  @PostConstruct            ◁——————┘
  public void useService() {
    inventoryService.prepareInventory();
  }
}
```

The `main()` method changed compared to the previous solution. Also, we need to delegate the start to the Spring `Application` class annotated with `@SpringBoot-Application`. It scans all the beans' annotations and handles the injections of all components where needed. Only after all components are ready, the final `prepare-Inventory()` method is called.

There are a couple of important observations to make. First, the actual creation, lifecycle, and ordering of initialization are hidden from us. Everything is handled internally by the Spring DI framework. As long as everything works as expected, we will be fine. However, as we continue developing our application, we observe some lifecycle problems. They may be a lot harder to debug because all the logic is implicit. Previously, we had control over everything, and we used the code that we own for it. Debugging such code is substantially easier.

The second aspect that we should take into account is the tight coupling with the Spring framework. Because of the annotation-driven DI, all our classes and components will be *polluted* by the Spring framework classes (or annotations). Besides that, our application is no longer a simple `main()` function. We now need to delegate the starter logic to Spring. This is also hidden from us, and we need to rely on this mechanism if we want to use the DI.

Finally, previously, all the components initialization logic was in one place. Now, the initialization is distributed among our codebase. It is not easy to see the whole picture of components' lifecycle without analyzing a substantial amount of code.

Let's get back to the main argument for why we decided to change the DIY solution to Spring DI. We started using the `@Scope("request")` in the `InventoryService` to achieve one service per request behavior. However, there is one big caveat here. The new `InventoryService` will indeed be initialized per request as long as we use the Spring DI-compatible web framework. In practice, this means we end up using

Spring REST. This is yet another dependency, so we need to adapt our application to work with it. Once we implemented the first step of using the Spring DI, we were forced to take a second step and migrate our web controllers to a Spring-compatible framework. The more such steps we take, the more tightly coupled our application and the given framework become. Also, more complexity will be imported to our application.

It is important to note that both Spring web and DI are well-proven and high-quality frameworks. However, if your use case is simple or you strive to have a limited number of external dependencies (for a variety of reasons, see chapter 9), picking some specific DI framework over a simple DIY solution may not be a good decision.

Instead of trying to solve an initial problem with some third-party framework, we can rework small parts of our DIY solution. For example, we could build an `Inventory-ServiceFactory` that creates a new instance of the actual service every time it's called. We can call it from the place where the new request arrives at our web service. Just because everyone is using some specific framework does not mean we should use it without taking the complexity and other factors into account. On the other hand, if we need the proven framework features, we should consider using a third-party solution, despite some of its shortcomings.

This concludes our analysis of dependency injection as an approach to changing our applications' structure. In the next section, we will look at reactive programming.

13.2 *When to use reactive programming*

The main idea behind reactive programming is to make it easier and more efficient to process incoming data. Usually, the reactive flow transforms the data and then emits the results. The results can be saved somewhere (to a sink) or consumed by other code interested in those results. The reactive model is nonblocking, meaning the processing needs to be done asynchronously, and the results can be emitted sometime in the future. Also, reactive processing can work on an infinite stream of data and processes it on demand as the data arrives (or when the consumer requests it).

Reactive programming gives us functional, data-driven processing that works in a nonblocking way. It allows us to highly parallelize our processing. The parallelization is achieved by splitting the work into multiple threads. However, the thread model is decoupled from the processing. We cannot make any hard assumptions about threading and which thread will process which parts of our processing.

One of the essential characteristics of reactive processing is its back-pressure support. When we have a stream of events emitted by a producer, it is expected that the consumer may not be able to process all the emitted events simultaneously. This can be caused by some intermittent consumer problems. If the producer keeps emitting the events at the same speed, when the consumer cannot process them, the events need to be buffered somewhere. As long as the buffer fits in memory, this is not problematic. When the consumer resumes processing at a normal speed, it may process the buffered events and get back to normal. Unfortunately, if the buffer is filled, or there is a failure in a node, we are also risking a failure in processing and will lose some events.

In such a case, reactive processing offers a mechanism called *back pressure*. The consumer can communicate the need for more events to process. The producer receives the signal, and it emits the number of requested events. This workflow is pull based. The consumer *pulls* events from the producer only if it can process them. This provides a natural back pressure mechanism.

As we can see, the reactive model offers a lot and solves many complex problems. However, this comes with a cost. The reactive API is not easy to learn and reason about. It may look easy for simple use cases, but for custom processing, it gets complex. It's not a one-solution-fits-all use case approach. To understand that, let's implement a data processing pipeline and evolve it to a reactive one.

13.2.1 *Creating single-threaded, blocking processing*

Let's start by implementing a processing workflow, where each user ID first executes the blocking HTTP GET. This is our I/O operation that will involve blocking, waiting for the response to come. The second step of our processing is a CPU-intensive task, which performs some advanced arithmetic calculation on the number returned by the blockingGet() method. The final response is returned to the caller. Figure 13.2 shows this use case.

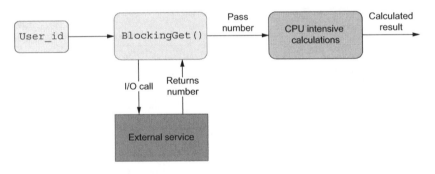

Figure 13.2   I/O and CPU-intensive tasks

Let's say our first try to implement this processing is simple. We will use a Java Stream API to chain those processing operations one after another. (There are APIs similar to the Java Stream API on other platforms, such as LINQ on .NET.) The following listing shows this initial processing.

Listing 13.9   Creating our initial processing

```
public List<Integer> calculateForUserIds(List<Integer> userIds) {
  return userIds.stream()
     .map(IOService::blockingGet)
```

```
        .map(CPUIntensiveTask::calculate)
        .collect(Collectors.toList());
}
```

Once all `userIds` are processed, the results are returned to the caller. It is important to note that the implemented logic is blocking. That means when the caller calls this method directly (without wrapping it in an asynchronous action), it will need to wait until the method finishes. Both `IOService` and `CPUIntensiveTask` log the thread on which the operations are executed, as the following listing shows.

Listing 13.10 Logging the operation's threads

```
public class CPUIntensiveTask {

  public static Integer calculate(Integer v) {
    System.out.println("CPUIntensiveTask from: " +
      Thread.currentThread().getName());
// ...
}

public class IOService {

  public static Integer blockingGet(Integer userId) {
    System.out.println("IOService from: " +
      Thread.currentThread().getName());
// ...
}
```

Let's write a unit test for our logic. We create a list of 10 elements using the `Int-Stream.rangeClosed` generator. Next, we pass all the data to the `calculateFor-UserIds()` method. Finally, we assert that it returns 10 elements. The following listing shows this approach.

Listing 13.11 Unit Testing for the processing logic

```
@Test
public void shouldCalculateNElements() {
  // given
  CalculationService calculationService = new CalculationService();
  List<Integer> input = IntStream.rangeClosed(1,
      10).boxed().collect(Collectors.toList());
  // when
  List<Integer> result = calculationService.calculateForUserIds(input);

  // then
  assertThat(result.size()).isEqualTo(10);
}
```

What's more important here is that, when running this test, we would be able to observe the thread on which the processing is executed. The following listing shows the expected output.

Listing 13.12   Viewing the log from our initial processing

```
IOService from: main
CPUIntensiveTask from: main
IOService from: main
CPUIntensiveTask from: main
```

All the processing is executed in the context of the caller thread. This test confirms our processing is blocking and also single-threaded. This means our processing is not parallel.

13.2.2 Using CompletableFuture

We can solve both aspects, blocking and single-threaded, by reworking our flow to use asynchronous abstraction available with the Java class: CompletableFuture. There's also a high probability that the language of your choice offers a promise–future API that lets you submit an action without blocking its results.

By using this pattern, we can submit *N* tasks in parallel. Each of those tasks can execute on a different thread or set of threads from a thread pool. We will use the CompletableFuture API that is built into the Java SDK because it is available out-of-the-box without the need for any external library.

Let's see how our method from the previous section will change. For every user ID we get, we start a nonblocking task that is executed on a separate thread (the noncaller thread). We achieve this by using the supplyAsync() method and invoking the first I/O blocking operation on it. Next, we need to chain a subsequent CPU-intensive operation. However, it should be called only when the first method (blockingGet()) finishes. We can achieve that using the thenApply() method, as the following listing shows.

Listing 13.13   Async implementation using the CompletableFuture

```
public List<CompletableFuture<Integer>> calculateForUserIds(List<Integer>
    userIds) {
  return userIds.stream()
      .map(
          v ->
              CompletableFuture.supplyAsync(() -> IOService.blockingGet(v))
                  .thenApply(CPUIntensiveTask::calculate))
      .collect(Collectors.toList());
}
```

It is important to note that the CPU-intensive task is executed after the I/O intensive task finishes. This means both stages for the same ID cannot be parallelized. Also, the supplyAsync() method has a variant that accepts the executor service explicitly. This allows us to provide our own thread pool. If not passed explicitly, then the common fork–join pool is used.

The `CalculationService` works now in an async and concurrent way. It returns the list of `CompletableFuture` tasks that contains the results we'll see sometime in the future. However, it is up to the caller to decide whether to wait on the result and block or chain subsequent async actions. For example, the caller may invoke the `get()` method on all operations and collect results to a list. The following listing provides the code to test this.

Listing 13.14 Creating an async implementation test

```
@Test
public void shouldCalculateNElementsAsync()
    throws ExecutionException, InterruptedException {
  // given
  CalculationService calculationService = new CalculationService();
  List<Integer> input = IntStream.rangeClosed(1,
      10).boxed().collect(Collectors.toList());

  // when
  List<CompletableFuture<Integer>> resultAsync =
      calculationService.calculateForUserIds(input);
  List<Integer> result = new ArrayList<>(resultAsync.size());

  for (CompletableFuture<Integer> asyncAction : resultAsync) {
    result.add(asyncAction.get());      ⟵┐
  }                                        │ Waits for the results
  // then                                  │ in a blocking way
  assertThat(result.size()).isEqualTo(10);
}
```

It is important to note that the transformation between async and sync API can be done quite easily. Let's assume the new async implementation of the `calculateForUserIds()` method is called in multiple places in our code. In that case, we do not impose on all callers to use the async `CompletableFuture` abstraction. If the caller's code works in a blocking way, it can easily extract the values from the list of `CompletableFuture` and continue using the blocking API. We achieved concurrency in our component, but we are not imposing the async workflow on all callers. If we run the test in listing 13.14, we may notice an output similar to what the following listing presents.

Listing 13.15 Viewing threads output of the async processing

```
IOService from: ForkJoinPool.commonPool-worker-9
IOService from: ForkJoinPool.commonPool-worker-2
.....
IOService from: ForkJoinPool.commonPool-worker-1
CPUIntensiveTask from: ForkJoinPool.commonPool-worker-2
CPUIntensiveTask from: ForkJoinPool.commonPool-worker-9
...
CPUIntensiveTask from: ForkJoinPool.commonPool-worker-1
```

Note that the actions are executed in multiple threads. Even if the caller blocks the results, the actual calculations are performed concurrently. Suppose we want to achieve *thread affinity*—the behavior when both I/O- and CPU-intensive tasks are executed in the same nonmain thread. In that case, we can pass the single-threaded executor to the `supplyAsync()` method.

The approach we currently have is relatively straightforward. We are using a Java API that's available to all potential callers. We have a direct influence over the threading model, and we can customize the behavior quite easily. We are also not imposing on our callers the need to implement all processing in an async way. It is effortless to wrap and to transform the `CompletableFuture` to a blocking workflow.

13.2.3 *Implementing a reactive solution*

Let's assume we want to make our code more up to date, and we decide to rework it to a reactive approach. Our processing executes transformations on *N* input elements, so the reactive approach seems to fit it well. We still want it to be asynchronous and concurrent as in our previous approach. We choose to use the Reactive API that gives us the `Flux` abstraction (http://mng.bz/jyMP). This is a reactive stream of *N* events. Other platforms provide other libraries and frameworks for reactive programming. The https://reactivex.io/ website provides options for several different platforms.

Let's see how the new processing looks. Our flow is split into *N* steps. Each action from the map is executed after the previous step finishes, as the code in the following listing shows.

> **Listing 13.16 Implementing the reactive flow**

```
public Flux<Integer> calculateForUserIds(List<Integer> userIds) {
  return Flux
      .fromIterable(userIds)
      .map(IOService::blockingGet)
      .map(CPUIntensiveTask::calculate);
}
```

We construct the `Flux` from a list of elements by using the `fromIterable()` method. In real-life reactive processing, the `Flux` is created from external sources and consumes emitted events as they arrive into our system. The events will likely be emitted constantly without a way to stop them (a hot datasource). The reactive stream is an abstraction that allows us to model such behavior.

As you can see, we return the `Flux` from our method. The caller of our method needs to use this API when interacting with our code. Returning the `Flux` from our method signals the caller that the data can be emitted *indefinitely* (in a streaming way). Due to that fact, all the `Flux` consumers need to migrate their flow to be reactive as well. This is not easy, and it's not safe to transform the `Flux` elements into a blocking abstraction. When using a potentially infinite data producer, we may risk blocking indefinitely as well.

Such a change is quite invasive. Suddenly, the redesign of our component and the fact that it uses the reactive approach leaks to all callers. The reactive processing should be implemented from the producer to the last consumer. It does not play well if we want to use it for parallelizing only small parts of our code.

Our goal is to have a method that doesn't block the main thread and parallelize computations. When we run our new reactive code, we will notice a weird behavior, as the following listing shows.

Listing 13.17   Output from a reactive single-threaded processing

```
IOService from: main
CPUIntensiveTask from: main
IOService from: main
CPUIntensiveTask from: main
```

All the processing is executed from the `main` caller thread! Although we are using the reactive API, our processing is single-threaded, and it blocks the caller because it uses the main thread. How do we alleviate that problem?

We can use the `publishOn()` method to specify the executor on which the specific part of the reactive workflow is executed. However, we need to remember that the `blockingGet()` method contains a blocking I/O call. According to the reactive specification, the actions used in the reactive workflow shouldn't be blocking. If this is necessary to invoke the blocking action, we may use a particular executor for it: `boundedElastic()`. It is designed for working with blocking calls. Unfortunately, it does not perform well when executing CPU-intensive calls that use the thread for a substantial amount of time. For that reason, we should use the `parallel()` executor optimized for our CPU-intensive use case. The following listing shows this implementation.

Listing 13.18   Reactive concurrency

```
public Flux<Integer> calculateForUserIds(List<Integer> userIds) {
    return Flux.fromIterable(userIds)
        .publishOn(Schedulers.boundedElastic())
        .map(IOService::blockingGet)
        .publishOn(Schedulers.parallel())
        .map(CPUIntensiveTask::calculate);
}
```

The following listing shows the output when we run this code. In the listing, note that now both I/O- and CPU-bound tasks use different threads. The actions are interleaving, meaning we have achieved some level of parallelism.

Listing 13.19   Viewing the reactive processing threads output

```
IOService from: boundedElastic-1
IOService from: boundedElastic-1
CPUIntensiveTask from: parallel-1
```

```
IOService from: boundedElastic-1
CPUIntensiveTask from: parallel-1
```

When following the reactive threading guidelines, it is hard to achieve thread affinity. If using both I/O- and CPU-intensive tasks, these both should be executed on separate thread pools. Therefore, it is not feasible to execute them on the same thread, as we can do using CompletableFuture and single-threaded executors.

We achieved our goal, but the current approach has a couple drawbacks. First, the configuration of threads is implicit. We are able to pass the parallelism levels to both schedulers, but this is not easy to tweak and configure. Our performance analysis and tests should back it up. Moreover, the threading model in the Flux API is not simple. Once we expose this API from our component, we are imposing that everyone who uses this API needs to understand the reactive API. When exposing Flux, we don't influence the way it's used. The caller can impact our processing by using the subscribeOn() method to change the thread pool used by our code.

Also, the caller cannot change the thread and chain a subsequent blocking action directly on the Flux returned by calculateForUserIds(). Such an action would be executed using the parallel() thread-pool, impacting the execution of CPU-intensive tasks.

Those are the only problems that can arise when using the Flux API. Of course, they all can be solved, but we need to ensure that all team members know the reactive API. If our goal is to parallelize only a small part of processing, reworking the whole application to reactive API may be too invasive. On the other hand, if we plan to rework the whole application workflow to reactive, we should tackle this problem in an end-to-end fashion instead of reworking one subcomponent to this API. In the next section, we will analyze functional programming usage.

13.3   *When to use functional programming*

The functional programming approach has many benefits, such as an easier concurrency model (due to the immutable state), more concise code, and easier testing (no side effects and no global state). However, overusing functional programming approaches in languages (such as Java) that are optimized for object-oriented development may be problematic in some situations. Let's consider some of those problems when trying to write 100% functional code in a mainly object-oriented language.

Java was created as an object-oriented language. Fortunately, in recent years, some functional programming constructs were added to the language, such as lambda functions and the Stream API. Although those concepts are well-known in functional programming, they are only a small subset of functional language constructs. It may be tempting to write all your logic in a functional way because those constructs are available. However, Java is still an object-oriented language at its core.

There are a lot of traps we can fall into when trying to write purely functional code using an object-oriented language. Let's assume we want to write a reduce() function using recursion. In the next section, we will use an object-oriented language for that.

13.3.1 *Creating functional code in a nonfunctional language*

Our goal is to write a reduce() function that should take a list of values, apply the reducer function from all of those values, and return the caller's result. This function should be generic, meaning it should work for any type of argument.

Also, let's assume we are inspired by functional programming, and we want to implement this logic in a functional way. We can use recursion and list decomposition. Every list can be presented as a head and tail, as figure 13.3 illustrates. The head is the first element of the list, whereas the tail is the rest of the values.

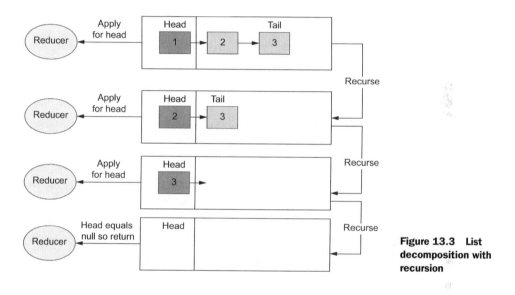

Figure 13.3 List decomposition with recursion

Once we get (and remove) the head from the list, we can apply the reducer function to this element. Next, we can pass the tail to the same function again. The list decomposition happens again, and we get the head, apply an operation, and pass the tail further. This logic is repeated (recursed) as long as the tail is not empty. Once the list is empty, we return the final value from our recursive function. Let's see how to implement this logic in the Java programming language with the method signature that the following listing shows.

Listing 13.20 Creating the reduce() method

```
public static <T> T reduce(List<T> values, BinaryOperator<T> reducer,
    T accumulator){
  return reduceInternal(values, reducer, accumulator);
}
```

This reducer function takes the current aggregated value as an argument and the head of the list. For the first iteration, we don't have the aggregate value yet, so the caller needs to provide the initial value as the `accumulator` parameter. The `reduce()` method delegates the actual implementation to the `reduceInternal()` method. It is called recursively, so we should start from the end condition, which specifies when the function should return.

For our case, we want to return the accumulator when the values list is empty. Without this condition, the function will never return and will recurse indefinitely. Next, we decompose the list, extracting its head and tail, as the following listing shows. This is delegated to separate methods that we'll see in a moment.

Listing 13.21   Implementing the Java reducer, `reduceInternal()`

```java
private static <T> T reduceInternal
    (List<T> values, BinaryOperator<T> reducer, T accumulator) {
  if (values.isEmpty()) {
    return accumulator;
  }
  T head = getHead(values);
  List<T> tail = getTail(values);
  T result = reducer.apply(head, accumulator);
  return reduceInternal(tail, reducer, result);
}
```

Once we have extracted the head, we can invoke the reducer function, passing the head and the accumulator values. Lastly, we invoke the method again (recurse).

The head and tail extraction methods are relatively straightforward. The following listing shows this implementation.

Listing 13.22   Extracting the head and tail

```java
private static <T> List<T> getTail(List<T> values) {
  if (values.size() == 1) {
    return Collections.emptyList();
  }
  return values.subList(1, values.size());
}

private static <T> T getHead(List<T> values) {
    return values.get(0);
}
```

The `getTail()` method returns an empty list if the values have only one element (head). Otherwise, it returns all elements, except the first element. The `getHead()` method returns the first element of the list.

Let's implement a unit test that verifies our functional `reduce()` implementation, which we will use for summing up all elements in the list of values. The following listing shows the code for this.

Listing 13.23 Creating a Java reduce unit test

```
@Test
public void shouldReduceTenValues() {
  // given
  List<Integer> input = IntStream.range(1,
    10).boxed().collect(Collectors.toList());

  // when
  Integer result = Reduce.reduce(input, (value, accumulator) -> value +
    accumulator, 0);

  // then
  assertThat(result).isEqualTo(45);
}
```

The reducer function takes the accumulator and the head value and sums them. The initial accumulator is equal to zero because we start the addition from this value.

At this stage, we can be perfectly happy with our implementation. We were able to implement the functional construct using a functional approach (recursion) in a non-functional language. However, our approach has one big problem. We can catch that problem by writing a unit test that operates on a higher number of values. For example, when running our logic for 100,000 elements, as the following listing shows, we will observe that our code throws a StackOverflowError.

Listing 13.24 Testing the reduce() throwing StackOverflowError

```
@Test
public void shouldStackOverflowForALotOfValues() {
  // given
  List<Integer> input = IntStream.range(1,
    100_000).boxed().collect(Collectors.toList());

  // when
  assertThatThrownBy(() -> Reduce.reduce(input, Integer::sum, 0))
    .isInstanceOf(StackOverflowError.class);
}
```

What's the reason for this StackOverflowError? It turns out that recursion is not well optimized and suited for the Java language. Every recursive call needs to allocate a frame on the call stack. For the 100,000 elements to process, this requires the same amount of stack frames allocated. Every stack trace occupies some memory. The upper limit of elements in the stack trace is limited by the memory available to our program. Therefore, the stack trace can have limited depth. If our code involves too many calls, we will end up with the exception signaling the problem.

This is one of the functional programming edge cases in a nonfunctional programming language. The reduce() function can be implemented in an imperative way, using the standard for loop, and we should favor such an approach in object-oriented languages.

Note that the reduce() method is available in the Java Stream API, so it can be safely used from Java. The reason for this is that it is implemented in the imperative (for loop) and not in a recursive way. We implemented our own reduce() function to demonstrate one of the common functional programming problems (recursion) when writing the code in an object-oriented language, such as Java.

13.3.2 *Tail recursion optimization*

If we use a fully functional language, the problem with recursive implementation can be easily solved. For example, Scala language implements tail recursion optimization.

This compiler-level optimization allows it to unwind the recursion. This can happen only if the recursive call that we use is the last call of our method. In such a case, the recursion is changed to a for loop by the compiler. We can still write the recursive, fully-functional code without worrying about the stack growing too much. To see how simple the implementation of a functional recursive reduce() method in a fully functional language (Scala, in this case) is, let's see the implementation that the following listing shows.

> **Listing 13.25 Implementing `reduce()` in Scala**

```
@tailrec
def reduce[T] (values: List[T],
    reducer: (T, T) => T, accumulator:T ): T = values match {
  case Nil => accumulator
  case head :: tail => reduce(tail, reducer, reducer(head, accumulator))
}
```

Our code is more concise and perfectly safe for running with a huge number of input values now. The concise part is achieved by yet another functional programming construct: pattern matching with decomposition. The head and tail list decomposition is achieved by simply issuing head :: tail. Note that the reduce() method is annotated with @tailrec (http://mng.bz/W7J1). This tells the compiler to check whether the given method can be optimized into a look (tail recursion optimization). If this cannot be done, the compiler returns an error. But for our case, it can be done because the recursive call is the last statement in our method.

By analyzing this example and looking at both Scala and Java implementations, we can conclude it is important to pick the proper language and tools for the specific programming task. Functional programming provides many benefits. However, when using all its techniques and patterns blindly, we risk many potential problems. On the one hand, we should strive to adopt the best ideas from functional programming languages. On the other hand, we should also be careful when using functional programming constructs in a not purely functional language. By applying the best patterns, we can expose an API that plays well with functional programming (e.g., Stream.reduce()) but is implemented in the imperative way underneath.

13.3.3 *Leveraging immutability*

Immutability is a powerful concept, but it comes with a cost. The immutable object, once it's created, cannot be modified in any way. In the Java language, we can create an object that is immutable by making all of its fields final. However, the final reference states only that the reference cannot be reassigned.

The object can be changed if it is created in a way that allows modification. It is possible to create an immutable object, but it requires careful design of your classes. All the ways to modify it need to be hidden from the callers. If we use an API construct that allows modifications (e.g., List), we need to wrap the mutable structure into an immutable wrapper. Once it is wrapped, we need to prohibit calls to all methods allowing the modification of the underlying object.

Once our object is immutable, we can safely share it between components without worrying about thread safety. The object can only be accessed, so all threads will have the same visibility. Therefore, we don't need any synchronization when accessing the object. This impacts the performance of our code.

It is also easier to write such code and reason about it, so it's easier to write code without bugs. It is essential that the object state is filled at the construction time—no later.

In reality, even if the object is immutable, we sometimes need to alter its state. In the functional approach, this is done by creating a new object, copying the state of the original one, and altering what's needed. Once the copy is created, it needs to follow the same approach as the original object, however. It cannot be modified in any way. At this point, we can see that such an approach results in creating a lot of objects. Each object is allocating some memory space. The more deep copies of the original object we make, the more memory we will need. Therefore, the functional approach of writing our code may result in more memory pressure and a more costly garbage collection. The number of created objects and their impact over garbage collection should be carefully measured.

In practice, the number of copied objects can be reduced. For example, let's consider an immutable List implementation. The whole list is immutable, and it consists of nodes connected via pointers. Let's assume we have a list1 reference that points to a list with two nodes. Next, we want to create a new list2 that is based on the immutable list1 but has one additional node with value C. Figure 13.4 shows this implementation.

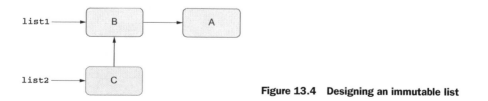

Figure 13.4 Designing an immutable list

We could copy all the nodes from list1 and add an additional node, but it will occupy space for three additional nodes. Instead of that, we can create one new node and point it to the head of list1. After that operation, we will have two immutable lists: list1 has two nodes, and list2 has three nodes. However, we only need a memory space for three nodes instead of five (the original list1 has 2 nodes, and the new list2 has 3 nodes). We can use patterns similar to this to reduce the memory overhead for other immutable structures and objects.

Functional programming is a complex topic and deserves a more profound understanding. The purpose of this section was to show only one aspect of it and analyze it in the context of an object-oriented language. If you want to learn more about functional programming, I recommend the book, *Functional Programming in Java* (http://mng.bz/8lVw) by Pierre-Yves Saumont (Manning, 2017). In the next section, we will look at two initialization approaches: lazy and eager.

13.4   *Using lazy vs. eager evaluation*

Our applications tend to interact with multiple components. Let's consider a web application that needs to connect to a database (opening the session) and populates the cache with the most recent user ID data. In an environment where we can have *N* instances of the service, all those tasks need to be executed on every node, as figure 13.5 illustrates.

We can choose to perform both operations lazily or eagerly. There is a recent trend of trying to make the application startup as fast as possible. This can be achieved by moving the time-consuming operations, such as initializing the database connection in a later stage of the

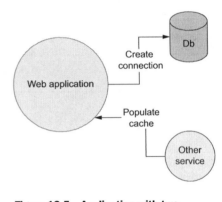

Figure 13.5   Application with two downstream components

application lifecycle. In such a pattern, the database connection is created lazily. This means that when we start the application, the connection is not initialized. By making it lazy, we postpone the initialization logic to be executed on the users' first request. However, it also means that the first user will pay the cost of initializing the connection on their first request. Figure 13.6 shows what lazy initialization might look like.

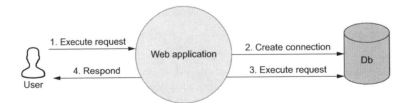

Figure 13.6   Using lazy initialization when connecting to a database

If we use the eager approach, initialization is paid once at the startup of the application. In this scenario, the first end-user request uses an already present connection without the need for initializing it. The connection is created at the application startup time (and kept in the connection pool). The first request takes this connection from the connection pool and uses it for executing the request. Figure 13.7 shows what eager initialization would look like.

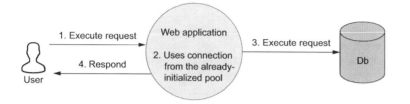

Figure 13.7 Using eager initialization when connecting to a database

In real-life applications, this effect will be even more noticeable. Often, there are N connections to the underlying system, and we keep a pool of N connections. The pool may grow dynamically, but it starts with some stable number of open connections. If we decide to have lazy initialization for all connections, the cost of initialization is paid with N requests, where N is equal to the number of connections in the pool.

We need to choose between increased startup time versus increased first (or more) request handling time. Assuming that our SLA has a hard limit and cannot exceed a specific request handling time, the lazy initialization may be problematic. On the other hand, if we need to start the application as quickly as possible, moving all the time-consuming logic to a later stage may be justified.

There is also a potential problem with eager initialization that may impact our application. Let's assume that we need to choose when to populate the cache. We can do this eagerly and prepopulate our app at startup, or we can do it lazily and populate the cache during the request execution. This decision obviously impacts the same aspect as the previous example: a time expense will be paid at startup or during the first N requests.

We should also be aware that there could be a problem with the external call. For example, the external call may fail due to an outage of a service. Therefore, there could be a situation when the other service used to populate the cache has some problems. Also, we may introduce some programming bugs when fetching this data.

When using the lazy approach of initialization, any initialization problem will be detected at our application's run time. It can also be a lot later after application startup. In such a scenario, we may deploy an application and observe that everything works as expected. Only when the application starts serving the traffic would we notice problems. This delay is caused by the lazy initialization and postponing the logic to a later time. If our application chooses to perform those actions eagerly (at startup), we can detect potential problems faster.

In case programming errors are introduced, we can detect them immediately when the new node with a new version is deployed. Having that information, we can rollback deployment faster. It can even be unnoticed by end users if we perform a rolling deployment, where the old version of the application is not deleted until the new nodes are up and running. With the lazy approach, the failure may go unnoticed during the deployment time. Only once all nodes are deployed, we (and our end-users) may start to notice a problem. Table 13.1 sums up our findings.

Table 13.1   Lazy vs eager initialization

Initialization phase	Startup time	Time for first *N* requests	Error detection
Lazy	Faster	Impacted; slower	Later, when the service is operational
Eager	Slower	Not impacted	During deployment

As you can see, lazy initialization offers faster startup time. However, this time overhead does not disappear, and it will be paid for by the first *N* request to our service. Also, the potential errors are detected later when the service is operational.

The eager initialization moves the time expense to startup. Therefore, the startup of an application that does initialization eagerly is slower, and because this cost is already paid, the first *N* request is not impacted. Also, some of the potential errors can be detected during the deployment process.

The decision whether to move initialization of your application to eager or lazy stages should take these factors into consideration. You may also choose a hybrid approach, where some actions are executed in an eager and some in a lazy way.

Summary

- With dependency injection, all dependencies needed by a specific component should be injected from the *outside* and can be done at any level. In this chapter, we learned when to use DIY versus existing solutions to implement this pattern.
  - Although the method injection pattern is a valid technique, it is not well suited in object-oriented languages, such as Java. A solution for this is to inject components at a higher level using constructor injection.
  - There are a few production-proven dependency injection frameworks, such as Spring, Dropwizard, or Guice. These provide a lot of possibilities, but they also rely on implicit assumptions and introduce tight coupling in our codebase.
- Reactive programming gives us functional data-driven processing that works in a nonblocking way, which allows us to parallelize our processing. However, the parallelization is achieved by splitting the work into multiple threads.

- Using a single-threaded processing as an example, we evolved it to work in an async and concurrent way. This allows us to parallelize our processing and handle higher throughput.
- Based on the recent trends, we reworked our solution to a reactive flow, as this seemed to fit our execution of transformations on N input elements.
- Learning about the threading model of all solutions, we can better analyze the pros and cons of this approach.

- The functional programming approach has many benefits, such as an easier concurrency model, more concise code, and easier testing, but using functional programming approaches blindly in languages that are optimized for object-oriented programming may be problematic.
  - We were able to implement a functional construct with Java using recursion as a functional approach. We then compared this approach with tail recursion in Scala.
  - Immutability is a powerful concept, but it comes with a cost. Once we create the immutable object, it cannot be modified in any way. As an example, we implemented an immutable list.

- Because our applications tend to interact with multiple components, we learned about lazy and eager initialization and their tradeoffs: initialization time, request handling time, and detection of errors.

index

379